I0837293

ART AND INDUSTRY

AS REPRESENTED IN THE

EXHIBITION AT THE CRYSTAL PALACE

NEW YORK—1853-4

SHOWING THE PROGRESS AND STATE OF THE

VARIOUS USEFUL AND ESTHETIC PURSUITS.

FROM THE NEW YORK TRIBUNE.

REVISED AND EDITED

BY HORACE GREELEY.

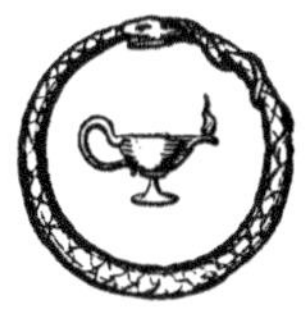

REDFIELD,

110 & 112 NASSAU-STREET, NEW YORK.

1853.

Entered, according to act of Congress,
in the year one Thousand Eight Hundred and Fifty-three,
By J. S. REDFIELD,
in the Clerk's Office of the District Court of the United
States, for the Southern District of New York.

A. CUNNINGHAM,
STEREOTYPER,
No. 183 William-street, New-York.

PREFACE.

It has been well observed by EDWARD EVERETT—who, almost alone among our public men, has achieved eminence alike amid the amenities and generous rivalries of Literature and in the sterner collisions of Statesmanship—who in the Republic of Letters has long been a critic and a censor without wounding a just susceptibility or provoking an undesirable enmity, and in Politics has been for thirty years a decided partisan, without limiting or qualifying the esteem and admiration with which he is regarded by his countrymen generally—that "It is remarkable that many of the best books have been written by persons who, at the time of writing them, had no intention of becoming authors. Indeed, with slight inclination to systemize and exaggerate, one might be tempted to maintain the position—however paradoxical it may at the first blush appear—that no good book can ever be written in any other way; that the only literature of any value is that which grows indirectly out of the real action of society, intended directly to effect some other purpose; and that when a man sits doggedly in his study, and says to himself, 'I mean to write a good book,' it is certain, from the necessity of the case, that the result will be a bad one."

Whether the unpretending work herewith submitted shall or shall not serve to illustrate the justice of Mr. Everett's observation, it is very certain that nearly all of its contents were written in exact accordance with the spirit of his suggestion; namely, by men intent on setting forth something which seemed to them deserving of public attention, but without a thought of book-making. Their incitement was as follows:

In anticipation of the opening of our Crystal Palace, the Editors of THE NEW YORK TRIBUNE determined that there should, from time to time, be given in the columns of their journal, accounts of the various contributions to this Exhibition of the World's Industry, as classed in their several Departments, not according to Geography or Nationality, but according to essential likeness or assimilation. Their idea was, that accounts should successively be given of whatever the Palace might contain in any important Department of Industry, with a retrospective glance at the origin and growth of the art or arts involved in its production; so that, when these sketches should be completed, their readers would have obtained an integral conception—crude and imperfect, perhaps, but vivid, practical and suggestive—of the means whereby mankind are fed, clad and housed, and of the various staples, wares and fabrics which give employment to Industry and Commerce, insuring material comfort to civilized communities and diffusing luxury and taste among their members. Hence grew the essays which, revised and somewhat modified, form the body of this volume.

That they should be unequal, alike in the interest of their respective topics and in the merit of their execution, was unavoidable. They are the work of at least a dozen different hands, about half of them employed on the Editorial staff of THE TRIBUNE; the residue specially employed to elucidate such departments of Industry as they were severally presumed well qualified to describe. No one of them wrote with any expectation that his article would have an existence less ephemeral than that of the daily broadsheet wherein it first met the public eye. The series had nearly been completed, when, at the urgent suggestion of readers who deemed them worthy of a more enduringly accessible form, the publisher was induced to make proposals for their collection and revision, whereof the result is herewith submitted. If this work of many hands shall induce, as we trust it may, some thousands of our younger mechanics, artisans and laborers, to regard the mighty Exhibition, not as a vast curiosity-shop or raree-show, nor yet as a mere Arch of Triumph, erected in honor of Labor, but as the grandest and most instructive University ever opened to themselves and their children on this continent, or ever but once in the world, then will its end have been accomplished, and our labor abundantly rewarded.

NEW YORK, NOV. 1ST, 1853.

CONTENTS.

INTRODUCTION.

A brief historical sketch of the origin and construction of the Crystal Palace may properly precede the notices of its contents embodied in this volume.

The first idea of an Exhibition of the Products of the Art and Industry of All Nations, was carried into effect in London in 1850–1. In 1849, however, the French Minister of the Interior sought to give a cosmopolitan character to the great quinquennial Exhibition held that year in Paris ; but he was overruled by the native exhibitors ; so the suggestion thus made was left to be first realized in England.

The Exhibition in London, from its inception to its completion, was sanctioned and upheld by the Court and Parliament. The Queen took the liveliest interest in it ; Prince Albert was its technical head and originator ; its interests were discussed in Parliament ; and, in a word, it was a favorite Government enterprise. Herein it differed radically from its copy in this country, erected at New York during the years 1852–3—the American Crystal Palace being exclusively a result of private enterprise. Great applause was bestowed on the Secretary of State, Mr. Webster, because he agreed to make it a Bonded Warehouse ; but we apprehend that Mr. Webster did not need encomium for so common-place and simple a proceeding. Equally easy of course was the action of the New York Municipality, in granting the site : if this had been refused, the omission would have been unworthy and unprofitable Whatever credit accrues to the idea and outworking of the Crystal Palace in this City, is purely and absolutely private and not political. *Suum cuique.*

On the 3d January, 1853, the Corporation of New-York granted a free lease for five years of Reservoir Square, upon two conditions: first, that the building should be composed of Iron and Glass; and, secondly, that no single entrance-charge should exceed fifty cents. On the 11th of March, the Legislature enacted a charter of Incorporation for the ASSOCIATION FOR THE EXHIBITION OF THE INDUSTRY OF ALL NATIONS. The main provisions of the act ran thus: capital, two hundred thousand dollars, with permission to increase it to three hundred thousand: authorization to the Directors to occupy any real estate that might be granted to them: power to award prizes, and to all necessary things for the completion of the project. The charter was not easily obtained, objections being made that it was hostile to domestic industry, and state-constitutional provisions being likewise interposed.

On the 17th of March, the Board of Directors met, elected THEODORE SEDGWICK, President, and WILLIAM WHETTEN, Secretary, and then issued the following general statement:

ASSOCIATION FOR THE EXHIBITION OF THE INDUSTRY OF ALL NATIONS.—A Charter having been granted by the Legislature of this State, for the purposes of an Industrial Exhibition; and the Corporation of the City having, with great liberality, granted the use of Reservoir Square for five years, the parties associated in the enterprise are now prepared to invite the co-operation of their fellow-citizens.

In doing this, they think it proper to state, at some length, the motives which guide them, and the objects which they hope to attain.

It is scarcely necessary to say, that the idea was suggested by the brilliant success that attended the London Exhibition of last year.

That Exhibition, prompted by enlarged and liberal views, and carried out with energy and skill, was crowned with the most triumphant results; and a just pride authorizes us to assert, that, in all that vast array of the triumphs of genius and industry, no nation gave more striking proofs of intellectual capacity and vigor, applied to the useful arts, than were manifested by our own people.

It was, therefore, a natural suggestion of patriotic and national feelings, that we should not only wish to see a like Exhibition in our own country, but that we should desire to re-produce in it the beneficial effects that had resulted from its great prototype.

It is generally acknowledged, that the London Exhibition marks an era in the progress of the world—an era, of which the distinctive characteristics are the advance of those arts which increase the comforts and heighten the delights of life, the spread of amicable relations among rival countries, and, above all, the elevation of labor to its proper dignity.

The difficulties apparent at the outset of the enterprise have been overcome; the liberality of the English Government has been emulated by the respective authorities of our country; and a correct appreciation of the objects of the Association seems to be entertained by those to whom they have been communicated; and we are satisfied, that the more generally these objects are made known, the more favorable will be their acceptation by our fellow-citizens, whose sagacity can foresee, as their co-operative energy can achieve, the results at which we aim.

In an edifice which, of itself, will be a noble monument of skill, we hope to bring together the choicest productions of the Old World's industry; thus not only opening a fair field for the competition of the productive talent of America, but enlarging its scope and multiplying its aims; and, at the same time, presenting to all classes of the community such rare and novel objects of attention, as cannot fail to widen the sphere of general knowledge.

It is well known, that in London a great portion of the building was occupied by objects of but little interest, and that American Industry entered into the competition to a very small extent. It is believed that by a more careful selection of articles, and by a larger introduction of our own products, the interest of the Exhibition, in these two essential particulars, can be greatly increased.

In a statement of this kind it is impossible to introduce full details; but we may say, in general terms, that we have such assurances, not only from England, but from the principal countries of the Continent, as justify us in the expectation of bringing under the eyes of our fellow-citizens not only such specimens of the industrial arts as shall generally interest the practical American mind, but such rare products of industry and skill as have never been seen among us. Some of these were among the choicest articles of the London Exhibition, and others are now being prepared abroad expressly for exhibition here. And, more than this, we hope to bring within the reach of all, such wonders of the Fine Arts as have hitherto been approached only by those of our countrymen who have been able to seek them abroad.

The Corporation is authorized by its charter to award prizes among the exhibitors; and in discharging this part of their duty, the Directors will hereafter invite the co-operation of the most eminent and capable of their fellow-citizens.

If we effect our object, we shall not only have imparted a fresh impetus to the career of our great metropolis, but we shall have given an impulse to mechanical skill and manufacturing industry; we shall have raised higher the standard of taste; we shall have extended and diffused the knowledge of the various families of the Old World; and, in so doing, we shall have strengthened the great bonds of peace and good-will.

The Association is incorporated, by an Act of the Legislature of the 11th March, 1852, for the term of five years.

The capital of the Company is $200,000, to be divided into shares of $100 each, and may be increased by the Directors to $300,000.

The price of admission to the Exhibition is limited to fifty cents, and the cost of the building is restricted by the charter to $200,000.

The Act of Incorporation provides that, for one day at least, the children and scholars of the schools of the Public School Society, of the Ward Schools, and of the Free Academy, of the Deaf and Dumb and Blind Institutions, and of the Orphan Asylums in the city of New-York, shall be admitted free of charge.

It also provides, that the nett proceeds of one day's exhibition shall be appropriated and paid over to the Treasurers of the Fire-Department Fund, for the benefit of Widows and Orphans of deceased Firemen in the cities of New-York and Brooklyn, and divided between them in the proportions of three-fourths to the former and one-fourth to the latter.

THEODORE SEDGWICK, *President.*

WM. WHETTEN, *Secretary.*

This was accompanied by the following call for subscriptions to the stock:

ASSOCIATION FOR THE EXHIBITION OF THE INDUSTRY OF ALL NATIONS.—Capital $200,000, with liberty to increase it to $300,000.

This Institution being organized under a Charter granted by the Legislature of the State of New-York, the Company is now ready to receive Subscriptions to the Stock. The books will be opened at the office of Messrs. DUNCAN, SHERMAN & Co., of 48 William-street, Bankers to this Company, from and after Friday, the second day of April, 1852.

Ten per cent. on the amount of subscriptions to be paid at the time of subscribing. No subscription to exceed Five Thousand Dollars.

THEODORE SEDGWICK, *President.*

WM. WHETTEN, *Secretary.*

The stock was not sought for in large sums, and this happily secured its distribution among many holders. It was taken by more than one hundred and fifty individuals and firms. On the 24th of May, 1852, Mr. Maxwell, Collector of the Port, stated that the General Government would consider the building a Bonded Warehouse, for which favor the Directors had applied.

In order to arrange the Foreign Department, CHARLES BUSCHEK, of London, well known as a Commissioner in the Austrian Department of the Crystal Palace there, was appointed an agent to secure the co-operation of the manufacturers of Europe. The architectural staff was then appointed, as follows: C. E. DETWOLD, Superintending Architect and Engineer; HORATIO ALLEN, Consulting Engineer; and EDMUND HURRY, Consulting Architect. Matters were now so advanced that the Directors were enabled to issue the following circular:

OFFICE OF THE ASSOCIATION FOR THE EXHIBITION OF THE INDUSTRY OF ALL NATIONS, NEW YORK, July 12th, 1852.

THE ASSOCIATION FOR THE EXHIBITION OF THE INDUSTRY OF ALL NATIONS give notice, that the Exhibition will be opened, in the City of New York, on the 2d day of May, 1853.

The Municipal Authorities have granted to them the use of Reservoir Square, and they are proceeding to erect thereon a building worthy of the purpose to which it is to be devoted.

The Association desire to make the Exhibition, in fact as well as in name, a representation from other countries as well as their own, of Raw Materials and Produce, Manufactures, Machinery, and Fine Arts.

To this end, they have made arrangements with CHARLES BUSCHEK, Esq., late Commissioner of the Austrian Empire at the Industrial Exhibition of London, whose skill, experience and high character offer the most satisfactory security to contributors from abroad.

Mr. Buschek is the authorized Agent of this Association, for all countries other than the Continent of America, and as such has received its instructions.

All communications from Contributors abroad must be addressed to him at "The Office of the Exhibition of the Industry of all Nations in New York," No. 6 Charing Cross, London. He will state to them the nature of the powers given and authority conferred, and will also explain the great inducements offered by this enterprise to European Exhibitors.

This Association will correspond with all persons in the United States, the Canadas and British Provinces, the West Indies, and this Continent generally, who may desire to contribute to this Exhibition.

All such communications must be addressed to "*The Secretary of the Association for the Exhibition of the Industry of all Nations, New York.*"

The Association is now ready to receive applications, and it is desired that they be sent in immediately. Due notice will be given, hereafter, when the building will be ready for the reception of articles.

Application for the admission of objects to the Exhibition must represent intelligibly their nature and purpose, and must also state distinctly the number of square feet, whether of wall, floor, or counter, required.

Machinery will be exhibited in motion—the Motive Power to be furnished by the Association—and applications for the admission of Machinery, to be so exhibited, in addition to the general description and the requisition for space, must set forth the amount of Motive Power required.

The Association deem it proper to announce, that Paintings in Frames will be exhibited.

As, notwithstanding the magnitude of the proposed building, there must, necessarily, be a limitation of space, the Association reserves the right to modify or reject applications, but, in so doing, will be governed by strict impartiality, looking only to the general objects of the enterprise.

The Association also reserves the right of determining the length of time, not to exceed in any case one season, during which objects shall, severally, form part of the Exhibition.

Exhibitors are requested to designate an agent, to whom their contributions shall be delivered when withdrawn from the Exhibition.

Prizes for excellence in the various departments of the Exhibition will be awarded under the direction of capable and eminent persons.

With this statement the Directors solicit the co-operation of the Productive Intellect and Industry of their own and other countries.

THEODORE SEDGWICK, *President.*

WM. WHETTEN, *Secretary.*

This was sent to the Foreign Ministers at Washington, who all responded favorably and cordially.

As no building of the kind contemplated had been erected in the United States, the want of experience in regard to it was felt. Sir JOSEPH PAXTON, who designed the plan of the London Crystal Palace, very liberally furnished one for our edifice; but the shape of the ground prevented its adoption.

Mr. DOWNING, since deceased, also offered one much admired, but it was excluded on account of its incompatibility with the terms of the city grant, which required an edifice of Iron and Glass. LEOPOLD EIDLITZ offered a plan with a suspension roof, designed to obviate the necessity of arches with wide spans. JAMES BOGARDUS presented one of a circular building with successive colonnades, one over the other, resembling, in a degree, the Coliseum. J. W. ADAMS sent in a plan of a great octagonal vault or dome, supported by ribs made of fasces or clusters of gaspipe. Other original and excellent plans were offered; but, after due deliberation, the board accepted that of CARSTENSEN and GILDEMEISTER. Mr. Gildemeister had been for some time established in New York as architect and artist; Mr. Carstensen designed the Tivoli and Casino of Copenhagen, the chief public grounds of that city, and had but lately come among us. This plan was accepted on the 26th of August. It was slightly changed from the original for the sake of economy, a basement story being omitted. The work was immediately commenced. Masonry contracts were signed with Smith & Stewart, and Lorenzo Moss on the 4th of September; and on the 25th of the same month, the chief part of the iron work was contracted for. The foundation and castings were contracted to be delivered on the 21st of October. To secure uniformity, a pattern-shop was established in this city, under Sheppard & Purvis, and the iron contractors were several, in order to expedite the work, as follows: Jackson; Stillman, Allen & Co.; Hogg and Delamater; Buckup & Pugh; and F. S. Claxton, of New York; Slater & Steele, of Jersey; the Matteawan Company, of Fishkill; Templins, of Easton, Pennsylvania; Betts, Pusey, Jones, and Seal, of Wilmington, Delaware; and Miller and Williamson, of Albany.

It is not necessary to trace here all the details of the building processes, or the means employed to secure the co-operation of artists and artizans in worthily filling the edifice. A few particulars will suffice.

The erection of the first column of the Palace was honored by appropriate ceremonies on the 30th of October, 1852. On that occasion the Governor of New York and other notabilities were present; and Mr. Sedgwick made an address to the Governor, of which the following is an extract:

Permit me, sir, to say a word respecting the building itself. We intend, and I believe it is not too much to claim, that the palace itself shall make an epoch in the architecture of our city. We believe that it will give an impulse to construction in the material of iron that will be of the greatest service to that interest. Iron constructions have already been carried far forward by a most intelligent and accomplished mechanic—Mr. James Bogardus—and I believe that the experience of this building will give it a great additional impulse. Its superior lightness, durability, cheapness, and facility of construction, give it immense advantages over any other material. We are erecting an edifice that will cover, on the ground floor, two and a half acres, and it will be done in the winter, in about six months, for a sum not much varying from $200,000. If any one compares this time with what would be required for a building of any other material except wood, the immense superiority of iron is most perceptible. [Applause.] But there are, sir, ulterior considerations which I wish clearly to state. The large cities of the elder world, especially on the continent, possess great galleries for popular instruction and entertainment. It is at first sight remarkable, though in fact easily intelligible, that in a country reposing entirely on popular power, comparatively nothing is done on a great public scale for the pleasure and instruction of our adult people. We have no galleries, no parks. This is not the place to say anything in favor of a park, though an object which should be dear to the heart of every New Yorker. But I desire, in regard to the other objects, to point out how easy it will be hereafter to convert this building into a great People's Gallery of Art. Its structure is eminently adapted for the purpose. We stand here on the city's ground, and it will be completely in the power of the city hereafter to accomplish this result. Long after our Association shall have disappeared, I hope this building may stand—as long as yonder massive and majestic creation; and like that, in the hands of the public authorities, be one of those monuments which make the Government dear to the people. [Cheers.] Allow me to say a few words of our purposes. The undertaking is a private one—fostered by no governmental aid; but the interests are so numerous and divided, that not the slightest color is afforded for the charge of speculation. There are, I venture to say, very few undertakings of equal magnitude which are represented by so large a number of parties, and it thus becomes practicable to impress upon the direction and management of the enterprise, that broad, liberal, impartial, and, as it were, national character, which is essential to its proper development. If our success is what we expect and intend it shall be, we shall claim the honor of it for our institutions—those institutions which enable private individuals to accomplish what in other countries vast governmental efforts are required to effect. We shall claim the honor for the country and for the people; for that mixture of individual energy and practical accommodation which gives such wonderful efficiency to the American character; for that public spirit and private good feeling of which we have such striking evidence here to-day—bringing together at this moment men of all parties, to work together for a common object of general interest.

The building progressed steadily, though impeded by certain delays, which seem to attend all such undertakings in a greater or less degree. The ceremonies of its inauguration and its appearance and contents are described in the extracts from THE NEW YORK TRIBUNE, which appear in this volume.

As we write, the organization of the Juries to award Medals to, and make honorable mention of, the best contributions to the Crystal Palace, has taken place. This work was confided to Messrs. B. Silliman, Jr., B. P. Johnson, and Samuel Webber, who have the entire control and management thereof, and are styled the Commissioners on Juries. There are fifteen Juries; and the number on each Jury is intended to be regulated by the amount of labor, and the greater or less diversity of subjects assigned to each. The choice of Jurors is made from the entire Union, and from foreign countries in proportion to their contributions. No exhibitor can be on a Jury, if competing for a prize to be awarded by it; nor can firms to which a Juror belongs receive awards. The decisions of each Jury will be final in its own groups of subjects or classes. No portion of a Jury can award a prize, though it may act in detail or by Sub-Committees. The Presiding Officer or Chairman of each Jury must be chosen by its own members; likewise the Reporter. There will be two classes of Medals—Silver and Bronze; beside an Honorable Mention. On this head, the precedent of the London Exposition will be adopted.

That precedent is as follows: The London Commissioners considered it inexpedient to establish beforehand rules so precise as to fetter the discretion of the Juries upon which the task was to devolve. They simply laid down general principles. For example, in the department of raw materials and produce, prizes were awarded in reference to the value and importance of the article, and the excellence of the sample; as regards prepared materials, important novelty, skill, and the ingenuity displayed were considered. In machinery, novelty, efficiency, economy, and social utility. In manufactures, increased usefulness, permanency of dyes, improved forms of arrangements, superior quality or skill of workmanship, new use of known materials, new combinations of the same, beauty of design in form or color, or both, in reference to utility, and cheapness relatively to excellence of production. In sculpture, models, and the plastic arts, rewards were given in reference to beauty and originality, improvements in mode of production, application of art to manufactures, and in case of models, to the interest attaching to the subject which they represent. The higher medals were awarded equally to cheap and dear things, provided the former had the merit of utility or beauty.

The award of the American Crystal Palace will be accompanied by a document of attestation, bearing the signatures of the President of the Association, and the Chairman of whatever Jury. The silver medal will be given only for originality of design, or invention, or discovery, coupled with due skill of fabrication and excellence of material. Their first meetings for the transaction of business were on the 9th of November, at ten o'clock in the morning, at the Crystal Palace. Those not resident in New York have their travelling expenses paid, but not their expenses while here.

The Directors of the Crystal Palace are as follow:

Mortimer Livingston,	Philip Burrowes,
Alfred Pell,	Johnston Livingston,
Auguste Belmont,	Chas. W. Foster,
Alexander Hamilton, Jr.	Theodore Sedgwick,
Geo. L. Schuyler,	Wm. W. Stone,
Elbert J. Anderson,	Wm. Whetten,
Henry R. Dunham,	John Dunham,
W. C. H. Waddell,	Wm. Kent,
Jacob A. Westervelt,	Watts Sherman,
James A. Hamilton,	F. W. Edmonds,
Samuel Nicholson.	J. J. Roosevelt.

The following are the JURY LISTS:

JURY A—CLASS I.

Minerals, Mining and Metallurgy, and Geological and Mining Plans and Sections.

Prof. James D. Dana, Yale College.
Dr. F. A. Genth, Philadelphia.
Baron Von Gerolt, Prussian Minister, Balt.
Prof. James Hall, Albany.
Wm. C. Redfield, Yew York.
Prof. Henry D. Rogers, Philadelphia.
Prof. Benjamin Silliman, Yale College.
Geo. Sumner, Esq., Boston.

JURY B—COMPRISING CLASSES II. AND IV. AND PART OF CLASSES X. XVIII. XXIV. AND XXV.

Chemical and Pharmaceutical Products and Processes, Vegetable and Animal Substances employed in Manufactures; Chemical and Pharmaceutical Apparatus; Dyed and Printed Fabrics, shown as such, Glass for Chemical Utensils made both in Stone Ware and Hard Porcelain:

Prof. James C. Booth, Philadelphia.
John F. Currie, Esq., No. 55 Prince st. N.Y.
John Cornwall, Esq., Louisville, Ky.
George W. Cushing, No. 43 Broad st. N. Y.
Henry Coggell, No. 78 Broad st. N. Y.
Dr. Wolcott Gibbs, New York.
Dr. A. A. Hayes, Boston, Mass.
Dr. Jenkins, Natchez, Miss.
Dr. B. W. McReady, No. 8 Ninth st., N. Y.
H. Planten, New York.
Dr. J. Lawrence Smith, Louisville, Ky.
Dr. John Torrey, No. 91 Wall st. N. Y.
Dr. David A. Wells, Springfield, Mass.

JURY C—COMPRISING CLASSES III. AND IX.

Substances used as Food, and Agricultural, Horticultural, and Dairy Implements and Machines.

John Anderson, New York.
George W. Dobbin, Esq., Baltimore.
Dr. A. S. Elwyn, Philadelphia.
William Evans, Esq., Montreal, C. W.
Major Philip R. Freas, Germantown, Pa.
Watson Newbold, Esq., Columbus, N. J.
James B. Oakley, Esq., No. 15 South st. N.Y.
M. Edmond Poirier, No. 120 Pearl st. N. Y.
Prof. John A. Porter, Yale College.
Col. John W. Proctor, Danvers, Mass.
Henry Wager, Esq., Western, Oneida, N.Y.
Dr. Arthur Watts, Chillicothe, Ohio.
H. D. Telkampf, No. 85 Beaver st. N. Y.

JURY D—CLASSES V. VI. AND VII.

Machines for Direct Use, including Steam, Hydraulic and Pneumatic Engines and Railway and other Carriages, Machinery and Tools for Manufacturing purposes, Civil Engineering, Architectural and Building contrivances.

Prof. A. D. Bache, LL.D., Coast Survey, W.
N. Victor Blaumont, No. 650 Houston st NY.
John B. Bell, Esq., Pittsburgh, Pa.
James Bogardus, Centre st., N. Y.
James Brewster, New Haven, Conn.
Samuel Chase, Holyoke, Mass.
Charles W. Copeland, No. 66 Broadw. N.Y.
George Geddes, Fairmount, Onondaga Co.
Col. G. W. Hughes, West River, Anne Arundel Co., Md.
Gen. Charles T. James, Providence, R. I.
Daniel Tredwell, Boston.
Samuel Woodruff, Hartford, Conn.
W. R. Wright, Bureau of Agriculture, Qu.

JURY E—CLASS VIII.

Naval Architecture, Military Engineering, Ordnance, Armor and Accoutrements.

Sir James Alexander, Quebec.
E. K. Collins, Esq., No. 56 Wall st. N. Y.
Capt. Cullum, U. S. A.
Col. A. G. Hazzard, Enfield, Conn.
T. W. Lenthal, Naval Constructor.
Donald McKay, Esq., Boston.
Major Mordecai, U. S. A.
Capt. Morris, U. S. N.
Col. James Page, Philadelphia.
Hon. Jas. T. Pratt, Rocky Hill, Conn.
Maj. Gen. Winfield Scott, U. S. A.

JURY F—CLASS X. Xa. Xb.

Philosophical Instruments and Products resulting from their Use, Daguerreotypes, Maps and Charts, Horology, Surgical Instruments and Appliances.

Prof. Louis Agassiz, Cambridge.
Prof. J. H. Alexander, Baltimore.
Prof. J. W. Baily, West Point.
Samuel W. Benedict, Esq., No. 5 Wall st.
Capt. Chas. H. Bigelow, Lawrence, Mass.
Geo. W. Blount, Esq., 179 Water st. N.Y.
J. L. Buckingham, Esq., Philadelphia.
Dr. Burnet, Boston.
W. Darling Campbell, Esq., M. P., Quebec.
Prof. John W. Draper, New York.
Col. J. D. Graham, U. S. A.
Dr Guyardetti, Leroy-place.
Prof. Joseph Henry, Sec. Smith. Inst. Was.
Dr Leidy, Philadelphia.
Dr. Samuel Parkman, Boston.
Prof. James Renwick, Columb. Coll. N. Y.
Mr. Muller, No. 166 Broadway.

JURY G—CLASSES XI. XII. XIII. XIV. XV.

Manufactures of Cotton, Wool, Silk, Flax and Hemp, Mixed Fabrics, Shawls, Vestings, &c.

Mons. Albinola, No. 54 Pine st. New York.
Samuel Batchelder, Esq., Cambridge, Mass.
Ward Cheney, Esq., Manchester, Conn.
Frederic A. Concklin, Esq., No. 6 Park-Pla.
Amory Edwards, Esq., No. 9 Park-Place.
Samuel C. Frothingham, Jr. Boston, Mass.
Jules Griollet, Courier des Etats Unis, N. Y.
N. Stanton Gould, Esq., Hudson, N. York.
John B. Hall, Esq., No. 42 Beaver st. N. Y.
N. Kingsburg, Esq., Rockville, Conn.
A. Laurie, Notre Dame st., Montreal.
Wm. Mali, Esq., New York.
Edward Christ, No. 68 Broad st., New York.
Oscar Zollikoffer, No. 107 Liberty st.
M. Muhling, No. 21 South William st.

JURY H—CLASSES XVI. AND XX.

Leather, Furs and Hair, and their Manufactures, Gentlemen's Wearing Apparel.

George S. Beardmore, Esq., London, C. W.
Seth Boyden, Esq., Newark, N. J.
Charles Field, Esq., Philadelphia.
Wood Gibson, Esq., No. 362 Broadway, NY.
W. Hoyt, Esq., No. 40, Spring st. N York.
Chas. M. Leupp, Esq., No. 20 Ferry st. NY.
John C. Lord, Esq., No. 164 Water st. N.Y.
John T. Pray, Esq., Boston, Mass.
David Samuel, Esq., Philadelphia.
Thomas Smith, Esq., Hartford, Conn.
Charles St. John, Esq., 142 Water st. N. Y.
George Taber, Esq., Philadelphia.
Nathaniel Wildman, Danbury, Conn.
E. M. Young, Esq., No. 37 Ferry st. N. Y.
D. Wallenstein, Esq., No. 34 Beaver st. N.Y.
F. Ludwig, Esq., No. 56 New st. N. York.

JURY I—PART OF CLASS XIX. AND CLASS XX.

Tapestry, Decorative Furniture and Upholstery, including Papier Mache, Paper Hangings and Japanned Goods, Marble Ornaments and Marbleized Irons.

Daniel Bixby, Esq., Bixby's Hotel.
Julius Catlin, Esq., Hartford, Conn.
Mons. Cotta, New York.
Wm. Gibson, Esq., No. 374 Broadway, N Y.
C. W. Meakim, Esq., No. 44 St. James st. Montreal.
Henry Pettis, Esq., Boston.
George Platt, Esq., No. 53 Broadway, N.Y.
George Ponsot, Esq., No. 562 Broadw. N.Y.
A. T. Porter, Esq., Philadelphia.
John Sartain, Esq., Philadelphia.
W. Sloane, Esq., No. 245 Broadway, N. Y.
Prof. Van Der Weyde, No. 35 Washington-Place, New York.

JURY Ia—PART OF CLASS IX. AND CLASS XX.

Lace, Sewed and Tamboured Muslins, Embroidery, Fringes, Fancy and Industrial Works and Female Wearing Apparel.

John Beck, Esq., No. 355 Broadway, N. Y.
Thos. C. Doremus, Esq., No. 21 Park-place.
S. R. Downer, Esq., No. 44 Beaver st. N. Y.
A. Kunsler, Esq.
Thomas Lowndes, Esq., No. 49 Exc.-place.
John Neil, Esq., Philadelphia.

JURY J—CLASSES XXI. AND XXII.

Cutlery and Edge Tools, Iron, Brass, Pewter and General Hardware, including Lamps, Chandeliers and Kitchen Furniture.

E. W. Blake, Esq., New Haven, Conn.
Erastus Corning, Esq., Albany, N. Y.
Wm B. Dinsmore, Esq., No. 59 Broadway.
H. N. Hooper, Esq., Boston.
Professor, E. N. Hosford, Cambridge.
Adam Norrie, Esq., No. 90 Broadway, N.Y.
Samuel Steele, Esq., Cincinnati.
Wm. H. Scoville, Esq., Waterbury, Conn.
E. F. Sanderson, Esq., No. 16 Cliff st. N.Y.
Matthias Stratton, Esq., Philadelphia.
R. S. Luqueer, Esq., Hanover-square, N. Y.
Chas. Zollner, Esq., No. 221 Bowery.

JURY K—CLASSES XXVIII. AND XXIX.

Manufactures from Animal and Vegetable Substances not Woven, felted or otherwise specified, Miscellaneous manufactures and small wares, Confectionery, Toys, Taxidermis, &c.

Gen. Avezzana, No. 103 Pearl st. N. Y.
Chas. Ahrenfeldt, Esq., No. 56 Maiden-lane.
W. H Cary, Esq., No. 245 Pearl st.
Dr. Wm. H. Ellet, N. Y.
A. D. Erson, Esq., Hartford, Conn.
John Gebhardt, Albany.
Edward Lamarche, No. 80 John st.
W. T. Porter, Esq., Park-place.
Geo. Reed, Esq., Deep River, Conn.
Robt. L. Stuart, Esq., cor. Gr. and Ch. sts.
Thomas Shortts, Esq., Toronto, Canada.
Philip Saunders, Esq., New Haven, Conn.
Henry Wurtz, Esq., Newark, N. J.

JURY L—CLASS XXIII.

Work in Precious Metals and their Imitations, Jewelry and other Personal Ornaments, except Bronzes and articles of vertu, which are transferred to the action of Jury O.

Samuel T. Crosby, Esq., Boston.
Geo. P. Curtis, Esq., No. 406 8th Av.
Ferdinand Eaysten, Esq., No. 146 Pearl st.
Mons. Pastacaldi, No. 87 Pearl st.
Robert Rait, Esq., No. 261 Broadway.
Wm. Stebbins, Esq., No. 264 Broadway.

SUB-JURY L—CLASSES XXIV. AND XXV.

Glass Manufactures, Porcelain and other Ceramic Manufactures.

Ebenezer Collamore, Esq., No. 293 Broadw.	Andrew T. Wale, Esq., Boston.
Benj. M. Mumford, Esq., No. 101 Pearl st.	C. C. Bechet, Esq., No. 24 Exchange-place.
John C. Jackson, Esq., No. 113 Water st.	Earl Douglas, No. 81 Pearl st.
P. C. Dummer, Esq., Jersey City.	Mr. Heye, No. 183 Pearl st.
Richard Burlen, Esq., No. 98 Pearl st. N.Y.	

JURY M—CLASS XXX

Musical Instruments.

Geo. F. Bristow, Esq., Director of Sacred Music Society, N. Y.	Mons. Jullien.
	Max Maretzek, Director of the Italian Op.
I. S. Dwight, Esq., Boston.	Leopold Meignen, Philadelphia.
Theo. Eisfeldt, Esq., Director of Philharmonic Society, N. Y.	William Norris, Philadelphia.
	R. Storrs Willis, New York.
Wm. Henry Fry, Esq., New York.	William Hall, New York.
Æmilius Girac, New York.	

JURY N—CLASS XVII.

Paper and Stationery, Types, Printing and Bookbinding, and Specimens of Ornamental Penmanship.

Wm. H. Appleton, Esq., No. 200 Broadway.	Mr. Lewis, No. 48 William st. N. Y.
Henry Butler, Esq., Paterson, N. J.	Mr. Ortell, Brooklyn.
A. B. Clark, Esq., Brooklyn	Charles Sherman, Esq., Philadelphia.
E. I. Danforth, Esq., No. 1 Wall st. N. Y.	Chas. Van Benthuysen, Esq., Albany.
Geo. Desbarats (Queen's Printer,) Quebec.	R. Grant White, Esq., No. 70 Wall st. N.Y.
James Fields, Esq., Boston.	Mr. Bell, No. 304 Fulton st. N. Y.
Robert Hoe, Esq., No. 31 Gold st. N. Y.	

JURY O—CLASS XXXI.

Fine Arts, Sculpture, Paintings, Engravings, etc.—Bronzes and Articles of Vertu from Class XXIII.

Mr. Edward Antonisson, No. 406 4th av. N.Y.	Henry Greenough, Cambridge, Mass.
A. M. Cozzens, Esq., No. 89 Water st. N.Y	Prof. S. F. B. Morse, Poughkeepsie.
Chas. A. Dana, New York Tribune.	Mons. Sebron, No. 4 Leroy-place.
A. B. Durand, Esq., No. 91 Amity st. N. Y.	Wm. Young, Esq., Editor of the Albion.
Chas. Elliott, Esq., New York.	Henry Ulke, Esq., No. 196 Grand st. N. Y.
Hon. Edward Everett, Boston.	Henry K. Browne, Esq., Brooklyn.
Prof. Foresti, No. 258 19th st. New York.	

It is the glory and strength of every truly great work, whether in the visible or audible form of Art, or in the intangible nature of enterprise pure and simple, or in the combination of thought and expression, that it is not adequately understood on being first presented to the world. Not counting the tears, disappointments and struggles of genius which cannot find a public plummet to reach the profundities of its conceptions, but coming to works absolutely born and placed within the range of public vision, how few great things are really apprehended! Take the Public Press, for example. It is but a few years,—some ten or so,—that it has been put upon a basis wide enough for the wants of the community, or in its division of labor, accuracy of information, earnestness and independence of thought, and mechanical resources, has merited the abstract claim set up for its grandeur.

Take, then, any other great thing—the Electric Telegraph for example. This discovery, though its value was mathematically demonstrated, went begging for years. Congress, although the working model was in a lower chamber of the Capitol, could not be induced to look at it. And, when it began to work, so little was its worth understood, that the cost of transmitting messages was placed, under a supposed necessity, beyond the means of ordinary people—(in Europe this cost is still frightfully high)—and it is only after some ten years' working that the sentiment of the grandeur and utility of the thing begins to lower the tariff of prices by outside pressure.

So, too, in the last important thing before the public, the ignorance in many quarters, as we see by the press, of the value of such a common centre of art and invention is remarkable. But the inherent resources of the Crystal Palace are so grand, and, if sustained, its novel results are so vast, that, with the view of widening such a contracted estimate of its values, we shall offer a few remarks on it.

The great utility of the Crystal Palace consists in its forming a standard of Art, and an exchange for testing the values of Industry. It is now rated as a thing for the moment; a house is built, and so many industrious or clever people have been induced to put in their productions as a cheap mode of advertising them. But that were a narrow view of the enterprise. We must accustom ourselves to look upon the Crystal Palace as a permanent institution. We must feel the necessity of not letting it die out. We need it woefully. We need a broad national and cosmopolitan platform whereon genius or ingenuity may at once place its productions and obtain the highest sanctions; or where pretence may meet with a decisive check. It is in vain to speak of the Patent-Office at Washington as a proper place. Washington is not a metropolis. Without disparaging its claims, suffice to say it wants the houses and the multitudes to make a metropolis. Neither is Boston, with its Mechanics' Institute; nor Philadelphia, with its pioneer Franklin Institute; nor New-York with its American Institute, fully equal to the national wants of such an art and industry show-house. But particularly are Patent-Office and State Institutes unequal to the indispensable part of cosmopolitanism which a World's Fair can alone play. A nation, like an individual, requires many a hard rub before the conceit can be taken out of it; on the other hand, it requires equally to measure its strength with others before it can be made truly aware of its strength. Doubts of the naval superiority of the Americans at sea were set at rest by the war of 1812; though it was deemed presumptuous to cope with the Briton on his traditional element. So, too, in England at least it was thought pert for the yacht America to walk the waters with unblenched courage, and challenge the swiftest of the swift of England's craft to decisive contest. But when *The Times* reported that the lagging yachts of its nation were so far behind that they were "nowhere" as to distance, the revolution of opinion was complete. We believe there are things—artistic things, in which America may measure her powers with Europe, which now, owing to their being above the standard of vulgar objective determination, are not recognized by their countrymen. Let it then, be fairly and fully understood that the Crystal Palace is a permanent foundation. Let it be recognized that every possible artistic, scientific and industrial production can be sent there, and seen and adjudged by competent persons. Whether it be iron, wood or ivory, gold, silver, velvet, woollen or cotton; whether it appeal to the eye, or the ear, or the palate, or to economics general or special, let there be a standing Court and Jury to determine, or seek to determine, its relative and positive value; its realities, its suggestions, its deficiencies, its triumphs. Then the sickening delays which talent or genius suffer would be greatly done away with. If the public cannot be taught to embrace a great thing at once—as they never have been—there may at least be great labor-saving machinery in processes leading in part to such a result. The best, largest and most potent machine for such a desideratum is surely the Crystal Palace,—not simply in its present moral and physical state, but connected with the possible extensions which are inherent in its national and cosmopolitan character.

In another point of view, the Crystal Palace, as a standard place of Exhibition, is of the highest value. The original acquaintance which the American public at large had with a good statue may be dated from the exhibition of a single one by Powers some few years back. Now, however, we have in the Palace a whole gallery of statues (not to mention paintings,) and the force of comparison, without which works cannot be tested, is thus available. The reasons, too, appear for our pursuing high art in order to produce works wherein our inferiority is evident. We cannot survey the rich collection of articles which Europe presents without being made acutely sensible of our shortcomings. We must feel, too, the economical beauty of achieving ourselves whatever noble art is practised in other countries.

The persons, it may be appropriately stated, who have accepted the office of Jurors to determine Prizes and Honorable Mentions for the contributors of the Crystal Palace are now actively engaged in their work. Those who have not looked into the matter cannot fully imagine the extent of the labors so cheerfuly assumed by a considerable number of our fellow-citizens. Besides the toil of travel—and the Jurors must often come from a distance, as they have been designedly chosen from various parts of the Union, in order that all may have a fair chance—there is a degree of separate and collective labor required that must prevent rapid decisions, however desirable, from taking place. We are particularly cognizant of one Jury, the individual members of which spend much of the day examining carefully and systematically the hundreds of things within their bailiwick, taking down at the same time copious positive and comparative notes. Besides this, they hold during the day a secret session where the utmost latitude of debate is indulged in, the Chairman maintaining due order and seeing that every one has a full chance for equal discussion. This morning session lasts sometimes three hours or more, and it is an excellent study to learn the vast amount of information then brought forward. Whole cyclopædias of knowledge come forth; the most accurate and ripened experience of men, almost every one of whom is a celebrity in his department, are detailed; and often a discussion of an hour is held in unbroken continuity upon the more intricate parts of the question. We could also name a Jury that meets at ten o'clock at night and goes through, in combination, the work of investigation which had been pursued by its members individually. This procedure is the most piquant of all. Rival projectors, inventors, artisans, artists, are summoned on the stand in their works, at least before this puissant body; how different the high-priestly talk on this occasion from the ordinary superficiality which passes with the world! Reputations deemed inexpugnable are shattered by a single keen, retrospective and prospective remark; some unexpected requirement is suddenly suggested; some new and more difficult standard of excellence agreed upon. And then the great works for competition, already winnowed, are placed side by side for comparison, sometimes. Ranged as in battle-array come the industrial and artistic hosts of France, Britain, Germany, Italy, America. Carefully cold is the decision now. Enthusiasm is out of the question. The words are few and peremptory. The Chairman's measurement-book is out. The various shades of excellence and inferiority are determined by a list of adjectives of genial or merciless import as they elevate or depress the object before them. The opinion of each Juror is separately asked. Is this or that quality a pretension of the work examined of the first, second, third, fourth, or fifth order? Is this other quality so and so? Is this requirement at such or such a point of excellence? And so through the whole searching catalogue.

If the reader, in his more inquiring moods, has ever attended a dissecting-room; if he has seen the fearfully-made body laid, its vitality fled, on a deal table; if he has observed the surgeon's knife piercing the wondrous texture of the outward skin, and all the startling economy of glory and beauty which God has arrayed to perfect his greatest work, Man, revealed; heart, brain, spine, ganglionic tissue, all patent to the eye, and the mysteries of their appearance and relations developed as they lie almost undisturbed, save as to their outward covering—he can by comparison imagine the materialized body of an Idea laid before such a Jury in such a place. Nothing is allowed to escape them. No partiality, no flattery to win the dull cold ear of death is needed for the first; and in its way the last hears naught but words of searching truth.

The vapid puffs of the venal or foolish, to vaunt this or that thing, are in especial contrast with the analytical scenes we have hinted at. The great force and dignity of truth are here exhibited. The value of such a high Court of Appeals—classifying in the face of the public and of the world, the great works that genius or labor may offer—weighing the saliencies and splendors of whole nations—describing a circle of economics and esthetics—cannot be over-estimated. We must see in it the vestibule to a permanent institution, whose tribunals will try reputations in art and labor, habitually—whose decisions America and the world will respect—whose wholesome advice, though it may grieve aspirants at the moment, may prove to them the cause of ultimate and indisputable superiority—whose abnegation of vulgar nationality may stimulate our countrymen into speedy and successful competition with Europe in all those arts wherein she is now our superior.

The Crystal Palace, we would remark, is inadequately visited by our city people, while country people and those from other towns than New York flock to it. How is this? Is it the old story, that "the stranger knows more of the sights of a town than residents?" If so, or from whatever cause, the city folks do not throng the Crystal Palace, are greatly the losers. The chance to study these art and industry wonders of the world may never occur again. Some wiseacres, never having seen it, have called the Exhibition a humbug. A humbug! Why, if the Crystal Palace had nothing in it, not even the Police on guard, it would be a—or *the*—lion of the thirty-one States. The building is magnificent. The dome ranks only after such as St. Peter's, at Rome. The splendid innovation on stale precedent, in the materials of the building—iron and glass: the types of solidity and lightness united, would alone recompense any person of ordinary taste and curiosity for a long journey in order to reach the premises. But once inside, what a brilliant, heroic revelation of human skill, devotion, industry, combination, versatility, and genius does it present? What is not there? From the huge labor-crushing, time-deriding machinery which promises the millennium of comparative repose to the under-fed, over-worked toilers of thousands of years—to the delicate and tiny missionary of beauty in diamonds, gold, silver, or colors—what a startling array there is of superb works! How rich and suggestive, too, is the contrast of the various powers and performances of different nations! How naif the outworkings of their respectively indigenous minds—as natural as the forest's growth or the water's fall! How national prejudice dwarfs and dwindles in the contemplation of such works as Paris, London, Milan, or Berlin sends forth.

Look at yonder collection of French skill. Examine those Gobelin tapestries—so dwelt upon in novels and travels—but now first revealed to us in this new world in all the plenitude of fabric, color, and design. What a lesson do they afford of the extent of human perseverance! Here is a great painting copied faithfully. But every tint in full and all its dying glories, is exactly imitated by the magical skill of the loom. A whole day will not exhaust the contemplation of its beauties. And then regard those Sevres Vases. What perfection! Can form or design, or color further go? We say, no. The Parthenon has never been eclipsed in architecture: neither has a Sevres Vase in the constructive and decorative beauty which it displays. It is perfection. Contemplate it for at least an hour. Time well spent. There learn to respect the French people who can habitually produce such Olympian-like miracles of art. Stop, too, before those French bronzes. Can anything be finer? They are diminutive in size, but gigantic in composition. That horse fairly leaps and snorts; that wounded bird seems lifted up in its dying agony, and heavy bronze transmuted into feathery waves of hovering tragedy. Wondrous art! Who is the great man who made it?

"The world knows not its greatest men."

Enter likewise the department of the sturdy Briton. How the Graces at last are playing over the foggy island! Just look at that Silver ware. Uncover yourself, for you are in the holy temple of art, and a god of beauty present. Look at those vases. They seem to have been made for the delicate hands of Hebe. Contemplate that prize silver work. Look at the men, the horses, the palm-trees. Ask yourself, is it mechanics, is it artists, is it special inspirations which have produced this?—what has, or rather what has not been called into action to produce these radiating splendors of imagination and execution? But how are such men honored in England? Could the Herald's office tell us?

But step over to the Thorwaldsen Gallery of Statues. Here is the Christ and his Twelve Apostles. They may not be—they are not—works of the highest order of originality—but what a lesson they teach of artistic devotion and religious sublimity? Mark the soft rays as they stream through the veiled sky-light and reveal the figures placed against the dark background. What a serene, holy influence is thus cast around! How it yields up this onward, impulsive, material epoch to the dreamy mistiness of the middle ages, when the sculptor's and architect's skill taught the Redeemer's love and agony, and life was seen through the heaven-wreaked splendors of the great cathedral window—circular type of eternity, and lustrous mimic of glad tidings of salvation!

THE

GREAT EXHIBITION

OF

ART AND INDUSTRY.

I.

THE PALACE.

THIS edifice starts in its delicate beauty from the earth like the imagining of a happy vision. Viewed at a distance, its burnished dome resembles a half-disclosed balloon, as large as a cathedral, but light, brilliant, and seemingly ready to burst its bands and soar aloft. In every sense, the Crystal Palace is admirable. To us on this side of the water, it is original. Nothing like it in shape, material, or effect, has been presented to us. If it were to contain nothing, it would alone be an absorbing attraction, and be beyond all else in New York, an architectural curiosity.

The building is two stories high. The first is in the form of an octagon, the second of a Greek cross. The centre of this is a dome, one hundred and forty-eight feet high. The four corners of the octagon are furnished each with two towers, seventy feet high. These towers support flag-staffs, adding to the lightness of their appearance. The construction of the building is similar to that of the original in London, so far as the connection of iron columns, girders, and so forth, go ; but the principal parts of the rest, the dome included, were fashioned by the architects, Messrs. CARSTENSEN and

GILDERMEISTER, who devised the plan of the whole structure as well as the details. The main building covers 173,000 square feet, galleries included; and the additional building 33,000, being 206,000 in all. The additional building is composed of a first and a second story gallery, 21 feet broad and 450 feet long, lit from above, the sides being quite closed up, so as to form a suitable place to exhibit pictures and statues. This additional building is connected with the main building by two one-story wings, which contain the refreshment rooms, and the mineralogical department under the charge of Prof. Silliman, Jr.

There are twelve stairways, the balustrades of which are light iron tracery, in accordance with the general spirit of the designs. The stairways are at each point of the compass, on the sides and under the dome. The great circular windows, facing at four points, add much to the charm of the effect.

Walls, properly speaking, the building has not, being enclosed with glass sustained by iron pillars. This vast mass of crystal occupies 45,000 square feet.

The cast-iron, weighs 1,200 tons; the wrought, 300. Each pane of glass is 16 by 38 inches. The prevailing style of the architecture is Moorish, and Byzantine in its decorations. The ceilings are painted in octagons, in blue, white, red, and cream-color. The single fault we find with the colors of the other portions of the building is, that the supporting pillars are of the same color with the other solid works, while if they were bronzed, a certain sameness would be avoided, and the impression of their character for strength be distinctly conveyed.

The decorative artist is Mr. Greenough. The offices of the directors and artists are in imitation of satin-wood, their appearance being very neat.

The entrances of the Palace are three, all alike: one on the Sixth Avenue, one on Fortieth, and one on Forty-second street. Each entrance is forty-seven feet wide, the central nave is forty-one feet wide, and the aisles fifty-four feet. Within, at the entrance, the visitor sees an arched nave forty-one feet wide, sixty-seven feet high, and three hundred feet long. The dome is one hundred feet across. The building, though not near so large as its prototype of the London Exhibition, is superior in architectural beauty. It is a magnificent ornament to the city, by which it should be purchased as a permanent property. Various ovations could be fitly celebrated in it. The work assures a national renown to the architects, Messrs. Carstensen and Gildermeister. The plans were submitted in July, 1852, accepted in August, and operations commenced in November. After delays, which should have been expected, the formal opening took place on the 14th of July, 1853, though the building itself was not then completed, while barely half the articles intended for exhibition were in position. For some weeks the leakage of the roof on every recurrence of violent rain was excessive, threatening to destroy the more perishable goods, many of which were doubtless seriously damaged.

A comparison of the American with the British Palace of Industry is by no means damaging to the former. True, we miss here the noble transept of the London edifice; we miss its stately, graceful elms, so admirably testifying of Nature in the very metropolis of Art; we miss its superb Glass Fountain, with its abundant flow of leaping crystal water. There is no single view in our Exhibition equal to that from the crystal fountain east and west through the grand aisle stretching one hundred rods on either hand and replete with the grand achievements of Genius and Labor. But the lofty, magnificent Dome of the American Palace has no parallel in the British, and probably has none in the world, unless it be that of St Peter's at Rome. Then the brilliant and generally judicious coloring—on the inside as well as externally—of the glass and iron composing our Palace, is a great improvement on the Quaker-like plainness of its London exemplar, which seemed but a paler reflex of those leaden British skies. Ours is said to cover but one-fifth the space engrossed by its prototype; but the actual difference in their relative capacity must be far less than is implied in this proportion. We judge the capacity of our Crystal Palace to be about one-third that of the British. Its galleries are relatively finer and more spacious. The eye is better satisfied with its symmetry, its decorations, and its colors. We were agreeably disappointed in its capacity, so far as the accommodation of visitors is regarded. As the London edifice was pretty full when sixty thousand persons were in it, and it was said to have been absolutely crowded by one hundred thousand, we had supposed fifteen thousand as many as our Palace would comfortably hold, and twenty thousand the utmost extent of its capacity. Experience proves that twenty-five thousand may meet in the New York edifice, without serious inconvenience or pressure. The lack of seats, which was a serious defect in the London Exhibition, is noted here also. There are many thousands so unaccustomed to constant walking that a single hour's locomotion fatigues them. These should have ample opportunity to rest without leaving the edifice, so as to renew their observations without inconvenience. The retiring-rooms, refreshment saloon, &c., which are such indispensable adjuncts of such an Exhibition, were not ready for weeks after the opening, and then the charges for refreshments were the subjects of general complaint. Of course the Managers had no interest in these exactions, but they might have foreseen and prevented them.

The few last days of preparation for the opening were signalized by the most untiring exertions within, around, and upon the Palace.

Besides an army of workmen in shops and factories preparing the materials for the building, there were at work upon it between six and seven hundred. It was a scene of rare industry. Thickly resonant blows from the stalwart arms of industry greeted the ear in wild confusion. Workmen perched, like autumnal pigeons on lofty boughs, clustered within and without the vast edifice, and the magic web of improvement each day proceeded. Each man appeared to be enthusiastically engaged on his task, forming a rivulet to meet in a wide sea of triumph. And not alone was the cunning hand of the artisan displayed in works of iron, wood, or colors; for here were now assembled the sons of toil and taste from all parts of Europe. The Russ, the Italian, Briton, Teuton, were all busily engaged in the work of arranging their contributions. It was a great battle of industry and love, and the God of such battles surely observed and blessed it.

II.

THE OPENING.

Notwithstanding the immense confusion of the Palace on the day preceding the Inauguration, we were surprised on entering it the next morning to find the dome completed, and glorious in its artistic beauty; the stairways arrayed with their crimson and gold, and many of the divisions elaborate in their ornamentation, completely arranged and containing their various contributions.

The vastness of the City of New York was strikingly illustrated by the weather of that day. The President and his suit were caught in a heavy rain in the lower part of the city, lasting an hour, while the early visitors at the Palace were ignorant of the circumstance, the atmosphere being dry and the sun bright in that quarter.

The approaches to the Palace were very much crowded as we proceeded there about eleven o'clock. The thickly-studded drinking shops were flaunting in their intemperate seductions. The various shows of monsters, mountebanks, and animals, numerous as on the jubilee-days of the Champs Elysées, opened wide their attractions to simple folk. Little speculators in meats, fruits, and drinks, had their tables and stalls *al fresco*. A rush and whirl of omnibuses, coaches, and pedestrians, encircled the place. But amid all this were plainly discernible the excellent provisions of the police to maintain order. The entrances to the Palace were kept clear, and no disturbance manifested itself through the day. Different colored tickets admitted the visitors at three different sides of the Palace, the fourth closing up against the giant Croton Water Reservoir.

There were two platforms partially under the dome, the centre point under which being occupied by Baron Marochetti's exceedingly absurd statue of Washington, with Carew's indescribably absurd statue of Webster—the worst calumny on that great man ever yet perpetrated, or that can be perpetrated—standing behind it. One of these platforms was toward Forty-second street, or, the north nave; the other toward the Croton Water Reservoir, on the east nave.

According to the programme, they were filled by the following classes of persons:—

ON THE NORTH NAVE PLATFORM.

Gen. FRANKLIN PIERCE, President of the United States.

MEMBERS OF THE CABINET.

Jefferson Davis, Secretary of War.
James Guthrie, Secretary of the Treasury.
Caleb Cushing, Attorney-General.

SENATE OF THE UNITED STATES.

Salmon P. Chase, U. S. Senator from Ohio.
Richard Brodhead Jr., U. S. Senator from Pennsylvania.

OFFICERS OF THE ARMY.

Major-General Winfield Scott, Commander-in-Chief.
Major-General John E. Wool, and a few others.

OFFICERS OF THE NAVY.

Commodore James Stewart.
Commodore Boorman, of the Navy Yard.

There were several other naval and military officers present, but their names are not recollected.

GOVERNORS OF VARIOUS STATES.

Horatio Seymour, Governor of the State of New York.
George F. Fort, Governor of the State of New Jersey.
Howell Cobb, Governor of the State of Georgia.

THE CLERGY.

Rt. Rev. Jonathan M. Wainwright, D.D., Provisional Bishop of New York.
Most Rev. John Hughes, D.D., Archbishop of New York.
Rt. Rev. Henry J. Whitehouse, D.D., Bishop of Illinois.
Gardiner Spring, D.D.; William Adams, D.D., and others.

THE JUDICIARY.

Judge Betts, Judge Edmonds, Judge Oakley, Judge Roosevelt, Judge Sandford, Judge Emmett, &c.

MILITARY, &C.

Maj. Gen. Sandford, Brig. Gen. Hall, Brig. Gen. Morris, with the Staff of the Major-General.

FOREIGN COMMISSIONERS.

Messrs. WHITWORTH and WALLACE, of the English Commission, were present; Lord ELLESMERE we did not see; he had not arrived in town at 10 o'clock. Lady ELLESMERE and daughters were present.

FOREIGN MINISTERS, &C.

Gen. ALMONTE, Minister Plenipotentiary from Mexico.

M. DE SARTIGES, Minister Plenipotentiary from France.

M. DE OSMA, Minister Plenipotentiary from Peru.

ON THE EAST PLATFORM.

Officers of the Army and Navy—a considerable number.

Officers of the Leander. (We are not sure that any were present—the ship is not here.)

Foreign Consuls resident in the city—a number present.

Judiciary of the Southern District of New York.

JACOB A. WESTERVELT, Mayor of New York.

FRANCIS R. TILLOU, Recorder of the city of New York.

RICHARD T. COMPTON, President of the Board of Aldermen.

JONATHAN TROTTER, President of the Board of Assistants.

The Common Council were rather thinly represented in numbers.

ISAAC V. FOWLER, Postmaster at New York.

Rev. Dr. FERRIS, Chancellor of the University.

CHARLES KING, LL. D., President of Columbia College.

Members of the Press, the Clergy, Officers of the American Institute, &c.

We believe there was no Foreign Commissioner, who came from Europe to be present at the exhibition, but the Earl of Ellesmere. The absence of this Commissioner at the opening, was much to be regretted—the more so, as he was prevented from coming by indisposition. Lady Ellesmere and her two daughters were present, however.

There were three military bands. Dodworth, stationed in the west gallery; Bloomfield's U. S. Band, in the south gallery; and an orchestra, with Noll's Military Band, and a grand chorus, composed of the members of the New York Sacred Music Society, conducted by Mr. Bristow, accompanied also by an organ in the east gallery.

The President, being detained by the storm, did not arrive at the appointed time of one o'clock, being delayed till about an hour later. When he did come, however, with his suit, civil and military, he was warmly greeted by the people within the building, who amounted to some 20,000, as far as we could judge.

The United States Band struck up Hail Columbia, and finished with Yankee Doodle. This part of the day's proceedings was extremely interesting. When the shouts had died away, and thousands of fair hands, waving their handkerchiefs, had exhausted their first burst of enthusiasm, Bishop Wainwright delivered, in a full, round voice, his appropriate prayer. It was in the following words:

PRAYER OF BISHOP WAINWRIGHT.

We praise Thee, O God; we acknowledge Thee to be the Lord. All the earth doth worship Thee, the Father everlasting. To Thee all angels cry aloud; the heavens and all the powers therein. To Thee cherubim and seraphim continually do cry, holy, holy, holy, Lord God of Sabaoth: Heaven and earth are full of the majesty of Thy glory. We, O Lord, Thy humble and dependent creatures would now join with Heaven and earth to praise Thy holy name. Thou art the Father of our spirits, and the bounteous source of all our blessings. While we adore Thy majesty and praise Thee for Thy goodness, we at the same time, in all humility, acknowledge our own sinfulness and unworthiness, and implore Thy forgiveness through the merits and intercession of our Lord and Savior Jesus Christ. As we thank Thee, O Lord, for all Thy mercies vouchsafed to us and to all men, especially at this time do we make to Thee our grateful acknowledgment for blessings Thou hast conferred upon us as a nation. We praise Thee for the goodly heritage Thou hast given us, for the civil and religious privileges which we enjoy, and for the multiplied manifestations of Thy favor toward us. Grant that we may show forth our thankfulness for these Thy mercies, by living in reverence of Thy Almighty power and dominion, in humble reliance on Thy goodness and mercy, and in holy obedience to Thy righteous laws. Preserve to us, we beseech Thee, and grant to all the nations of the earth the blessings of peace. Grant that the Kingdom of the Prince of Peace may come, and, reigning in the hearts and lives of men, unite them in holy fellowship, that so their only strife may be who shall show forth with most humble and holy fervor Thy praises, and most entirely and affectionately obey Thy laws. O, Lord, our governor, who hast been mindful of man and visited him; who hast made him lower than the angels, to crown him with glory and worship, and hast made him to have dominion of the works of Thy hands, and hast put all things in subjection under his feet, we devoutly thank Thee for the favor and protection Thou hast extended to this great and benevolent enterprise, to inaugurate which we are now assembled. We acknowledge that it is Thy spirit which hath given to man understanding. In these manifestations of skill, genius, enterprise, and industry, we would ask Thy inspiring power. In all this fertility of invention, these powers of combination, these hands and fingers of dexterity, and this abundance of materials, furnished from the inexhaustless treasury of nature, we would see Thy hand. We pray that the happy influence of this undertaking may be to incite a generous and laudable competition among the sons of science, art, and labor, throughout the world, and that we may all look upon it as a demonstration of the wisdom and goodness of God in endowing man with rich and manifold gifts, which, faithfully exercised, will contribute to the comfort, the happiness, and the moral elevation of the great family of man. O Lord, our Heavenly Father, the high and mighty Ruler of the universe, we implore Thy blessings upon the President of the United States, and upon all in authority over us, and so replenish them with the grace of Thy Holy Spirit, that they may always incline to Thy will and walk in Thy way. Give grace, O Heavenly Father, to all bishops and other ministers, that they may, both by their life and doctrine, set forth Thy true and holy word, and rightly and duly administer Thy holy sacrament. Prosper, O Lord, our schools, academies, and colleges, and cause them to be more than ever the promoters of sound learning, of pure morals, and undefiled religion. And we beseech Thee pour the quickening influence of Thy Holy Spirit on all the people of this land, and save them from the guilt of abusing the blessings of prosperity to luxury and licentiousness, to irreligion and vice. May the devout sense of Thy manifold mercies, as vouchsafed to us as a nation, renew and increase in us a spirit of love and thankfulness to Thee, a spirit of peaceable submission to the laws and government of our country, and a spirit of honest zeal for our holy faith. May we constantly improve these inestimable blessings for the advancement of religion, liberty, and knowledge, throughout our extensive land, till the wilderness and solitary places be glad for them, and the desert rejoice and blossom as the rose. And now, O God, vouchsafe to us Thy presence in the remaining services of the day—direct us in all our doings with Thy most gracious favor, and further us with Thy continual help, that in all our works begun, continued, and ended in Thee, we may glorify Thy holy name, and finally, by Thy mercy, obtain everlasting life.

Almighty God, the fountain of all wisdom, who knowest our necessities before we ask, and our ignorance in asking, we beseech Thee to have compassion upon our infirmities; and those things which for our unworthiness we dare not, and for our blindness we cannot ask, vouchsafe to give us for the worthiness of Thy Son, Jesus Christ our Lord, in whose name, and in whose holy words we sum up our petitions unto Thee, saying:—

Our Father, which art in Heaven, hallowed be Thy name; Thy kingdom come; Thy will be done on earth as it is in Heaven. Give us this day our daily bread, and forgive us our trespasses as we forgive them that trespass against us; and lead us not into temptation but deliver us from evil, for Thine is the kingdom, and the power, and the glory, for ever and ever. Amen.

Then came stealing through the vast aisles the Hymn of Old Hundred set to semi-secular words. The effect where we stood under the dome was mystically grand. It might be imagined to typify the voices of distant nations rolling in harmonious vastness through the aisles, and bearing the accents of gentleness and beneficence. Their artistic interpretation was entrusted to the ladies and gentlemen of the Sacred Harmonic Society, and admirably did they execute their task. Mr. George Bristow was the conductor of the body. Mr. Timm, however, was the chief director of all the musical arrangements. The hymn ran thus :—

Here, where all climes their offerings send,
  Here, where all arts their tribute lay,
Before thy presence, Lord, we bend,
  And for thy smile and blessing pray,

For thou dost sway the tides of thought,
  And hold the issues in thy hand,
Of all that human toil has wrought,
  And all that human skill has plann'd.

Thou lead'st the restless Power of Mind
  O'er destiny's untrodden field,
And guid'st him wandering bold but blind,
  To mighty ends not yet revealed.

Next, Mr. Theodore Sedgwick, the President of the Crystal Palace Association, rose and addressed President Pierce in the following language :—

Mr. President: Amid this concourse of people, in this assembly of personages collected from all parts of the world, eminent in every department of human skill and genius, surrounded by the trophies of intellect and industry, the eye and the mind naturally, inevitably rivet themselves, sir, upon you. [Applause.] Upon you, the head of that political system to which, under God, we owe our choicest public blessings—of that vast confederacy founded by the immortal man whose effigy stands before us, and the chief executive powers of which have been transmitted through a long line of illustrious statesmen to your hands. [Renewed applause.] It has fallen and will fall to the lot of others to welcome you in other capacities. It is my duty, sir, as the presiding officer of the Association which has raised this edifice, to thank you most cordially, most respectfully, for the honor you have this day done us—we feel it deeply. It was perceived by us at the very outset of our enterprise, that it was essential to our complete success to obtain the approbation, and secure the confidence of our own Government—that while we were of course mainly to rely on our own energies, it was at the same time indispensable to create a general conviction that our objects were public, and our aims national. The work of impressing on this undertaking the seal of national approbation, as far as that can be done under the restrictions of our form of government—and I recall the circumstance with gratitude mingled with pain—was begun by an illustrious statesman now no more —a son, sir, of your own State. He had a mind large enough, and a heart broad enough, to perceive, even in its infancy, the development of which this undertaking was capable. How much of interest his presence would have added to this occasion, I need not say. Alas! his image only is among us. Genius knows no country. The monument of Daniel Webster, hewn out of French stone by English hands, rises here most appropriately to contemplate the work to which he gave the first great impulse. What he commenced was continued by the eminent gentleman who succeeded him in the last high office which he filled—a gentleman of whom I may be permitted to say that the country is still fortunate in commanding in another department his experience and ability. And finally, you, sir, have this day consummated the work, by permitting us to greet the Chief Magistrate of the Republic within our walls. We once more thank you, sir, for the honor you have done us. [Applause.] Your presence here to-day proves the close and friendly ties between the Government of the United States and the happy people whom its power protects—[applause.]—the cordial sympathy entertained by the highest functionaries of the Republic for any legitimate popular undertaking—the intimate connection between labor and honor; while, at the same time, it is proper here to state, most distinctly and most emphatically, and especially to those not so familiar with the frame-work of our system, that the government of the Union is not in the most remote degree responsible for our short-comings in this matter, whatever they have been, whatever they may be. With the great objects of our enterprise, sir, you are already familiar—to bring before our countrymen the choicest productions of the genius and skill of the Old World—to make a first exhibition on a national scale of the trophies of the inventive spirit and restless energy of our countrymen—on a national scale to collect (in the poetical language of a most distinguished stranger, this day for us unhappily not here) a full representation of

"The arts for luxury, the arms for strife,
Inventions for delight, and sight, and sound ;——"

to bind together the two hemispheres—to extend the area of commerce and the fraternity of nations. These have been our aims. How far they have been, or will be attained, it would be most presumptuous for us to say. Recalling to mind the gorgeous and gigantic pageant exhibited in Hyde Park two short years ago—knowing what French genius has undertaken to establish in the capital of continental Europe, that centre of intellectual life and artistic luxury, it is enough to say, that we have desired to do something for the art, for the architecture, for the industry, of our beloved country, and that if we shall be hereafter pronounced by competent judges to have succeeded, our dearest wishes will be answered. On some particulars, however, I may for a moment be allowed to dwell. Incomplete as our exhibition yet is, we have, what are to us, abundant proofs of the interest which it has excited, and the results which it will accomplish. The flag of England, borne by a vessel commissioned by that royal lady who commands the respect of foreign nations, as she does the affections of her own people—[applause]—has waved in our waters on this peaceful errand. The national vessel of France is on her way—that of Holland will almost immediately follow. Old armor from the old Tower of London, frowning here, as it did perhaps at Cressy or Poictiers; tapestry and porcelain from the imperial manufactories of France; porcelain and iron from the royal work-shops of Prussia, are here, or actually on the water bound hitherward, and I cannot express too strongly our sense of the kindness and courtesy with which our foreign agents have been received abroad, no less than our respect for that liberal and enlightened policy, in obedience to the dictates of which the sovereigns of Europe have vied with each other in sending offerings which in other periods of the world would have been made to crowned heads alone. [Applause.] Nor, sir, are our greetings or acknowledgments yet concluded. I have still to express the extreme gratification which we feel in the presence of so many distinguished agents—distinguished by social position, by character, by attainments—from all parts of Europe, from all parts of this continent. The dwellers on the eastern shores of the Atlantic are here mingled with the representatives of our own empire on the coast of the Pacific, and there are, I believe, here to-day twenty chief magistrates of as many states of the confederacy—lights of that constellation of which you, sir, are the central star. [Applause.] We are deeply sensible of this courtesy and kindness, while, sir, we are not so blind or so vain-glorious as not fully to understand that the honor is done not to us, but to you,—[renewed applause.]—and that the homage of their respect is above all poured to the governing power and majesty of the Republic. May that power and majesty—and I say it with the profoundest reverence—be ever united to and governed by that spirit of peace and good will which is our direct command from on High, and to contribute to which, in the great family of man, is the best, and purest, and wisest action that can bring us together in this temple of industry—in this palace of labor. But, sir, I detain my hearers from the pleasure that I hope awaits them. Hereafter, I may take some more fitting occasion to state in detail what we have done, and what we desire to do; the difficulties we have encountered, and the obstacles we have surmounted. To-day, my voice is of little moment, except for the echo and the response which, I hope, it is fortunately destined to awaken. Permit me then, sir, to ask you to let your voice be heard beneath our dome, and to request that you will, by words, as well as by your presence, inaugurate this exhibition of the industry of all nations.

Mr. Sedgwick speaks emphatically well. His manner is practiced and self-possessed, and he was much applauded. The President replied, evidently impromptu, and his words were well chosen. He appeared fatigued in the previous efforts he had made in public speaking during his journey, and was very brief. Mr. Pierce, however, most favorably impressed his auditory. He was fluent, earnest, and unabashed before so vast an auditory. We subjoin here the words of his speech :

Sir,—I return you, on behalf of those of my constitutional advisers who are with me, and on my own account, my warm and cordial thanks for the reception you have been pleased to extend to us. I have come, Sir, to testify the interest I feel in, and the respect I entertain for, this great Industrial Exhibition—designed and calculated to promote all that belongs to the interest of our country. You, sir, and the gentlemen who have been and are associated with you, have imposed upon all of us a deep debt of gratitude for your energy and perseverance in this great enterprise. Whatever the shortcomings of which you have spoken may be, I can only remark that they do not appear here ; and, so far as I have been able to perceive, they are lost in your complete and transcendant success. [Loud and continued applause.] Everything around us reminds us that we live in an utilitarian age, where science, instead of being locked up for the admiration of the world, has become tributary to the arts, manufactures, agriculture, and all that goes to promote our universal prosperity. Sir, if you had achieved no other good but that which you have in bringing together, in this metropolis, citizens from all parts of the Union, you would have fulfilled, perhaps, one of the most important of missions—that of strengthening and perpetuating that blessed Union. [Great applause.] But you have done more, and you have nobly alluded to it. Your Exhibition has been the means of bringing here, from all the civilized countries on the face of the globe, men most eminent in all the walks of life ; and thus you have done more than could be done, in almost any other manner, to promote that great object dear to you, dear to me, and dear to my venerable friend near me, [Bishop Wainwright,] peace and good-will among men. [Applause.] I have not the voice, at this time, to address you at any greater length, and conclude by again returning to you my thanks for your generous reception, and tendering my heart's best wishes for the success of your praiseworthy enterprise. [Applause.]

Mr. Sedgwick, when the President had finished, proposed three cheers for the President, which were heartily given by the multitude.

No other speeches were made, but various pieces of music were sung and played by the army of artists present. The effect of these was magnificent. At one moment, a resonant March, in all the stately force of double-time, painting the tread of armed and plumed hosts ; this, after its echoes had died away, and ceased to weave their beauties through the arabesque aisles and the soaring dome, would be responded to by another band, pouring forth some sensuous Waltz, full of youth and love, and the spirit of early hearts and gentle hands ; then these souvenirs "of the earth, earthy," would cease, and the religious idea of the glories of Art would culminate, as Handel's masterpiece, the Messiah chorus, came forth with the colossal effect of a multitude of singers, running through fugued, lyrical windings, typical of the circularities of the soul, boundless and sublime, and shouting the old church words and music—" Hallelujah ! Hallelujah !" as adopted by the genius of the composer, and turned into transcendental ecstatic declamation.

STRICTURES ON THE OPENING.

In commenting upon such an ovation, it would be a grateful task to us to speak with unqualified praise of all the proceedings, but we feel it a duty to make an exception, and one of the most positive and condemnatory force.

We do not in these remarks make much account of the Crystal Palace and its contents not being ready. Let any one enter the premises and see the apparently infinite detail of beams, rafters, pillars, arches, partitions, glass, tints ; and add to that the care, trouble, and calculation, to place in their proper positions, and under their best phases, all the goods from six thousand contributors, and the vulgar complaint against the place and its treasures not being ready, will be swallowed up in admiration of the architectural and general esthetic splendor of the scene. Of its beauty, there is but one opinion. Gen. Pierce, and all those who came with him, seeing it for the first time, were evidently thrilled with delight. No words are too strong for admiration ; first, for Messrs. Carstensen and Gildermeister, the Architects of the Crystal Palace, and then for Mr. Sedgwick, and the gentlemen connected with him, in the elaborate and difficult work of supervision. Under these circumstances, the triumph of the scene, so thorough and so far exceeding expectations, must silence all reflections on the delays as to the time of the Exhibition, and the public agreed fully with the President, when he would not admit of the existence of shortcomings as regarded the aspects of the scene.

Our objections lie in another way, and we shall explain them. We hold that the Crystal Palace is, if anything, the most eminent tribute to Art and Industry that this country and this century can pay.

We hold its Inauguration should have been the occasion for artists and mechanics to occupy the highest representative seats on the platform; but both were absolutely ignored by the Committee of Arrangements. We saw fighting men in abundance, politicians, and place-holders, but not a single man eminent for the arts which the Crystal Palace was opened to celebrate. At the opening of the Crystal Palace of London, although it was a purely Norman exhibition, clergy, soldiers, and politicians, occupying the seats of honor, and the working-men, who built and stocked the wonderful edifice, were kept like Roman slave-artists and laborers in the servile back-ground of swinish caste, yet there, even amid the shams of state, Mr. Paxton, the genius who waked it to life, was on the platform. But we would ask, where were the architects of our Palace, Messrs. Carstensen and Gildermeister? Why were they not on the platform? What had any military personage, or the Reverend Doctor this or that, to do in the face of the public in comparison with the men who created the edifice which dazzles and delights all beholders? Yesterday was their triumph, and they should have been seen and heard. But, true to the barbarism of this country, every one overlooked them; they were not mentioned in terms; they were not greeted by the President of the United States; and if the Crystal Palace had built itself there could not have been a more ignorant, stupid, vulgar omission of their names.

Again: of the thousand workmen who spent their skill and strength, and showed their courage in building the dome,—as great as that renowned by the capture of Mexico,—there was not one representative on the stage. Labor was practically ignored and thrust aside for epaulettes and white cravats,—for men who had nothing particular to do with the Palace, and have every day or week opportunities of appearing fitly and professionally before the public.

Again: of all the exhibitors, not one was allowed to be on the platform sacred to clergymen, soldiers, and politicians. On the contrary, we find among the printed orders of the day the following sentence :—

" Exhibitors will be admitted at 8 o'clock A. M., and will remain in their respective courts during the ceremonies."

Now, we are quite of opinion that a delegation, at least, of these exhibitors should have been on the platform. We looked in vain for such men as McCormick, who saved the American Department from disgrace in London, and whose Reaping Machine *The London Times* pronounced so important, that if the Exhibition had done nothing else but make that invention known, it would repay England for all its cost. An American who had borne his country's honor so loftily abroad, might have been a fit invited guest on such an occasion ; but neither he, nor any other ingenious man like him, appeared on the scene.

But we do not wish to condemn the Committee of Directors for the contempt which they displayed for artists and working-men on the occasion. They merely chimed in with the filthy barbarisms of society around and about them. We may say in this country that we respect Art, and Work, but we do not speak the truth. We *do not* respect them. Our measure of honor is almost exclusively political. Then, out of the piddling-peddling little wars that we have, we contrive to manufacture military heroes, and so politics and the sword carry the day. In the proceedings we see no exception to this rule. General Scott, who appeared on the platform long before the President, was cheered, and very appropriately; but no one of the twenty thousand present demanded that the men whose genius, art, industry, and courage had called that gorgeous scene into life and beauty, should present themselves and receive homage. No Artist was there. No Mechanic. No Laborer. The scene calling itself industrial was simply a continuation of the dreary annals of humanity—of State Craft, over-riding the majestic Individualism of the true creation, Man. We see less and less reason for paying respect, as it is called, to public functionaries, when we find that every department of Government which the boldness of private enterprise has snatched from the insolent hands of prescription, has flourished truly, for the first time, in private hands. The Crystal Palace, an evidence of pure, unaided personal enterprise, is a case in point. The same thing in Europe, is made a Government affair. Long slang-whanging speeches, "master-pieces by great statesmen," precede, accompany, and follow its creation, and its completion is made the reason for fresh loyalty, and additional self-abasement on the part of the people toward their hereditary masters. Here, however, it is suggested, planned, pursued, completed, and sustained by private enterprise. All that the Government ever did for it was to say that it should be considered as a Bonded Warehouse, and to write a few letters to foreign countries, where the sanction and coöperation of Governments are thought to be a necessary thing.

We regret to speak thus; but the Crystal Palace has signally failed to crown Labor and Art in its proceedings of yesterday. Its ovation was to anything else but the building and its contents. It was to Daniel Webster, the President, or whatever else, but not to Labor and Art, represented and honored on the platform. The dignity of the creative functions of a nation's genius has yet to be truly recognized. It has not yet seen the light in Europe nor in this country. When wars and preparations for wars shall cease; when the operations of government shall be reduced to their least proportions; when professional or technical combinations cannot create shams whose celebrity is false, then the true era for Industrial Jubilees may come, but it has not yet arrived. Let us hope, however, that even these Exhibitions may do much to hasten its advent.

In the mere proprieties of the day, apart from these objections, the scene passed off well. The speeches had the excellence of brevity; the music was fine and varied, great rivalry evidently existing between the different bands and orchestras; the audience was unexceptionable in its deportment; the appearance of the feminine portion was brilliant, and, it must be added, that the directors liberally provided a ladies' refreshment-room; the attention of those in authority, the new uniformed police included, was unremitting; the progress made in decorating, finishing and arraying the details of the building and its contents in the few last days, when all seemed to promise disorder and defeat on the promised day of opening, was a veritable wonder of industry; the arrangements of tickets, places, entrance, exits, were admirable; the accommodations for the corps of reporters were liberal and thoughtful; the positions of the sculptural attractions were well chosen as to locality, light, and combined effect; and, in a word, the whole was arranged, as to outward show, with a skill that was unsurpassable.

It was a thing to be seen once in a life-time. As we grow in wealth and strength, we may build a much greater Crystal Palace, and accumulate therein more imperial treasures than we could now afford to purchase; but it cannot have the effect of this one. This has been the first love of its kind. The second cannot bring the exhilaration and glory of the first, though exhausting the wealth of Genius in its production. In this we behold the first decided stand of America among the industrial and artistic nations of the earth. In this we see a recognition of her progress, power, and possibilities. In this we find a yearning after Peace—Peace which shall dimple the face of the earth with the smiles of plenty, which shall join the hearts of nations, which shall abolish poverty and servitude. God's earth loves Man to her innermost depths;—treat her well with Peace, and she will reward him as a generous mother; abuse her with War, and she will drive him from her presence. Such History has proved; but we may fairly believe that the recorded vicissitudes of the past may be avoided in travelling the placid and generous path pointed out by the CRYSTAL PALACE.—*July* 15.

III.

THE BANQUET.

THE opening of the first American Exhibition of the Industry of all Nations, was celebrated in the evening of the opening day by a superb entertainment, given by the Directors of the Exhibition to the President of the United States and other distinguished personages who had favored the ceremonial by their attendance. The Metropolitan Hotel was the scene of this festival.

Arrangements were made for six hundred guests, and nearly that number participated in the feast. Everything proceeded with regularity and good order ; and, although the notice given the hosts was absurdly brief, the whole affair was got up in a style highly creditable and agreeable.

ARRANGEMENT OF THE GRAND BANQUETING HALL.

This hall presented a most splendid view. The walls were covered with American and other flags, under the superintendence of Mr. Hayden, upholsterer at the establishment of A. T. Stewart & Co. Over the chair of the President was a tent formed of two large American flags, handsomely draped from the ceiling. On the right, this tent was supported by the flags of England and Russia ; on the left, by those of France and the Netherlands. Along the wall, on the left side, were the flags of Bohemia, the Papal standard of Rome, the Republic of Peru, &c.

The orchestra-box, in which was ensconced Harvey B. Dodworth, with his admirable band, was festooned with the flags of Hungary, Turkey, and Prussia, supported on either side by the stars and stripes. Next came the royal standards of Portugal and Japan. The flags of the German Confederation and Saxony occupied the lower end of the hall.

On the right hand side were the Italian, Sardinian, German, Switz, Danish, French and English (union jack) standards.

Over all, in the centre of the room, was a Maltese Cross, formed of beautiful festoons of American flags.

THE TABLES—CONFECTIONERY.

Along the head of the room, on a raised daïs, was a splendidly furnished table for the leading dignitaries of the occasion. At each end there were tables for reporters, where accommodations of the first order were provided—pens, ink, paper, &c.—in such a manner as to call for the especial gratitude of those members of the press whose most tedious labor commences just when other guests get at the flood-tide of enjoyment. Such courtesies are not too common, and the Messrs. Leland are entitled to our warmest thanks therefor.

Down the room ran four tables of great length, furnished in capital style. The confectionery, or fancy sugar-work, was very fine. Before the President sat a capital representation of the Crystal Palace, surmounting a parti-colored pyramid of fruit. On his left was an exceedingly fine piece, made of flags of all nations, surmounted by a figure of Liberty, holding her cap and staff. On the right was a Grecian temple, with a figure of Washington, holding the Declaration of Independence and a sword. On the other tables various fancy pieces, of appropriate character, such as Gothic temples, arches, &c.; pyramids, a bird cage, and other articles.

The *coup d'œil* of the room was very fine, and called forth many commendations for the excellent taste by which it had been created.

No less than a hundred and fifty waiters were employed to attend to the guests, being one to every four.

ASSEMBLING OF THE GUESTS.

The hour for the dinner was six o'clock. The guests, however, were, as usual, an hour behindhand. By half-past seven o'clock, the seats were filled, and the gastronomical exercises commenced.

Among the distinguished guests, we noticed :

THE PRESIDENT OF THE UNITED STATES.
The Secretary of the Treasury.
The Secretary of War.
The Attorney General.
The Governor of the State of New York.
The Governor of the State of Georgia.
The Sardinian Chargé des Affaires.
The Prussian Minister.
The French Minister.
Senator CHASE, of Ohio.
Sir CHARLES LYELL, English Commission.
Chancellor WALWORTH.
Chief Justice OAKLEY. Judge EDMONDS.
Recorder TILLOU. Ex-Mayor KINGSLAND.
ABM. HILLYER, U. S. Marshal. Gen. JAMES TALLMADGE.
Rev. Dr. GARDNER SPRING. Rev. Dr. KNOX.
Hon. Mr. EDGERTON. Hon. OGDEN HOFFMAN. Dr. J. W. FRANCIS.
Col. J. W. FORNEY, Clerk House of Representatives.
W. W. CORCORAN, of Washington. E. K. COLLINS, of New York.
Com. SHUBRICK, U. S. Navy Maj. Gen. WOOL, U. S. Army.
Col. WALKER, U. S. Army. Maj. SPRAGUE, U. S. Army.
Gen. J. A. THOMAS, Engineer. Gen. E. WARD, N. Y. Militia.
Major General SANDFORD, First Division N. Y. State Militia.
Col. J P MUMFORD, N. Y. S. M. Col. E. CORNING, Jr., N. Y. S. M.
Col. H. S. LAINSING, N. Y. S. M. Lieut. Col. CHAS. E. SANDFORD, N. Y. S. M.
Maj. E. SCHENCK, N. Y. S. M. And a large number of other notabilities whose names we did not get.

THE DINNER.

The guests having assembled, a blessing was invoked by Rev. Dr. Spring and then a very dainty Bill of Fare was carefully discussed. This being of greater interest to partakers than to readers, we spare the latter a recapitulation. Suffice it that the dinner was very good, well cooked, well eaten, and seemed to give general satisfaction. The truite was especially commended.

TOASTS AND SPEECHES.

Dinner being over, the toasts and speeches came in their order as follows :—

THEODORE SEDGWICK, Esq., President of the Association, and officiating Chairman at the Dinner, gave the first regular toast, which he prefaced substantially as follows :—

In rising to propose the first toast of the evening, and after reverting to the obligations conferred on them by many assembled in carrying out the great enterprise in which they had engaged, remarked more particularly the assistance received from the press of the United States, to whom they were under the deepest obligations—but to preface the introduction of any toast individually would be impossible, but if they were to select any one, it ought to be those gentlemen who came from the other side of the water, and who, after all the annoyances they had been subjected to, had materially assisted them in reaching the point to which they had already gained. It had been often said that the feeling of loyalty finds no proper response on this side of the water, but looked at in its proper sense, it was one of the deepest implanted feelings in the human heart. The soldier is loyal to his flag—the true-hearted lover to his mistress—and if the Englishman is loyal to his Queen, the American is at all times loyal to the Union. You have here to-night the head of that Union,—[loud and repeated applause.]—and in proposing to you "The President of the United States," I would add the Anglo-Saxon expression, also, and "God bless him." [Nine cheers.]

By the Band—*Air*, "Hail, Columbia."

The President then rose and spoke as follows :—

Mr. President and Gentlemen: In responding to the sentiment you have pronounced, my own thoughts, I confess, dwell upon a circumstance which mars, and, so far as I know, the only circumstance that does mar, the festivities of this joyous occasion. I allude to the illness and absence of Lord Ellesmere. Gratified as we are all that he came, how much has that gratification been enhanced by the fact that he came not alone, but that his family graced and honored the Inauguration of your Exhibition by their presence yesterday. I am sure I should hardly be excused if I were to fail here to refer to a gentleman who has paid to our country and countrymen many pleasant compliments—more, I have sometimes thought, than we deserved—a gentleman who, if his reputation depended merely upon the cultivation of science, would stand at the head of the men of science; but his fame rests upon a broader and ampler basis—upon this: that he has himself contributed largely to the sum of useful human knowledge. You cannot mistake me, sir; I refer to Sir Charles Lyell. [Loud cheers.] His country and ours are now within eleven days, is it? No, nine days of each other—[A voice—Ten days.]—by steamers.

As an illustration of what this Exhibition was likely to do, I was very much impressed by what Sir Charles Lyell himself told me, that an eminent inventor and machinist discovered, upon visiting the work-shops of Lowell, that while they accomplished in the working of iron in one hour what it takes us five to perform, yet in the cutting of wood, the advantage is just as great in favor of our machinery. While we return our grateful acknowledgments to all the governments and nations here represented, I am sure that all the gentlemen here assembled will unite with me in the expression of the hope that the only rivalry which may ever spring up between them and us shall be the rivalry of earnest, determined, steady effort to promote the elevation of the race, and peace and good neighborhood among nations and men.

The President sat down amid a perfect storm of cheers.

Mr. SEDGWICK then remarked :—

We must not forget that the President is not here alone. Other gentlemen have accompanied and assisted him in his arduous journey, and have done us the honor to be present here to-night. I propose, gentlemen,

The Secretary of the Treasury—James Guthrie, Esq. [Cheers.]

Mr. GUTHRIE replied :—

Though a public speaker, he had never been so much abashed. He came to see the Opening of the Exhibition of the Industry of all Nations, this commendation of all Art, this toleration of all religion, this extension of commerce, this meeting and agreement of all arts and sciences. He had little to say, nothing to offer, except the examples of his countrymen in arts, and in agriculture. They had felled the forests, and made in their place cultivated fields; they have added state after state to our glorious Union, until the bright galaxy of stars now numbers thirty-one. Seventy years ago the city where we now are was a mile and a half long, and half a mile broad, and contained twenty-one thousand inhabitants: now it is more than five miles long, and two wide, with a population of six hundred thousand. Then, there were only wooden houses, of one and two stories—now it is a city of princely palaces. Her commerce whitens every sea, and she draws to herself the rich products of every clime. By her Railroads and Canals she has given the farmers of the western wilderness the world for a market. She now offers the Crystal Palace, wherein are the evidences of her Art and Industry, and invites her sister states and all the nations of the earth to come here and join in the Exhibition. She has won her wealth and renown by the arts of peace, and while peace exists, New York and her example will extend, until other cities emulate her independence and enterprise—that enterprise, industry, and integrity, which, guided by her merchants, have made her preëminent. [Cheers.] Mr. G. expressed his thanks for the complimentary toast, and sat down.

[During this speech the President left the room with Gen. Wool, and his Secretary, Mr. P. S. Webster. The party immediately proceeded to the Opera at Castle Garden.]

Mr. SEDGWICK then gave, after some complimentary remarks upon his course in the Mexican War,

The Health of the Secretary of War—Jefferson Davis. [Loud Cheers.]

Mr. DAVIS responded :—

He spoke in eulogy of the National Flag, under which his father and himself had fought, and went on to show that war and its accoutrements were not out of place on such an occasion. War was a school of reality, that taught the value of peace. He then went on with an out and out Free Trade speech, and concluded that, by throwing open the ports of all the world, perpetual peace would be secured. He thought we should declare, that what could be bought more cheaply in another country should be bought there. Free Trade was the rising sun which was to illumine the globe. Thence he proceeded to speak of the Pacific Railroad, which he thought to be the problem of the age, which we were to solve.

Mr. Sedgwick then gave as a toast :—

The Health of Gen. Cushing—Attorney-General of the United States.

Mr. Cushing made a brief reply :—

" Peace hath its victories, no less renowned than war," said he ; this Temple you have reared to a divinity unknown to ancient mythology—a Temple to Industry and Art. He admired the triumphs of Peace, yet held to the necessity of force. True, there was sometimes force in reason, but there was always reason in force.

Mr. Sedgwick, then, by what he called a *coup d'état*, reversed the order of the toasts, and, after speaking highly of the character and power of the Press, gave the fifteenth toast :—

The Press :

He called upon Mr. Raymond of *The Times.*

Mr. Raymond, in rising to reply, said that, while he had never regarded with the slightest favor *coups d'état* of any sort, he felt bound to say that the one which our President has effected on this occasion, contradicted all his notions of propriety more distinctly than any other he had ever known. The military gentlemen present would bear him witness, that bringing the rear of an organized force into the front, in the midst of an engagement, was such an utter breach of all rules, that it deserved to be taken notice of in higher quarters than he could pretend to represent on this occasion. [A laugh.] Mr. Raymond said he was sure he did not know for what the President had felt it his duty to apologize on this occasion, nor what it was that he had explained. But certainly, after the very handsome manner in which it had been treated, he felt quite safe in considering it as being now, at all events, *all right*, and in dismissing all notice of it accordingly. I feel quite certain, he added, that I shall have the assent of that great, laborious, and, I may venture to add, influential profession to which I belong, in returning their cordial thanks for the complimentary terms in which their services had been acknowledged, on behalf of that Great Industrial Exhibition of which you, sir, are the official head, and the preparation of which you have now brought to so noble a termination. [Cheers.] It is the special duty of the Press to spread intelligence of important facts before the public, and to accompany them by such comments as truth will sanction and the public good requires. [Cheers.] And I cannot but feel that the highest compliment which can be made to the power of the Press, and the general beneficence with which that power is exercised, is to be found in the fact, that it is the first source of influence at which ambition always strikes in its march to arbitrary sway. [Cheers.] Whenever any usurper, on either Continent, seeks to subvert Constitutions, abolish laws, destroy public liberty, and make his own will the sovereign public law, the first thing he does is to crush the Press. In that fact alone, sir, I find a grateful and an emphatic tribute to the influence of the public Press. [Cheers.] And not less highly do I appreciate the fact, that on such an occasion as the present, when the industry of all the nations of the earth is represented here, the services of the Press, in the promotion of the great ends for which this Association has been formed, should be so cordially acknowledged by the able and intelligent gentleman at the head of that great movement. [Cheers.] I cannot say, sir, that I felt specially flattered by his remark, however kindly intended, that on this occasion there had been no attempt on the part of the Press to levy "black mail" for services rendered to this great work. I am sure, however, that he did not design that his remark should suggest any inference which its language would not warrant — and that he would freely say that he had never known any instance, or any occasion, in which any respectable portion of the American or of any other Press, had ever demanded payment for the statement of important facts, or for advocating great measures demanded by the public good. [Cheers.] I had hoped, Mr. President, (said Mr. R.) that the original design would have been carried out, and that the duty of responding to this toast would have been discharged by a gentleman of whose former connection with the Press all its present members were justly proud, and who now fills an important post at the head of one of the principal literary institutions of the land. I feel ashamed that so honorable a task should have been so suddenly and unexpectedly cast upon one so unable as myself to perform it aright; and I can only ask the indulgence of the company, and especially of the Press, for the imperfect manner in which it has been discharged. [Cheers.]

Returning to the second toast, the Chairman gave:

The Senate of the United States.

Hon. S. P. CHASE, Senator from Ohio, replied very briefly. He thought the acts of the Senate might speak for the Senate. He gave:

The Legations of Foreign Governments near the Government of the United States—Representatives of the ties by which the States of the Union are linked in amity with the nations of the earth.

Baron GEROLD, the Prussian Minister, responded very briefly, but we could not hear a word that he said.

In response to the third toast:

The Governments of Foreign Nations—which have contributed to our Exhibition—

M. Sartiges, Minister from France, made a reply in the following words :

Sir,—My colleagues here present have requested me to be the interpreter of our common thanks for the toast and friendly sentiments expressed in honor of our respective Sovereigns and Governments. And now, sir, I have a kind of personal ardor to tend you relative to the French Commissioner, whose mention had been made yesterday by the eloquent speaker who had the honor to welcome his Excellency the President to the Crystal Palace. Having, six weeks ago, had occasion to visit the ground of the Crystal Palace, and having been brought to the conclusion that the intended building would not be in order before the end of August, I have communicated to Paris my impression, which, perhaps, may have produced some modification in the first intended arrangement.

I think I had not sufficiently accounted for the marvellous rapidity with which everything is accomplished in your country. I will take care, in future, to include in my calculation of probability this element of rapidity. Well, I ask you to consider me, in your high or friendly re-union of to-day, as representing more specially commercial France. I am as proud to represent commercial as political France, now that through the entire world, to the old adage—"If you wish for peace, prepare for war," this one may be substituted: "If you wish for peace, multiply your 'commercial relations'"—indeed, the Congress the most universally interesting, is the Congress of Commerce, the exhibitions of universal industry. In assuming boldly the initiative of an enterprise whose theme was certainly grand, but whose success, undoubtful to-day, was not so at first, the gentlemen Directors of the Association for the erection of the New York Crystal Palace have rendered a service not only to their own country, but to the commercial and political world. They must be proud of their success, and they have a right to unanimous applauses. I beg leave to offer them mine, in which the French commerce will thank me to include his own. I will, therefore, conclude by proposing, on behalf of my diplomatic colleagues here present,

The Health of the President and Directors of the Crystal Palace Association.

The fourth regular toast was then given :

Prince Albert—The originator of the great Industrial Exhibition of 1851.

Responded to by Mr. Hamilton, one of the Commissioners to the London Exhibition ; but, as he was unfortunately at the far end of the room, we were unable to catch his remarks.

The fifth toast :

The Foreign Commissioners, who have honored us this day with their presence—

Was received with loud applause, and responded to by Sir CHARLES LYELL. After alluding to the lamented absence of the Earl of Ellesmere, who, notwithstanding his indisposition, had pressed on his journey from Canada, in the hope of being present, proceeded to say how gratified the noble Earl would have been, could he have participated in their festivities, but fate willed otherwise. He, (Sir Charles Lyell) however, was commissioned by his noble friend to say, that in his travels through some parts of this country, he had been received with the most cordial (yet unobtrusive) hospitality ever extended to him. The President of the United States had spoken of him (Sir Charles Lyell) in terms of no measured eulogy. He received them gratefully indeed, as intended at least to convey his kind feelings toward him for the little part he had taken, whether in the advancement of science or in making Americans and American genius and skill known to his own countrymen. His friend, Mr. Whitworth, in his travels through many parts of the manufacturing districts of this country, had been struck more by the labor-saving inventions and the beautiful machinery than by its soil, and to which they must ascribe the great wealth which it had already exhibited; and he trusted that this Exhibition would be the means of sooner making known those inventions and improvements which it was most desirable his countrymen should become familiar with.

The next toast, (the sixth):

The Governor of the State of New York,

was responded to by Hon. HOWELL COBB, Governor of Georgia, who expressed the hope that the result of this Exhibition would not only encourage, but increase the paternal intercourse of this government with the government of the whole world, and give a stimulant to industry, the arts, and sciences, and thus promote the best interests of the whole human race. The Hon. gentleman resumed his seat amid enthusiastic cheers.

The seventh and eighth toasts were united—while the ninth,

"The Fraternity of Nations,"

was ably responded to by Dr. FRANCIS, who, in his concluding observations, reminded the gentlemen present, and, more especially Sir C. Lyell, that in the city of New York, where Shakespeare's works were first interpreted and used for the grammatical instruction of youth, Lyell's works were freely used to instruct them in geology. [Loud laughter.]

The tenth regular toast,

The City of New York,

was responded to by Chancellor WALWORTH, but we were quite unable to glean a stray passage from anything he said.

The eleventh toast,

The Arts of Peace,

brought up OGDEN HOFFMAN, Esq., who, after complaining of indisposition, proceeded to say:

What are the Arts of Peace but those that man's own skill, his own genius, has lifted up? We live in times now when men are not torn by conscription from the plow-tail, the student from his studio, the painter from his easel, or the sculptor from his statuary, to swell the army to invade some foreign land, or it may be, to defend our own—no; the Arts of Peace are those which repose in the hour of man's rest, not those which flourish under wronged humanity. No, sir; they are the elements of humanity, which teach men that dependence on one another alone can secure prosperity, happiness, and comfort. To create this—to ennoble the feelings of our common nature, this association was formed, and invitations extended to people of other climes to offer their productions. This was not done for the purpose of exciting feelings of rivalry, but to teach us our own deficiency. This Society was not the creation of any Government—no man in authority stood sponsor for it, but it was the offspring alone of the enterprise and skill of a few noble creatures, and brought into existence to redeem a promise made to this community.

There were several more toasts, and further speaking; but our object is not to embalm all that was said, but merely to give a fair idea of the spirit and drift of this festival. It faded out some time after midnight, leaving a grateful quiet behind it.

IV.

STRICTURES ON THE BANQUET.

The great Dinner was given last evening by the Directors of the Crystal Palace to the President of the United States, and the Commissioners to the Exhibition. Messrs. Leland prepared it in splendid style, and it was spread in Niblo's Saloon, adjoining the Metropolitan Hotel.

The President, his Cabinet and suite, and the other invited guests, entered the room between six and seven o'clock, Dodworth's Band playing the National Hymn. Mr. Theodore Sedgwick, head of the Committee, presided on the occasion. There were fifteen regular toasts. If all the speeches had been as short as Mr. Pierce's, the Dinner would have been of reasonable length, but as the eloquence was profuse, and not a little of it of the stump-political order, as to topics—there being much of the Union, of Free Trade, and little of arts or æsthetics—it lasted till half-past twelve. Some of the speaking was good, some bad, some indifferent. Gen. Davis treated us to a Free Trade harangue, forgetting that the reason why we have anything to show at the Exhibition is owing to Protection.

The Press was put down as the last toast, No. 15, in the list printed and placed on the table. Mr. Theodore Sedgwick, who is evidently a man of tact, expressed his regret that such a blunder should have been committed—that he thought he was right in rating the Press as he had, but that he found out it was an error. As Mr. Sedgwick made the amende honorable very handsomely, we have nothing to say, except if we find the Press snubbed in future at dinners, we shall treat the delinquents as they deserve. The time has gone by, when the business of the Press was to swell small men into great, and then take their dirty leavings at public feasts. The Press, according to the change in the

Programme, was given about No. 4 of the list, and Mr. Raymond, of *The Times*, responded to it in a fluent and elegant manner.

We sat close by the two most eminent men in the room, the occasion considered. We mean Messrs. Carstensen and Gildermeister, the Architects of the Crystal Palace—the men whose genius planned, and supervised it from floor to dome. As nearly everything under heaven was introduced into the political harangues of the evening. we thought that by some stray chance the names of these eminent and splendid artists might be mentioned, but no more notice was taken of them than if they had been two hod-carriers. The reason was, they were neither Generals, Colonels, Captains, Lieutenants, Judges, Congressmen, Office-hunters, or Quacks—but simply creative Artists.

Such is the taste and enlightenment of New York in the nineteenth century! We have heard of the play of Hamlet, with the part of Hamlet omitted: it was paralleled last night.

The venerable Dr. Francis gave us a good, cordial historical tribute to New York. Ogden Hoffman spoke brilliantly to the toast on the Arts of Peace. Lord Ellesmere was not present, but Sir Charles Lyell made an address in his absence, full of genuine pith. Mr. Morton McMichael responded on the part of the Commissioners from the states. There were much international courtesy and comity displayed. Mr. Theodore Sedgwick showed unsurpassed ability in prefacing all the toasts with appropriate remarks. The company numbered some five or six hundred.

The room was very elegantly decorated with flags; on the table was every conceivable dainty; the judicious orchestral and military music of Dodworth aided digestion, and ladies in limited numbers looked on the scene, which was very gay.—*July* 15.

HONOR TO ART AND INDUSTRY.

We have received various communications, and read numerous notices in the Press, approving of our remarks of Friday, included in the description of the opening of the Crystal Palace. The subject, indeed, which we touched upon, namely, the ignorance, vulgarity, stupidity, and barbarism which overlooked Labor and Art on the occasion, and gave all the places of honor on the platform to clergymen, soldiers, politicians, and shams, is one of such solemn import, that we may be permitted, under the extended notice which our remarks have received in public and private, to dwell on the subject again.

We may as well confess the truth, that we do not live in a civilized country. The mere possession of edifices, grand and diminutive, public and private, and the production of articles of food and raiment, do not constitute civilization. The Romans, who had white slave-artists, men of genius or talent, were also civilized in the same sense. They could build a matchless Coliseum—still standing—a wonder of strength and design—but they also could make it the arena of gladiatorial combat, designedly ferocious and tragic. In this country, also, we have yet to see Labor and Art rewarded—we have yet to see an intelligent Mechanic, or Artist, as such, elevated to eminent office, though if his blows and strength had been devoted to battering down ensanguined walls, and he had a chivalric title, he might have been selected, other things equal. We constantly hear it quoted that Franklin was advanced because he was a Mechanic. It is a falsehood. He was advanced because he became first, Editor, then Postmaster, or professional politician ; and this and the sword, are almost the only road to advancement known in this country.

Our public festivals are countless. On all national jubilee-days they spring up by tens of hundreds over the land. They are made the occasion of national glorifications, or in other words, things and persons are supposed to be dwelt upon in toasts and speeches, which are honorable to the country, and enable it to hold its head up among others of the earth. But we record as a dismal fact, which taken singly would place America among barbarous nations, that never, never on these occasions has any man been signalized, individuated, honored, or elevated by notice in toasts or speeches, who was not connected with politics, either civil or military. We challenge proof of any such official notice being taken of Rumsey, Fitch, Evans, Fulton, Whitney, Morse, McCormick, Ericsson, Allston, Sully, Inman, Hicks, Powell, Powers, Greenough, Bryant, Willis, Irving, Anthon, Dr. Thomas Jones, Sears Walker, Silliman, Hare, Wells, Haviland, Strickland, Renwick, William Norris, David Dale Owen, Franklin Bache, Ralph Waldo Emmerson, H. C. Carey, or any other of the historical names of the country—names which will live when the work of political shams will be reduced to their least elements, when Army and Navy shall be abolished, when the Mint shall be in private hands, when the Post-Office shall also be so directed, when Foreign Missions shall be done away, when the dignity of the citizen shall be truly eliminated from the huge load of ancient and mediæval oppression, form, and falsehood, and individualism assert its proper claims to notice, profit, and honor.

This fact of political function over-riding and stifling worth, work, and genius, upon all occasions of a public or national character, was simply carried out in full deformity at the opening of the Crystal Palace; and, in order that the barbarism of that occasion might not be contrasted with its opposite, at the public banquet at Niblo's Saloon, on the day following, the same ignoring of all names and persons not political was repeated.

Let us consider the real condition and philosophy of the occasion:—

In presence of twice ten thousand spectators, of Commissioners from Europe and America, of the Chief Public Servant of the Republic, of a corps of journal-reporters taking down notes to be reproduced within a few days in thousands of newspapers at home and hundreds abroad, the ceremonies of the inauguration took place. There soared above them the vast dome: there loomed around them the great structure, covering five acres, and seemingly light as a dream; in which the might of engineering and the splendor of architecture resonant of the triumphs of the nineteenth century are combined—an architecture no stale iteration of the ever-present and under-done rendering of Grecian orders in this country, but palpitating with the courageous and advancing heart of the age—of the age when iron wrenched from the stubborn earth, is made to work with the genius of the nation—to cut its way in the aboriginal forest; to redeem from swamp and pestilence the richest land; to wreathe great staples into form and value; to cleave in the steamer the angriest seas; to support with the strength of fabled deity whatever incumbent massive structure; and, in the last capacity, threaded through fields of crystal, to solve a new problem in the builder's skill. This all was before them—not the names of politicians who did nothing toward it, not the prides of men paid out of the public purse, not the precedents and actors of Church and State—but Art and Labor, so displaying its calculations and proportions, and so opening its doors to the world. But no Art or Labor was there represented in person, while the Roman ideas which confined greatness to the politician, warrior, and priest—combined in the high patrician person—were absolutely carried out, and the world did not appear to have advanced for two thousand years. And the Banquet, which followed, was full in keeping with the Inauguration. Sir Charles Lyell, being a foreign Commissioner, (Lord Ellesmere, a Norman nobleman, being absent, owing to severe indisposition,) was called upon to speak, but that was the only real tribute to science on the occasion. We wished on that occasion to have something except from politicians, in power or out of power, but, with the above reservation, we did not hear a word. We would like to have seen the company rise up *en masse* and cheer the architects who planned the building, and thus receive the homage which was so ungallantly withheld from them at the Inauguration—in the same manner that Mr. Paxton was thanked and honored in public. But there they sat—countrymen of Thorwaldsen—unnoticed and unknown—no more named than they are in the official catalogue of the Crystal Palace.

We have no patience with such proceedings. Rhetoric is palsied in characterizing them as they deserve. Fejee Islanders would honor a Robinson Crusoe who would give them a new string to their bow; but on the greatest occasion of Art and Industry this continent has ever known, we thrust both into the background—we wrench the claims from genius—we drive the laborers among the rafters of the dome, to look down like blackguard boys on the official crowd beneath—we tell the makers of the treasures of the Exhibition to keep by their wares "during the ceremonies," as though they were not fit to sit alongside of cassocks and soldier-clothes—we follow out the uniform political fraud that prates of this or that speech in Congress saving the Republic, that omits, on every public occasion, to signalize Genius, that never mentions the Inventor, Painter, Composer, or Poet, that is circumfused in a sea of Roman and Norman lies!

The time has come when the Artists and Laborers of this

country must seek to redeem themselves from the fardels of caste. They must make themselves represented on public occasions. They must not forget politics or the practice which overrides their claims. Politics have hitherto almost revolved in a circle. There is as much villainy in the government of this city as in either House of Parliament. But it is genius outside this that shapes the destiny of nations. It is a Columbus, a Newton, a Fulton, a Whitney, that re-writes the history of nations. Carolina, adoring Calhoun, forgets Whitney, whose contributions to her wealth and glory are as a million to one of Calhoun's—and so runs the parallel.—*July* 18.

THE MORAL OF THE PALACE.

It is Gibbon, if we remember aright, who suggests that an Arminian commentary on the Epistle to the Romans must be one of the severest tests of human ability and ingenuity. That may or may not be ; but it is certain that there is a charm in paradox for men of lively imagination, and audacious self-confidence. Hence, Secretary Cushing signalizes his progress to, and appearance at, the opening of the Crystal Palace, by speeches in favor of Filibusterism and War—these being the two National follies and crimes which would seem of all others most pointedly rebuked and stripped naked by an Exhibition of the trophies of Industry. " There is *sometimes* force in reason," is Caleb's generous concession ; " but there is *always* reason in force." That is to say—Might makes Right ; and Slavery is divinely sanctified, until the slave is able to cut his master's throat ; *then* Slavery becomes diabolic, and the ex-slave is rightfully and religiously free. Slavery is right in South Carolina and Cuba, but horribly wrong in Hayti and Jamaica, until the Filibusters shall be strong enough to overrun those Islands, when Slavery will again be sanctified in both. Freedom is the right of white men in this country ; for our fathers, with French help, flogged the British, and made them acknowledge our Independence ; but Freedom has no business in Poland, Hungary, Lombardy, because of the weight of invincible logic hurled against it in every death-dealing discharge of Suwarrow's, Paskiewitch's, and Radetsky's batteries. Who says there are no Atheists, when an American Minister of State dares to utter a sentiment so infernal ?

Col. Jefferson Davis, being Secretary of War, very properly irradiated the Palace Banquet by a rhapsody on the blessings of Peace, to be secured through universal Free Trade! To stop Nations fighting (so runs the argument) we must set them fiercely to dickering and swapping jackets. Of course, then, Carthage of old, and Great Britain of modern times, must be exceedingly peaceful and lamb-like, while Japan should be a rapacious, aggressive, bullying, and annexing power. Of course we ought to have been very belligerent under the Protective Tariff of 1842, but meek as a dove after reducing it to the standard of 1846. Of course we are a very harmless, pacific, non-covetous people, now that we are all glorifying Free Trade, and its eloquent devotee is our Minister of War! Mexico and Cuba may rest in perfect security, since no truculent, grasping Protectionists are likely to be in power here for years, but such apostles of Peace as Davis and Cushing fill our National Councils! Men who let each other alone are in danger of fighting; set them to underworking and underselling each other in common markets, and they will love each other supremely! Huzza for perpetual and universal Peace!

'But," say Davis and his echoes, "the Crystal Palace preaches Free Trade." Then why are you not willing to trust to its preaching? Why so eager to interpose your own especial spectacles between the observer and the object of scrutiny?

But *does* the Crystal Palace preach Free Trade? Look at the contributions from European Nations always devoted to that policy—from Holland, Portugal, Naples, Turkey, &c.,—compared with those from Great Britain, France, and Belgium, whose manufactures were notoriously built up under the auspices of Protection. Consider how poor and rude German manufactures were prior to the formation of the Zoll-Verein, or Tariff-Union, and what immense and rapid strides they have since made, and the excellence they have now attained. Before the Zoll-Verein, Germany in her poverty bought most of her better fabrics from France and Great Britain; now she rivals both in many of the finest in our own, and other important markets open on equal terms to all.

Do you say these comparisons are far-fetched? Then contrast the products exhibited in the Crystal Palace from that section of our Union which adopted and acted upon the Protective Policy, and that which, though originally its advocate, long since repudiated and has so bitterly resisted it. Massachusetts and South Carolina have specimens of their respective products in the Crystal Palace; scrutinize them, and give the facts fair play. They are mightier than the rounded periods and glittering declamations of Col. Jefferson Davis.

"Ah!" says a middle-man, "Protection was a good thing in its season; but Great Britain has outgrown and discarded it; other Nations have discarded it; we too have outgrown and may now repudiate it." This way of talking without thinking is very common now-a-days with people who suppose it squares with their personal interests as traders or political aspirants: let us consider it:—

Does any man now regret that we have, by the aid of Protection, built up the manufacture of Cotton and Woolen fabrics in this country, so that they now give employment to many millions of capital, and tens of thousands of our people? Does any man believe that we are now paying more for these fabrics than we should be if we imported them? Would any American really rejoice to see these vast and prosperous branches of American Industry put back to the point where our feeble manufactures of Silks and Linens are now struggling? We do not believe there is one. Nor do we believe a candid, intelligent man can doubt that the main reason *why* our Cotton and Woolen manufactures are now relatively so strong, and those of Silks and Linens relatively so weak, is just this—that we have systematically and determinedly protected the former, while we have failed to protect the latter.

Now admit, for argument's sake, that our Cotton and Woolen Manufactures, like those of Great Britain, have outgrown the need of Protection—say, if you will, that our Iron Industry has very nearly reached the same point, and may, if the present abundance of Gold and consequent demand for Iron continue, soon pass it—does that prove that we may now discard Protection? On the contrary, should not the fact that such results have been attained, encourage us to attempt still more? What American heart would not rejoice over the fact, if it only *were* a fact, that we could show Linens with Ireland, Silks with France and Switzerland, Bronzes with Paris, Laces with Belgium, Steel with England; &c. &c., as we can show Plain Cottons, Prints, Ginghams, Satinets, Flannels, Delaines, Kerseys, &c. &c., with any country in the world? What American would not hear with exultation of the growing of Ten Millions' worth of Raw Silk by our countrymen this year, and its subsequent elaboration into rich and elegant fabrics worth Thirty Millions? Would not a show of American Silks in the Palace equal to the French, be hailed with National pride throughout the country? How is it, then, that we desire the end but reject the means? How do we construe the fact that our past efforts have been crowned with success into an argument for stagnation hereafter? How is it, in short, that Labor never thinks for itself among us, but allows itself to be for ever led blindly about by monopolizing traders and scheming politicians? —*July* 20.

WHAT THE EXHIBITION TEACHES.

The immediate practical uses of the Exhibition will be largely dwelt upon by the usual exponents of public sentiment, by the journals and by the occasional orators; but there are other aspects of it more important, perhaps, but not so likely to arrest attention. These we propose to notice.

Let us premise, however, that we would not, by any means, overlook the more practical bearings of a display of this kind. As an epitome of the experiences of a traveller who should pass his time in examining the workshops of the world, as a collection of the finest specimens of industrial art, as a record of the progress of human development in some of its most significant elements, as a tide-mark of the height of perfection to which mechanical processes have been carried, it cannot fail to be instructive.

It must be particularly instructive to Americans, because it will furnish them with evidences of a skill in many branches of creation beyond their own, and of models of workmanship which are superior, precisely in those points in which their own are most deficient. No one, we presume, will push his national predilections so far as to deny that, in the finer characteristics of manufacture and art, we have yet a vast deal to learn. Stupendous as our advances have been in railroads, steamboats, canals, printing-presses, hotels, and agricultural implements—rapidly as we are growing in excellence in a thousand departments of design and handicraft—astonishing as may be our achievements, under all the difficulties of an adverse national policy—adroit, ingenious and energetic as we have shown ourselves in those labors which have been demanded by the existing conditions of our society, we have yet few fabrics equal to those of Manchester, few wares equal to those of Birmingham and Sheffield, no silks like those of Lyons, no jewelry like that of Geneva, no shawls like those of the East, no mosaics like those of Italy. But, in our rapid physical improvements—growing as we are in prosperity, in population, in wealth, in luxuries of all kinds,—these are the articles that we ought to have and must have, to give diversity to our industry, to relieve us from dependence upon other nations, to refine our taste, and to enable the ornamental and elegant appliances of our life to keep pace with our external development. Mere wealth, without the refinements of wealth—barbaric ostentation, prodigal display, extravagant self-indulgence—can only corrupt morals and degrade character. But the cultivation of the finer arts redeems society from its grossness, spreads an unconscious moderation and charm around it, softens the asperities of human intercourse, elevates our ideals, and imparts a sense of serene enjoyment to all social relations. Our common people, immeasurably superior to the common people of other nations, in easy means of subsistence, in intelligence, as in the sterling virtues, are yet almost as immeasurably behind them in polished and gentle manners, and the love of Music, Painting, Statuary, and all the more refining social pleasures.

These Exhibitions, then, which make us acquainted with the superlative arts of other nations, cannot but be highly useful to us. But they have also another use—a moral, if not a religious use, in that they teach us so powerfully the dependence of nations upon each other—their mutual relations, and the absolute necessity of each to the comfortable existence of all the rest. There is hardly an article in the Crystal Palace to which the labor of all the world has not in some sort contributed—hardly a machine which is not an embodied record of the industrial progress of the world—hardly a fabric which, analyzed, does not carry us to the ends of the earth, or which does not connect us intimately with the people of every clime—with the miners who tortured its raw material from the dark cave, or the diver who brought it from the bottom of the sea—with the solitary mariner who shielded it from the tempests—with the poor, toil-worn mechanic who gave it form or color, or with the artist who imparted to it its final finish. Thus, no man liveth to himself alone, even in his most ordinary occupations; he is part and parcel of us, as we are of him. A wonderful and touching unity pervades the relations of the race; all men are useful to all men; and we who fancy that, in some important respects, we stand on the summit level of Humanity, have a deep interest in the laborers of the vales—in the celerity, the excellence, and the success of what they do—and in the comfort and happiness of their general condition. As Emerson has wisely sung, in that sweet poem of his—

All are needed by each one;
Nothing is fair or good alone.

There is also another thought suggested by our topic which contains a world of meaning. We are apt to speak, in our discussions, of the progress of Industry; but do we always ask ourselves wherein that progress consists? Is it in the greater perfection to which, in modern times, we have carried the works of our hands? Look at the elegant tissues of Persia and India, or at the flexible blades of Toledo and Damascus, and say in how far we have surpassed these works of semi-barbarous ages and people, with all our boasted mechanical improvement! Can we imagine anything more splendid, more rich, and more delicate, than the clothes in which the Oriental princes still array themselves, as their forefathers used to array themselves centuries ago? Have we yet a dye more brilliant than the Tyrian, a sculpture equal to that of Greece? an architecture better than that of the "Dark Ages?" paintings on glass to compare with those in the old cathedrals? workers in bronze to rival a Cellini? Is it not the highest compliment that we pay to a product of skill or genius, to say of it that it is "classical,"—that it is worthy of the models that have been preserved for ages in our galleries and museums? What, then, do we mean when we speak of ourselves as more advanced than former nations? What is that difference between us which authorizes us to use the word progress, and to look back with a complacent, half-pitying eye upon the attainments of the generations that have passed away?

It is this: that in our discoveries in science, by our applications of those discoveries to practical art, by the enormous increase of mechanical power consequent upon mechanical invention, we have *universalized* all the beautiful and glorious results of industry and skill, we have made them a common possession of the people; and given to Society at large—to almost the meanest member of it—the enjoyments, the luxury, the elegance, which in former times were the exclusive privilege of kings and nobles. Formerly, the labor of the world fed and clothed and ornamented the Prince and his Court, or the warrior and his chieftains; but now it feeds and clothes and ornaments the peasant and his family. Then the ten thousand poor, miserable wretches worked for the one, or the few; but now the ten thousand work for the ten thousand. Then the wealth of provinces was drained to heap up splendors for the lord of the province; but now that wealth is multiplied and diffused, to give happiness to the commonalty. All the concentrated capital of Lyons and Leeds and Lowell, all our complicated machinery, while it creates new demands for human labor, is intended to cheapen manufacturing products, as the effort of that cheapness is to put the fabrics of woollen and silk within the reach of the poorest classes. Our books, at this day, may not be individually superior to the books of the days of Elzevir, but millions of men now possess books, where hundreds only possessed them formerly. Our vases and cups may not be more exquisitely wrought than the vases and cups of Benvenuto Cellini; but they are wrought, not like his, for Popes and Emperors, but for Smith and Jones, and all the branches, collateral and direct, of the immense families of Smith and Jones. Our roads are not built at a vast expense, for some royal progress, or the passage of a conquering army; but are built to roll from house to house the precious treasures of industry, or a happy freight of excursionists, giving their hearts a holiday of merriment and innocent delight.

Our progress, in these modern times, then, consists in this, that we have democratized the means and appliances of a higher life; that we have spread, far and wide, the civilizing influence of Art; that we have brought, and are bringing more and more, the masses of the people up to the aristocratic standard of taste and enjoyment, and so diffusing the influence of splendor and grace over all minds. Grander powers have been infused into society. A larger variety and a richer flavor have been given to all our individual experiences; and, what is more, the barriers that once separated our race, the intervals of time and space that made almost every tribe and every family the enemy of every other tribe and family, have been annihilated, to enable the common interests and common enjoyments to renovate and warm us into amity of feeling and the friendly rivalry of fellow-workmen, pursuing, under different circumstances, the same great ends.

Legislation, rightly directed, might have done, and may yet do, much for the civilization and advancement of society; but, unfortunately, in most nations of the earth, the legislation, having been under the exclusive control of a self-styled higher class, has impeded rather than hastened the movement. Yet, in the face of this terrible obstacle, under all the evils of the insular monopoly of Great Britain, seeking to aggrandize her own manufacturing industry at the expense of the industry of the rest of mankind, the genius of practical art has triumphed, and will triumph still more, over every difficulty. It is raising the laborer to his true position; it is facilitating the association of men; it is harmonizing their interests; and whether legislation helps it or not, it will ultimately redeem our race from dependence and slavery. And herein is the chief reason why we salute with satisfaction the opening of the Crystal Palace.—*July* 14.

V.

SCULPTURE.

So infantile is the Sculptor's art among us—so absolutely unknown to the great mass of our people—and so meagre and poor have been its products hitherto accessible to the American public—that the display of statues, busts, and of other works in the Crystal Palace may be said to work an era in the recognition and appreciation of Sculpture in this country. To it the post of honor in the Exhibition has palpably been assigned; and no visitor can have spent even a half hour in the Palace without having his attention forcibly arrested by its numerous specimens. With these, then, let us begin our analytical account of the articles exhibited; and, since it is important that a severely correct taste should be acquired and cultivated by our countrymen—since hardly can human effort be worse directed than to the production of defective, indifferent works of Art—works which display no genius and enkindle no lofty aims—we shall speak of them with entire frankness and with relentless justice.

First, then, let us observe, that there is no sphere of art in which the public is so much imposed on, and, if we may say it, so extremely humbugged, as in sculpture. The reason is palpable. Sculpture brings before us forms without color, a thing unknown to nature. It deals only with outlines and surfaces, having abstracted therefrom the mass of qualities that the common eye beholds in external objects. Consequently, the common eye is unable to judge of its excellence. The mass of people, when placed before a statue, are about as incompetent to estimate and feel its worth or its defects, as a blind man would be to decide about the correctness of a model of the Parthenon or of Mount Blanc. They have not observed and studied nature in that aspect, and accordingly cannot tell whether its representation is faithful and artistic or the contrary. But they know that the work before them is sculpture; that it was carved by the illustrious Mr. Thing, or the famous Baron Thung, and so they go into raptures about it. They are, simply, thoroughly humbugged, and think they enjoy themselves in proportion.

A striking illustration of the truth of these remarks may be had by whomsoever will take the trouble to stand for a little while near Baron Marochetti's equestrian statue of Washington, which is in the place of honor under the dome of the Palace. It is bad, unqualifiedly and entirely; it is beneath mediocrity; and yet it seems to be a source of pleasure to many humbugged people. We are told that the same horse was employed by the artist to mount the effigy of Richard Cœur de Lion, which he exhibited at the London World's Fair, and which was so much admired that a movement has been set on foot to erect it in Hyde Park as a public monument of that Exhibition—which movement, by the way, will fall through, under the vigorous opposition of the London Press. But this proves nothing more than that the admirers of Marochetti in England are as easily deluded as those in this country. For, though we never saw that statue, we dare pronounce it intolerable. No group of which such a horse forms a part, could be worthy of any criticism except to explode its pretensions. It is an ungainly, wooden, lifeless, and ill-proportioned animal. Its action would be impossible in a real horse. The fore foot is lifted as if to paw the ground with violence, while the raised hind foot is going upon a gentle trot. But this colossal abortion is nothing to the figure astride of it. The attitude of this figure is about that which would be assumed by a bag of meal on horseback. The body is short and squat and the legs long, while the head is out of proportion with either. The face has not the least resemblance to that of Washington, and looks more like Franklin, than any other of the American revolutionary patriots, though we should hate to believe it a likeness of any. The head is bare, and the right hand, resting on the thigh, holds the three-cornered hat. This hand is twisted in a manner which suggests the idea of palsy or some other preternatural flexibility of the muscles. The palm is turned outward, and the fingers are quite out of proportion. In short, we are unable to find in this colossal work a single point worthy to be admired or even tolerated, and if the artist enjoys, as we are told he does, a European reputation, it must be among a very limited circle.

But, if we are obliged thus to speak of this statue, what shall be said of the image behind it, called by the name of Webster? This is certified to be the production of Mr. Carew, an English sculptor, whose name had been heard on this side of the Atlantic, though his works had never been seen here. Absolutely, this statue is a disgrace to its maker, and an outrage on the memory of its subject. We have used pretty severe language on the Washington, but it is a genuine work of art compared with the Webster. We do not believe there is in town a wood-carver, who cuts figure-heads for ships, who would not lose all his customers if he supplied them with such work as this. The head is deformed; the forehead bulges as with hydrocephalus; the features are feeble and expressionless; the body, the arms, the legs, the draperies, the pose, the action—all are not only without merit, but so far replete with its opposite as to be beneath contempt. Indeed, it is a pity that the thing stands in the Exhibition.

From these two unfortunate productions we turn with satisfaction to the Amazon by Kiss, which has its place near them, as if to render their want of every artistic quality only the more salient. This is a work of undeniable ability, which has achieved a good reputation for its author. The original stands in the open air by the door of the Museum at Berlin, and has long been an object of admiration in Germany. At London, too, it received the medal given to the best piece of sculpture in the Exhibition. The subject has great capabilities. A young Amazon on horseback, armed with a spear, is surprised by a tiger leaping upon the breast and neck of her horse and fixing his claws and teeth in the flesh of the frightened and suffering animal. Undaunted, she levels her spear at the tiger, and her face and movement indicate a courage superior to his ferocity. It is a conception full of the elements of life and interest. The beautiful woman, whose costume and movement reveal at once the vigor and the grace of her form, the wounded and desperate horse, the tiger clinging madly to his prey, and the bold heart and firm hand of the rider, all powerfully appeal to the feelings of the beholder. There is also great merit in the execution. Contrast this living and well-shaped horse with that deformed one by Marochetti, and you will easily get too high an idea of the work of Kiss. Certainly it is far superior to the mediocrity that prevails in the mass of recent sculptures. There is in it the evidence of power, knowledge, and sense, on the part of the artist. It deserves to be admired. But we do not pronounce it faultless. There are serious defects in it as a composition. For instance, if you stand directly in front of the group, you will be unable to form an idea of what it represents. The back of the tiger is so curved by the animal's posture on the chest of the horse, that you cannot tell that it is a tiger, and at the same time it hides from you both the Amazon and the horse, with the exception of the head of the latter—which, however, is turned aside, so that you are not sure that it belongs to the same body to which the tiger is hanging. Now, it will not do to say that it is not necessary that this front view should be perfect; because the group stands in Berlin with that view directly presented to the public, and it should, therefore, have been composed so as to make that view a good one, if not the best of all. On the whole, it is an interesting and pleasing work, but by no means a first-rate one.

The view of this work is somewhat impeded by the crowd constantly gathered about the four works of HIRAM POWERS, which adorn the Exhibition just at the beginning of the east nave, and at the point where the Amazon can be seen to the best advantage. We have here a copy of the Greek Slave, the Eve, the Fisher Boy, and the bust called Proserpine. The Eve alone is entirely novel to the public, the others having been repeatedly exhibited here before. It is marked by the general characteristics of its author's productions. In some respects, it is superior to the Greek Slave, though, as a whole, it is not so successful. Mr. Powers is absolutely unequalled in the perfection with which he re-produces nature, and in the exquisite elaboration of the surfaces of the body. No artist, since Greek sculpture was at its climax, has so given us the convolutions and rounded swell of the muscles, and the beautiful quality and delicate variations of the skin. In what we may call the *execution* of a statue, we cannot too much admire this conscientious and nature-loving worker. Give him nature to put into marble, and he is peerless. For the same reason, his busts of living persons are admirable. They not only are good likenesses, containing the character, features, and temperament of the original, but they derive a certain air of vitality and power from the artist, which, in the case of strongly-marked individualities, such for instance as Gen. Jackson, gives the beholder something of the higher pleasure belonging to the ideal, and that without any violation of artistic truth. This sort of excellence is well illustrated by the Eve. The body of this statue is finely modelled, and replete with a feeling of life and movement; the muscles of the trunk are alive, and its forms satisfy the desire for beauty. The legs, however, are too heavy, and the head is totally destitute of meaning. Not only is it not Eve, the Mother of Humanity, with the destinies of a world foreshadowed on her features, but it is not even a tolerable face which might pass for any ordinary person. Instead of going to nature, and finding among her living types the elements of a head and face befitting such a character, Mr. Powers has resorted to the conventional classic model; and, with that for his guide and standard, has attempted the strict ideal. Now, this is where his ability is deficient. He cannot create; his imagination is not of that power and temper which we call original genius; and where he undertakes the ideal he lamentably fails. Every work here exhibited proves this. Here are four heads, and every one of them is flat, barren, soulless, senseless. The statues, if the heads were knocked off, would command universal applause; but the eyes which can see meaning in either of these four faces, must be greatly aided by the fancy of their possessor. Nor in respect of originality in their conception can we award the highest praise to these statues. They are rather re-productions of the antique than new works, and we cannot behold either Eve or the Greek Slave without feeling that the Venus de Medicis has not only been thoroughly studied by their author, but that its suggestions were never absent from his mind while modelling them. So, also, the Fisher Boy is a derivative of the Young Apollo. This criticism, however, applies to others, the most eminent modern sculptors, and is dwelt on with regard to Mr. Powers only, with a view to fixing his place in the history of art. What that place is we think is not doubtful. In the manipulation of marble, and in the representation of muscular action and surfaces of flesh, he is supreme, among modern sculptors; in portraiture, he has but one or two equals; in imaginative and creative power, there are few, of any note, who do not surpass him.

A statue of Flora, by CRAWFORD, is to be shown here before the Exhibition closes, but as it had not arrived when these lines were written, we can only speak of the design. The figure is to occupy a place in the conservatory of a wealthy and tasteful citizen of New York. The goddess is represented as lightly moving forward, scattering flowers with both hands. It must be a graceful and pleasing work. Crawford has that quality of imagination which Powers has not. He conceives large and complicated works, requiring great constructive and combining genius. His mind is affluent in artistic ideas of grand and varied beauty. Witness the design of the monument to Washington he is now executing for Virginia. We hold him to be the first of American sculptors, and, in his peculiar line, to have no superior among his living rivals of other nations.

Opposite to the Amazon, and near the Powers' collection, is an equestrian statue by OTTIN, a French sculptor, representing an Indian shooting an arrow into the throat of a snake, which has coiled its folds around his horse, forcing the animal upon its haunches. The snake has its head raised and its mouth opened to strike its enemy, who improves the moment to pierce the reptile through the head and neck. The work has more the air of a sketch than a finished statue. The figure of the Indian is spirited, and shows careful study of human anatomy. In an out-of-the-way corner of the Palace is another group, by a French artist, representing a fisherman in the hug of a polar bear. The man has planted his knife in the bear's neck, but the latter crushes him to death in that resistless grip, and his head already droops in the exhaustion of death. There is a good deal of power in the treatment of this subject, but it is repulsive. It is contrary to the internal truth of art to represent man falling a helpless victim to an inferior animal; the struggle between them may excite interest and pleasure, as we see in Kiss's Amazon, but the total defeat of the human combatant is simply painful and disagreeable.

There is a great variety of other large works by French artists, but none that requires particular remark.

In the South Nave stands Müller's group of the Minstrel's Curse. Mr. Müller is a young German sculptor, trained in the best schools of Europe, who has come to establish himself in this country, bringing with him this group as an evidence of his capacities. We fear that his talents have not been recognized here at their true value, for we see in the Exhibition nothing else from his severe and vigorous chisel. Nor are the charms of elegance and beauty lacking to him. In this group, the boy, fainting in the languor of death, droops, with touching grace, to the earth; while the father, standing upright, raises his right hand to launch the imprecation at the tyrant who has slain his son. The story is told in one of the beautiful ballads of Uhland, and the sculptor has admirably caught its spirit. A wandering minstrel and his son sing before a king and queen; the queen is pleased with the boy, and the king, in a paroxysm of jealousy, slays him; thereupon the father launches a weighty imprecation at the murderer. We see him here with his right arm raised aloft to pronounce the curse, while his left sustains the youth smiling in death at his feet. The figure of the father is full of dignity and strength, and his face is inspired with the just rage natural to one who has lost so much by such a crime. This group is not yet placed upon a permanent pedestal, and does not stand high enough to be seen to the best advantage. It is an ornament to the Exhibition, and will carry the fame of its author over the United States.

In the North Nave is a bronze figure by Mr. H. K. Brown, apparently designed for a monument. If we mistake not, it is essentially the same statue as we saw last year, by Mr. Brown, called the Angel of the Resurrection. At any rate, the two have a family likeness, though this one has no wings, while the other was well furnished in that respect. It is a female figure, draped to the feet, with the right hand raised and pointing up, and the left suspended and pointing down. It has little meaning and no beauty. By the way, why will Mr. Brown provide his statues with such big feet? The draperies are very commonplace and insignificant.

Not far off is the great attraction among the sculptures of the Palace, next to the works of Powers. We refer to Thorwaldsen's Christ and Apostles. They are all large, but the Christ is colossal. These figures were designed to ornament a church, and can be perfectly appreciated only in combination with architecture. The Christ, for instance, should stand so far from the others as to reduce the excessive difference in their size, but here the want of space necessitates crowding them together. And so of every one of the thirteen statues; each can be properly judged only in connection with the objects and uses for which it was made. But they all betray the hand of a master. Thorwaldsen was not a great original genius. He is not to be classed with the first sculptors of history, with such men as made the Venus of Milo or the frieze of the Parthenon. Among modern sculptors he has superiors in some respects. He could not have made Houdon's Voltaire, or some of the busts of Powers. But he was a man of broad, powerful, generous nature, and of exhaustless fertility. He could grasp and combine a complicated work, and take hold of it with mastery and ease. What a life of happy activity was his! what a crowd of productions he left behind him! ranging through almost every sphere of his art, marked generally by the freshness of a broad and untiring imagination, and executed in a large and facile manner. He was rich in resources, and his mind and hand were fraught with erudition. There is much learning in these thirteen figures. Take the draperies, for instance, and see how artistically rich and graceful hang their folds. These details illustrate the superiority of the accomplished artist. If you would know their value, turn from Thorwaldsen to Brown, and contrast the draperies of the Apostles with those of the bronze figure above referred to. In point of expression, we find these statues not inadequate to their subjects and their purpose. The general treatment must of necessity be somewhat conventional, and based upon the traditions and sentiments of the religious world. An entirely new conception of the Savior and his followers would have been unsuited to the purpose for which the group was made. Within these limits, then, lay the problem to be solved by the artist; and his work, if it does not attain ideal perfection, is worthy of his fame. If not a great and faultless work, it is one of eminent merits, and we predict will continue to be the most generally admired feature of the Exhibition.

A considerable number of Italian statues are exhibited, mostly in marble, but they are uniformly very poor. Italy is now not rich in either sculpture or painting, and has by no means sent here specimens of her best. In Industry she has beautiful products in the Exhibition; but in Art we cannot boast for her. One statue, however, has a pleasing character: it is of a child threading a needle, and the intent expression of the face makes it prominent among the dreary blankness of its neighbors.

A bust, called Ariadne, is exhibited by the American sculptor Ives, now in Italy. It is carefully and nicely wrought, and forms a pleasing ornament for a parlor, but why it is called Ariadne we are at a loss to discover. There is nothing about it which would not answer as well to the name of Daphnis, or Cybele, or any other classic appellation. The face is regular enough, but has a great deal less meaning than Undine's had before she became endowed with a soul, for that was full of the life of the external elements, and poor Ariadne has no life at all. We have little respect for these fancy heads which are like nothing in nature. It is a pity that sculptors of talent should waste their time on such nonentities.

Mr. Ball, of Boston, exhibits a Statuette of Webster, in terra-cotta, which has a great deal of merit. The likeness is good and the pose dignified and natural. The great orator, standing, and with his head erect, seems about to enounce some weighty proposition. His right hand rests easily in his vest, as it was wont to do when he uttered the general idea on which whole periods of reasoning declamation were to be based. No other sculptor has so well succeeded in pourtraying Mr. Webster.

But after all, the large works in bronze and marble must yield the palm of perfection to some animals and birds in bronze in the French department. In this line, excellence here seems to reach its boundary. There is a heron trying to extract an arrow which has pierced its body, by Comolera, which we do not think could be improved, either in vivid truth to nature, or in the details of its execution. There are partridges, wolves, and other animals by Delabriérre, with cats, monkeys, and birds, by Fremiet, which, though of less magnitude and pretension, are remarkable for beauty and artistic finish of work. It is perhaps not singular that in these small and comparatively easy subjects such excellence should be reached, while the nobler horse is so rarely modelled with truth and life, and the still nobler creature, man, rarest of all. It was not so in the palmy days of Greek art. The horses on the Parthenon are beautiful, but the human figures are more so. Then the artist seemed to gain in power as his subject rose; now it is the reverse.

We cannot properly close our notice of the statuary in the Crystal Palace, without reference to the Equestrian Jackson, by Clark Mills, which, though not exhibited beneath its roof, is exhibited in the neighborhood, and with reference to the crowds attracted there. This work has been excessively and ignorantly praised, and will stand as a monument of the absurdity of trying to do what you don't understand. It has two points on which it has been lauded; one is, that it was made by a young man who knew nothing of sculpture but what he taught himself, and the other is that it stands unpropped on its hind legs. Both are foolish, but the first is preposterous. You might as well expect a young man with an ear for music, but no instruction, to compose an opera like Don Juan, or an unlearned carpenter to build an edifice like St. Peter's, as to expect a good equestrian statue from a tyro, though he had a genius like Michael Angelo. Such a statue requires all the discipline, all the learning, all the resources of the art, of which it is one of the most difficult productions. Why, a man is not trusted to make a watch, or forge a horse-shoe, till he has gone through an apprenticeship; and yet we are told that he can accomplish a work infinitely more difficult without any apprenticeship at all! This is the summit of nonsense, and merited the endorsement of the last Congress with a premium of $20,000. But let us look at the statue which has thus been rewarded. Here we are met by the second point of excellence, the rearing of the horse on his hind legs without any prop to hold him up, such as is employed in other equestrian statues where the horse is represented in that position. Now this is not an artistic but a mechanical point, and might have been gained by any former artist who had enough ignorance, or want of conscience. There is no difficulty whatever in standing such a statue on the hind legs, and never was any difficulty, if artists would have adopted the manner of Mr. Mills. His secret consists in substituting for the legs of a horse those of a gigantic ox or a moderately sized elephant. On supports like those a world might stand alone, without any special glory to the builder; indeed, if he boasted of it as a beauty, it would rather turn to his shame.

In the Jackson, this disproportion of the horse's hind legs and quarters is excessive; seen from the rear or the front, it becomes a deformity which would be glaring were there any beauty in the work with which to contrast it. The equipoise of the statue is, no doubt, also maintained by casting the rear parts much heavier than the front. The figure of the rider is mainly back of the apparent centre of gravity, and does its part in keeping all straight. It is a stiff, awkward, graceless, and undignified figure. Nothing could well be less pleasing than the angular, elbow-crooked sort of way in which the right hand holds the military hat. But we cannot go over the work in detail. Nor does it need such criticism. It speaks for itself. It is the work of a novice. It is not a work of art. It knows nothing of art. It has no artistic features. It is, no doubt, an ingenious production for a young man under such circumstances, but it is most unfit for Congress to pay for, or to be set up as a national monument. Still, if it is any consolation, we will add that it is not so poor as Marochetti's Washington.

We state these plain truths with sorrow, but they need to be stated, not only for the sake of Mr. Mills, but for the sake of the country. It is a national misfortune for an American to produce a work so beneath criticism, at a large expense to the National Treasury. It is a personal misfortune when it is grossly and falsely praised, for such delusion cannot last, and the waking up from it is intensely painful. Mr. Mills has a contract to make a statue of Washington. We earnestly counsel him to doubt his own powers; to begin the modest and difficult career which alone can elevate even a man of genius into an artist; and to qualify himself for so arduous a work before he undertakes its execution.

VI.

REAPING, MOWING AND THRESHING MACHINES.

WHETHER we regard the ingenuity of their contrivance, or the practical services they render, the machines for Reaping and Mowing naturally take the first rank among farming implements, and first of these machines, because more widely known, is McCormick's Reaper, of which, since 1846, Mr. McCormick has sold at his manufactory, at Chicago, Ill., upwards of seven thousand. This Reaper is also used for mowing; the price for the Reaper is $115, and when arranged for mowing, $140. About 1200 a year are manufactured and sold at these rates. The cutting principle is that of a sickle-edged knife, which is slightly indented on the edge, working in combination with fingers which hold the grain up to the knife. Twenty acres can be cut in a day.

Next to this may be seen Ketcham's Mowing Machine, the best known and most approved for merely cutting grass, of any of the family. The cutting principle of this machine is that of shears. The blades are like large saw-teeth, being some four inches long, riveted to a bar, and working through stationary fingers, cutting very smooth and close to the ground, and not liable to clog. The motion is given by a cast-iron driving-wheel and gearing, done by two horses, the driver sitting upon a safe and comfortable seat, while a swath about five feet wide is cut at his right hand as fast as his horses can walk. We are not able to give the price or performance of this machine, as we found no one present to answer any questions. We happen to know, however, that it is a very valuable farm implement, and can be worked upon tolerably rough ground. They are manufactured at Buffalo.

Manny's Reaper and Mower is a western machine, invented and patented in 1851, by J. H. Manny, of Freeport, Ill. In public favor, it is likely to become a strong rival of some of the older inventions in the same line. Readers will remember that this is a premium machine, as a combined Mower and Reaper.

Burrall's Convertible Reaper, as most of our agricultural readers will recollect, took the first premium as a Reaper, at the great trial last year at Geneva, New-York, where they are manufactured by Thomas D. Burrall, and sold "cheap for cash," but how much is not made apparent. It is undoubtedly a good Reaper, and the inventor thinks it is now so perfected that he can also compete successfully with others in mowing. This machine is made to discharge the grain like Hussey's, in the rear, or like McCormick's, at the side. There are some advantages claimed for this convertible principle, upon the merits of which we shall not attempt to decide. The cutting principle is similar to Ketcham's or Manny's, by triangular-shaped knives moving between stationary fingers.

Hussey's Mowing and Reaping Machine should properly have been named first, as it is the original of all the Reaping Machines in America. The inventor (one of nature's noblemen) is a resident of Baltimore, where he manufactures his Reapers, not on quite so large a scale as some of his more successful imitators, for he does a portion of the work with his own hand, and, like many other benefactors of his race, although he has been the cause of others gaining fortunes by his machines, we believe he has not himself been so successful. The wheat-growers of this country, whether using Hussey's or any other Reaper, ought to know and remember how much they are indebted to this humble mechanic for the advantages which they now enjoy in being able to substitute horse-power for manual labor in cutting grass and grain. At the South, Hussey's machines are more generally approved than McCormick's, notwithstanding the latter is a Virginia invention, and took the great medal at the London World's Fair. In some respects, and in some situations, one is better than the other, yet it would be difficult for impartial judges to decide which *par excellence*, should be preferred, where both are so good. This and McCormick's are considered the great rival machines, in consequence of the glory gained in England and the noise made in the world, by the American reapers. The price of the two is about equal.

Fairbanks' Reaper and Mower is next to be noticed. What particular superiority this machine has over the others we are not able to discover, unless there is an advantage in the fact that the wheel which supports the end next the standing grain is larger. The width of the swath appears to be narrower than the others, the cutting principle the same as all the others, except McCormick's. The inventor is evidently indebted to Obed Hussey for the idea of this part of his apparatus. The raker sits on this machine riding backward, and rakes off the grain at the side behind the horses.

The Self-Raking Reaper was invented by Charles Denton, of Peoria, Ill., and is manufactured at that place by Gregg Denton. This is the second machine of the kind ever built; the first, which was proved in last year's harvest, has been sent to England, to be tried and patented there. The cutting principle is the same as Hussey's, but the swath is eight feet wide. The grain is pressed up to the knives by a wheel like McCormick's, and falls on the platform upon a cloth band which carries it up over the driving wheel and gearing, and drops it into a *dumper* holding enough for a good sized bundle, and then empties itself ready for the binder, cutting twenty-five acres a day—the team required is four horses. This machine seems very heavy, but the inventor claims that in consequence of being supported on both ends by wheels four feet in diameter, it does not run much harder than the narrow machines, and that four horses can work it easier than two horses can any other yet invented. It seems peculiarly adapted to operate on the vast prairies where it originated. The price is not yet fixed, but it is thought to be about $160.

The Reaper of Seymour & Morgan, Brockport, N. Y., here exhibited, is now under injunction for an alleged infringement of McCormick's patent. The principle of the gearing and cutting is much alike in the two machines; there is in each the same style of serrated sickle-edged knife, working between guiding fingers, the wheat being pressed up to the knife by a reel. The cutting edge of this Reaper is a little wider, and is set off about two feet further from the gearing than Mr. McCormick's. The raker rides at the back of the platform, pushing the grain off with a fork behind the horses, so that it is out of the way of the next through.

The California Reaper is only the model of an immense double machine, represented to be capable of cutting, raking and binding the wheat all at the same operation. Without some further information than can be obtained from the model, it is impossible to learn enough about its working to give our readers any practical ideas. The cutting is upon the same principle as in those already described.

The Horse Cradle is the name we should give the model of another grain cutter here exhibited. Two horizontal cylinders, mounted upon a pair of wheels, are geared so as to revolve toward each other. The cylinders, we believe, are to be four feet diameter, and about the same length. On the bottom of each cylinder a set of knives, like short sythe-blades, are set, and out of the surface of the cylinder, fingers like cradle-fingers project, which carry the grain as it is cut by the knives and discharge it behind. What is to become of it then, is more than the model, without a word of explanation, makes apparent. Col. Johnson, the Superintendent of this Department, informed us that the exhibitor assured him that the machine had worked successfully, and cut the grain as fast as any other machine with one horse. The model exhibited shows it is intended for only one, as it has a pair of thills, which, by-the-by, like the proportion of parts of a great many models, are represented about sixty feet long. We don't know the inventor's name, as he does not see proper to inform the public by any written memoranda who he is, where he is, or what his machine is for. And this is the case with nearly every implement in the Exhibition. There is nothing to indicate to a visitor whether he is looking at a Reaping Machine or some contrivance to sweep the streets. We heard the inquiry made fifty times while persons were looking at the most simple farm implement, such as a corn-sheller, "What is this?" A man who had lived on a farm all his lifetime, and kept a large dairy, did not know what a self-acting cheese-press was for, and any Hottentot from Africa could have given quite as good an account of the purpose of the machine. Thousands of people will look upon these things who cannot tell a fanning-mill from a balloon, or a corn-sheller from a new patent rat-trap. Farmers who wish to buy better tools will come here and cast their eyes upon the very things they want without knowing it. Exhibitors need not say they are stupid if they cannot tell what such common things are. How can they tell until they learn? Pray what do you exhibit your goods for? We need not tell you, but we *will* tell you, that it is a piece of excessive stupidity to send things here without having the name of every article just as plainly printed thereon as you are careful to have your own. There is no interest in looking at a thing, the use of which we cannot comprehend. At the very moment of writing these notes, a woman, who looks like a farmer's wife, is turning a sausage-meat cutter over and over, and wondering what on earth it can be for. Her husband is equally puzzled with a new, and, as we think, valuable improvement in the threshing-machine—of which more hereafter. And so of a dozen others all around us, looking with a sort of vacant stare at things whose use is familiar to those who sent them there, for the purpose it would seem of puzzling every body who does not happen to possess the same knowledge with themselves. It is no excuse that things are not yet arranged, for the same exhibitors have done the same thing for years. It is full time that they were taught better by a little gentle castigation, of which we here present them with a specimen, to be renewed from time to time until the lesson is taken to heart and made to bear practical fruit.

Next after the Reapers come Threshing Machines, and that of Palmer may be appropriately named first in the list, because it is a recent invention and novel in construction, differing in all respects totally from any one heretofore invented for threshing grain, and being in some respects as greatly in advance of all others as the ordinary kind is in advance of the flail or trampling of cattle. It does not thresh by a spike-toothed cylinder working into a spiked concave, like the ordinary machine, which is fed by a man who stands in front, feeding it with wheat and himself with dust, to which is sometimes added a flying tooth or other death-dealing object. The grain is put into this machine upon aprons on both sides, as fast as four men can handle the unbound sheaves, which pass through a hole upon each side of the case, which is circular, about four feet in diameter and six inches thick, the hole being about the size of a bundle of grain, and situated at the outer edge of the circle, about half the height from the ground. Here the heads of the grain are struck by four iron arms of one and a quarter inch round iron, which are firmly set in a hub that is made to revolve with great speed. This blow or blows, falling rapidly upon the heads as they project from a square corner, knocks out a great portion of the grain; the straw is then carried forward by the arms through the lower half of the circle, the sides of which are waved plates of iron, which give the straw a tortuous motion, whipping it from side to side until every kernel is whipped out. The straw is still carried forward by the arms over the upper part of the circle and thrown out at the same side it entered, a little above. These plates are adjustable, so as to be set close for timothy, or wide for coarse straw, or of wheat, rye, oats, rice, buckwheat, or peas, either of which it will thresh perfectly clean. This machine, as exhibited with its most elaborate finish, might be taken as a mere model of the conception of some visionary patentee, but such is not the case; numerous machines have been fully tested by large planters in North Carolina, where it was invented, and there is not a shadow of doubt upon our mind, that with the same power, this machine will thrash more grain than any other; and we think no one who has had much experience in threshing, can examine this model without coming to the same conclusion, even before he sees it in operation.

We beg all grain-growers who read these notes, to make it a point to see this new thresher; and we beg the inventor to put a card upon it, to tell those who stare with wonder at it, without knowing what it is, that it is Palmer's Threshing Machine.

The same man has made a valuable improvement upon the old-fashioned spike cylinder machines, to prevent danger to the person tending them, when a stone or other hard substance happens to be in the sheaf. This is simply by cutting off the apron just before it reaches the cylinder, so that all heavy substances drop down. There is also a roller in front of the cylinder to prevent whole sheaves from passing, or the feeder getting his hand caught. These inventions are valuable improvements for the farmer, and this inventor, like all his class, is doing more good to others than himself. At least do him the honor to examine his inventions.

There is another newly invented machine of this class, the improvement of which is in the attached apparatus for cleaning grain. This is the invention of E. S. Snyder, of Jefferson County, Va. It is known as the "Farmer's Labor-Saving Machine," being designed to thresh, clean, and put the wheat in bags, ready measured for market, all at one operation. The machine exhibited is intended for two horses, and is represented as being capable of threshing and cleaning one hundred bushels of wheat a day. This we do not doubt; but that it will, or any two-horse machine, when in operation on the farm, continue to do as much, day after day, we shall not believe; because, by somewhat long experience, we have never been able to find such an one. That it is a good machine, and worthy the attention of farmers, we have no doubt, and hope all who visit the Palace will give it a fair examination.

The same patentee has the model of a threshing machine, in which the cylinder stands upright. This, the patentee thinks, will work so much more easily than the horizontal cylinder, that it will save the power of one horse in four. The plan is worth a trial, the only means by which the value of improvement in all machinery is determined.

In connection with these threshers, the patentee exhibits a model of a machine much needed at the South. It is intended to separate garlic from the wheat, which no common cleaner will do. In this the wheat is washed and the garlic taken out, and the grain dried by hot air or steam. It can be operated by hand, horse, or any other power. Planters who suffer from this pest of the Southern wheat-grower, will do well to inquire into this machine.

But we are straying from the subject of Threshers, which are well represented in the Exhibition. Having already spoken of several, we will now give such descriptions of others as will enable such of our readers as may not be familiar with this kind of labor-saving farm machinery, to judge how much space may be required, and also what constitutes a threshing-machine, or a thresher and cleaner combined.

We will first describe one of medium size which we find in the collection of R. L. ALLEN, on the north side of the gallery. This is simply for threshing out the grain, without separating it from the straw and chaff. Machines for that purpose are much used by large wheat-growers; some of them depositing it in bags ready for market.

This machine is a stout frame, thirty-four inches high, forty-six inches long, and twenty-eight inches wide, which supports a cylinder twenty-three inches long and sixteen inches diameter, made of wood, covered with sheet-iron, in the periphery of which short iron teeth are set, so as to run between corresponding teeth in a concave bed. This is called an under-shot machine. An over-shot one has a similar concave cap over the cylinder. This cylinder is driven with great speed by a band running over a pulley on the end of the stout iron shaft upon which it runs. The bundles of grain, with the bands cut, are laid upon a platform about three and a half feet long, attached to the frame in front of the cylinder which carries them through, and out at the other end of the machine, where the straw is raked from the grain by hand, or sometimes separated by machinery attached and driven in connection with the thresher. On the same floor is a machine called "Gilbert's Excelsior Thresher and Cleaner." This term, *excelsior*, so often misapplied, means "more lofty, more elevated, higher;" and seems to us to have about as much to do with a threshing machine, as with the pile of straw after being threshed.

The frame of this machine is necessarily a good deal higher than the other one described, because it has a fanning-mill directly under the cylinder, similar in all respects to those noticed in a former article. The grain and straw as it passes from the cylinder, is driven upon a revolving band made of small sticks somewhat resembling a Venetian window-blind, such as those arranged to draw up by cords on the inside of windows. This band is some five or six feet long on its upper surface, and, as the straw is carried up, the slight inclination at which it is placed, and over the end, where it falls six or seven feet to the ground, the grain falls through the slats of the band on to the screens of the fanning-mill, where the chaff is blown away, and the grain delivered in bags for market; that is, in about as clean a state as slovenly farmers are apt to send it to mill, or for sale. It is represented that a No. 3 machine, costing $110, will thresh and clear ten or twelve hundred bushels in a day, with two horses. If it will do three-quarters of that, the purchaser may rest assured that he has got a good article.

The cylinder is driven by a band, and the straw-elevator and fan by small bands from the cylinder, so that all operate together from the same power.

The peculiarity in this threshing machine, and upon which the inventor claims a superiority over all others, is in the formation of the threshing cylinder, which certainly, we believe, unlike any of the somewhat numerous family. It is thirty-one inches long, and sixteen inches in diameter, measuring from the extremities of the teeth, and is composed of a centre-shaft, surrounded by eight round bars, which support five teeth, or rather clusters of teeth, to each bar. These clusters are made of a piece of thin flat bar-iron, two-and-a-half inches wide, and sixteen inches long, through a hole in the centre of which runs the shaft, and equi-distant on each side a smaller bar. Each of these flat bars has two pieces riveted on each side, the ends of each cut into four saw-like teeth, and each plate bent out from the other, thus forming the cylinder all of wrought iron. The concave is composed of eleven three-quarter inch bars of square iron, set with the corners to the teeth, which pass very close to their surface. There are no teeth in the concave. The height of the cylinder shaft is four feet three inches above the ground, rendering it necessary for the feeder to be elevated. The width of the frame is three feet eight inches, and its length, independent of the feeding platform and straw-carrier, four feet four inches. The height from the ground to the top of the cap over the cylinder is five feet, above which is a dust-chimney, which may sometimes benefit the feeder a little.

Never having seen this machine in operation, we cannot express ourselves quite as sanguinely as the inventor, that it is the best of all, not only in the Exhibition, but out of it. The opinion of several gentlemen of good judgment, who have examined the machine, without seeing it work, is that it will break the grains of wheat. If it does that any worse than any other thresher, it will spoil it for seed. Our impression is that it will not. However, it is our candid opinion, from long and careful examination, that about one-fourth of the grains of wheat, and those of the largest size, are ruined for seed, in their passage through any threshing machine. We believe every grain that is struck a fair blow by one of the teeth has its germinating power destroyed, even when it shows no external breakage. And this, in our judgment, is one of the causes of degeneracy in many sections of the country in the quality of this grain. It has long been remarked by wheat-growers, that it is not as round and plump as it used to be. It is also a subject of remark that it takes more seed lately to produce the same crop, than it used to do thirty years ago. We meet now occasionally with an old farmer who contends for three pecks of seed to the acre, because that used to be sufficient. But that was when threshing was all done by flails, as all wheat for seed should be threshed. This is a subject worthy of very serious consideration by all farmers.

We hope wheat-growers will give the machine above described a share of their attention, because it is something new, and may be thought, on examination, better than any of its predecessors. They will find it in the extreme end of the agricultural gallery, next to the reservoir; and in the same vicinity they will find another, called Hathaway's Combined Machine for threshing, separating and cleaning all kinds of grain, clover, and grass-seed. The inventor, like all other inventors, says, "its capacity for threshing excels all others now in use." So it does, if it will thresh and clean, as he states, "six to eight hundred bushels of wheat per day." The machine is undoubtedly a good one, and, with very short straw, in good condition, *may* be made to thresh eight hundred bushels in a long day, with double sets of teams and hands. But that is not a fair day's work of any threshing-machine, and the public should not be told so. The story is too big for one who has had as much to do with threshing-machines as the writer of this article.

The dimensions of Hathaway's machine are as follows:

Height of frame, forty-nine inches; height of cap over cylinder, twelve inches; height of edge of feeding-apron, fifty-one inches; height of extreme end of straw-carrier, eight feet; width of frame, forty-one inches; extreme length of machine, fifteen feet. There is a little contrivance for cleaning out the straw that falls through the slats of the carrier, which will be very useful. It is a band, with small iron-teeth, which runs crosswise through the machine, between the upper and under part of the carrier.

The threshing-cylinder is driven by a band, and bands from the cylinder-shaft drive the fanning-mill and straw-carrier. This is as well made a machine as there is in the Exhibition. It is strong where strength is needed; and where light-wood will answer, pine is used; in other places, oak. The inventor says it will clean clover-seed to perfection. If it will, that will add to its value. It will be well for all who feel an interest in such things, to compare these two machines, one having the common cylinder with spike-teeth, and the other those very singular ones described.

On the lower floor, next to the machine-arcade, stands another thresher and cleaner, called "Moffat's Patent," from Piqua, Ohio, which differs from any of its predecessors—so much so, as to be well worth careful attention. We will endeavor to describe it, so that our readers can form some idea of its appearance and dimensions:

The cylinder is thirty inches long and sixteen in diameter. It is made of eight flat bars of iron, half inch by two inches, fastened upon iron heads with four strong iron bands. In each of these bars are seventeen flat teeth, fastened by nuts on the ends, on the back-side of the bars. The teeth pass between one row of teeth in the concave, which is made of bars of iron, open so the grain may fall through. The shaft of the cylinder is thirty-four inches above the ground, and is driven by a spur-wheel on the left hand side of the machine, which works into a pinion on the cylinder-shaft. On the right of the machine is a bevel-pinion, upon the end of the shaft which supports the spur-wheel, which is driven by a wheel set at right-angles upon a short shaft, to which the power is connected by a universal joint. The width of the frame is forty inches; height over top of cylinder, forty-two inches; height of straw-carrier at extreme end, six and a half feet; extreme length of machine, nineteen feet. The straw-carrier is made of round rods and iron links, so as to form an endless band. Underneath the straw-carrier, there are two screws, six feet long, eight inches diameter, running in sheet-iron troughs, which carry up the grain and chaff that falls through the concave and short of the straw-carrier, and drops it upon the screen of the fanning-mill, which is under the back end of the machine. On the left side of the frame, there is another similar screw on the reverse angle, which brings back from the fanning-mill the unthreshed heads, and drops them into a spout which leads them back to the threshing-cylinder. There is another screw, running across under the fan-mill screen, which brings the clean grain out through a spout on the right side of the frame, to which a bag may be attached, and, for aught we know, tied up after it is filled without the aid of hands.

There is a wheel over the straw-carrier that assists to push up the load. The fanning-mill is in the usual form, similar to those described to work by hand. The objection we have to this machine is, that it has too much machinery—is too complicated, and probably too expensive, and requires too much power. If driven with sufficient power, it will undoubtedly do good work, and a good deal of it; but we prefer a more simple machine, even if it should not be so effective.

In the Canadian Department, there is another thresher and cleaner, hailing from Brantford, Canada, which will undoubtedly strike the fancy of some visitors, because it is much lower than either of the others, and apparently more convenient. The height of the edge of the feeding-apron is only forty inches from the ground. The height of cylinder-shaft is only thirty-three inches. Diameter of cylinder, sixteen inches; length, thirty-two inches. It is made somewhat like Moffat's, only the bars are broader and thinner; the teeth are two and a half inches long, about three-quarters of an inch square at the butt, flattened out toward the end to three quarters of an inch, and turned back hooked, for strength, and giving but a very small surface to strike the grain. The concave is cast-iron, with small teeth. The width of the frame is forty inches; height, thirty-three inches; height of extreme end of straw-carrier, six feet; extreme length of whole machine, seventeen feet. There is a double apron to carry the straw and grain, the upper one of small, square rods, on leather bands, at each end; the under one flat slats set edgewise on a cloth band, so that all the grain, falling through the open work of the straw-carrier, is taken by the grain-carrier, dropped down upon the shaking-screen of the fanning-mill, which is at the end opposite the cylinder. The thresher is driven by a band, and the other parts by bands from the cylinder-shaft. This has the appearance of being a very strong, simple, effective, good machine.

We have now given our readers, we think, such information as will enable them to understand these very great labor-saving implements. The price varies from thirty-five to probably one hundred and fifty dollars for some of the largest. We hope all grain-growers will give the machines we describe a careful examination when they visit the Exhibition, and not take our word for any one, as it is not our intention to commend one above another, but simply to describe them in such a manner as to attract the notice of those who are interested, and set them to thinking and inquiring which is best, or whether it would not be more to their interest to purchase some of the good new machinery lately invented to facilitate the labors of agriculture, than it is to continue to use the old tools of their fathers and grandfathers' time. Although we contend that seed-wheat should be threshed by flails, we know that no farmer can be successful in growing rich by raising grain, who adheres to that antiquated fashion. Farmers should try to inform themselves, in some way, whether it is for their interest to continue to beat out their seed by flails, or tramp it out by horses, when they can so easily procure a machine that will do the work so much faster and cheaper. In what way can they gain that information so cheaply as by visiting this Exhibition, with this paper in their hand, and thus giving each machine a most careful and scrutinizing examination? See for themselves—take no one's opinion as an *ipse dixit* upon anything they see, until they can satisfy themselves by the exercise of their own judgment that the article before them is well calculated to perform all that the builder claims for it.

Farmers should visit the Exhibition with particular reference to the Agricultural Department, and for the purpose of making careful examination of implements that are new to them, and they certainly will find a great many which they are as wholly unacquainted with as though they had not been all their lives tillers of the soil.

It is true that this part of the Palace is not as well filled as we had good reason to expect, from the large number of agricultural implement manufacturers which have lately sprung into existence in the United States. There are four or five establishments, some of which are doing a very large business in this city, engaged exclusively in making and vending farming-tools, who are exhibitors, and whose warehouses, always open to visitors, contain almost as great a show, in their line, as the Crystal Palace.

VII.

PLOWS.

In ascending the great stairway from the dome, leading north-east, on your way to the gallery of the Agricultural Department, the visitor will find in the angle, between the two flights of stairs, a collection of Plows from one of the oldest and largest manufactories in the United States, among which are some of the best, perhaps, that he has ever met with. On examination he will notice upon the inside of the mold-board of every one, the name of J. Nourse, who is the senior partner of Messrs. Ruggles, Nourse, Mason & Co., of Worcester and Boston. Their names are almost world-renowned as manufacturers of this indispensable farm implement. Mr. Nourse was one of the first to improve the plow upon scientific principles, having been more than a quarter of a century engaged in the business; first as an apprentice to his father, and afterward devoting many of the best years of his life, and the strong energies of a mind determined to succeed in producing a perfect plow, of every size and shape required. Hence his partners have nobly determined that his name shall be known and remembered by every one as a man justly entitled to be honored by every American farmer.

Probably the first plow that will attract attention in this collection is that numbered 77, because it is the largest and the last perfected. The beam is five feet long, and the whole length from end of handle to point of beam nine feet. These are made of the best of tough oak and ash timber, all the rest of the plow being made of refined cast-iron, the cutting-edges cold-chilled in the mould till they are harder than tempered cast-steel. This is called the deep-tiller and sod-plow. It is intended to turn a furrow from nine to thirteen inches deep and fifteen to seventeen inches wide; and such is the perfection of its construction that it can be done easily by two yoke of oxen, such as are in common use all over the New-England States. If the soil is very stiff and hard, an extra yoke is added. At the end of the beam there is a cast-iron wheel, by which the required depth is guaged. The draft is from a rod attached to the beam at the standard and leading under the beam through a guide, by a screw upon which the rod can be raised or lowered four or five inches, thus varying the line of draft. Between the wheel and share a coulter is fixed, with a sharp steel edge. From the point of the share to the heel, along the land side, it measures three feet; width across the heel, 15 inches; across the wing, 22 inches; from the point to upper angle of the wing, 4 feet 5 inches; height of standard to under side of the beam, 19½ inches. The handles are braced with iron rods, and the whole is made as strong as wood and iron combined can effect. No doubt, those who read about this iron plow will naturally imagine it must be a very ponderous article, and many of those who looked at it while we were present, thought it was too heavy for one man to handle. To satisfy them of their miscalculation, we had scales brought up, and the weight ascertained to be only 205 pounds. This lightness is produced by the most careful and exact calculations in making the patterns, so as to dispense with every grain of iron not necessary to the perfect construction of the implement. You can hardly imagine the perfection of the curves of the mold-board, until you apply a two-foot rule upon its polished surface, in the direction of the line of draft, and find that it touches the whole length. All parts of the iron subject to friction are ground smooth before leaving the factory.

The minute description of this plow will serve for all. Constant improvements are made, perhaps trifling in appearance, in fact really imperceptible to the casual observer, yet, by the mere change of one-eighth of an inch in the curve of the mold-board, a vast saving of labor to the team is effected.

Not finding in this collection one of the smallest sized cast-iron plows, we procured one known as No. 60, from among the plows of R. L. Allen, of this city, to weigh in contrast with the large one described, and found the weight only 39 pounds. This is a plow much used by cotton and corn planters in the light lands of the South, where more land is plowed less, than more than two inches deep. The price of the large plow is $19—the price of the small one, less than that for a dozen. The dimensions of this small one-horse plow is five feet from point of beam to end of handles; length from point to heel on the land side, one foot six inches; same length from point to upper angle of wing; height of standard, 14½ inches. Between this and the first, there is to be seen almost every size and shape that could be wished for. There is one of the same style and general appearance with that first described, known as deep tiller No. 71½, with wheel and cutter, but with a dial clevis instead of centre-draft rod, and much lighter, weighing only 108 lbs., and which was designed expressly for plowing loose, porous, dry, sandy and gravelly loams. Its mold-board has a long, gentle curvature, and turns sod furrows five to eight inches deep and eleven to thirteen inches wide, with such a long, easy twist that, notwithstanding the friable nature of the soil, the furrow-slice is completely rolled over, burying the grass, or weeds and stubble, and still leaving the surface in a measure compact, and in much better condition than it would be if plowed with No. 70, which is made expressly for the purpose of stirring up stiff soils and leaving them in a light, mellow condition. Such soils as No. 71½ was made to plow, require to be laid over in perfectly flat furrows, with the edges closely matched, and the natural cohesion of the parts preserved, thus promoting condensation rather than evaporation of moisture. This tends to prevent the withering influences of our excessive drouths; and yet, from the depth of the furrow of such a plow the earth is in fine condition for growing plants. In direct contact with the above are the stubble-plows, Nos. 31 to 39. They are made with high standards—that is, high beams, and short-high mold-boards, and wide in the heel, by which the furrow-slice is broken up in such a manner that the course of the furrows is indistinguishable, though from five to ten inches deep and ten to thirteen inches wide. Some of this class of plows were got up expressly for the use of broom corn growers, by which they can effectually bury stubble and stalks beneath the surface.

Another implement, which promises to be very useful, is called the Double Plow, or sod and subsoil combined; known in some parts of the country as the Michigan Plow. Its peculiarity consists in this: upon the beam about where the cutter or coulter is usually fixed, there is a common cast-iron plow-share, which cuts and turns the sod any required depth, while the main share takes up the earth from the bottom of the furrow, four or five inches deeper, and lays it in a completely pulverized state on the top of the inverted sod. This Plow attracts a good deal of attention, and, generally, commendatory remarks. Another exhibitor has given a prominent position to one of the same sort, which the original inventor thinks is a plagiarism upon his; or at any rate so nearly like it, that, without the original, the other would never have been conceived.

The subsoil plow is so little known to a majority of those who till American soil, that a more particular description and slight history of its introduction will be found interesting. In the year 1840, Messrs. Ruggles, Nourse, Mason & Co. imported from Scotland the first subsoil plow ever seen in the United States. It was a complicated, expensive, cumbrous affair, as most of the Scotch plows are, and could not be patterned after with any hope of successful introduction among farmers. Feeling satisfied of the benefits that would result to them from the use of a good subsoil plow, that good genius of American farmers, Joel Nourse, set his mind to work and produced one, more simple, lighter, and cheaper than the imported article. It was tried, proved satisfactory, and the manufacture of various sizes, suited to a team of one to six horses, soon introduced this new farm implement to the notice of many farmers who never had seen or heard of the thing before, but soon learned to profit by its use. This plow has no mold-board; the use of it is to enter the bottom of the ordinary furrow, and stir up and pulverize the hard subsoil from four to twenty-four inches deep. Upon this the next round of the turning plow lays its usual thickness of furrow-slice, thus doubling the depth of tilth. It is especially valuable in land which has a natural hard-pan, or in which one has been formed by the trampling of the plow-team, or the sliding of that instrument for a hundred years on the bottom of furrows always plowed just the same depth. Some idea can be formed of the shape of this plow by supposing the land side of the common cast-iron one continued in a smooth plate up to the beam, the handles being riveted upon that, like those of a common shovel-plow. On the mold-board side of this plate, there is a shelf projecting a couple of inches, running in a gently inclined plane from the lance-head-like point to the heel, producing exactly the effect that a wedge would do if drawn through the earth, lifting it up and dropping it over the butt, which is two to four inches high. Such is the subsoil plow, in use in most of the Northern States; and from its efficiency, strength, ease of draught, and cheapness, (from five to fifteen dollars,) it was thought that perfection had been obtained in that farm implement. Not so. For this very reason these great plow-makers have brought out a new subsoil plow, as much more simple than their first one, as that is more simple than its Scotch prototype, and yet more effective, and not requiring more than one-half the force to propel it; besides which, it is a self-sharpener.

A perfect idea of the shape of this plow can be got in the way it was first obtained by Professor Mapes, to whom are the manufacturers indebted for the original, by taking a piece of paper twice as long as wide, and folding it first end to end, then side to side, then cut off the corners from side to end-fold; now make a slight lap at the side-folds and lay it down upon the table; the edges will touch all round, while the middle is slightly elevated. Now fancy a smooth piece of hardened cast-iron of this shape, twenty inches long and seven and a quarter wide, with an upright part, eighteen inches high, made broad and thin, with edges alike, so that it makes no difference which goes forward, screwed to a beam, five feet long, with handles four feet long, bolted upon the sides of the beam, held in place by an iron supporter, with a centre-draft rod and dial clevis, movable four or five inches up or down, or upon either side, and the whole only weighing eighty-four pounds, and yet strong enough for two yoke of oxen, but not of too heavy a draft for one yoke, when run up to the beam in the ground, producing such an effect as to shake bushes or plants several feet upon each side, and you will have some idea of a new subsoil plow, now publicly exhibited for the first time.

By the side of this last-described implement stands another

which, from the oddity of its appearance to a very large portion of those who have been acquainted with these farm tools all their lives, attracts a great deal of attention. This is nothing more nor less than the common Scotch plow, in almost universal use in its own country. It is made all of wrought iron; the beam and handles, which are almost on a line, giving it an appearance of great length, are ten feet four inches—the beam five feet, and right-hand handle, from where it is bolted to the mold-board to the upper end, is seven feet. From heel to point, on the land side, two feet ten inches; from point to upper angle of wing, three feet seven inches; width of heel, eight inches; width from land side to point of wing, one foot seven inches; length of standard, fourteen inches. There is no wood, except the end of the handles, in its construction, which is the case with all iron plows. The weight of this plow is two hundred and seven pounds—two pounds more than the one first described, which will cut a furrow about double the size of this; and some, who have tried both, say with the same team.

The next curious affair in this collection is the side-hill plow. It is so contrived that by unhooking a stout hook and a little exertion of the plowman, while the team is coming about, the whole share, mold-board and all together, is rolled over, and again fastened with the hook, so that the furrow is turned the other way. These are made of different sizes, turning a sod from five to seven inches deep and ten or twelve inches wide, and, notwithstanding their awkward appearance, work equally well on level or hill-side land. The same scale of proportions and carefully laid down principles, in regard to curved lines, is preserved in all the plows coming from this manufactory; so that all work alike as to tractile force, whether great or small, according to the work required of each kind.

With a side-hill plow, the plowman may commence on the lower edge of a hill-side, turning all the furrows down the slope, going back and forth, changing his plow to the right and left at the end of each furrow, or in the same way he may plow a level field.

Another side-hill plow stands just across the stairway toward the dome from the last described, which attracts much notice from its curious, unique appearance and neat construction. It is all iron, stands on a bench flanked by two others of the same material, in the common form of turning plows.

The peculiarity of this side-hill plow is, that the beam and handles together turn round upon a pivot formed of the top of the standard. The share has a straight land-side, two feet ten inches long, with points at each end exactly alike. Suppose you are turning a right hand furrow, and wish to change to the left, you give a rod under the right handle a little jog, which unlooses a catch, and you walk round with the handle in your hand till the beam points directly the other way; now pull the rod and close the catch, stoop over and give the mold-board a flap, and it turns back bottom up, disclosing another under it exactly like the other, also bottom up and pointing forward; turn this also, and you have before you as neat looking a plow as you will find in the Exhibition, the reversed mold-board lying under the other, quite out of the way, and the reverse point forming the heel of the land side. The length of the beam is four feet; handles, four feet six inches; width of share, nine inches; length from point to upper angle of wing, two feet nine inches; length of wing from the joint to upper end, one foot seven inches; height of standard, one foot two inches; height of fin-cutter, nine inches. The weight not ascertained, but, from the neatness and perfect workmanship, we judge it is light for an iron plow of the same cutting width.

There is one defect in the one exhibited, which is easily remedied. The pintle upon which the beam turns around is not strong enough; and it should be made with a shoulder for the nut to screw down upon without touching the beam. It is a recent invention, the patent bearing date the present month, granted to L. Hall, of Pittsburgh, Pa. This plan completely obviates the objection to the other side-hill plow, that is, that it requires a very strong man to hold it, or rather to shift the share which rolls under, in changing from side to side. This turning-beam plow can be operated by a small boy, and we cannot help thinking will prove a very acceptable improvement to the large number of persons interested, who, in their visits to the Exhibition, we hope will give it a critical examination.

VIII.

OTHER AGRICULTURAL IMPLEMENTS.

Among the many inventions and contrivances for the use of farmers exhibited, are several not fairly embraced within the foregoing classes, yet which seem worthy at least of consideration. We now proceed to speak of them.

One of the new things which seems to attract the most observers, is Atkins's Automaton Raker—one of the most simple and yet most effective pieces of machinery we ever saw in operation. It was invented last year by Jearum Atkins, of Chicago, a bed-ridden cripple, who had not been in a harvest-field for years, and who has never yet been able to witness the operation of his ingenious and useful invention. This Raker can be attached to any of the half score of Reapers on exhibition, as there is nothing peculiar in the construction of the machine upon which it is now shown, unless it is peculiar to see one exhibited just in the condition they are all built for sale to the wheat-growers of Illinois, without any tinsel, or extra gew-gaw show, such as some exhibitors seem to think make their articles more attractive. The attachment and operation of the Raker is by a bevel-wheel, about twenty-three inches diameter, upon a spur of which, on the inside of the rim, is a knob, working into the hollow end of an arm, and by the mere turning of that wheel, without any other means, that arm in its circular motion creates a motion of the rake, which is exactly what the two hands of a man would be if he stooped down and scraped up the grain with his hands which the reaper has cut and laid upon the platform. The rake then turns round, opens its fingers, lays down the wheat ready for the binder out of the way of the next through, stretches out its arms, turns back to the platform and takes up another load, and thus goes on his ceaseless round, the motion of the reaper keeping the raker performing its work with unerring certainty. If there was not another article in the Palace of interest to the farmer, this one would be sufficient to pay him well for a journey of a thousand miles. Machinists will be equally interested with the wheat-grower, for they will see a complicated movement produced by the most simple and ingenious piece of mechanism perhaps in the whole Exhibition.

By the side of the last-described machine, stands another odd-looking concern, unlike anything else in the Palace, and, for aught we know, anywhere on earth out of it. This attracts a great deal of attention, and bears the name of Gibbs' Rotary Spade. It has long been a desideratum among farmers to produce a machine which would perform by team-power, and produce the same effect upon the earth that is produced by the operation of spading. It seems very probable that this result has at length been reached. The implement before us is the invention of a plain, practical, common-sense man, who, unlike many of his co-exhibitors, has not attempted to get up something that looks more like a piece of parlor furniture than it does like a farm implement, but shows his machine in working order, with the dirt of the last trial still adhering to it. This spading machine is composed of two cast-iron circular plates, about two feet four inches diameter, and one inch thick. These are fastened upon a shaft about two inches apart, and working between them are eight stout, narrow, wrought-iron teeth, somewhat like the old-fashioned cultivator teeth. These teeth are hung, and have a trigger to throw the tooth out as the machine revolves. Two sets of these plates and teeth are set in a stout frame, and look like a pair of toothed wheels, of a very formidable appearance, the teeth projecting about nine inches. The operation is thus: A pair of oxen, which are sufficient upon ordinary soil, are hitched to the frame, and, as it is drawn forward, each tooth in succession is pressed into the earth by the weight of the machine, and as it rolls forward the weight falls upon the trigger, and that throws the tooth out with its load, turning and pulverizing the earth as though spaded, or, more properly, forked over. The two wheels cut a furrow about two feet wide and nine inches deep, which can be increased by an enlarged machine to any desirable width or depth. It requires no holding, yet is provided with handles so fixed as to throw the teeth out of the ground by the weight and motion. It is a very strong and apparently a very efficient farm implement, unlike anything else heretofore offered; and if it proves to be as good as it promises, it is possible that it foreshadows a rotary steam-working implement, for doing the work of the plow. The greatest objection we see to it, is, that it hails from Washington—and we cannot help thinking of a text of Scripture which says, "Can any good thing come out of Nazareth?" If any good thing agricultural, either as machines, or an intellectual production, has come out of that place with this implement, it ought to be set down to the credit of that centre of everything that is notoriously old fogy about agricultural improvement. On this account, if nothing else, that farmers may say they have seen one thing from Washington which was intended for their benefit, we bespeak them to look at the Rotary Spade. They will find it in the gallery of the east nave, nearest the Reservoir.

Properly following this implement, as it might do in practice, we will notice another curious rotary machine, called a Ditch-Digger. This is another new farm implement, patented this present month, by R. C. Pratt, of Canandaigua, N. Y. It is also iron, the frame about five feet high, with twelve spades arranged around a circle, which revolve as it is drawn forward. Each blade, which is eight inches wide and twelve inches long, enters the ground and takes up its load, carrying it round to the centre on the top, where it is discharged upon conductors which carry the dirt off upon each side. It looks well, is strongly built, and the exhibitor is entitled to one credit which many are not: he tells the public what his machine is for. On a card attached is neatly printed in large letters these words:—"This Ditch-Digger requires but one span of horses and one man to work it, and where the ground is favorable, will cut one hundred and fifty rods a day, not less than two feet deep. In hard and stony ground, it will cut fifty to one hundred rods, by using an extra man in the ditch with a pick." That tells the story in a very plain, comprehensive manner. Of the truth of it, those who want such a machine can inform themselves.

Arnett's Improved Road-Scraper is another entirely new farm implement. It was thought when the cast iron scraper was substituted for the wooden one, that further improvement upon so simple an article as this very much neglected, and yet very useful farm implement, would not perhaps be attempted. Yet we believe wrought iron has been successfully substituted, without, however, altering the form. All who use this implement are aware that it is no child's play. Strong arms are required to discharge the load of dirt after it is accumulated and carried to the place. Perhaps a few who may read this article do not even know what a road-scraper is. Fancy a shovel big enough to hold a hundred hand-shovels-full of dirt, with one or two horses, or a yoke of oxen attached by a chain to an iron bail, pulling it forward. A man behind, takes hold of two projecting handles, and guides the point into the loose plowed-up earth, and the concave of the shovel is soon filled. The dirt is to be deposited a few yards off, and it rides easy to the spot. There the man takes hold of the handles again, and gives them a lift and a jerk forward, upsetting the contents upon the desired spot. It is now drawn back and turned over, and refitted, and so on. The working of this new implement is the same, until it comes to the unloading. As the handles are raised, the hind part of the shovel opens by ingeniously arranged hinges, and lets the great bulk of the load out behind; doing (apparently) as much work as the old-fashioned scraper, or ox-shovel, with less labor to the operator. This is an Iowa invention, just patented. We advise farmers and others interested in this class of labor-saving implements, to give this one their attention. They will not only find the name of the article conspicuously inscribed on it, but the inventor present, ready to impart all information required; and that is more than we can say of more than half the things exhibited. There is an improvement, however, in this respect since our former castigation of the stupidity of those who send articles here to be gazed at in silent wonder by the thousands who do not happen to know all that the inventor knows of his own idol. It does appear to us past belief how any one with the intellect of a donkey could place an article, particularly a new invention which he wishes to sell, here for people to wonder over, most unprofitably to themselves as well as the exhibitor, without giving it a name. In this connection, it is due to Messrs. Longett & Griffin to say, that since our former visit, they have lettered every article most conspicuously; for instance, Corn-Sheller, Straw-Cutter, Fan-Mill, &c., with gilt letters. Some other exhibitors have taken the hint, and if all do not, in the department of Agriculture, they must expect what sometimes follows a hint, when that is not taken. In this, exhibitors are not only in fault, but the Managers are lamentably so.

We witnessed to-day an amusing scene over a pair of snow-shoes. Of some twenty curiously excited men and women, not one of them had ever seen, or had any conception of the appearance of an article which all had read of, and which, when they knew what they were looking at, became the object of intense curiosity. It is reasonable to suppose that twenty thousand gazers at these very articles will be in exactly the same condition as the twenty whom we had the satisfaction of informing to-day, that they were looking at a pair of Indian snow-shoes, instead of "a sort of fish-net," or "may be a strainer, to strain maple sap through;" or some of the other odd uses we heard named for these very necessary appendages to a Northern voyager's outfit. How much would it cost the managers to write "Indian Snow-Shoes," and pin to these, before we see another group of wonderers around them? How much will it cost other exhibitors to put a card upon each article, to let those who come to look, know whether the box before them is a churn or a beehive?

Redding's Corn-Sheller and Separator is another new machine, patented last year, for which the owner claims some advantage over any other, principally on account of a self-adjusting rest for the ears of corn, formed by the cobs. The machine is a stout sheet-iron case, four feet long, and fifteen inches diameter, in which revolves a wooden shaft, seven and a half inches diameter, covered with iron, and armed with four rows of teeth, set spirally. The shaft runs near the bottom of the case, leaving a space above and on the sides, which fill up with cobs, which form the rest for the ears while being shelled. The corn is shoveled into a hopper at one end, and the grain falls out at the bottom of the case, and the cobs at one end. The inventor says he has shelled seven hundred bushels in four hours, with a common four-horse power.

This machine was patented last year by William Redding, of Flemington, N. J.

The same patentee has the model of a kiln for drying grain, which it will be well for those interested to examine. The arrangement seems well calculated to do a great amount of work with but little fuel, the grain being constantly stirred by machinery.

A patent Pig-Pen is not the least curious of the new inventions to be found in the Agricultural Department. It is a model of an improved plan for feeding swine. Instead of a feeding trough, there is a series of cast-iron basins set in a bench about a foot high, over each of which is an iron frame to keep every pig in his own dish. Over these basins there is a roof, and the side of the pen in front of them is hung upon pivots, so it can be pushed back at the bottom, shutting the pigs in the pen and the troughs out. When they are filled the bolt is withdrawn, and the force of hunger pushes it back to its original position. It is worth looking into, if it is nothing but a pig-pen. The inventor has given his name; but we won't mention it, because he did not put the name of his invention, as well as his own, where visitors could see it.

A patent Broom is worthy of notice, if for no other reason, because it is, we believe, the first patent ever granted for making corn-brooms, and because it is an article that our female friends in the country will highly appreciate; for it will enable them at any time when the old broom is worn out, to make a new one, without depending upon "the men-folks," or waiting for a rainy day. If they have the broom-corn, which every farmer *should* have, and every good one *will* have, the "women-folks" can make their own brooms, which is a vast step toward their independence. There is no twine, no wire, no stitching, about the patent broom. There is a flat steel spring, six inches long, with a T head inserted in the handle, and over that is a hinged socket, which, being opened, the broom-corn is laid upon the spring, with the butts in the socket, which, as well as the cross-head of the spring, is covered with teeth, which hold the corn. To keep it in place, now shut down the hinge of the socket, and slip a ring down over the corn to about the point where the twine is generally stitched through, and the broom is done. One handle will last for years, and is not very expensive. There is a very decided advantage in these brooms in this: that the handle does not project down into the broom, but the steel spring gives it a pleasant elasticity, until it is completely worn out. For those who do not, or cannot raise their own broom-corn, it will be easy to buy it when they buy their broom-handles. It is usually worth about six cents a pound. We bespeak the attention of the farmers' wives to this improvement; knowing, as we do, that many do not grow broom-corn, because it is so much trouble to make brooms, or because they do not know how.

A machine to cut vegetables for feeding stock is worthy of the attention of all root-growers. They will find it in the collection of Ruggles, Nourse, Mason & Co., just at the left hand of the right branch of the stair-case landing, north-east from the rotunda. On a frame about 2½ feet high, the same length, and about half that in width, is hung a cast-iron wheel, in a manner similar to a common grindstone, and turned by a crank in the same way. This wheel is about two feet in diameter, and has, in four equidistant mortises, each about 8 inches long and 1½ inch wide, one blade as long as the mortises, and five cross-knives. On the side of the frame is a hopper, which will hold a bushel and a half of turnips, beets, or whatever may be desired to cut. The operation is thus: The wheel being turned, the roots in the hopper press down against the side of the wheel, and are first struck with the long knife, which cuts off a slice three-quarters of an inch thick. This is pushed up the blade, which is set at an angle with the plane of the wheel's face, and meets the cross-knives, which cut it into squares ¾ by 1½ inch. A stout man can cut a bushel a minute, with a hand to feed the hopper, and continue the operation as long as would ordinarily be required to provide a day's feeding of a large stock. The price of this useful machine is within reach of every farmer who keeps a horse and cow.

There is another machine on the platform over the Reapers, which seems to be designed for the same purpose, or rather to cut up the roots into much smaller pieces. This is a conical roller, 18 inches in diameter at one end and about 10 inches at the other, and 12 inches long, which runs at the bottom of a hopper, mounted on a frame some 2½ feet high, the same length, and 16 inches wide. On the outer face of the roller there are twelve slats, upon which are screwed the cutters ; the edges are shaped exactly like the edges of a ruffle, the crimps of which are about three-quarters of an inch wide, so that the pieces cut are like a slice from the side of a small potatoe, say a quarter of an inch thick. We know nothing of the operation of this machine ; it does not, however, look as if it were as effective as the other, which we know is worthy of the notice of every farmer.

On the same platform with the last-named machine, is a common wooden frame-expanding cultivator, to which is attached a drilling apparatus for planting any kind of seed. Attached to the hind end of the centre-beam, is a wooden wheel twelve inches in diameter, and four inches thick, upon the shaft of which is a driving-pulley. A band runs from this to an iron shaft on the former, also made to expand, and this shaft carries the seed-droppers in tin boxes on the ends of the side-piece of the frame. This looks like a very simple mode of drilling seeds, two rows at a time, combined with an implement which ought to be much better known and more generally used. Besides the advantage of drilling, the same tool answers for tending the crop in the course of its growth, by simply removing the driving wheel of the drilling apparatus. Any one who owns a cultivator—may attach the drill to it, at much less expense than he could buy a separate machine.

We have seen a drill attached to a plow, but like this better. We are in favor of drilling all kinds of seeds, and hail with pleasure any improvement that will lessen the expense of the machine necessary for that purpose.

One of the small articles, well worth a passing notice, because it shows a decided improvement, is a common grocer's or household funnel, which measures the liquid just as correctly as can be done in a separate measure. This is accomplished by a spring valve which keeps the spout closed while the liquid is poured or drawn in from the cask till filled up to a ring, marking the desired quantity, when the valve is opened by a slight touch on a thumb-piece, letting the liquid down into the receiving vessel. This convenient new implement belongs to that universal Yankee genius who invented and exhibits the curious revolving-spade before noticed.

The same man has a bit made to expand and bore a hole of any size, from ¾ to 2¼ inches diameter, which is strong and easily adjusted. He also has a very simple washing-machine. A grooved bed is placed in a wash-tub, and on this a cap is made to revolve upon a centre post. The clothes are put in and the cap put on, the operator taking hold of a handle and making it revolve half round and back, which gives almost the exact operation of rubbing the clothes by hand over the washboard. The great advantage is the simplicity and cheapness of this labor-saving implement, to a class who are most in want of such labor-saving machinery. It need not cost over a couple of dollars to put one into any wash-tub, and it can be removed at pleasure. It is a very simple, cheap contrivance, and we hope those who dread washing-day will look at this machine, certainly the last of a numerous family, and tell us what is the objection to it, if there are any that are very serious. We recommend the inventor to make his rubbers of zinc, pressed into the proper shape, and then, as they are prevented by a shoulder on the centre-pin from coming together, no injury can come to the clothes which are rolled over and over, back and forth, by an easy rubbing process.

The hand corn-sheller is a very simple, effective, cheap farm implement, and yet unknown upon half the farms of the United States. These machines are made of different sizes; one of the smallest is a frame 38 inches high, 24 inches long, and 8 inches wide, in which the machinery is boxed. The largest size is 3 inches higher and wider, and 6 inches longer. On the top of the box there is a hole about 3 inches in diameter, into which the ears are dropped one at a time, which are held by a wheel and spring up to a cast-iron-toothed flat wheel, as large as will run in the box. This wheel is turned by a crank on the centre-shaft, and a man and a boy can shell from one to three hundred bushels a day. It makes no difference whether the ears are large or small, as the spring regulates the size of the opening through which the cob must pass. Some of the machines are so arranged that the cobs are separated from the shelled corn, but that is a matter of very little consequence. This machine is a very substantial one, and, the shelling apparatus being enclosed, the corn is not scattered. It does seem to us that every man who sees one of these very useful articles will never afterward feel quite easy in his conscience while he sits hour after hour, rubbing off a few bushels of corn upon the edge of a shovel laid across a wash-tub, when with one of these little machines he could do the same work in five minutes.

Among Grain-Cleaners, the common Fanning-Mill, in almost universal use among farmers, ought, perhaps, to be first noticed. We say almost universal, because it is not wholly so; for we know districts of the United States, where the old mode of cleaning grain by hand-riddles, and blowing the chaff out in the wind, is still practised. In fact, it is not many months since we saw a grain-grower hard at work with an old-fashioned Dutch fan, made of willows, trying to separate the grain from the chaff. Less than three years ago, we saw four stout negroes, upon a South Carolina rice plantation, tossing the grain up and down in a blanket, to blow out stuff lighter than the grain. It had been previously threshed with flails, and would be hulled by the equally primitive way of working, by beating in a hand-mortar. It is almost needless to say that it was cultivated entirely by hoes —no plow ever having been used upon the land where it grew. And these are not the only people who know nothing of machines for cleaning grain.

The fanning-mill, so well known to those who use it, is a plain wooden box, two or three feet wide, and three to four feet long and high, in one end of which is a wooden wheel with broad fans, which, being turned by a crank and iron cog-wheel on the outside, by which the velocity of the fan is increased, creates a current of air, which, blowing against the grain as it falls through the riddles near the top, at the other end of the mill, forces the chaff out that way, while the grain runs down an inclined screen, dropping small end through, and carrying the plump grains over and out at the end opposite from the chaff. The grain, as it comes from the threshing-machine, is shoveled into a hopper on top, over the riddles, which are shaken by a crank and awkward motion sidewise from the fan-wheel. There is a number of wire sieves and screens of different fineness, for various grains, and the machine, on the whole, is a very useful one ; but in all the "improvements" and new patents, the old principle seems to have been adhered to. There are three of these machines exhibited—one by Allen, in the plain style ; they are made for farmer's use, costing about twenty-five dollars ; one by Meyer, lettered in gold "J. T. Grant's patent, 1845," made of black walnut, and finished off as though for a piece of parlor-furniture, to the decided disadvantage, as we conceive, of the exhibitor, and him who may for the first time see a fanning-mill, in the Exhibition ; as on being told what it is for, he will at once conclude that he cannot afford to put such a piece of cabinet-work into his barn, or, what is much more common, by the side of a grain-stack in the field, exposed to all weathers. Another of these machines, exhibited by Longett & Griffin, is still more *outré* in its appearance ; for, beside the polished black walnut, it has sides of glass, by which its interior is rendered very much more visible than the design of the builder, in making a farm implement so unlike anything which will ever be used in practical operation.

Having described the common fan, we shall try to give an idea of an entirely new machine for the same purpose. It is called "Salmon's Improved Excelsior Grain and Grass-seed Separator" —a very objectionably long name. How much better would have been "Improved Grain-Fan," or "Excelsior Grain-Cleaner !" The same objection, also, rests against the finish of this machine as the others. As it is something new, and we really believe, something very good, it ought to have been shown just as it is intended to build them for the farmer. The builder says that it is not his fault—that the managers requested him to get up a machine to show fine workmanship rather than practical utility, and refused him room enough to show two, one plain, and the other as highly finished as they pleased. This machine is very unlike the fan-mill above described, though answering the same purpose, and even effecting much more ; for, by slight changes in the force and direction of the blast, wheat can be separated from chess, cockle, garlic, smut, white-heads, and other impurities, as well as from grass-seed, saving that, and separating the different kinds of grain and grass from one another. The wind-wheel is made of iron, sixteen inches diameter, eighteen inches long, and is placed in an air-tight iron trunk at the bottom of the frame, which is three feet ten inches high, two feet wide, and two feet ten inches long. The wind-wheel is driven by a cog-wheel two feet diameter, which gives the fan great velocity, sending the air up a tight trunk, through which the grain is falling from the sieves, which are not shaken sidewise, like the common fan-mills, requiring a good deal of extra room, but are jogged in front by a cam on the shaft of the driving-wheel. The sieves, five in number, for different grain, are made fine at the end where the grain first strikes them, to let through fine seeds, and coarse at the other end, through which the wheat falls on the inclined plane, and through the wind-spout into a receiver at the bottom. The wind-spout, at the back of the mill, can be closed in part, or wholly, by which a little blast is allowed, or all turned out through the sieves.

This machine is very simple in its whole construction and operation, and worth the attention of farmers and millers who desire something better than, and equally cheap as, the old-fashioned Fanning-Mill. It is quite portable, as may be seen by its size, and the weight of one the size of that exhbited, is from one hundred and twenty-five to one hundred and thirty-five pounds, only. It was patented in July of the present year, and originated in the great wheat region of Northern Illinois, where the want of a perfect grain-cleaner has long been felt—the wheat from Chicago being generally several cents below that of this state, on account of the very imperfect manner in which it is cleaned. This promises to be a very valuable improved machine for all wheat-growers. Let them look at it, and hear the owner's explanation.

There is another somewhat similar-looking machine by the side of the one described, which we have reason to suppose is intended for the same purpose; but as the owner has neither given it a name nor taken the trouble to be present to give explanations, we are unable to give our readers any information respecting it, besides telling them that such a thing is there, and, if they can reap any benefit from its examination, it is more than we have been able to do, or hear that any body else has.

By the side of that stands another secret mystery, which we have guessed is a clover-threshing and cleaning machine, but have never seen anybody who could say for certain. We have heard others "guess it is a carding-machine." Who knows? It has no name, and perhaps no owner. In connection with these nameless articles, we were pleased to find the following placard, lately posted up: "Exhibitors in Class 9 are requested to have the names of their implements, with their own names, placed upon them. Per order."

There is another machine called "Child's Separator," which has lately come into the Exhibition, from Rochester, accompanied by the inventor. It has been some years in use, and has gained a high reputation among millers. One of the principal improvements of this machine upon the old fanning-mill is an attachment which causes the grain to fall through a draft of air, created by suction of the fan, so strong that the grain is held in suspension until all the light particles are separated and blown out another way. This machine is worth the attention of rice-planters, as we think its operation is such that it would be very valuable in separating the rice flour and broken rice from the whole grains, after they come from the mortars.

By-the-by, where are some of the much bragged-of rice-hulling machines, made in Brooklyn? We see none of them here in this Exhibition of all Nations. Is not Brooklyn one of the nations of the earth?

Another, which may probably rank as a grain-cleaner, is a very simple little machine for husking corn, invented by T. C. Hargreaves, in 1852.

A man stands by the side of a little frame and turns a crank, while a boy places the ears of corn in little troughs of a horizontal wheel on top of the frame. As they pass round, a chisel comes down, separates the stalk from the cob and pushes out the ear and returns ready for another, as it comes around. Another contrivance throws out the husk. In this way, says the inventor, two hundred bushels a day can be shelled, or with a large power-machine twelve hundred bushels in ten hours. The price of a hand-machine is eighteen to twenty-five dollars. This is an ingenious contrivance for lessening one of the very tedious operations of the farm, and was got up by a practical New York farmer. We advise corn-growers to look at it. They will find it on the platform over the reapers.

Having noticed several American and one Scotch plow, we looked about among the contributors of other nations, to find some of the same implements which we might describe by way of contrast with our own. On the north side of the Palace, a little to the west of the Sixth-avenue entrance, hid away among numerous unnamed, unarranged things, we found a solitary German plow, the dimensions of which we took, and now give to the reader. It has a wooden beam, six feet eight inches long, and one handle, a straight, almost upright standard, four feet four inches long, with a pin for the hand eight inches below the top, and three feet from the ground, the holder either taking hold of the pin or top of the upright, as he pleases. The land-side measures three feet two inches from point to heel, and from the point to the upper corner of the wing it is three feet three inches. The length of mold-board on the upper edge twenty-three inches, height thirteen inches. Width from top of mold-board to land-side, thirteen inches. Width from bottom of mold-board to land-side, eleven inches. Height of standard to top of beam, seventeen and a half inches. The mold-board is wrought iron, made with a very great twist, and held in position by one strong iron brace from the handle. The wing of the share is wrought, and the under side cast, and so is the landside and standard, in separate pieces. There is, about halfway between the standard and point of beam, another share, fastened to a cast standard and held by a clamp and screw on the right side of the beam, and movable up and down, very much like the Michigan plow, heretofore described. Did the patentee of that get his idea from this? Both shares have coulters, fastened in cast-iron clamps on the left side of the brace by a wedge. Instead of a gauge-wheel on the forward end of the beam, like our best plows, this has a wooden post with a set of sled-runners on the bottom, shod with iron. On one edge of the post is a toothed rack, so it can be gauged by moving a pin and slipping up or down. The clevis is a quarter circle, with holes to attach the chain by which the draft is regulated. The whole is rather roughly made, and we noticed one great defect in the workmanship; the standard and pin of the handle, through necessity but little crooked, are cut across the grain of the wood, very unlike anything to be seen among the American plows. It is a pity this could not be placed among those, that it might be seen and better judged of by contrast.

In the Canada Department, there is a plow which in shape much resembles the Scotch plow, but has a cast-iron beam from the standard forward, and wood behind, and wooden handles. The land-side and standard are cast in one piece, and the two parts of the beam, wood and iron, bolted to the standard, giving it a very unique appearance, and, so far as we can see, without any advantage over wooden beams.

Near the German plow, stands a hand seed-planter, with handle and wheel like a wheel-barrow; the seed being placed in an iron hopper on the frame, is taken out by twelve little spoons on circular plates, which are moved by small chain-bands connected with the wheel. It is very roughly and strongly built, and may answer a very good purpose; but it does not strike us as being fit to compare with some of our machines for the same purpose.

Corn-Shellers of larger size, to be driven by horse, or other power, are of various forms. We have described one already. Another form somewhat resembles a threshing machine. A toothed cylinder, twelve to sixteen inches in diameter, and thirty inches long, is mounted on a frame, with a large hopper, into which the corn is shoveled, or poured out of baskets, and as the cylinder is made to revolve rapidly by a pulley and band on the shaft, the ears are carried under the cylinder, and the grains scoured off between that and the concave bed. Some of the largest sizes of this description of corn-shellers will shell two bushels a minute, or twelve hundred bushels a day, with a four-horse power.

While you are among the farming-tools, don't overlook the numerous specimens of spades, shovels, forks, hoes, scythes, and such minor tools, but equally important as those of larger dimensions.

As you pass along almost over the statue of Daniel Webster, cast your eye into a couple of cases of tools from the Tuttle Manufacturing Company, Naugatuck, Ct., which we believe is one of the oldest, as well as most extensive, manufacturing establishments in this country, of hoes, forks, garden-rakes, root-diggers, &c. You will certainly see in these cases, some tools which show a degree of skill in their formation and finish, not easily exceeded, in this or any other country. Perfection in the art of working the steel out of solid bars, into hoes, rakes, or forks, with two to fourteen tines, has been reached, and the way they are finished is equally perfect, and highly creditable to American manufacturers. The Tuttle hoes have long had an enviable reputation. One, called the concave hoe, is sold in almost all hoe-using countries. The greatest skill is required in the manufactory of the many-tined forks, all out of one piece of cast-steel, without a single weld. This is not accomplished without the aid of tools which have taxed the ingenuity of many, and the skill in their use, of many others. Those who can contrast these tools with such as we used thirty or forty years ago, will acknowledge that our country is progressive. Hoes and forks were then very roughly made in a common blacksmith's shop, at more expense to the farmer than the beautiful polished articles.

Among other things, we ask farmers to look at manure-forks, of any number of tines required, which are light and strong; at spading-forks, with flat tines, half an inch thick; at hay-forks, with two, three, or four tines, which you may lay down under the wheels of a loaded wagon without injury. Look at the potatoe-hooks, somewhat like the tines of a fork, turned round so as to set like a hoe with a handle. Note the tools made in the same way, but stronger, for digging manure. See also what timber is used for the handles—ash that is almost as strong as steel. These tools are just as they are sold to farmers. In the hoe-case there is a little extra show about the gold and silver ferules.

In regard to the extent of the business of this company, a few facts will be interesting. In the first place, the power in its factory is equal to one hundred horses, and is so arranged as to be permanent, which is very useful. The number of hands employed in all the various departments is something like one hundred.

The quantity of steel used is over two hundred tons per annum, and this will be greatly increased the present season. The goods turned out per year amount to something like fifty thousand dozen of various descriptions. Each hoe, fork, and rake, requires a handle and ferule, making one hundred and fifty thousand dozen pieces. Persons examining these cases may be struck with the style, variety of goods, and finish. They are not confined to one particular description of articles, but make to order any quality or style, their prices varying from $2 to $75 per dozen.

Next to the case of forks, there are two cases of shovels and spades, from the Old Colony Iron-works, Taunton, Massachusetts. In the manufacture of this description of tools, that state has long held a preëminent position. We are not aware that any country in the world exceeds ours in the good quality of its shovels. In these cases, may be seen pretty much all sizes and shapes, and great skill in the manufacture and finish. Some of them have brass blades, for handling sugar, meat, or such stuff as iron-rust might injure.

There are a good many other cases of similar gardening and farming tools, many of which, we doubt not, will be seen for the first time by old farmers, who may profitably spend a day in the agricultural department.

One of the advantages of the Exhibition will be, if the opportunity is rightly improved, to compare such tools as farmers have in use with such as they may see here, and also such as they see one with another, and finally select the best. A determination to improve by a visit to this great collection of good, bad, and indifferent tools, should influence every farmer who comes to the New York World's Fair.

IX.

PRESERVED FOOD.

THE art of preserving food as much as possible in its original state, is one of very great importance. It is at present in a state of high perfection, and has been gradually improved by various discoveries in chemistry, and still more by the diffusion of chemical knowledge among those engaged in the useful arts. We do not suffer the deprivations which our forefathers underwent; the common articles of food may be obtained at all seasons; the delicious fruits of our gardens may be made to contribute to our health and refreshment at a time when the trees which produced them are surrounded with snow; and the sailor, or he that makes long voyages, is not necessarily confined to salt meats,—he may, on the longest voyage, enjoy meat and vegetables apparently as fresh as if he were in port; he can have a dish of white cabbage with his corned beef, and good milk with his tea; and that scourge and dread of sailors, scurvy, need no longer be entailed upon the mariner's life, except by wilful neglect.

Appert, whose collection is in the French Department below, is the Nestor of food preservers. So far back as 1810, M. Appert received a reward of 12,000 francs from the French Government for his method of par-boiling provisions and inclosing them in earthenware vessels in such a manner as to exclude the air. This constitutes the great difficulty of any process for preserving food. The chemical elements which enter into the composition of food substances are placed together in such proportions that their union is held very loosely together, and, as soon as the forces of life which held them together are removed, the tendency to rearrange their particles in a more stable and permanent manner commences—this constitutes putrefaction. For these changes to go on, it is not necessary that the substances be exposed to the air permanently; if exposure to a small extent at the commencement occur, decomposition will set in, and considerable changes ensue without any further assistance from the external air. This change is common to fruits and flesh; if before being packed, decomposition have set in, even to a very small extent, no after-packing will check the progress of change up to a certain point; were it not for this occurrence, the preservation of fruits would be a very easy, whereas it is at present a very difficult process, and limits the exportation of the valued fruits of this country to Northern Europe. In both vegetables and meat it is in the juices containing albumen (a substance resembling the white of an egg) that fermentation or decomposition first sets in; and, could this be moderated or checked, the after preservation might be more manageable. By exposing the meat to a heat of 150° to 200°, the albumen is coagulated; and, as this is much slower to putrefy than when liquid, it explains the common observation that cooked meat will keep longer than raw. But it will not keep long so; it must be now excluded from any further action of the air, both internally and externally. The air in the internal parts is removable by boiling, and that on the exterior by packing in air-tight cases. The following out of these principles in practice constitutes the process of M. Appert, who is enabled to pack large cases of provisions and meat freed from bone, which, from the trials which have been made with them on long voyages, fully justify the high estimation in which the process is held. The original process has been improved by the inventor in France and in England, by Douken and Bevan, and Appert is now able to box up in one case one hundred and fifty pounds of flesh, which may be kept sweet indefinitely long. There is one case preserved in this way in his collection.

In the French Department, also, is a collection of dried vegetables, prepared after Masson's process, which preserves the texture, flavor and qualities of the vegetable exceedingly well. This process consists in slicing cabbage, turnips, apples or whatever vegetable may be selected, and drying them in an oven until about eight per cent. of the water in them is driven off; this drying must not be conducted either too rapidly or too slowly; after drying, the vegetables are packed into a very small compass by the intense pressure of a hydraulic press: then squared and trimmed with a knife, packed up in tinfoil, and stored in boxes. Specimens of various vegetables, beans and pulse, are exhibited in this department; and of the value of this mode of preservation we can speak in the highest terms, having during last year tasted the articles when cooked.

Rodel & Sons, Bordeaux, have a collection of preserved meats and vegetables, with fruits in brandy. Fiton & Son, and others, have similar collections. This department is rich also in its exhibition of preserved sardines. Taken as a whole, the collections of preserved food are creditable to the exhibitors.

We have searched the American Department, and have not found any exposition from two of our countrymen, whose skill in this department is not inferior to any of our transatlantic friends: we refer to the meat-biscuit preparation of Gale Borden, and the preserved fruits of Wm. Smith* of Macedon, N. Y. The meat-biscuit is now an approved food, having received a prize at the London Exhibition: it is formed by boiling down the strong beef of Texas, and mixing into the strong beef-tea thus formed a certain proportion of the finest flour. Four ounces of this biscuit are sufficient food for a man on active service: it is light, portable, and keeps without change: owing to the profusion of the cattle in Texas, the manufacture of the meat-biscuit is carried on in that State near to Galveston.

The preserved fruits of Mr. Smith are perfectly unrivalled by any other specimens of their kind. His process is different; he preserves the fruit neither in syrup nor in brandy, but in its own juices or a fluid of the same density. By this means, the bursting or the shrinking of pulpy fruits is prevented, and the flavor preserved by careful peeling under water and preservation from contact with the air in all its stages. The fruit is of the same whiteness as in its fresh state. Why are not these in this Exhibition? Even here they would stand unrivalled, and may anywhere challenge competition.

There are a few specimens of preserved milk in the American department, as also exhibited by Chollot & Co., who show all

* Afterward exhibited. Mr. Smith has removed his manufacture from our State to Wilmington, Del., in order to be where fruits grow more abundantly and luxuriantly.

kinds of preserved vegetable aliments. These are useful preparations on shipboard. They are made solid by partial evaporation of the milk and the subsequent addition of farina and sugar until the whole solidifies. Perrin, of Paris, displays chocolate and some unpalatable-looking preparations from the blood of domestic animals.

X.

PRODUCTS OF THE SOIL.

OUR first survey of the Exhibition gave us the impression that there was absolutely *no* display of the agricultural productions of the United States, in the raw or natural condition of their growth. Not finding them in the Agricultural Department, we had supposed there was an entire want or unfortunate omission in this, to us, and many thousands of other visitors, most interesting part of any Exhibition that professes to present a view of the industry of *all* nations—which we are just simple enough to suppose should include our own.

We can, however, now report that there *is* a show of substances used for human food. It may be found on the lower floor, next to the wall upon the north-east side, looking out towards Forty-second-street. As you enter from that street, turn to the left, and you will soon see all that we have seen. The first articles in this collection that you will be likely to notice, are a baker's dozen of very large and very ancient-looking edible roots. There is no name, nor anything to indicate what they are, or where they are from, or why they are there, the sole representatives of their numerous family, and it is very difficult for lookers-on to guess. We happened to be able to tell sundry inquirers that they were California potatoes; whereat they stared and wondered amazingly.

Next to these are seven ears of Missouri white-dent corn (maize), of large size, small cob and long grains, produced, as a label tells us, by careful selection of seed. This is right, and really useful, interesting information. Next to these are nine other ears in the husk, of similar white corn, which we *guess* came from the South or West. Next are three ears of corn, also white, which any one who knows can say was grown somewhere in the Northern States, from its general appearance and round, smooth grains. Then comes a Minnesota collection—four white ears, twelve yellow ditto bastard gourd-seed corn; half an ear mixed blue and white, and three quart boxes full of shelled corn; one striped dent, one purple flint, one yellow ditto; one quart of barley; one of spring wheat; one of winter ditto, and one of wild rice; also a mocock (Indian pack) of the same—exhibited by M. Le Duc, D. Gilman, Captain Todd, of the Army, and Sylvanus Lowry, whose names are an honor to Minnesota, the only section of the United States making any pretence toward a show. There are also two quarts of common field beans, and two other little sacks, which may possibly contain some very uncommon ones, or something else. There is a beautifully arrayed case of ears and grains of Indian corn, intended to show all the kinds grown in this State, for which we are indebted to Col. B. P. Johnson, Secretary of the New-York Agricultural Society; as well as for two other cases of English grain. This case of corn would be very interesting, but it is placed in such a bad light that nobody can see it to any advantage. Now tell it not in Gath, but hear, ye Farmers of the United States, and listen, ye Managers of this Exhibition of Industry, this is the sum total of your agricultural products, in the raw state!

There is in the same neighborhood a good show of highly finished Flour Barrels, which probably contain very white Flour. There are several neat-looking bottles of Pickles, and a hogshead, said to contain Sugar from a Southern plantation. There are some very white refined Sugar, and some pure-looking Potato Starch, and possibly a few other edible things. There is a case with some samples of yard-long Wool—the animals which produced it are among the outside shows; one glass case of what probably may be eight fleeces of fine Wool, but as yet invisible; one case of fine Cotton, and several bales of that article; and also some bales of Hemp and Flax. If this does not comprise the sum total of the farm, we hope somebody will correct our list, which in fact includes manufactured articles—as refined Sugar, Starch, ginned Cotton, and dressed Flax and Hemp. There is one dry limb of a Cotton-stalk, showing the

Cotton as it appears when ready to pick; but that is stuck up almost out of sight, with no name to tell what it is, or where it grew, or whether it grew at all—a fact about which many who look at it are quite uncertain.

And this is the New York World's Fair Exhibition of Industry and Production of American Farmers! Can anything more disgraceful to that class of our citizens, upon whom all other classes are dependent, be conceived? Is there any one thing in the Crystal Palace of so much importance, or that would have been so interesting to so many people, as a collection of Indian Corn from every state in the union, showing at a glance all the varieties grown, both in plants and ears, from the eighteen-feet-high stalks of the Ohio valley, to the little dwarf of Lake Winnipiseogee? It is of no use to repeat that stale falsehood, "want of room," for an excuse for this outrageous neglect, because hundreds of feet of bare walls are too palpable a contradiction of such an assertion. Room could be found for an ordinary Broadway omnibus; for every-day-seen fire-engines; for common brass cannon and oft-exhibited gun carriages and ammunition wagons; but are these, one and all, of one hundredth part as much importance or interest to visitors, as would be a stalk of growing cotton in full bloom and bearing.

How many of the visitors to this Exhibition of Industry ever saw that product of an American farmer's industry, a stalk of growing Sugar-Cane? With what delight thousands would gaze at it! and it is not too late, perhaps, now, if the managers had half the desire to do honor to those who cultivate the soil, that they have to court the favor of men whose trade is in blood, guns, swords, and powder; or who work in marble, precious metals, and fine linen, in foreign countries. There would be no clap-trap about the announcement of an arrival of Indian Corn and very superior Seed-Wheat, from John Smith's farm in Oquaquanock; and no need of the humbug of a Bonded Warehouse, and highly-paid officers of the Custom-House, to receive and take care of a collection of American farm-products. Yet, in such a collection, those who live by industry, and grow produce for the sustenance of those who do not even know the meaning of the word, might learn lessons never to be forgotten; for they might learn how to improve the quality of their seed, and make two blades grow where but one grew before.

It is not yet too late to remedy this great oversight and total neglect of the most important branch of American industry. Give an invitation to farmers to send in samples of every choice kind of seed, plants, and valuable farm productions, and let them be carefully arranged so as to show the varied productions of different states, and then there will be an Agricultural Department worthy the name, in an exhibition of industry, the managers of which seem to have forgotten that the productions of the soil are the base of all wealth, and that mechanical industry is of but little use when the soil and its cultivators are neglected, or treated as though they were not considered of any importance to the rest of the community.

NOTE.—We believe a few articles were added to this department after the above was written; but not enough to change its general aspect from barrenness to plenty. This chapter is given as a hint to future managers of Exhibitions. Display all the rare fabrics and curious devices you can gather, but do not forget to exhibit also specimens of all the important products of the soil.

XI.

PORCELAIN.

THOSE who witnessed the London Exhibition of 1851, and examined the products of manfacture there, must be struck with the difference which exists between that and this in our city, in at least one particular. There the raw material was exhibited in both its crude and dressed forms, and portions were selected at the various stages of perfection, in which its progress or alteration could be made manifest. The whole process of manufacture was thus exhibited at a glance, and the mind not only became aware *of what* the manufactured article was made from, but it became impressed with the improvement, the skill and the taste, which mark our own times. Here, however, this is rarely to be witnessed. The fine article is exhibited without the course material. In the expositions of Iron and Steel, the ore, or native source from which it is obtained, might with advantage be placed in juxta-position, so that the Crystal Palace might be a school of knowledge, as well as a theatre of admiration. This remark applies with especial force to the exhibition of Glass and Porcelain. The contrast between the raw materials and the beautiful products is startling, but it is not here visible. "Who," says Johnson, speaking of Glass, when he saw the first sand or ashes, by a casual intenseness of heat, melted into a metallic form, rugged with excrescences, and clouded with impurities, "would have imagined that in this shapeless lump lay concealed so many conveniences of life as would in time constitute a great part of the happiness of this world?"

The formation of earthen vessels, or the *ceramic* art, divides itself into two branches—that of Pottery, as it is commonly termed, and that of China-ware. There is not so much difference in the materials employed in each branch, as in the manner of treating them, the material for porcelain being semi-fused, and thus more nearly approaching in its nature to glass. It is curious to see, by the articles exhibited, how zealously these two branches have been cultivated by rival nations, the excellence of the British department being in the articles of *delf* or common household ware, while the taste and skill of France have been devoted to the perfection of Porcelain. The show of these articles lies chiefly with these two nations, for the samples of ware fabricated on this continent are few, and not of a high degree of perfection. It cannot be said to be an indigenous art, although Vermont and the other New England States, as well as New York, furnish an abundance of very pure materials. The wealth to patronize extensively exists here, perhaps, but the skill to execute is yet a desideratum. Nor is this absence of manufacture peculiar to our people. If we put aside the Chinese, there are but three nations who can export pottery to any extent—first, England; then, France; and lastly, Germany.

The fabrication of Porcelain is an art half chemical—half mechanical. Transferred from China, to which by prescriptive right it belonged, it has been imitated as an art in Central Europe, with little advance beyond the Asiatic originals. It is not a century since the strangest views were entertained respecting the composition and nature of China ware. Reaûmur proved that the mixture of two peculiar earths found in China, called *petun-tse* and *kaolin*, produced porcelain. The next step in advance was to discover if any earths similar to these existed in Europe. The Jesuit, Francis Xavier d'Entrecolles, who was residing as missionary in China, contrived to elude the jealous vigilance exercised toward strangers, and not only forwarded to France the specimens of the earths, but also the knowledge of the manufacture, which he had acquired. They were, however, worthless, owing to his want of practical intelligence. Much about the same time, Baron de Botticher, a German alchemist, established the porcelain manufacture in Saxony, by accident. While following out some vain researches for the philosopher's stone, he prepared some crucibles, and, having burned the clay over much, he observed it had all the characters of Oriental porcelain. He saw the importance of this real discovery, and, abandoning alchemy, he commenced the manufacture of Dresden porcelain. The secrecy attempted in the processes could not be retained, and with partial knowledge and national rivalry, the establishments of St. Cloud and the Faubourg St. Antoine were commenced about 1719. White porcelain only was manufactured in these places. It was of beautiful appearance externally, but wanting in all that constitutes good china.

The manufactory at Sevres, in France, was started and maintained under royal auspices, and the works there produced specimens of art which vied successfully with Dresden and China. When Frederick the Great conquered Saxony, he forcibly carried away several of the best workmen from the manufactory at Meissen, near Dresden, and conveyed them to Berlin, where, since that time, a considerable manufacture has been carried on. As many as five hundred men are employed in the Royal Prussian establishment; but the quality of the porcelain fabricated has never equalled that of Dresden.

The manufacture of coarse earthen-ware in Staffordshire, England, goes as far back as the time of the Romans. In the year 1690, two brothers, named Elers, from Nuremberg, settled at Bradwell, where they made an improved red-ware, and introduced the glazing of the vessels by throwing common salt into the oven. Jealousy succeeded in driving these two men out of the country, after the secret was stolen from them. Astbury succeeded them in the manufacture, and introduced a white stoneware, which, it is said, accident brought under his notice. In travelling on horseback to London, his horse's eyes became attacked with some disorder ; an ostler of the inn where he stopped, cured them by burning a flint, and reducing it to a fine powder before he blew it into the horse's eye. The potter, observing the beautiful white color of the calcined flint, immediately saw how it might be applied as an ingredient in his own business. This step in advance, led the way to the improvements of Isaiah Wedgewood, with whose name this beautiful art, in England, is indissolubly linked. Of the seven various kinds of ware introduced by him, two are of especial value : one, his table ware, or Queen's-ware, as it is commonly known, and the porcelain biscuit or

Wedgewood-ware, of which mortars and other chemical utensils are made. These inventions of Wedgewood showed that porcelain could be made in England. Cookworthy discovered the earths in Cornwall, and, having secured to himself, by patent, the exclusive right of using these materials, was the first person who made true porcelain in that country. This was in 1768. It is now manufactured at Derby, Coalport in Shropshire, Worcester, and Swinton in Yorkshire.

Porcelain is a mixture of earths, which, by subsequent heating, is semi-fused. Reaumur's experiments show this clearly: he took the two earths from China, called *petun-tse* and *kaolin*, made a small cake of each substance, and exposed them to the heat of a strong furnace; the *petun-tse* was fused by this means without any addition, while the other, the *kaolin*, gave no signs of fusion. He then intimately mixed them both, and found, when the mixture was baked, that it had acquired all the qualities of the finest Chinese ware. It is thus by a mixture of an earth which is fusible by heat, (*petun-tse*) and one which is infusible, (*kaolin*) the whole, being semi-vitrified, becomes partially transparent. Porcelain stands intermediate between pottery and glass; were it wholly infusible, it would be earthen-ware; were both materials fusible, it would be glass.

These two earths are obtained in China, and are produced by the decomposition of granite. Latterly, in some instances, the Chinese use a coarse granite, in which the crystals of feldspar are arê large, (pegmatite) which they reduce to powder, form into shapes, and submit to the furnace, and from which a very good porcelain is made. Mr. Ebelman, a distinguished chemist, and director of the porcelain works at Sevres, has made a series of experiments on the materials used at present by the Chinese, which are of great value to the manufacturers. Kaolin is a very fine clay, or silicate of alumina, which the shores of Lake Champlain, both on the New York and Vermont side, abundantly supply. It is also found in every New England state, and in the valleys of districts surrounded by granite rocks. It is derived from the action of the atmosphere upon the mineral feldspar. Petun-tse is the fine silicious matter of the granite rocks, and is in all other countries, except China, superseded by ground flint or opaque quartz in very fine dust. These materials are ground to impalpable dust, made into a cream with water, some calcined bone added, and the water is then evaporated off until the mixture has the solidity suitable for working it into shapes. It is then placed upon the wheel and lathe to be turned into form. Sometimes it is pressed into shape in plaster moulds. It is then placed in the ovens or biscuit-kilns to be fired. Here it must neither be soiled nor overheated. To avoid these, it is enclosed in "seggars," or earthen vessels. After being baked, it is gradually cooled, and appears as what is termed biscuit-ware, being of a soft, dead-white, delicate appearance. It is then glazed by dipping the articles into a vessel of water containing the materials of glass in a pulpy state. When coated with this, they are replaced in the oven to be fired a second time, by which the glass materials are melted, and a thin varnish of glass is thus spread over the outside of the ware. It is subsequently painted, gilded, and enamelled, by beautiful processes. It is now that finished and *recherchè* article, of which there are exquisite specimens in the Exhibition.

Of the porcelain, the large majority is in the French and British departments.

In the former, the collection of L. Andre, Pilliougt & Co., deserves inspection ; the assortment of colored and gilt china dinner service and vases ; a dessert service, of low comporter pattern ; a toilet-set, in blue and gold, with flowers, is among the beautiful contributions from this establishment. In the article of vases and in fancy porcelain, there is nothing in the Palace which approaches the specimens shown by Messrs. Haviland & Co., of Limoges, and of John-street in this city ; the large size of these ornaments, the beauty of the coloring, clearness of the picture, and the chasteness of the designs, place them in the first rank. The representation of the dancing girl, from Victor Hugo's novel of *Notre Dame,* is well executed on the body of the vases. The collection consists of a centre-piece, two larger and four smaller vases, and a dinner-service in pink and gold.

Rees & Co., of Limoges, exhibit specimens of their ware. With the exception of one noble vase, the articles are not of the first quality ; a collection of Parian statuary is upon this stand.

In the English department, Sampson Bridgewood & Son, of Staffordshire, exhibit a good collection of delf and soft china. Ridgeway, of Staffordshire, has a collection of gilt china. It may be stated here that the English porcelain is almost always what is termed *soft* porcelain, or made of materials which melt or form a semi-fused mass at a lower temperature than those manufactured in France. This is due to the employment of bones by the British manufacturers, which give a kind of semi-transparent enamel; this compensates to some extent for the incomplete fusion of the clay in the British porcelain. From this it may be perceived that French porcelain, as a ware, is a superior article, quite independent of the superior taste exhibited in the ornamentation.

Rose & Co., of Coalport, Shropshire, have an extensive collection of gilt and vari-colored china, in dinner and tea-services, urns, vases, pitchers. Some jewelled vases and some with two-necked swans are of great beauty; a queen's pattern vase, painted and gilt, is an object worth inspecting. This collection eminently displays the superiority of Great Britain in the design and manufacture of domestic wares, which do not imply elaborate design and ornament. Minton & Co.'s, Stoke-upon-Trent, occupy a very respectable position in the Exhibition. Among the most prominent articles in their collection is a dessert service of great beauty; it is a combination of statuary porcelain, which is of the hard kind, with the gilded and colored porcelain, which is of the soft kind. The ground of turquoise almost approaches that on the Old Sevres. The service consists of a hundred and sixteen pieces. They are flower-stands, with figures emblematic of the seasons; wine-coolers, with hunting groups; oval baskets, with eastern figures; many of the pieces are supported by Parisian figures. The plates (six dozen) are perforated and highly ornamented, each differently. Queen Victoria purchased the original collection (of which this is a duplicate) for one thousand guineas, and made a present of it to the Emperor of Austria.

The most useful articles in Minton's collection are the samples of encaustic Venetian and other ornamental tiles for flooring. These pavements are now used in the flooring of churches and other buildings in this city and elsewhere on this continent. The encaustic tiles are made from the wet or slip clay, pressed into blocks, and faced with a finer clay, colored to the desired tint. The whole is then put in a box-press, and a plaster slab, containing the pattern in relief, brought down with force upon the face of the tile; upon this, deeply indented surface clay, in a semi-fluid, is poured. This clay is generally of a deep color, and, after lying twenty-four hours on the tile, becomes hard. The superfluous clay is scraped off, and the surface mechanically cleaned and smoothed, and the tile is then baked in the oven. This process is almost similar to the mediæval one, and Mr. Minton is entitled to the credit of having revived it with increased beauty and utility.

The Mosaics are made from stained dry clays, which are pressed and baked, and afterward formed into moulds by mixing with plaster or Roman cement. The variety of uses and the beauty of patterns are well shown in Minton's collection, which consists of slabs for fireplaces, jambs, and other branches of house ornament. The pressure exercised to form these dry tiles is immense, being, in the steam machine working by Prosser's patent, equal to four hundred tons. Each machine can make five thousand tiles an hour, and but one man is required to take out the finished article. A Council Medal was awarded to Messrs. Minton in the London Exhibition. Minton & Co. have also a collection of Parian figures of great variety and excellence.

The introduction of statuary porcelain, or Parian figures, is a branch of porcelain manufacture in which Great Britain has advanced beyond France and Germany. This imitation of marble was originated in Alderman Copeland's works (Stoke-upon-Trent), early in 1842. It is now fabricated in almost all the factories of Staffordshire, but excellence in the finish, and beauty in artistic design, are still maintained by Mr. Copeland, and the collection of Parian statuettes on his tables are the gems of their kind in the Exhibition. Parian material is a porcelain in which a soft feldspar is used instead of the more silicious Cornwall stone. The dulness of the tint, which adds to its beauty, is due to a little oxyde of iron accidentally present in the clay. This, uniting with the silica of the clay, forms a silicate of peroxyde of iron of a light yellow color. These figures, instead of being pressed into moulds as in the case of porcelain, are cast with the materials in a liquid state, or plaster with water. As all clays contract in drying, when these are fired they contract as much as one-fourth, and, what is more difficult to manage, they contract unequally, in proportion to the mass of material in different parts of the figure. Hence, dexterity and a good knowledge of the human form are requisite, as the subjects are cast in separate pieces, and have to be united afterward by a skilful artist. Besides the beauty of this kind of biscuit-ware, the fidelity with which the *chef d'œuvres* of sculptors are copied by Copeland, enhances the value of this collection. Among the fine statuettes, we may mention the groups of the "Prodigal Son," an imitation of a Cellini vase; "The Struggle for the Heart," consisting of two cupids from Flamingo; "Ino and Bacchus," from the original marble of Foley, the reduction being effected by Cheverton's process,—a very pretty group twenty-four inches high; "The Return from the Vintage," a fine group of seven figures, twenty-six inches high; "The Love Story" and "Paul and Virginia," two small groups; "Eve Tempted," is a beautiful design, the apple being presented in the serpent's mouth; and the four Children of Queen Victoria emblematizing the four seasons, after Mrs. Thorneycroft's originals. Besides there are some fine chivalric groups. In the same ware is a complete tea-service, which appears to us a very interesting application of biscuit. Copeland also exhibits porcelain dinner and tea-services; two pink Etruscan vases, jewelled, and extremely beautiful small jewelled vases; these last articles fetch a high price. We have lingered over the collections of Parian ware with great pleasure, as the introduction of this material is destined to effect for statuary what electrotyping accomplishes in the harder metals; it facilitates the reproduction of the works of the finest artists in a material less costly than marble, with their multiplication to any number of copies, and the elevation of the public taste in articles of fancy. We cannot have manufactures of the kind in this country without a cultivation of taste as well in the public to foster, as in the artist to produce and for the latter, Schools of Design are absolutely necessary. We have stated that the porcelain and earthenware in the Fair is almost exclusively foreign; there being no articles of fine manufacture in the American Department which are native; those of Dailey and Haughwout being imported, though the ornamentation is done here, but mostly by foreign artists; nor can such a branch of industry exist in all its departments until we have the means of technical education afforded by Polytechnic Schools and Galleries of Art and Design.

In the United States Department is an exhibition of a similar manufacture, which is well worthy of observation by all those who take delight in the progress of American art and skill. This is in the space allotted to the United States Pottery Company of Bennington, Vermont, who display Porcelain, Parian, Lava and Enamel Flint Wares. The articles are not only manufactured in this country, but the materials from which they are made are of this continent exclusively. Indeed we have not only no lack of good delf and porcelain material, but a surplus of mineral matters of a character very superior to the European minerals, and which have now become an article of export trade to England. Such is our feldspar, which is very abundant in the northern New England States, from which the decomposition, of which the kaolin or fine clay, which enters into the composition of China wares, is derived. The European kaolin contains a small trace of iron derived from the mica which the original feldspar always possesses. This metal, when not separated from the powdered mineral, communicates a light tint or cream-color to the ware. For white wares, the iron has therefore to be removed by chemical washings, which increases the cost of the articles. The feldspar from New Hampshire is remarkably free from mixture with iron, and is therefore well adapted for the manufacture of a white body without any purification. The neighborhood of Bennington, Vermont, is one well adapted for the establishment of a pottery manufacture, as there is a considerable deposit of plastic clay, which is met with in large quantities, and of great purity, in at least a dozen other places in Vermont.. Indeed, there is no State in the Union better adapted for manufacturing porcelain and other earthen wares, containing, as has been stated, all the mineral elements, and also ores of iron and manganese. These, however, in themselves, constitute but a portion of the success of any branch of manufacture, and it is to the untiring industry and skill of Mr. C. W. Fenton that this country is indebted for the establishment of this art at Bennington. He has labored over thirty years to advance the manufacture, and with great pecuniary expenditure has advanced it to the condition in which it is exhibited in this collection from Bennington. At the sacrifice of time and health, he has also succeeded in introducing the manufacture of Parian Ware in this country; produced the Flint Enamel Ware, for which he has secured a patent; and is engaged in the extension of porcelain manufacture, which has been followed by other establishments in this country, but by no means to the same satisfactory development as by him. The United States Pottery Company are now erecting a very large manufactory at Bennington, which, when completed, will furnish porcelain or Parian wares equal to French or English, at a more moderate price, owing to the cheaper cost of the materials, the facilities possessed to prepare them, and the superior construction of the kilns, in which an economy of fuel, with a more steady and clearer heat, is obtained. To the artist and superintendent of the premises, Mr. D. W. Clark, the Company owe much of their success in the beauty and execution of the designs and articles.

The articles exhibited by this Company are of porcelain and Parian ware, lava and enamel flint wares. Among the articles the most prominent is a tile floor, which underlies the whole of the articles, embracing a space of seven square feet. The tiles are inlaid with variegated colors, the borders displaying the American flag. Upon the centre of the floor stands a monument ten feet in height. The first or lowest section represents the "lava ware" or variegated stone; the second section their "flint ware;" the third, open columns inclosing a bust of Fenton, the designer of the articles on exhibition; the fourth section crowns the monument, and is a Parian female figure presenting the bible to a child on a monument by her side.

Around this monument are displayed table and scale standards, Corinthian capitals, figures, vases, urns, toilet-sets, and a great variety of other specimens in porcelain, plain and inlaid. The pitchers in porcelain are deserving of notice, as a branch of national industry; though not decorated beyond a gilt molding, and, therefore, not attractive as china, yet they possess the

6

first elements of good ware—that is, an uniform body without any waving, and of well-mixed and fine materials. It is upon such ware only that ornaments or decoration can succeed, and Mr. Fenton has overcome the great obstacle in the producing of ornamental china, namely—the formation of a ware having the essential properties of good porcelain—density, whiteness, and transparency.

The superiority of the Flint Enamel Ware over the English consists in the addition of silica combined with kaolin, or clay from Vermont, which, when in properly adjusted proportions, produces an article possessing great strength, and is perfectly fire-proof. Telegraph insulators in white flint are on exhibition; this material being one of the best electric non-conductors that can be found. Various forms of insulators are in the collection. This ware has been employed on the telegraphs in the vicinity of Boston: among these specimens is a patented form, recommended by Mr. Batchelder, which has a shoulder with a re-entering angle of forty-five degrees; this angle causes the wind and rain to pass downward, and prevents the inside of the insulator from being wet. This enamel ware comprises a variety of assorted articles, candlesticks, pitchers, spittoons, picture-frames, tea-pots, &c. This ware has become a favorite article in New-England, and possesses much merit as cottage furniture. The lava ware is a combination of clays from Vermont, New-Jersey, Carolina, &c.; composed of silica and feldspar, intermixed with the oxydes of iron, manganese and cobalt. It is the strongest ware made from pottery materials; the glaze upon this lava-ware and upon the flint-ware, is chiefly of flint and feldspar, and has, therefore, to be subjected to such an intense heat to fuse it, as would destroy the glaze upon common crockery. The colors upon the flint-ware are produced by different metallic oxydes applied on the glaze, which latter serves as a medium to float them about upon the surface, while in a state of fusion, thus producing the variegated tints.

The Parian ware of this Company is remarkably fine, especially in the form of pitchers. They are light in material, of graceful outline, and of two tints—one fawn-colored, from the presence of a little oxyde of iron, and the other white, from its absence. To us, the former appears the more pleasing to the eye. These are made of the flint from Vermont and Massachusetts, the feldspar from New Hampshire, and the china clays from Vermont and South Carolina. This Company has the credit of first producing Parian ware on this continent. China has been heretofore made in Philadelphia, and also at Green Point, L. I., but the manufacture is now only carried on in the latter locality. The United States Pottery Company are at present enlarging their works at Bennington, owing to the increased consumption of their wares, where they are fitting up a main building, 160 feet in length, and giving employment to one hundred operatives, using water-power for grinding the materials, and six kilns, of an improved construction, for the firing of the wares. With the increased facility of manufacturing which this extension affords, this market will be supplied with China wares of a superior kind manufactured at home, and which will no doubt remunerate the Company for the outlay incurred, and add another to the new manufactures established among us.

Haughwout & Daily have in the gallery of the American Department a very fine collection of decorated Porcelain, among which are some pitchers with salmon-colored ground, and lotus leaves—a pretty toilet set; a china set, made for Baron de Longeuill, C. W., the labor and design of which occupied many months; each article having a separate pattern. There is also a beautiful dessert service, a centre-piece and a service with a crimson ground, gilt and with varied devices on each article. The whole collection reflects credit on the exhibitors, who have established the art of decorating china in this city. Haughwout & Daily also exhibit on the lower floor a collection of Cornelius's Gas Fixtures. Cornelius, of Philadelphia, obtained, in 1851, a prize medal in the London Fair, for the best bronze chandelier. There are very beautiful specimens of these articles here exhibited, one of which is a twenty-one-light gilt gas Chandelier, with mermaids of artistic bronze, surmounted by Parian china, and opal glass shades. This is the finest thing of its kind in the Palace, not being excelled by any in the Foreign Departments. Besides this, there are eight light green bronze Candelabras, with dark lacquer—a specimen of a pretty Hall Lamp, with cupids and masks—Brackets in artistic bronze and gold—Chimney Girandoles—Chandelier Brackets, with glass of lotus leaf pattern —Candelabra and centre ornament for flowers—Solar Lamps in black bronze—Gilt Lamps on Corinthian capitals, with a peculiar style of ornamentation.

The other display of strictly American Porcelain is from the manufactory of Messrs. Cartlidge & Co., at Green Point, Williamsburgh. Mr. Cartlidge is an Englishman, formerly engaged in this manufacture in his native land, and first brought to this country on business growing out of that manufacture. He decided to remain here, and commence the manufacture of Porcelain from the clay—no one in America, we believe, being then engaged in that manufacture. One result of this enterprise has been the discovery in this country of the most valuable earths and other materials not previously known to exist here. He has gone on steadily and prudently, extending and improving his works as he could afford to do so; and now his Tea-sets, Pitchers, Bowls, &c. &c., are equal in strength and beauty of form, though not in fineness of material nor in neatness of ornamentation, to the best imported. His Door-knobs, Door-plates, &c., are not surpassed by any other, no matter where fabricated.

XII.

GLASS.

The chief expositions of Glass are in the French, Austrian, and the United States departments. Considering the various kinds of Glass that are now used both for the comforts of life and the finer purposes of art, there cannot be said to be either a varied or an extensive exhibition. There is a much greater supply of painted and ornamental glass than of the plain article, and the plate-glass seems only to be shown in the mirrors in the room. We had expected our own country would have sent in a larger collection of crown, window, and plate glass.

Glass is an abstract term for a composition of earths which fuse to form a transparent compound. This character of fusibility is the only point which distinguishes it from porcelain. The latter, composed of silica and fine clay, never melts in the fire. To convert those ingredients into Glass, it is necessary to add some earths or metallic oxydes which give it that property. Such are potash, soda, lime, oxyde of lead, and a few other bodies. The cause of fusion appears to be an effect of any one of these last bodies upon the original mixture of clay and sand, in dividing the silica or sand between the alumina (clay) and it self, forming what are termed double silicates. Thus, crown or window-glass would be a silicate of soda and silicate of lime; bottle-glass, a mixture of silicates, of alumina, iron, soda, and lime; and flint-glass, a silicate of potash and silicate of lead. Those which contain alumina, lime, or iron, are hard glasses; those having potash or lead are soft, and more easily fusible. Any one of these can be substituted for the other when a corresponding change in the glass is desired. The materials, generally pure and in powder, well mixed, are placed in vessels termed glass-pots, in a furnace heated up to a white heat, where they melt, and are taken out on the ends of tube-rods when it is desired that the articles should be of blown glass—such as decanters, tumblers, and window-glass. It is only of late that window-glass has been melted in plate, as it is termed, or on a level surface; the usual mode being to blow a sphere upon the tube, and, by a skilful hand, to throw the two sides together, by flattening the sphere down the point. Where it was attached to the rod of the workman is near the centre, and is termed the bull's-eye.

Window-glass has been found in Herculaneum, which must have been formed by being blown. Layard, in his discoveries in Nineveh, found a glass bottle in the ruins of Konyinjink. This shows at how remote a period the knowledge of glass and its early application to drinking-vessels existed. From the Assyrians, the manufacture of Glass passed to the Phenicians, from them to the Crusaders, and thence was carried to Venice in the thirteenth century, where the processes were long kept secret, and formed a monopoly. In ornamental glass, Venice excelled, especially, in that variety termed *mille-fiore*, in which a number of colored flowers and glass ornaments are imbedded in a lump of transparent white glass. This ornament has been revived lately in the form of letter-weights, and beautiful specimens are exhibited in the French Department. Bohemia and France imitated the Venetians with success, and transplanted the art into their soil. In the latter country, the first works were established near Cherbourg, because in topographical position it resembled Murano in Venice. In 1688, Thevart introduced the art of *casting* glass, or making it assume the form of a mold. He established works at Paris for the manufacture of plate-glass. In England the first window-glass was made in 1557; but it was more than a century later when drinking-vessels were made there. In 1771, the St. Helen's glass-works were established at Ravenswood, Lancashire, and now supply more glass of its kind than any other manufactory in the world.

All the materials for a manufacture of good glass exist in this country. The silicious sand is generally that brought from the banks of the Delaware. In Berkshire, Mass., and North ern Vermont, beautiful white sand is obtained and used, and the other materials are as cheaply obtainable here as elsewhere; in some departments of the art, considerable progress has been made. The collection of the New-England Glass Company exhibits a very good display of molded glass in one case and cut-glass in another. The same company have a collection of decanters and vases, plain and colored, and a series of glass-ware silvered; one of them is a centre-piece, which is also cut. The mode of obtaining these silver surfaces is simple. The glass vessels are double, and between the layers the silver solution is poured in, and a solution of grape-sugar added. The latter reduces the silver in contact with it, and it is thrown down with a bright metallic surface on the glass. When the deposit is complete, the liquid is poured out, the inside cleaned, dried, and then sealed up from contact with the air. We do not consider silvered glass a beautiful article; instead of resembling a silver article, it more resembles a mirror, and the general effect is not so pleasing as if it were colored instead of silvered. Beside the foregoing, the Boston Company have an assortment of fruit-stands in colored glass, *liqueur* bottles, and their specimen of enamelled glass. This is the largest glass collection in the American Department; beside it is a small display from the Baltimore Glass Works, chiefly of crown-glass, being an assortment of window-glass and druggists' phials. An assortment of black bottles is among the list, which are purer and lighter than these are usually blown. We do not perceive any exposition of the glass manufactured in the vicinity of New York, at least none direct from the works and so labelled. Stouvenel & Co., Vesey-street, have a very fair assortment of cut-glass, mixed with porcelain articles. We have already alluded to the advantage which a display of a process of manufacture offers both to the exhibitor and the observer. Could not glass-blowing and glass-cutting be both exhibited on the small scale in this as well as in the London Palace? The glass-blower's corner is always an amusing and an instructive spot. We submit it to the exhibitors.

Colored and decorated glasses are well exhibited in the French Department. The collection of Mr. Maez, of Clichy, near Paris, is a very extensive and beautiful one. Beside being a manufacturer of glass, he is also well acquainted with the chemical department of his art, as is evinced by the beauty and novelty of some of his productions, for which he has received two medals from his country and from England at the London Exhibition. The latter was given for lenses and glass for optical instruments; a Council medal for novelty of chemical application, and a prize medal for a prism of zinc glass. There are two flower-vases in the collection in which the glass is not as crystal usually is, but is a zinc glass—oxyde of zinc replacing the red oxyde of lead. The glass is brilliant and undistinguishable to the common eye from the lead glass. There is a considerable display of lenses both plain and ground and of all sizes, from that of the large Daguerreotype camera to the smaller lenses of the botanist. Most of the best cameras of our skilful Daguerreans are fitted with German lenses (Voigtländers). Here in the French Department is presented another source whence to obtain good lenses.

Not only is the ornamentation and coloring of Mr. Maez's collection of great merit, but in the design and form of the vessels there is great taste. The forms of the claret-glasses are very pretty, with a variety of flasks, both plain and gilt. The imitation of Venetian glass and filigree work, is very good. The paper-weights, already alluded to, are here in innumerable variety. The articles worth notice are a celestial blue and white vase; vases in three colors—maroon, white, and gold; a Beauvais vase, red and gold, surrounded by a vine; flower-vases, made to imitate lava; an *eau sucré* service, in gold, chalcedony and chrysoprase colors. This last set is of great merit, and shows the close imitation of the natural stones. The combination of several colored glasses in the one specimen is a very beautiful process, which, with cutting, produces infinitely various effects, which may be studied to advantage in Maez's collection. The manner is simple. The object being first formed in white, transparent and colorless glass, is allowed to cool until solid, and is dipped for a moment in a pot of colored glass in a state of fusion. It is then suddenly withdrawn, when it carries with it a thin film of colored glass, which immediately hardens upon it and is incorporated with it. The article is then shaped by the glass-maker; and, if it be afterward cut, the cut parts will disclose the clear transparent glass, while the parts not cut remain coated with the color. The great Portland Vase, in the British Museum, was colored in this manner, by which several colors may be laid on without difficulty. The metals used for coloring are gold, iron, copper, manganese, cobalt, and uranium. The rose and ruby colors are due to oxyde of gold. Uranium gives the topaz tint, and it and copper the emerald green. The other green is produced by copper and iron, the first giving the glass a blue, and the latter a yellow tint, and the combination of both producing green. Mr. Maez has some pitchers and vases in opaque glass of very great beauty. The effect of the opacity is to give the material all the appearance of porcelain. Some of the specimens exhibited, besides being opaque, are gilt and painted, producing a pretty effect. Card-tables, toilet articles, and other small ware, are decorated in this fashion. Glass is rendered opaque by the addition of arsenic, and the opacity is still further increased by the use of phosphate of lime (bones) and oxyde of tin. The painting on the enamelled glass of Maez's collection is extremely well executed. Indeed, the examination of the works at this table will reward the time devoted to it.

On the lower floor of the French department, Mr. La Hoshe has a collection of cut-glass claret, Madeira, and other wine services, the patterns of which are very pretty, and the form and finish of the glass such as to please the most fastidious. La Hoshe has some drinking-pitchers, ornamented with an opaque medallion of *the* Napoleon on one side, and a copy of the ribbon and seal of the Cross of the Legion of Honor. This design is unique : the cutting of the glass in La Hoshe's collection is of a very pretty design, peculiar to himself, one service of which he decorated for the Court of Russia, and received, we believe, forty thousand dollars for it. Several of the specimens in these collections are of a lace pattern, some of net or muslin, and a few present the appearance of stuff goods.

We could have wished to have an exhibition of plate-glass, such as used in windows, and of crown glass of superior quality. We do not think the samples of American production in the Palace fairly represent the condition of the art among us ; for, although we are still dependent for most of our plate and superior window-glass upon France and England, we yet produce specimens such as are not yet shown in the American department. In the Holland department is a small display of glass-shades of tall dimensions, and of window-glass made in Dort. With this we have gone through the entire show of crown-glass. In the Austrian and German department is a collection of what is termed *Bohemian* glass, which is, for the most part, highly colored, and exhibits some peculiarities of form not hitherto noticed. For fancy sets of table and side-board glass, for the wealthy and luxurious, this display has merits; but the taste and skill evinced therein do not, as a whole, equal those displayed in the French department; and we do not deem necessary any further observations on this manufacture.

XIII.

FIRE-ARMS—RIFLES AND REVOLVERS.

THE rivalry of arms has long been a principal theme of historical record and national ambition. The glory of a nation or a race has consisted, not in the lives it has made happy, and the beauty, grandeur, or greatness of its public institutions, or in the extent of its benevolent enterprises, but in the power and ingenuity with which the lives of neighboring nations or races could be sacrificed, and empires destroyed. We speak of this kind of glory not to join in the war-cry, nor to augment the desire of conquest or annexation, but in order to record a growing belief in the minds of all thinking men, that it is in fact the *shame* rather than the *glory* of the past, the great impediment of true civilization and social reformation, rather than the promoter of public order and advancement. We confess, therefore, that we have no sympathy with the rivalry of arms as it regards their use, and the purposes to which they are applied. We believe the time is approaching when rulers must find a better game than war, and when the greatness and power of any country can be more completely enjoyed and appreciated in the cultivation of humane and friendly feelings, rather than in the destruction of human creatures. But, as the world will probably pass through many changes of character ere this millennium of humanity and universal benevolence shall be established as the practice of mankind; as we live now in the age of *intellectual* enterprise rather than of positive brute force on the one hand, or of high moral refinement on the other, we find it our duty to describe to this intellectual age the achievements of its inventive heroes, its schemers, its mechanics, and its practical men. Rivalry in the invention or manufacture of arms, is of a different order to the rivalry of which we have been speaking; the man who can invent a rifle, who can patiently toil at the vise, to complete with his own hands the idea which has irresistibly forced itself upon his mind, is not the man who would delight in the destruction and demolition of life or property; no, he is one whose mental qualifications and persevering industry place him above dependence upon this particular branch of mechanical ingenuity. He could turn his hand to other and more useful pursuits. Although, therefore, we avow our pacific principles, we, at the same time, confess our interest in the various schemes for the improvement of fire-arms which are presented in the Crystal Palace. We have carefully examined the merits of each complete invention, and we here present a description of all those that are so similar in their construction and purpose as to be considered as rivals. We make use of this term on our own responsibility, each inventor being unwilling to acknowledge that there is anything in the market which can bear any comparison with his own.

The cases in which the American Fire-arms are exhibited, are placed on the left-hand side of the north nave, near the centre, marked in the Catalogue Class 8, Division A, Courts 1 and 2.

In considering the relative value of rifles, the following are points which are principally involved, and the piece which will bear the test of the most of these points will be regarded as the most complete:

I. *Safety in firing.*—It must be obvious that this is the first consideration, because if either a ball, or a piece of the steel breech-pin, or of the barrel, should happen to take a contrary course from that intended, the enemy would soon exult over the suicidal action of his foe, or the day's sport would come to a sudden, and in some cases melancholy termination.

II. *Certainty of firing.*—To miss a fire, according to the experience of those engaged in personal encounters, is to give an enemy an opportunity to do to his foe just what his foe would have done to him, if he could. This point, therefore, is frequently a matter of life and death. Or if, after wandering about for miles up the hill and down the vale, the sportsman, at last, finds the object of his pursuit, and then, when he attempts to fire, simply makes a snap or a flash, the partridge or turkey will have sense enough to take advantage of the signal, and the game is lost, with some risk, perhaps, of losing the good temper and equanimity of the sportsman.

III. *Facility of loading and rapidity of firing.*—These two points are closely connected, because the latter depends mainly on the former, although not entirely so: the perfect action of the lever and trigger, and the condition of the touch-hole, of the cap, or of the primer, being essential to rapidity, as well as to certainty of firing; and to fire rapidly, with good aim, is to gain great advantage over an enemy. It is of little advantage, however, to fire with great rapidity, unless there is sufficient time for taking an aim.

IV. *Simplicity of construction.*—Complex guns, more than complex machinery of any kind, are most liable to get out of repair.

V. *To keep constantly clean.*—If a gun will become clean after every charge, by its own operation, without any especial cleaning, it is an important advantage.

VI. *To have facility in loading, during a shower or in unfavorable weather*, without producing derangement or causing a miss-fire, and general cleanliness in loading and action. The other qualities of range and penetration have relation more to skill, and the amount of powder employed, than to construction.

Now, it is in relation to these six points of excellence, that we proceed to discuss critically the relative merits of the principal rifles professing to be newly invented.

The first case which invites especial attention, is labelled, "Sharp's Patent Rifle," which was patented in 1850; since which time it is said eighteen hundred cases, each containing two dozen pieces, making forty-three thousand two hundred in all, have been sent from the manufactory. The peculiarity of construction consists in a square movable breech-pin, which is constructed of solid, well-wrought metal, about three-quarters of an inch thick by an inch and a-quarter square. On turning down the lever or guard, this breech-pin is lowered, leaving a breech of its own size. A ball-cartridge is pressed with the thumb into its seat. The breech is then closed by pulling back the lever, and the sharp edge of the breech-pin, in rising, cuts off the rear-end of the cartridge, exposing the powder to the action of the "Maynard's Primer" or common cap, either of which can be used. Although the ball-cartridge prepared for this piece is best, those in common use by the U. States Government, will answer; and in case of being out of cartridges altogether, as will sometimes happen in the far-west, the ordinary powder flask can be applied to the breech end with almost equal facility. This we have witnessed, and all that is required to work the gun in this way, is care in not scattering the grains of powder where they are not required. But, even when this is done, the construction is so simple that there is but little probability of its lodging in sufficient quantity to produce unpleasant effects. For sporting purposes, therefore, it is a favorite weapon.

Our good opinion of this rifle is founded on a careful examination of its construction in comparison with others, and we find it will stand the test of the first five most important of the points of excellence above enumerated. It is *safe in firing*, because it contains but one charge at a time; and the breech-pin, when made of sound metal, is of great strength, and sufficient to resist ten times the force of the heaviest charge; and in speaking of the construction or strength of any piece, we must of course calculate on the soundness of the metal used. The facility, too, with which the condition of the barrel can at any time be ascertained, by looking through from the breech end, is an additional reason why this rifle is safe in using. The *certainty of firing* is best proved by experience, and a report of the Board of Ordnance Officers states that it was "fired several hundred times without cleaning, during which the movements of its machinery were not obstructed." The *facility of loading* and *rapidity of firing* are certainly equal to all that can be truly said of other single-barrel guns, not revolvers, while it possesses the advantage of greater safety than can be claimed for any revolver. We have not seen its equal for simplicity of construction. It is not professed that this gun will do without occasional cleaning; but it is found that by tallowing the ball, which is purposely grooved, the barrel can be kept clean during several hundred successive firings. We have tried the range of this rifle from one of the piers into the river. The ball seemed to fall into the water at the distance of about one thousand yards. The price of this rifle is forty dollars.

Marston's Breech-loading and Self-cleaning Gun and Cartridge next comes under notice. Mr. Marston's invention consists in a breech-bolt or slide which, by *drawing the lever forward*, is brought back from the breech end of the barrel a sufficient distance to allow space in the breech in which to place a ball-cartridge. When the cartridge is placed in this chamber through an opening on the right hand side of the gun, the lever is drawn back, and the ball-cartridge is forced by the pressure of some forty or fifty pounds into its seat in the barrel. The piece is now loaded, and, by placing a cap on the nipple, it is ready to be discharged. The fire is communicated to the rear end of the cartridge by a small hole running through the nipple to the breech-bolt and thence to the cartridge, which is perforated in the centre, as will be presently described. The most ingenious part of the construction is at the top of the lever, where there is a slat or slide in the shape of a knee-joint, in which the pin of the breech-bolt works. When the lever is brought forward in drawing back the breech-bolt, the top of the lever slides along on the pin connecting it with the bolt the whole length of the slat, and the lever then hangs at right angles with the breech-bolt, and offers no resistance to the backward motion of the breech-bolt. But so soon as the lever is drawn back, and the cartridge driven into its seat, the lever and breech-bolt being at an angle of one hundred and thirty-five degrees, and formed at their connection so as to fit at that angle, the resistance to the backward force produced by the fire is complete, the two pieces of metal fitting each other in a similar way to that of the keystone of an arch fitting the stones on each side. A small round bush enters the breech end of the barrel, and surrounds the cartridge and breech-pin at their junction so as effectually to prevent the leakage of smoke or fire when the piece is discharged. We can testify that this is effectual to this end, having seen the gun fired several times by Mr. Marston.

The cartridge deserves special attention. It is composed of

the usual materials with a conical ball cemented into it. The rear end, however, has a leather button or disc attached to it, of somewhat larger diameter than the bore of the barrel. This is why a lever is employed to force it into the barrel. This leather button is perforated in the centre to receive the flash from the cap, as above described. The first fire of the gun will leave this leather button (which is previously greased) in the large end of the barrel, and the second fire will force the button through the barrel, thoroughly cleaning it for the discharge which immediately succeeds. The result of this ingenious arrangement is to secure what we have classed above as the fifth point of excellence in a rifle, viz: "To keep constantly clean." However, as the leather button is left in, every time, it would seem to be necessary to expel it, or draw it out by some other means than by firing, when it is intended to lay by the gun, otherwise the effect of the last shot would still remain in the barrel. A ramrod is furnished with each gun for this purpose, or for uncharging, or for loading the gun at the muzzle in the old way.

The lock is a slight improvement upon the ordinary locks; the lever hangs upon a pin with an elongated hole, which allows it to rise and fall so as to avoid the necessity of another piece of metal between it and the piece which works the tumbler, simplifying that which has always been the most complex portion of fire-arms. The same lock is applied to the Marston patent revolving pistol.

The inventor has produced a pistol on the same principle as his rifle. Having visited the manufactory of Marston's arms in Jane-street, corner of Washington-street, we may say that it occupies two floors ninety feet by seventy feet, besides the forges in the sheds below; that since the date of the patent in 1850, the average sale has been about forty a week; that one hundred and forty men are employed on the manufacture of this and of the small rifle and revolving pistols, producing, in addition to the above, one hundred and fifty revolvers, and four hundred rifle-pistols a week.

Colt's Revolvers are displayed in a number of beautiful specimens, the case being arranged with great taste. The construction and general efficiency of these pieces are so universally known, that we need do no more than place this mention of them first among our notices of *revolving* fire arms. Many new inventions on the revolving principle have appeared, some of which we are enabled to describe. If we omit any mention of others, it is either because they are not essentially new, or because we could find no one at the Crystal Palace to exhibit them or afford information with regard to their construction.

"Porter's Patent Revolving Fire-Arms" come next in our notes. Their peculiarity consists in a cylinder two and a half inches diameter, fitted vertically in the breech of the weapon. The thickness of this cylinder is about three-quarters of an inch, and it revolves upon a journal so as to present its face close to the end of the barrel which fits it nicely and is thereby closed. The cylinder is made of solid steel, and the face is perforated with eight, and in the larger pieces nine chambers, large enough to receive a charge and ball, each corresponding, as it revolves, to the bore of the barrel, so as to present a charge in turn ready to be fired off. Thus eight or nine charges may be fired in such rapid succession as to produce astonishment in the mind of every spectator. Each chamber has a touch-hole communicating with the centre of the charge and opening on the right hand side of the cylinder, covered when in position by the end of the cap. Any number of these cylinders can be loaded and capped at a time, so as to produce a succession of shots, it being easy to replace one cylinder with another. When in its place, the cylinder rests firmly on its journals against the action of the discharge, and is also supported at its circumference by the iron portion of the breech in which it revolves. The cap is struck internally by a nipple-shaped hammer, working horizontally. The lock, a very simple piece of mechanism, is fixed at one end of the barrel by a hinge, closing and clasped upon the side of the cylinder when ready for use, but otherwise opening and allowing the cylinder to be taken out and charged or exchanged for another at pleasure. In the best rifles, a cap-box, accommodating thirty caps, and presenting one at the touch-hole of each chamber as it comes into place, is attached to the outside of the breech. In the carbine, however, the ordinary nipple receiving the cap is connected with each chamber. The trigger-guard is also a lever, turning the cylinder precisely one step at each movement and cocking the hammer at the same time. Three fingers of the right hand pass naturally through a loop in this guard, and, by a slight motion downward and back, the cylinder is turned the proper distance as often as the hand can move. This motion and the pressure of the trigger alternately are all that is necessary to discharge the piece, which may easily be done nine times in as many seconds.

These guns are also exhibited at the shooting gallery, Gothic Hall, 316 Broadway, where we have seen them in operation. We saw an unpractised hand fire the carbine sixteen times in thirty seconds, including the exchange of barrels, and we are informed that a skillful person can fire off the gun, in rapid succession, without moving it from its position on the shoulder. If this can be done, there is no doubt but that forty shots can be fired in one minute, including the replacing of four additional cylinders. During the experiments we witnessed, several charges missed fire, which we were informed arose from the dampness of the cylinder previous to being loaded. The greatest advantage secured by this invention above all others is its *rapid action.* We have seen none other fired in so little time. Its execution by a skillful shot would be fearful. In order to guard the touch-holes from ignition, a plate is fitted so closely as to prevent the contact of fire. And with the best rifles an arch-guard is supplied, which covers up the cylinder and prevents its liability to accident or wet. The cylinder, when loaded, is said to be water-proof, this depends however upon the accuracy with which the ball fits the chamber in which it is rammed. The cylinder can either be loaded before it is placed in its position in the breech, or it can be loaded in its position. In the former case, the ball would be rammed on to the powder by means of a mallet, and in the latter by means of a spring-hammer fixed on the barrel of the piece.

"Cook's New Revolving Rifle," an entirely new invention, is here presented for inspection, only. The novelty consists in a brass revolving apparatus inside the wooden stock, composed of five cubes, each capable of holding twelve cartridges, so that it is intended to fire sixty shots in succession in about two minutes and a half.

There is a beautiful case of Whitney's Revolver and Whitney's Rifle, and another of Allen & Thurber's Revolvers, manufactured at Worcester, Mass., but as we find no one to explain the pieces and to exhibit their construction, we have not become aware that they possess any particular claims to originality.

Gibbs's Patent Revolving Rifle and Pistol may be seen in the Agricultural Implement Department, up stairs, class 9, where Mr. L. H. Gibbs of Washington, D. C., exhibits a very novel Revolving Rifle. It differs essentially from Colt's Revolver, in having no centre-pin to the cylinder, which revolves on two raised bearers inside a fixed brass case, covering two-thirds of the cylinder above, and a slide bearing the weight of the cylinder below. This slide is easily withdrawn when it is desirable to take out the cylinder. The slide is so constructed as to continue under the barrel in the shape of a stock, leaving space sufficient between the slide and the barrel to permit of the exit of all the balls at once, should they all go off, without danger to the person, the covering above the cylinder protecting the eyes and face, and the slide below protecting the hand from the effects of such an accident. The inventor declares that he has fired five cartridges and balls at once, without harm. The cylinder is revolved in the most simple manner by a slide similar to a trigger, working in a slat in the underside of the case or breech, formed by the brass slide already described. This trigger is worked by touching it with the left hand, every motion of which acts upon the cylinder within, by means of a catch, of which there are seven round the cylinder. If the inventor should perfect his piece according to the drawing he has submitted to our inspection, in a similar manner to the principle of his pistol, which we have examined, there can be no doubt but his invention will be favorably received, as being more safe and simple in its operation than any Revolver yet invented.

The English, French, Russian and other foreign departments are nearly destitute of arms. There are some from Belgium, but nothing new. In fact, it is hardly likely that the old countries will attempt to compete with the United States in what has so long been the principal instrument of American warfare. The rifle of America has been notorious for nearly a hundred years. And, however much we may advocate the establishment of peace on earth, we can admire the talent and ingenuity of such men as Sharp, Marston, Colt and Porter, and would encourage in every way the exercise of such faculties, as when well directed, do honor to our country, and increase the wealth, prosperity and happiness of our race.

XIV.

LEATHER.

The visitor, who takes a general survey of the contents of the Crystal Palace before proceeding to inspect them in detail, as every person of sufficient leisure ought to do, will be struck with the degree of substantiality and practical utility evinced in the American Department, as a whole, compared with the foreign departments. Having entered into the reasons why this is the state of the case, in former articles, we here simply refer to the fact, in order to express our regret that there should be some remarkable exceptions to this statement. Among these, there is one deficiency on the part of American enterprise which is so observable, while so unexpected, that we deem it our duty to call special attention to it.

The reader will anticipate us as referring to the exhibition of American leather, and we say emphatically that the Tanners of the United States have fallen far short of their duty in suffering the show of their products to be so inexcusably meagre and deficient. In justification of our complaint, we state a fact—for which we feel sure the Leathermen of the land will not be, themselves, prepared, to say nothing of other classes of readers —which is, that only four of the thirty-one States of the Confederacy are represented in this department of the Fair. Were the exhibition one for the benefit of a single State, or of even a single nation, such a circumstance would not be excusable, and it is still less so here. Then, again, it would not be so bad were this mere trio of States represented severally, or even collectively, to an extent at all commensurate with the extent and spirit of their participation in this immense and important branch of industry.

The art of Tanning is, doubtless, a very ancient one, though the date of its origin is not known. In the popular acceptation of the phrase, it includes two quite distinct, though relative, branches of manufacture—that of the " currying " as well as the tanning process proper. The last named is merely a chemical process, although it requires more or less of manipulation in order to facilitate the chemical action on which reliance is primarily placed. The former is a mechanical process alone. The *modus operandi* of tanning is, simply the bringing of the vegetable principle of *Tannin*, or tan, into contact with the animal principle of *Gelatine*, whereupon a chemical change takes place, in obedience to the laws of affinity, resulting in a hardening and thickening of the skin subjected to the process. The infusion of the Tannin in the cellular coating and inner substance of the hide, is the mechanical part of the operation, which necessarily precedes the chemical. Gelatine abounds, in greater or less degree, in the skins of all animals, as also in their limbs, from which the culinary article of jelly is commonly extracted by a process quite familiar to all our lady readers. It is also resident in the other parts of animal bodies, including the horns and hoofs, which, as our readers are aware, largely supply the article of commerce known as glue.

Tannin is a principle found more or less in the barks of all trees, but the Oak is mainly that from which it is derived in this country. We say mainly, because there are portions of the country where this class of trees is so scarce as to render necessary a substitution of the bark of other trees. For instance, in New Hampshire, and other of the more northern tier of States, Hemlock bark is used by Tanners almost exclusively, many employing Oak bark very rarely, if at all, and then only to give a desired color to the leather after the actual process of tanning is considered complete. It is the universal abundance of Oak, and particularly the White Oak and the Chestnut Oak, in Virginia, Maryland, Pennsylvania and the other Middle States through which the spurs of the great Alleghany Mountains are extended, that has facilitated and rendered so largely profitable the business of manufacturing various kinds of leather, and especially sole leather and the heavier upper leather. In those States the traveller will be struck with the number of tan-yards which reveal themselves here and there in ravines along the high-ways and by-ways. They are almost as plentiful as the old-fashioned water-propelled grist mills, or the country taverns; and it is these that turn out the immense quantities of leather which find their principal dépôts at Baltimore and Philadelphia. The leather, and particularly the sole leather, manufactured among the oak-clad hills to which we have made allusion—those of the more western portions of the middle tier of States—may be generally known from Northern leather by its peculiar hue. This fact is, probably, what has induced the use of Oak Tannin, in other regions, for finishing purposes, amounting to a species of imitation.

It may be here stated incidentally, that the Quercitron Oak (*Quercus tinctoria*) has become a source of extensive profit in that portion of the Union referred to, where it is ground and packed in casks for foreign exportation. It commands very high prices in Europe, and may be found regularly quoted in commercial reports. It is exported, however, mainly for dyeing purposes, as the botanical name it bears indicates, for which it is indebted to Dr. Edward Bancroft. It may also be stated that *Catechu* far excels all other vegetable products in the amount of Tannin it yields. This has been clearly demonstrated by careful experiments instituted by Sir Humphrey Davy and others, whose analyses, by the way, have done justice to our native oaks. But Catechu is, of course, entirely out of the question for ordinary tanning operations, owing to the great price it commands as a medical drug. Our *Sumac* also, stands very high in the chemical scale, but owing to its scarcity it is too dear for employment on the coarser and more largely used kinds of leather, and hence it is mostly employed in the manufacture of the finer sorts of morocco.

We now proceed to catalogue, sufficiently for comparison and remark, the specimens of American leather so far on exhibition. Alfred Crawford, of "Shawangunk Tannery," has a lot of well-tanned and firm leather for boots and shoes. Edward A. Smith, of this City, exhibits a case of Moroccos of various colors and thicknesses, designed for boot-tops and book-bindings. They look well through the glass-case—particularly the specimens of Turkey Morocco. The same remark will apply to a case of more varieties from Cook and Mann, of this City. In this case we noticed every conceivable color of skivers, and some fine laid sheep-skins; also some superior American sheep-skins. There is a package of English colored calf and Russet calf (for law-books) among the collection of this firm. The American sheep-skins are not only a superior article of their class, but are remarkable for being the only thoroughly domestic product in the whole lot. They were manufactured in Massachusetts, and it may not be generally known that but a small proportion of the sheep-skins manufactured hereabouts for book-binders' use, are from the backs of American sheep. The reason assigned for this is, that they are too thin to split to advantage. The greater part of the book-morocco, even the Turki h morocco, is made from sheep-skins derived from the English markets. It gratifies us to be able to state that our country is fast being absolved from her dependence on foreign manufacturers for its supply of morocco. The raw kid-skins, which are very rare in this country—goats being nowhere raised for the sake of the skin—are imported very largely; and manufactured by American hands and improved machinery. There are several extensive manufactories in this City, whose moroccos will compare favorably with the best of their class produced elsewhere.

Though the tanners of this state make such a beggarly show in the Exhibition, it is not because they are beggarly themselves, if the statistics of their business are an indication. The number of tanneries in the state is about two thousand five hundred ; the number of men employed, ten thousand ; the amount of money invested, $10,000,000. The product of these, in sides of sole and upper leather, may be put down at $3,000,000 a year, at the lowest estimate. It is true that there are very few tanneries in the city ; but it must be remembered that this city is the great dépôt of most of this New York leather, and also of a large proportion of the products of the tanneries of the West, and even of portions of the East.

New Jersey, though making a show far beneath her real abilities, has done better than New York. J. Chadwick & Co., of

Newark, have furnished decidedly the greatest curiosity in the leather line, which attracts much attention. It is a single ox-hide, which contains one hundred square feet of leather; and good leather, too, it is justly considered. This firm have a large show-case, well filled with specimens of patent and enamelled leather of almost all conceivable colors. These are highly creditable to the state and the country. The extensive Carriage and Harness-Factories of the prosperous city of Newark alone require a large quantity of this species of leather, not taking exports into account, nor the wants of the other manufactories of vehicles, within the states, which are numerous and extensive.

Pennsylvania is still better represented than New Jersey, though falling far short of a correct idea of her immense production, the capital of which, footed up in 1840, at $4,255,055, by which, at that date, five thousand two hundred and twenty-six operatives were employed. H. M. Crawford, of Philadelphia, exhibits some samples of sole and uppers, the former of which is firm and durable. H. Brodt, of the same city, has a package of shoe-uppers, one article of which particularly deserves notice, as the result of an attempted imitation of the plain French calf-skin style. In this we consider him to have only partially succeeded. His own style presents a much more encouraging prospect of success, as the samples thereof clearly indicate. The reason of this we shall explain when we come to speak of the French and German Departments, which represent the only foreign nations whose Tanners and Curriers have deemed the Exhibition worthy of their attention. George S. Adler, of Philadelphia, shows a case of black morocco, which presents a creditable appearance through the glass doors. There are two other specimens of Pennsylvania leather, which are deserving of more special notice. One of these comes from the "Union Tannery" of Jacob Hoffman, of Juniata county, a fine grazing region, well adapted to the tanning business. It consists of sole-leather alone, and is decidedly of a superior sort. Its firmness and color indicate not only great care, but the taking of time. The latter is a great desideratum too seldom regarded by manufacturers of the present "fast" era, when the old slow but sure method seems to receive very little favor in any department of industrial enterprise. But the most noticeable sample of sole-leather is exhibited by James Clever, of Tannersville, Penn., under the designation of "American Oak-tanned Butt, for Belting or Soles." This is fully a third of an inch thick, and weighs forty-seven pounds. It is about as hard as a board, and of a darker hue than its neighbor, just noticed. It has evidently been subjected to a very slow process, after the old-fashioned mode, and it has not unlikely been four or five years in the yard. This may seem an altogether unwarrantable inference, in view of the rapid, machinery-forced processes now coming in vogue. But it is, nevertheless, probable. Not only are several years consumed on ox-hides, in many sections of this country, but the same is the case in England, whence the idea of its necessity was originally imported by the progenitors of the present race of rural tanners, who, in the language of one of their class, tan "just as fathers did fifty years ago." And, in fact, there is great reluctance, on the part of many of the most proficient tanners and capable judges of leather, including not a few of our best boot and shoemakers, to trust these recent time-shortening inventions. They regard such statements as the butchering of a kid, dressing the meat, and then tanning the hide, all in the self-same hour, as purely fabulous; and yet an intelligent German tanner, now in this city, actually performed this feat, while residing in Paris, where the question of how long it requires to tan perfectly has become one of days, instead of months, and even years, as of yore. There only remain to be noticed, among domestic articles, some very fine and beautifully colored buckskins, for gloves, &c., from the manufactory of Ramberry & Ebert, of Georgetown, D. C. These are highly creditable to this firm—particularly a specimen of "Daguerreotype Leather," which presents a remarkably fine-grained and smooth surface.

Here are also specimens manufactured at the tannery of Gideon Bantz, Jr., of Frederick city, Md. They were prepared expressly to test the availability of a new process of tanning without the use of bark, of which their exhibitor (David Kennedy, of Reading, Pa.) is the inventor and patentee. In the lot are all the usual sorts, from heavy sole and harness to the light and flexible calf-skin and the porous sheep. Some of the specimens of sheep-skins are finished so as to resemble calf-skins, and answer many of the purposes of that sort of leather. They certainly appear impervious enough for summer wear. There is also a hair-dressed deer-skin worthy of notice. It is smoothly finished on the flesh-side and blackened, leaving all the non-conducting qualities of the hide unaffected. For winter wear, in severe climates, it would be decidedly comfortable.

The calf-skins of this collection are remarkably firm and elastic, considering the rapidity of their preparation. They are said to have been tanned in from six to seven days. This celerity is the more noticeable from the fact that no machinery, beyond that usual in tanneries, has been employed. And here, it may be well to state, that seventy-one days were found sufficient, with this process, as we are assured, to turn out as firm and durable samples of sole as are usually met with.

Neither the manufacturer of these samples, nor the patentee of this process, has given us any insight into the particular styptic used, or the source of its supply. Bark is used to no greater extent than one-fourth the usual quantity, and not at all in tanning the lighter sorts of skins. As a matter of interest, we subjoin the inventor's own statement of the advantages of his process over the old method. He assures us that to "tan one dozen common size calf-skins, will cost from seventy-five cents to one dollar, and all other kinds of hides in proportion. It requires less room or space to carry on the business. The tanning can be perfected in one-fourth of the usual time. Sheep, goat, deer, and calf-skins, or any similar skins, can be tanned in from three to ten days; kip, upper, harness, skirting, and heavy sole-leather, in from twenty to eighty days. The process can be learned by any tanner in a very short time. It gives the leather more strength and durability, greater softness and pliability, more weight, and fills it up better, produces a finer texture, and, consequently, finishes much finer, and renders it much more impervious to water than leather tanned by the old method. Sheep and goat-skins, tanned in this way, possess the strength of calf-skins, and, in shoes and boots, will retain their shape equal to that of calf-skin. Deer-skins make a splendid article for gloves; calf-skins possess double the strength of those tanned by the old method.

The apparatus, and different stages of the process, are the same as, or analogous to, the usual method." Mr. Kennedy's patent was taken out in 1852.

James R. Smith, of this city, has done his part toward redeeming the credit of our leathermen, whose neglect of the Exhibition we remarked upon in our first article, by furnishing a case of buff and colored kid and sheep-skins, which are creditable for finish and coloring. They are of the sorts used by book-binders, hatters, &c. L. & T. Grosholz, of Philadelphia, exhibit a lot of plain calf-skins, designed as imitations of the French style of dressing; also a lot of sheep-skins. Jacobus & Utter, of Newark, N. J., have a couple of sides of light sole. They are smooth-grained and very fair and clean—the most so of any of their class in the building.

Having disposed of the specimens of Leather in the American Department of the Palace, we now come to the Foreign. France has sent a great profusion of specimens, particularly in the classes of Patent and Enamelled upper leather, and particularly in plain and enamelled calf-skins. In both these classes of boot materials, the French are, unquestionably, greatly in advance of the American tanners and curriers. Their plain-dressed calf-skins have always been in deserved repute, owing to their delightful pliability and softness, which are attained, together with durability as well as smoothness of grain. The secret of this excellence, unquestionably, lies chiefly in the cheap rates of wages prevalent in France. After the tanning processes proper are completed, the currying opens a field where patient manipulation can effect what once would have been considered wonders in the way of finishing. For example: it is said that the French curriers, after putting the tanned hides through the several usual processes, whereby every particle of lime and other residuary matter would be considered extracted, and the necessary degree of pliability attained, are in the habit of subjecting the leather to a milling or pounding process, which would be considered utterly destructive to the very substance of it by the old-fashioned members of the craft. Thus they not only give to their plain calf-skins the peculiar softness and pliability already noticed, but prepare the surface for the addition of the enamelling process. Contrary to all this, the American attempts at enamelling, or japanning, are too frequently made upon leather utterly unfitted for its reception, because of the roughness and porousness of the surface. This, and the failure to temper the heat of the composition, are, doubtless, among the chief points of failure in this country. The foregoing remarks will apply with equal force to the German processes, and their results in this line of practical art. There is little difference in the leather produced on the two sides of the Rhine. In fact, a large proportion of the French leathers is manufactured by Germans in Paris and other places in France. However, the French have secured the start in reputation, which is a great thing in a commercial point of view.

The following French manufacturers are represented by specimens of their skill, viz: Placide Peltereau, Jr., who has on exhibition well-arranged specimens of Black Harness Leather, numbered and classified as follows: Vache Lissée, 1 (smooth cowskins); Vache Lissée, 2; Bœuf, 3 (ox-hide); Vache, 4 (cowskin); Cuir Jusé, 5 (juicy leather); Vache Lissée, 6. These are very compact and thick samples. We have translated the indications of quality literally, as a matter of curiosity. The difference from the classification adopted by tanners and dealers in this country will be seen at a glance. For instance, we have no distinction between the hides of the male and female animals, when manufactured into the kind of leather for which they are best suited. By the term ox-hides we indicate all skins of full-grown cattle, while the phrase "cow-skin" would be taken to represent untanned or raw hides. Bayvet, Brothers & Co., Paris, have a large lot of buff and colored Buckskins. Every variety of tint is presented, among the rest a most perfect bronze. In this respect the excellence of French workmanship is shown, as in all fabrics where color is involved. A. Houette & Co., of the same city, exhibit a fine collection of patent and enamelled and plain calf-skins, and morocco. Nys & Co., have a collection pretty much the same as that last described, in variety and quality. A very superior lot of plain calf-skins is shown by Manson and Nantes. There is a case of skins designed for ladies' winter gloves, shown by T. Textier, Jr., of Paris, which for pliability and smoothness, as well as gloss and shading, we think it would scarcely be possible to excel. A. Petet Didier has sent a package of sole and upper leather, which presents very creditable varieties. Beside this, he has an unusually pliable and tough article of harness-leather, which seems to have been perfectly saturated with oil. It was produced by "Gerare," as nearly as we could decipher the pale and illegible chirography of the manufacturer. In the sole-leather line there are some pieces, designed for single shoe-soles, which give promise of rarest durability and imperviousness. We have never seen so much substance in so little bulk of leather. The name of the maker, with which we found the same difficulty as with the above, we read "Degrux Laceur." E. Courtois, Paris, has some fine samples of varnished calf-skins. J. Gautier, also of Paris, has on exhibition a collection of the best quality of moroccos and patent leathers. Of the same classifications there are fine samples from the factories of L. Deade; while Soucin Corbet and Chaney & Bouchet exhibit cases of plain black calf of the highest finish, and Tailbouis a superior lot of glove-skins. These are all Parisian fabrics. To these French deposits we have only one addition to make, which calls for special remark. We allude to the large collection of Charles Knoderer, of Strasbourg. Among his advertisements we find the following card:

"PATENT TANNED LEATHER: New process of tanning leather, almost *instantaneous* and *superior* to any known hitherto. It gives, in thirty to forty times less time, a product of much finer color, softer, heavier, and more water-proof."

As this vaunting piece of bad English bears the signature of "A. Barbey, Agent," we will not hold the manufacturer accountable for it, nor for the French-Yankeeism of this puffing card. But it should be added, that "three days in summer," and four in winter, are declared to have been sufficient for the manufacture of various specimens of upper leather, which, we must do this new process the justice to say, presents all the external marks of good stock and good leather, "whether tanned in three days or three years," to quote the frank remark of an old-fashioned tanner who stood by us, as we were examining them. The machinery-aided process by which these wonders have been accomplished, has been known and used in this country for some years. Its principle in bringing the skins into rapidly repeated contact with the tanning liquor by means of a revolving cylinder, which catches up and dashes them down alternately. The hint was, doubtless, derived from a fact well known among practical tanners, that the more frequently hides are "handled," as taking them out of the vat, and replacing them in fresh and gradually stronger bark, is called, the better the leather will be. Frequent exposure to the atmosphere is supposed to have more or less to do with the result aimed at, which is the introduction of the tannin as repletely as possible among the fibres of the skin. The great length of time, during which the hides were subjected to the action of the liquor, under the older and slower process, which is still followed in this and other States, finally accomplishes, with the aid of the tanner's hands, what is done by the machine. And while the old-fashioned plain way may suit the rustic tanner, whose operations are but limited, the heavy and progressive capitalist will naturally give his preference to this "almost instantaneous and superior" process; and it is already largely employed in this country.

The German Department is not near so full as the French, but highly creditable as to quality. Among the German exhibitors are Cornelius Weyl, of Worms, who shows patent leather, and Heintz and Frendenberg, of Weinheim, who show enamelled, both remarkable for softness and for fineness of graining. Doerr & Reinhart, of Worms, have much the largest and most varied collection. It consists of patent and japanned upper and calfs, and also kid, deer, and sheep skins. The latter are very noticeable for their extreme thickness, and velvet-like softness.

In the English Department some samples of Leather have now been placed. One of the lots has not been labelled yet. J. S. Dead, of London, exhibits a case of kid and sheep skins for bookbinders' use. They are of all the usual colors, and look well. Revington & Morris, of the same city, have a case of Uppers and

Sheep-skins—the latter of various colors. Their sheep-skins are the thickest in the building, perhaps, excepting some in the German Department. The same remark will apply to some of their Kid skins. Bayley & Shaw, of Nottingham, have contributed much the largest English collection.

These also are in a glass case, where a bad light does great injustice to them. Among their various sorts we find a specimen of embossed leather. Its raised figure-work gives it much the appearance of damask. We should think it capable of a greatly varied application to the manufacture of carriages and furniture.

From France there are some recent additions of plain calf-skins and other uppers, presenting those qualities which have given reputation to the French manufacturers of this sort of leather. They are deposited by Delon Alboy and F. Gaudelet. From Germany there, are also some additions to the specimens before remarked upon. Rupp & Bechstein, of Frankfort, exhibit specimens of enamelled calf-skins, which are very fine in texture and finish. The graining is well nigh perfect.

We come now to Austria. J. J. Pollak & Sons, of Prague, have a very large variety of leathers, including almost every conceivable kind and quality, some of which are decidedly novel. Their wagon harness leather is very heavy and durable, but rough and uninviting in color. Their patent or lackered leather, as they called it, is very thick, firm and smooth. An article of this sort designed for cap-fronts, and therefore black on one side, while of some other color on the opposite side, presents these qualities in great perfection. Some of their uppers are curious in the graining, giving a species of minute diamond-work. But the most remarkable of these Austrian specimens is a plain calf-skin dressed as morocco. While having the granular appearance of the latter, it is far more durable. Indeed, it is the most pliable article of boot-leather in the Palace, the best French not excepted. A pair of boots from it would be a luxury. The Messrs. Pollak are the patentees of a steam process of currying—a recent invention, as they claim. They state that with its aid, they can turn out calf or sheep-skins within two or three days, and the hides of oxen, cows or horses, within four or five days from the lime pit.

In the same department, F. Wolff exhibits some specimens of goat and sheep-skins of a decidedly novel style. They are printed in figures and flowers, so as to resemble the usual pattern of oil-cloth used for table-cloths and furniture covers, and would probably be found well adapted for car or carriage linings.

These results of practical industry are calculated to give a rather agreeable disappointment to the visitor who has not kept himself tolerably well posted as to the present developments within the vast dominions of Austria. There is a special reason for the success in the Tanning Art evinced by the specimens just noticed. The Imperial Royal Army affords an immense amount of patronage, by which competition is stimulated and rewarded. But, besides this factitious stimulus, the supply of native hides is very great in that country. It includes all the varieties of England and the United States, with many others of great value. The grazing advantages of a large portion of the country are immense, while every species of tree from which the principle of tannin is derivable, is at hand in the forests. The oak is plentiful, even at as great altitudes as 2,800 feet above the level of the sea. But although tan-bark is thus rendered accessible and cheap, it would seem that it is not much used in portions of the Empire, especially in Hungary. The process of tanning in this country is so different from that employed in the United States, that we add a brief description of it. It consists in impregnating the stronger hides with a mixture of alum, common salt, and suet. Two months are required for the process. The tanning apparatus employed consists chiefly of a furnace with an iron boiler for dissolving the alum, a vat for immersing the hides in the solution, and a copper boiler in a chamber, made close so as to retain a great degree of heat. In this chamber, although generally as small as five by six feet, there are usually, beside the copper boiler, which is capable of containing from one hundred and fifty to two hundred gallons, the following conveniences: A stove, in the middle of which is a stone slab, upon which stands an iron grate about a yard square. It is covered with charcoal. At each side of the stove are large tables, running the length of the chamber. On these the leather is spread to receive the grease. Overhead are poles on which the leather is hung while heat is being applied. The other parts of the operations are similar to those used elsewhere. The skins are washed in some river, on the bank of which the establishment is reared, next shaved, and then steeped for twenty-four hours in water. They are next cleansed with five or six pounds of alum to each side, and three or four pounds of salt, supposing the hide to weigh not more than seventy or eighty pounds. The salt softens the effect of the alum, while it attracts moisture from the atmosphere, and assists to preserve the desired suppleness of the leather. When the alum and salt are perfectly dissolved, they are poured upon the hides. These, being placed in the vat, are tramped upon by walking backward and forward. They are next transferred to a vat containing hot water alone, where they are again tramped.

Then they are steeped for eight days in the alum solution. All of this round of preparations is subsequently repeated, after which the skins are dried in the open air, or at a stove, but stretched at intervals to prevent them from wrinkling. Having been piled away, until they are considered dry, they are trampled for the third time. This is to open the pores and render the leather pliable. Bleaching in the sun is resorted to with the view of whitening them. But there is another novel step in the process, which must not be overlooked. It is the stretching of the skin over the burning charcoal, for about a minute, with the flesh side toward the fire. Having been thus "flamed," they are exposed to the radiation of the heat on inclined planes, while covered carefully with cloths. They are finally hung up, in order that the grease may dry in and harden. Instead of alum, sulphuric acid is used sometimes —of course, in a diluted state. This would seem to indicate that the sulphuric acid of the alum is the principle relied on, in the other plan, to effect a chemical interchange with the chloric acid of the salt.

Among foreign samples of leather, are those from our neighbors of the British American Provinces. Oliver T. Macklin, of Chippewa, [C. W.] has deposited several sides of superior sole, the weight of which runs from twenty-six to thirty-five pounds. It is hemlock-tanned, and therefore darker-colored than much of the leather manufactured in the States. The hemlock bark affords a cheaper astringent than the oak, and hence the hides tanned with it are used extensively at Lynn, and other shoe-manufacturing localities where cheapness is a leading object. It gives the mahogany hue to soles of the "Yankee shoes," as they are styled in the Southern markets. The Canadian sole leather differs generally from ours in one important particular. Its flesh side is generally left unshaved, and is merely rolled. The weight is thereby increased, but there is no actual gain, one would think, in sales to discriminating buyers. And yet to the manufacturer of Brogans there is the advantage of enabling him to give the appearance of greater thickness and substantiality to the soles, without the reality.

W. A. Clark, of Toronto, has on exhibition some good specimens of Roans, or Cape Sheep-skins, in which the beautiful tint imparted by the cochineal dye is displayed to advantage. The Sheep-skin Moroccos, colored with cochineal, are much more costly than any other Roans. They are worth in this market, from eight dollars to ten dollars per dozen, which is from one dollar to one dollar and fifty cents higher than even Imitation Russia. Mr. Clark exhibits also, a very soft and white Lamb-skin. There is a specimen of Buckskin in this department, tanned after the Indian process. It looks very rough, when compared with the finer specimens around it, giving no indications of trouble in shaving off the fleshy roughness usually supposed to require the aid of the currier's knife or roller; but it has evidently retained all the native strength and flexibility of the skin.

But the most remarkable sample in the Canadian Department, and we might perhaps add, in the whole Exhibition, is that of leather manufactured from the skin of the porpoise. Though aware of the general qualities of this animal, we were not prepared to see its skin turned to such an account as this. The texture is more porous than that of ordinary uppers, but it gives evidence of having all the other requisites of shoe-leather. In pleasantness of pressure it would be quite equal to buckskin for dry weather, while it would probably be more durable. This curiosity—for such it is—was tanned by C. H. Tetu. He calls his novel article "Patent Porpoise Leather." It took a premium in the London Exhibition.

XV.

SADDLES, HARNESS AND TRUNKS.

Under this head we propose to do justice to most of those heavier articles on exhibition, which are manufactured chiefly from leather. First of Saddles. The Saddle's origin is not known. It probably never had any distinct origin, but has been a gradual growth from the suggestions of necessity, beginning with a mere piece of some untanned skin, and progressing to the beautifully finished and comfort-assuring modern saddle. The saddle was not known among the Greeks, a sort of cloth, or housing, being all they used. By this latter name a portion of riding apparatus is known to the present day. The same was also used by the Persians. We have good inferential evidence that Saddles, in anything approaching the modern arrangement of stirrups, were totally unknown to the Ancient Romans in the description by the great physician of their time, Galen, of certain diseases caused among their cavalry by the pendency of their legs on horseback. The first mention of saddles is that we have in connection with the history of Constantine. Constantius, a brother of the first Christian Emperor, got up a plot to deprive him of his scepter. In the course of its attempted execution, he is represented as having made his way into the midst of the squadron where Constantine was, mounted on a saddle, from which he suddenly threw himself. Before that time, square panels were in use by horsemen, as may be seen represented in ancient statues, such as that of Antoninus, which still graces the Roman capitol. In the Theodosian code, there is a curious prescription of the legal weight of a saddle and bridle; they were to weigh not more than 60lbs! A law of the reign of Henry VII. shows that in more modern times attempts were made to regulate the use of saddles. The nobility were compelled to use them. The cost which they were made to incur must have been annoying even to their class, judging by the circumstance of Richard II. having bartered no less than four hundred cows for the saddle which he used in his expedition to Ireland for the purpose of chastising MacMorrogh for his assumption of the title of king—at least so runneth the history of the time. The earliest charter of a saddle-manufactory, of which we have any account, was granted in 1272, though one is said to have been in existence in England as early as 1190.

Great improvements have been made in saddles within fifty years, as a comparison of the specimens in the Exhibition with the relics of a former day will show. In this respect the English are behind the American saddles, although the manufacture receives great encouragement from the nobility and gentry, owing to their racing and fox-hunting habits. The same material (hog-skin) is used, for the best saddles, in both countries, on account of its softness, and capacity for exposure to the sun and rain. In this country, buckskin is frequently used, for the seat and the horns of ladies' saddles particularly. Among the samples of foreign saddles we find none but the plainest hog-skin—that is, no attempts at fine quilting, and other ornaments so common in this country. These come from the manufactories of Great Britain and Ireland, which are the only foreign countries represented in this line, except Germany. From the latter, there are some bridles of a very pretty and peculiar pattern, whose maker has not thought it worth while to attach his name. From London, Robert Blyth has sent two men's saddles and one lady's, and also a racing saddle. The latter is smaller and lighter than the others. The seats are all flatter than those of corresponding American articles, while the skirts of the side-saddles are narrower and shorter—a fault from which the soiled skirt of the fair rider would soon suffer. William Lennan, of Dublin, exhibits one man's saddle and one hunting-saddle. The weight of the latter is put down at 10 lbs., and the selling price at £5. This is certainly a well-made and neat article, but the price indicates that the user is expected to pay for his fancy. An equally good saddle could be furnished for $15 in New-York. Its light weight is certainly a recommendation, especially for hunting purposes, and contrasts curiously enough with the 60 lbs. legal rule cited above. But the price, high as it may now seem, falls a good way short of the worth of four hundred cows, at any valuation conceivable.

All the saddles in the American Department are of military patterns, as though fighting were really the chief employment of our horsemen. Thornton Grimsley, of St. Louis, has a case of dragoon equipments that are very showy, and no doubt well adapted to the "pomp and circumstance of glorious war." The embroidery is of wide gilded lace, and the quilting is very neat. The bridles appear much lighter than usual, which is a most merciful improvement. There is, in this case, what might be called an unpadded "tree," which is said to be much in use among the Mexicans, and which was adopted by Generals Scott and Taylor during their Mexican campaigns. Presenting no check to evaporation, while leaving the spinal column of the horse entirely untouched, it is also a humane Invention. A still more ornamental saddle is shown by Thompson & May, of Bridgeport, Conn., for whom it was manufactured, as their card informs us, by Benjamin Stevens. It presents the peculiarity of having no cloth upon it.

Before passing to the harnesses, we must mention an improvement in bridle-reins, of which W. A. Holwell, the Canadian Commissioner, is the patentee. It is designed for either riding or driving. He calls it the "Duplex Safety Rein." Ordinarily there are two reins to every bridle, one of which connects with a curb, and the other with a snaffle. This improvement proposes to dispense with one of these altogether. A single leather rein is attached to the curb-bit. A short elastic connecting-piece, or false rein, is attached at one end to the main rein, and at the other to the ring of the snaffle-bit. With this arrangement, so long as the horse moves gently, the driver or rider bears upon the connecting-piece only, and through it upon the snaffle-bit. If the horse is restive or hard-mouthed, his resistance stretches the connecting-piece until the pressure is thrown upon the main rein, and through it upon the curb or stiff-bit, thus bringing its lever power into play. The moment the animal becomes tractable again, the elastic piece contracts and transfers the natural pressure of the horse's mouth to the snaffle-bit, the lever-bit becoming instantly relaxed. The material used by Mr. Holwell, for his model, is a gum-elastic tube with a metallic hook at one end, to attach it to the snaffle or cheek-ring, and a little button at the other, for whose reception holes are punched along the main rein. The advantages proposed by this promising though simple invention, are a more natural, self-relying movement on the part of the horse, and greater sense of security to the rider or driver. For women, or inexperienced or feeble persons, it promises an exemption from the common risk of getting hold of the wrong rein, amid fright and confusion. Women are often thrown from their horses in this very way, when using double-reined bridles.

The term Harness anciently indicated the complete armor of a cavalier, including his casque and his cuirass. In our more modern sense, it signifies the trappings or furniture of the horse, or of a team of horses, or other animals used for draught of any sort. We have derived the word from *harnaes*, (Welch,) though the original is supposed by some philologists to have been a Greek root, *arnakis*, a lamb-skin, because the Greeks covered themselves with lamb-skins as a part of their protective armor. The near resemblance of the equivalents in various ancient and modern languages is so remarkable as to be worth citing here, as a philological curiosity, while at the same time indicating universal use. While the orthography runs as we have seen in the Greek, the Welch, and the English, in the German it is *harnisch*, in the Spanish *arnes*, in the Danish *harnisk*, in the Italian *arnese*, in the Armenian *harnes*, and in the Swedish *harnesk*. The first portion of our horse-harness used was probably the traces, in the shape of pieces of cord or raw hide. On the Eastern Shore of Maryland, where the draught is easy, owing to the level quality of the ground, and where the horses are poor and feeble, may be seen, at this day, these rope traces, with rude wooden hames, and a straw collar; whereas, among the ancients, a piece of cord was, most likely, thrown around the back to keep the traces from flying about and becoming entangled, while their front attachment was to the head of the halter-shaped bridle, such as is still used by some nomad tribes.

We have already mentioned that saddles were dignified by

various legislative enactments regulating their use among the English of former eras. In the reign of Richard II., the use of harness was also regulated by law, the persons being designated who might lawfully use them, and the time when, prescribed.

There are on exhibition only two lots of carriage-harness, or indeed of any sort of harness, we may say, with the exception of some collars sent in by John B. Seidenstricker & Co., of Baltimore, to show the utility of Taylor's patent spring-hames—an article, by the way, well worthy of attention. The first of these which we shall notice, is from the manufactory of Lacey & Phillips, of Philadelphia. They exhibit a case containing two sets of russet or brown single-harness, and one set of black; also three sets of double. The leather is very smooth and strong, and the stitching well done. The embroidery is of the neatest quill-work; and the mountings are of plated silver, with turrets set in gilt—all very heavy. The other lot, which is also arranged in a large show-case, is from Newark, N. J., from whose extensixe Harness Factories a representation was to have been anticipated, if from anywhere. It bears the name of Owen McFarland, one of those remarkable architects of their own fortune who abound among the industrialists of the country. He presents both double and single carriage-harness. The body is of plain leather, while the collars and blinds are of patent leather. The mountings of these are also partly golden and heavy, and the embroidery, which is beautiful quill-work, is well done. It will give the discerning some trouble to determine the comparative merits of these two lots. We shall dismiss them with a word of thanks for the care which both manufacturers have given to the reins—always a paramount matter in harness. These reins are apparently very secure, though of the round style, and very delicate-looking. We should take them in hand with a sense of reliance, behind the wildest horse, so far as their important office is concerned—which would be far from the case with a large proportion of the reins in the market, made as they are with but little regard, seemingly, to the quality or adaptation of the leather, or the safety of life or limb in their use.

Limited as is the display of the articles already named in this notice, the reader will hardly be prepared to learn that but a single travelling-trunk is to be found in the entire American Department. In a travelling age, such as this, we had a right to expect pretty fair samples from other countries; but how it happened that so immense a branch of business as the manufacture of trunks in this country should be represented by a single sample, and that exhibited merely for the sake of the secondary quality of its needle-work ornaments, we are at a loss to conceive. And this sample comes from St. Louis, a far-off Western city, where the want of manufacturing enterprise is a theme of loud complaint among her journalists. The article referred to was manufactured by S. F. Summers, of that city. It is a fair leather trunk, with heavy plated silver bands and mountings, which give it a strong exterior. It is locked so as to prevent inspection of its internal arrangements. But, as we have already hinted, it has evidently been sent in to show what the needle can do in the ornamental line. The wife of Mr. Summers is credited with this feature of its finish, by which she has won herself deserved praise. The value of this trunk is estimated at three hundred dollars, which, perhaps, may do for St. Louis, where everybody is rich. In the Italian Department, there is a single trunk, but it is remarkable for nothing except being made of patent leather, and having glaring brass bands and white stitching. Imagine such a trunk in one of our American baggage-cars, or at a railway station, amid piles of luggage, when the passengers are called on to "come forward and point out their baggage." We should expect to see the unhappy owner emerging from the *mêlée* a sadder and a wiser man, with his trunk banged to pieces, and not a trace of its pristine splendor remaining on the relics.

XVI.

ARTIFICIAL FLOWERS.

Of all the arts that are devoted to the mimicry of nature, there is none, perhaps, that approaches nearer to it in fidelity than that which counterfeits the perishable beauties of the Floral Kingdom. To such a degree of perfection have the imitative powers of man brought its productions, that could we but impart to them the delicious perfumes exhaled from the original, we should feel almost as exquisite a sense of enjoyment from the contemplation of their charms. We might then replace the withered rose which from time immemorial has been the emblem of "blighted hopes" and "crushed affections," by ever-blooming wax and muslin substitutes, whose freshness would not require to be kept alive by the artificial stimulants of our tears, and the tiresome applications of the watering-pot. Thus we might revel in the odor of *souvenirs*, and rejoice like Mark Tapley in the perpetual greenness of our sorrows. Why, amongst the numerous discoveries that are daily enriching the arts, this has not been already accomplished, it would be difficult to say. Since Genin has made an epic of his hats, and Phalon an eclogue of his hair-dye, it has become so much the fashion with our tradesmen to infuse a dash of sentiment into the calculations of the counting-house, that we can see no reason why the poetry of artificial floriculture should not seek its apotheosis in the full-toned fragrance of its bouquets.

When we consider, however, the influence for good or evil which a coquettishly-disposed bunch of artificial flowers has had on the destiny of some of us—when we reflect upon the seductive spells which lie lurking within its petals, and upon the cunning basilisks that are disporting within the dark ambush of its leaves —when we think, too, of the drain which the supply of these costly vanities (yielded in the abandonment of our weak moments to the salutations of some bright-eyed petitioner) entails upon our purse, we are disposed to take rather a more serious and philosophical view of the subject. We have been so cruelly deceived in the dawn of our first illusions by the apparent simplicity which this floral embellishment would seem to denote, that in the ripeness of our mature experience we have ceased to have any faith in it. When we now see a beautiful girl overladen with the treasures of the Vegetable Kingdom, like another Ceres, we cannot help deploring the taste which refuses to Nature the free display of her most precious gifts, and to Man the opportunity of forming an unembarrassed judgment. The melancholy picture, but too often seen, of tottering senility struggling to conceal the ravages of time under the freshness and bloom of the rose, only serves to awaken our pity, and to remind us at times of those garlanded skeletons which the Egyptians were in the habit of seating at their feasts.

As, however, the taste for this species of ornament is rapidly spreading among our feminine population, and as it bids fair to become an important branch of our commerce, we are bound to give to it that impartial consideration which our growing manufactures demand. We shall therefore now proceed to give a brief account of the early history of the art and of the progress which it has made within the last few years in the United States.

The art of imitating vegetable productions in a variety of materials, seems to have been practised among the earliest and rudest nations. The savages of South America are said, for instance, to excel in the manufacture of flowers made from the brilliant plumage of their own birds, and which bear a close resemblance to the originals from which they are copied. The Italians seem to have been the first European nation who attained any degree of excellence in the art, but they were soon surpassed by the French, who have ever since maintained their pre-eminence. Some idea of the importance of this branch of industry in France may be formed from the fact that her annual exports in this article alone amount to 11,000,000 of francs. The manufactures that she produces are the finest in the world, being unequalled for the purity and brilliancy of their tints, their delicacy and exquisite finish, and the fidelity with which they adhere to nature. Some of the flowers contributed from Paris to the London Exhibition were perfect marvels of ingenuity and skill, and the cases that contained them were continually besieged by admiring crowds. Among the productions which excited the most interest on that occasion were specimens of some rare exotics, exhibited by Madame Emma Fürstenhoff, a Swedish lady, who to the nicest observation of nature unites artistic talent of the highest order. High as was Constantin's previous reputation, and great as was the display which he made of the resources of his *atelier*, it was universally conceded that his lady rival bore away the palm. The houses in Paris which take the lead in the finest descriptions of goods are those of Constantin, Fürstenhoff, Sophie Perrot, Haraud, Huot, and Bortin. Of these, we only see the name of the latter in the list of contributors to our exhibition. M. R. E. Royer, of the Rue de Caire, exhibits several cases of artificial leaves and branches, some of which are beautifully executed, but which nevertheless present but little variety. In the American Department we observe one case, that of Madame Civatte, which are very beautiful, but which we suspect were not manufactured here, but in Paris. This suspicion is repelled by Mad. C., who insists that they were made by her in this city. Assuming this to be the fact, we feel bound to point out the manifest injustice done to our native manufacturers by having their goods placed in competition with foreign flowers, executed by some of the oldest makers in the French capital.

The commencement of our home manufacture does not date further back than about thirty years. The house of Christopher & Co. was, we believe, the first that engaged in it; but the progress made was slow, owing to the difficulty of procuring competent hands and proper materials. It may be necessary here to observe, that in Paris the preparation of the materials used in the manufacture forms several distinct branches of trade, and that the quality of the flowers depends, in a great manner, on the care used in the getting up of these materials. The New York manufacturers were reduced to the alternative of either preparing them themselves or of importing them from France, and for many years they were obliged to pursue the latter course. It was formerly, also, the custom of the manufacturer to import foreign flowers for the purpose of intermixing them with, and completing their own assortments. It is only within the last three years, in fact, that some few of them have commenced to make the complete flower, and to dispense with the aid of foreign accessories. Owing to the rapid increase of the manufacture in New York, and the formation of a large body of skilled hands, there is now no obstacle in the way of attaining its full development. Could the prejudices be got over that exist in favor of French goods, our manufacturers would, in the course of a few years, compete successfully with the Paris makers. As an illustration of the rapid progress which has been made in the finer branches of the manufacture, we may mention that in two specimens of the same flower submitted to us for inspection a few days since, the one made in Paris and other in New York, it was impossible for us to distinguish any difference. We were informed that even more skillful judges than ourselves were frequently deceived by the exactness with which the Paris patterns are copied, so that we may fairly assume that our flower-makers have acquired the taste and experience necessary to the successful prosecution of the manufacture.

There are now a great many flower-manufacturers in New York—we believe from sixty to seventy. In Philadelphia there are about a dozen, and in Boston only half that number. In the other leading towns throughout the states, there is not more than about one to each, the difficulty of procuring skilled hands operating as an effectual barrier to the extension of the trade. The consequence is that the home consumption is chiefly supplied by New York, the greater facilities of manufacture and importation which it possesses, giving it a natural pre-eminence.

The flower-trade gives constant employment throughout the year to a large number of women and children, the services of men being only required in the rougher branches of the manufacture ; such, for instance, as cutting out and stamping. The rates of wages average from one dollar to six per week ; and some children become so expert, after a short time, that they are enabled to contribute to the support of their families. It was found extremely difficult at first to train the American girls to that minute and patient attention to details which it is so necessary to observe throughout the different processes of this ingenious art; but, the school having once been formed, they fell naturally into the routine of the work, and brought to it a degree of taste and intelligence which peculiarly adapt them for this occupation, and which place them almost on a level with the best French hands.

The busy seasons in this trade are from the first week in February to the end of April (for spring goods), and from the first week in August until the end of October, (for winter articles). The spring trade commences thus early in order to give the buyers from the South and West time to make their purchases and prepare for the coming season. There are more artificial flowers consumed in New York, Philadelphia, Boston, Cincinnati, and New Orleans, than in the whole of the United States beside. The credit to purchasers is six months; but the leading houses take advantage of the discount, and pay at the expiration of the month. The goods that remain unsold at the end of the season, are generally disposed of at a reduction of twenty-five, and often fifty, per cent., the freshness of the article constituting one of its chief recommendations.

The leading manufacturing houses in New York, are those of Christopher, Saxton, Guillaume & Korn, Bassford, G. H. Smith, and Bianchi.

The importation of foreign flowers cannot be said to have occupied any place in our Treasury returns until about fifteen years since. Brun la Rosière, Jacquelin, and Strange Brothers, were the first houses that gave any development to the trade. Of these three, we believe, the house of Strange Brothers is the only one now in existence. The other leading importers are Messrs. Lowitz, Kahn, Henderson, and Smythe.

The total value of flowers imported does not exceed $250,000. Of these, the greater part comes from France. A few parcels are received from Vienna, but they are not as highly esteemed in the market. Neither the coloring nor the mountings are as true to nature, nor as graceful as those of French manufacture.

With these general preliminaries, we will now proceed to give some account of the progress of manufacture, which may be interesting to such of our female readers as occupy themselves in analogous pursuits. To make it as intelligible as possible, we will describe the progress of the raw materials, through the different stages of manipulation necessary to form them into the beautiful flowers which imitate so closely one of the most admirable productions of nature.

On entering the laboratory, we find several workmen engaged in the preparation of colors for the different tints, or in dyeing the muslins and crapes which form the material to work upon. After being saturated with the color, the stuffs are stretched on frames and left to dry; in this way, a piece of white crape can be dyed a beautiful emerald green, and, placed in the hands of the cutter, in the course of about half an hour, ready to undergo the next process through which it has to pass. The silk velvets used for winter goods are stretched on frames and stiffened with a coat of size. While the latter is wet, a piece of calico, of the same tint, is laid on to the back of the velvet, and another coat of size given to it. It is then left to dry before it passes into the hands of the cutter. None but white cotton velvet are ever dyed, the original color of these materials being sufficiently varied and brilliant to afford the different shades wanted. The leaves and petals of the flowers are tinted by the hand with a camel's-hair brush. They require great nicety of execution, the beauty of the flower consisting in the degree of artistic softness with which the different shades are blended into each other.

In the cutting-room, we find a number of boys engaged in cutting out with metal forms, having sharpened edges following the outlines of the object, the leaves, and other parts of the flower, which are susceptible of being thus treated. The material is laid on a lead block, to prevent the edge of the form from being blunted, and a blow of a hammer being given to the latter, eight folds of the material are cut at a stroke into so many leaves. If velvet be employed, its thickness will not admit of its being folded more than twice. The leaves being cut to the required form, the next process is to impart to them, by pressure, the different veins and fibres which exist in the original. For this purpose, dies or stamps are used, in conjunction with their matrix, the leaf being inserted between them and submitted to the action of a hand-press. Nothing can be more perfect or natural than the fibrous resemblance thus obtained.

The leaves are now shaded with a camel's-hair pencil, and sent into another department, to have stems attached to them. The wire used for this purpose is covered either with silk or cotton floss, and is imported ready prepared. It is pasted on to the leaf, and if the latter be made of muslin, it is then dipped into wax, to impart to it a smooth surface. Some of the leaves, however, (those intended for the finer descriptions of flowers,) require to be painted before they are waxed. None but a very expert workman can be intrusted with this latter process. It requires great delicacy of manipulation and acquaintance with the properties of the different colors. The latter are specially prepared for the purpose, and when laid on are fixed by means of gums.

We will now enter the flower-room, where the materials thus prepared are sent to be completed. Here we find between forty and fifty women and children employed in passing them through their different stages. Here, also, may be seen another illustration of the advantages arising from the division of labor; the materials being no sooner received from the cutting-room than they are worked up in an uncommonly short space of time, not only into single flowers, but into elaborate bunches ready for the warehouse. Let us take, for instance, a rose, and follow it from hand to hand until it arrives at maturity. One girl makes the heart of the flower, either with thread or raw silk, and dipping it in colored gum passes it on to the *monteuse*. The petals are gauzed by another, and sent to the same destination. The buds are intrusted to a third, generally an experienced hand; and, the separate parts of the flower being now completed, the *monteuse* groups and attaches them together. This latter is the most important person, perhaps, in the whole establishment; great taste and practice being required to combine naturally the different parts of the flower. In most of the European establishments, the persons employed in this capacity are French women, as they are considered to possess more talent in this respect than the natives of other countries. In most of the New York establishments, we are happy to say, our own countrywomen are to be found at the head of the department, a proof that they are not considered inferior in the qualities necessary to the successful discharge of their duties.

Having shown that this branch of industry is rapidly progressing, and that we are likely soon to extinguish the importation of foreign goods by the perfection of our own manufactures, it will be naturally expected that the results exhibited at the Crystal Palace will afford a fair index of its present prosperous state. Owing to some unaccountable feeling of apathy, however, on the part of the makers, or to some other cause which it is difficult to penetrate, we regret to say that this is not the case. With the exception of one house, that of Messrs. Guillaume & Korn, we do not see any of our leading makers who figure on the list of contributors. These gentlemen exhibit a case of artificial flowers, consisting of tulips, cacti, camelias, jacinthuses and garlands, composed of crape flowers and leaves, every part of which, they state, was manufactured and mounted in their factory in New York. They are most beautifully executed, and appear to us to combine lightness and freshness with a truthfulness of tint and fidelity to the originals, which render them worthy to be classed with some of the best French flowers. They also show a case of leaves, which comprise an immense variety of the different species of foliage, and which are characterized by the same careful attention to details. They were all made in their factory, and afford a valuable evidence of what enterprise and perseverance will do, these gentlemen being the first and only manufacturers who have attempted the fabrication of leaves in this country, and that in despite of obstacles which would have discouraged most other men. We have already noticed the very beautiful *etalage* of Madame Civatte, in speaking of the French department, and therefore shall not again advert to it here. Mrs. Vonskillen, of New York, exhibits a case of paper flowers of her own manufacture, which display considerable taste and skill. They appear, however, to be intermixed with French flowers. There are several contributions in wax flowers from different parts of the States, but they seem to be mostly the productions of amateurs.

In some of the specimens exhibited we observe a novelty

which seems to have been recently introduced, and which deserves a passing remark. We allude to the substitution of crape for the materials recently employed in the fabrication of the leaves. It imparts a soft and peach-like effect to them, which no other material is capable of producing, and forms a beautiful background to the bright tints of the flower.

XVII.

DAGUERREOTYPES.

If there be any one department in the whole building which is peculiarly American, and in which the country shines pre-eminent, it is in that of Daguerreotypes, which are exhibited below stairs; and the collection, which is an extensive one, is made up of contributions from almost every section of the Union where the art is practised. In contrasting the specimens of art which are taken here with those taken in European countries, the excellence of American pictures is evident, which is to be accounted for by several reasons. In the first place, American skies are freer from fogs and clouds—from bituminous coal not being much used, the atmosphere of our cities is free from smoke, at least upon the Atlantic coasts. Then the chemicals and processes are, generally speaking, of a more sensitive character, and the apparatus is more convenient and suitable than that of Europe. Our little inventions come into play and aid in saving time and developing a good picture; and last, though perhaps not least, our people are readier in picking up processes and acquiring the mastery of the art than our trans-Atlantic rivals. Not that we understand the science better, but the details of the art are acquired in a shorter time by us, while the enormous practice which our operators enjoy combines to render the daguerreotype a necessary contributor to the comforts of life. Does a child start on the journey of existence, and leave his "father's halls;" forthwith the little image is produced to keep his memory green. Does the daughter accept the new duties of matron, or does the venerated parent descend into the grave, what means so ready to revive their recollection? Does the lover or the husband go to Australia or California, and not exchange with the beloved one the image of what afforded so much delight to gaze upon? The readiness with which a likeness may be obtained, the truthfulness of the image, and the smallness of cost, render it the current pledge of friendship; and the immense number of operators who are supported by the art, in this country, shows how widely the love of sun-pictures is diffused. Several thousand industrious artists and artisans are occupied in the preparation of very pure chemicals, as bromine, iodine, gold salts, hyperphosphate of soda. Another class prepare silvered plates, cases, buffs, gilding, cut glass, and a hundred little addenda. Then the manufacture of cameras and the grinding of good lenses is an important branch of the business; for without a camera having good lenses, the best operator would fail to produce an image which would be distinct or saleable; and even with a good Voigtlander or Harrison camera, it requires great skill to focus the image; for, strange as it may appear, the point where a good view of the sitter is obtained is not the point best adapted for bringing out a good picture. In other words, the focus of vision and the focus of chemical action are not the same; and hence, when we have the one we lose the other. This is owing to the fact that it is not the rays of color on the solar spectrum which produce the image, but a different set of rays, viz., those of chemical action; and since this is the case, we submit the opinion that it is not possible to obtain a daguerreotype in its *natural colors*, as Mr. Hill and others have been trying to delude our operators into believing, and leading themselves and others by the ignis fatuus of plates tortured into iridescent colors by chemical oxydation. But we are getting discursive upon this beautiful art, which was intended to subserve many other useful purposes than that of portrait-painting.

Everybody knows how difficult it is to keep silver from tarnishing, and that the action of light tends to destroy all preparations of silver. Some of these are more readily acted on by light than others—are more *sensitive*, as it is termed. Such are the iodide, bromide, and chloride of silver. These salts cannot be kept exposed to the light for any, even a very short time, without undergoing some change; and when a plate of silver has a thin layer of iodine and bromine on its surface, and is placed in a camera, so soon as the screen is raised the image of the sitter falls on the plate. The silver plate is acted on unequally, producing the effects of light and shade when *brought out*, as it is termed, by exposure to the vapor of quick-silver. It is then fixed, or prevented from undergoing further change, by washing it with a solution of gold.

To produce a daguerreotype picture, there are five operations necessary. The first is cleaning the plate. This is the stumbling-block of most operators. They are not cleanly enough. Several views in this Exhibition show that the plates were not well enough cleaned. Never was a maxim more true than the old one, that "cleanliness is a virtue"—when it has reference to daguerreotyping. The second is the formation of the sensitive iodide of silver over the surface of the plate. The third is the adjusting the plate in the camera obscura, for the purpose of receiving the impression. The fourth is the bringing out the photographic picture, which is invisible when the plate is taken from the camera. The fifth, and last, is to remove the excess of sensitive coating, and thus prevent that susceptibility to change under luminous influence which would otherwise exist and ultimately efface the picture. The second operation is that which gives tone and warmth to the picture, and when performed by skillful hands, makes a daguerreotype a beautiful piece of art. The clearness and distinctness of the image is produced by the third process, when carefully conducted, and the whole picture should be distinct over the whole plate. These remarks will serve to illustrate the subjoined notes upon the collections in the Exhibition.

Mr. Lawrence exhibits a case in which softness of tone and distinctness of image are united with artistic arrangement. The latter quality is specially noticeable in "The Three Ages." The mechanical execution of these pictures is unexcelled. These pictures of Mr. L. were exhibited in London. Mr. Brady's collection is not very large, but there are a few very good pictures exhibited by him. In Gurney's collection the coloring of the back-ground has a fine effect; there are some very well executed portraits, among which is one of Mr. Forrest, worth notice as a work of art; taken as a whole, there is less softness and more distinctness in this collection than in that of Lawrence.

The picture of Ware and his sister is an instance of a picture well developed when the chemical action extends to the margin of the plate. The collection of Meade Brothers, taken as a whole, is fair, there being great variety in the display, and some pictures of merit. The portrait of Daguerre, in this collection, is the only one of the kind in this country, having been taken by one of the exhibitors when in France, in 1848. Shakespeare's "Seven Ages" are illustrated on as many plates, taken from life. The earlier pictures of this series are better conceived than the later ones, especially those representing the Soldier and the Lover. The Meades have also a number of heads on the largest-sized plates; some Daguerreotypes colored to resemble miniatures on ivory; and what are termed by them Instantaneous Daguerreotypes. These do not possess any remarkable merit. We perceive in Brady's collection some well-selected heads, among which are two of President Pierce and one of Lieut. Maury. M. A. Root has a large and respectable collection now on view, among which are many specimens of his Crayon Daguerreotypes.

D. Clark, New-Brunswick, N. J., has four pictures of merit; and Van Schneidan a small collection of well-selected heads. J. Brown has a collection of portraits of Commodore Perry and the officers of the squadron of the Japan Expedition, in half-sized plates; the interest of this collection is much marred by the names of the officers not being attached underneath the plate; it is not too late to rectify this omission. Haas has a whole-plate allegorical figure of a family man reading the paper at home—an excellent idea and well executed. Besides this, he has a couple of other pictures, though on the whole his show is mediocre. In the cases of Harrison & Hill there is displayed excellent artistic arrangement with very indifferent mechanical execution. In the mammoth plates occupied by allegorical designs, the back-ground is wretchedly brought out—the plates were not properly cleaned, and are full of scratches; there are a few half and whole-sized pictures set in gaudy frames.

Webster, of Louisville, Ky., has twenty-three pictures, possessing clearness. They have, however, been exposed a little too much to the camera; they lack warmth, but are otherwise well developed, and exhibit good mechanical execution. Alexander Hesler has a collection of whole plates handsomely executed, possessing a nice arrangement of the drapery, which has the effect of throwing the head out in good relief. There is artistic arrangement in this collection, especially evinced in the picture "Driving a Trade," one of a series illustrating character and passion. The panoramic views of Galena, Ill., show that city to advantage; and the three views of the Falls of St. Anthony possess great merit. Mr. North, of Cleveland, O., has a case of pretty fair likenesses, perhaps exhibiting the lights too strongly. Bisbee, of Dayton, O., exhibits a panoramic view of Cincinnati from Newport, upon six large plates. This view is, without exception, the finest thing in the whole room; we might even go further, and say that it is the finest view by the Daguerrean process ever exhibited. The mechanical execution is excellent, the perspective good, and the development unsurpassed. The effect of the smoke over the southern part of the city is very finely given. The distinctness of the letter-signs, three-quarters of a mile distant and across the Ohio river, is well brought out. The rest of the collection is fair, possessing no peculiar merit. Williamson exhibits a poor collection. Dobyn, Richardson & Co. have several whole-size, well-executed specimens, in which the mechanical part, the artistic arrangement, and the chemical effect, are good. The "Cupid Reposing" is a very ungraceful posture of an ill-formed child, and the coloring is bad. That of the Bateman Children, in character, is a good picture. There are some exceedingly well-executed heads in this collection.

Long, of St. Louis, has four frames of one hundred and eighty heads of Wyman's School, in that city, with the edifice and principal; they possess no merit. A likeness of Prof. Mitchell, Cincinnati, is well executed. Some of the pictures in this collection are invested with papier mache frames inlaid with mother-of-pearl and tinsel. As this style of frame appears in a few other collections, we may as well here express our dissent from the use of this material, as being too gaudy and wholly unsuitable for daguerreotype plates. These latter are difficult to be viewed except in one light, and from the brightness of their surface, are much set off by deadened color on the frames, while the glare and iridescence of the papier mache add to the difficulty of discerning the picture; the use of such implies bad taste in the artist. We felt this opinion growing upon us as we looked at them, and felt our view corroborated by a boarding-school miss, who whisked alongside of us, and, caught by the colors, exclaimed, "Oh my! aint those *frames* beautiful?" Fitzgibbon has the richest exposition in the Fair—the most expensive frames, with a large and passable collection. The mammoth plate of Judge Colt is very good—that of Jenny Lind the best in the Exhibition—those of McAllister, Julia Dean, Kate Hayes, and Kossuth, are good pictures. His collection of Indian Warriors is a very fine one, which we understand is to be forwarded to the Ethnological Society of London, to have copies and busts made from them. Masury and Silsbee, Boston, exhibit twelve very pretty and tasteful plates, with good arrangement, and well finished. The collections of Kilsey, Beals, and Howe, do not require notice. Whitehurst has a few good pictures in a large and passable collection; he has ten pictures illustrating the Falls of Niagara, which are very well executed. Some of his large heads have their features out of all proportion. Whipple, of Boston, has a collection of photographic pictures, which he calls Crystallotypes, taken from hyalotypes; there are a plate of the moon daguerreotyped, and one of the spots on the sun. McDonnell & Co., Buffalo, have a very poor collection—so poor as not to deserve a place in the Exhibition; the views of Niagara are fine. Hawkins exhibits photographs on paper. Drummond, eight plates of the Order of Freemasons in their lodge dress. Fitzgibbon (already noticed) exhibits a very interesting case, which is a frame of electrotype copies from daguerreotype plates, very beautifully executed. It should not be looked upon as a mere curiosity to place a daguerreotype plate in a copper solution and take a copper cast from its surface by means of electricity: the copper cast looks much warmer in tone than the original. It is to be regretted that Fitzgibbon did not complete this frame by the insertion of a third plate, by taking a second copy from the copper copy. This would be in relief, like the original silver-plate, and is susceptible of being treated like an engraved plate, yielding, when inked, prints resembling mezzotint. Beside the above collection of daguerreotypes, there is an assortment of cameras, lenses, stereoscopes, and photographic paper, which are of interest to those practicing these beautiful arts.

XVIII.

HATS.

In one of the principal arms of the Greek cross which describes the architectural form of the Crystal Palace, and immediately facing the entrance from the Sixth-Avenue, stands a monument of ambitious proportions and cunning detail, which overshadows in its pretensions, and in the importance of the locality assigned to it, most of the other objects in our Exhibition. The *exegi monumentum* of the Latin poet has so evidently suggested the conception and presided over the execution of this remarkable structure, that we should be wanting in duty as chroniclers of the glories of our industrial Pantheon were we to postpone examining the merits of the particular manufacture which this Temple of Fashion is designed to illustrate.

Smile not, ye worshipers of those refined arts which advanced the early republics of Greece and Rome to such a high degree of civilization. Sneer not, ye connoisseurs in Sevres tea cups and Dresden monstrosities. Bow down your heads reverentially, ye carvers in wood and workers in base metals, as ye pass this imposing fane, enduring monument of an ambition which, if we judge from the emblems by which it is crowned, would fain soar into the heavens and "cap" even the globe itself. Its architectural order may be somewhat too composite for your taste—its contents too familiar to excite your wonder—the reputation of its owner too much associated with previous feats of self-illustration to enlist your attention; but you would do well to remember that this man is a perfect type of the proverbial energy and enterprise of his country, and that he has done more to contribute toward its material prosperity by the extent and importance of his operations, than scores of the art-imitators who hold up their heads so high and turn up their noses so scornfully at a success which their incapacity forbids their achieving.

The professional critic must not, however, run away with the notion that the simple articles of every-day use, to the exhibition of which this pretentious looking temple is devoted, are in themselves unworthy of the prominent place which in its wisdom the Executive Committee has allotted to them. In all ages, in proportion as intellectual superiority has been appreciated, a significant importance seems to have been attached to the protection of the organ whence it was derived. It would seem, even, that the hat itself borrows something of the peculiar idiosyncrasy of the wearer. Thus, for instance, its firm set on the head is considered to indicate determination—its depression over the brows, pugnacity—its retreat from the forehead, carelessness—its jaunty inclination to the right or left *rouerie*—and its rough and negligent condition, slovenliness. What an important part does it play, too, in the courtesies of life? The relative degrees of respect and social consideration are in no other action more accurately defined than in the manner in which it is employed in the amenities of daily intercourse. In its nice adaptation to the necessities of the moment, the prejudices of rank are conciliated and the reverence due to age becomingly rendered. With women there is no surer passport to favor than its graceful introduction in those subtle evolutions which constitute in their eyes the test of gentle breeding. Of all nations the French are perhaps the most skilled in the use of the hat. In the air of profound respect with which a Parisian exquisite instantaneously uncovers on meeting a lady, and in the negligent grace of the position into which he throws himself as he balances it tenderly between the forefinger and thumb of his accurately gloved hand we recognize the very perfection of the *savoir faire.* He is so impressed with the advantages of the self-possession and concentration of ideas which its aid affords him that he carries it with him into the *salon*, and entrenches himself behind it as a species of breastwork. When his fair enemy's batteries are carried, he cautiously emerges from its protection and ventures on a sortie which secures a truce for the remainder of the visit.

What an infallible index, too, does the physical condition of the hat afford to the position and circumstances of its owner! The wholesome faith in this now generally received fact, makes men who are disposed to be slovenly exceedingly careful in this particular. It is an axiom in the economy of dress, that a gentleman may, without derogating from his social position, indulge in the luxury of an old coat, provided always that he complies with the cardinal conditions of a glossy hat, spotless linen and well-fitting gloves and boots. If you are too independent to submit to these conventional trammels, present yourself, by way of experiment, under the *debris* of a napless beaver, to one of those favored mortals whom luck, rather than merit, has placed within the category of the Upper Ten. The most sensible man is so apt to be swayed by external appearances, that it is next to certain that he will button up his breeches pocket and meet you with the uncharitable judgment of Pindar:

> "A rusty hat seems to contain
> A skull quite destitute of brain."

Why even the very porter at his door will measure you contemptuously from head to foot, and if he has a dog, there are ten chances to one that the aristocratic cur will fly at your legs and render your condition still more ruinous. With man and beast, the *date obolum* seems an inevitable conclusion from a faded hat.

That the fashion of the hat may convey a political meaning, the records not only of past but of our own times will show. Numberless instances might be cited of the important part which it played in the political troubles of both England and France, and we need only refer to the reign of Charles I. as a proof of the powerful influence which it exercised in keeping alive the bitterness and exasperation of the great parties which were then struggling for the mastery. Even within our own recollection, the Calabrian hat became not only the badge of a party, but an object of proscription to the tyrants of Italy. The cock of a revolutionary beaver was more feared by them than the click of a musket. To the credit of the French despot be it said that, if he has deprived the Socialist of every other privilege, he has not attempted to deprive him of this harmless means of vindicating his opinions.

With the assumption of a superior moral condition, the fashion of the hat has been also somewhat oddly associated. Previous even to the formation of the sect which has adopted as one of the cardinal points of its creed an unusual expanse of beaver, the Tartuffes and Cantwells of scenic representations were similarly distinguished. Why a more elevated phase of our spiritual nature should be indicated by an acre of brim, is, however, a question of too metaphysical a nature to be discussed within the limits of the present article.

We think we have said enough to prove that, independent of its material uses, there is a moral significancy in our subject.

Let us now view it in its commercial bearings, and see whether it justifies the importance we attach to it.

The public generally are so little acquainted with the material employed in the manufacture of the hat, and are so disposed to take in trust the assurances of the maker as to its quality, that a few details explanatory of both may prove useful to the uninitiated. The materials used for making hats are, beside silk, the fur of hares and rabbits, chosen from the long hair, together with wool, and beaver, and nutria. The finer descriptions of hats were formerly made of beaver, but since the introduction of "water-proofing," it is found unnecessary to use so valuable a material in the foundation. The body of a beaver hat is now made of fine wool and coarse fur, mixed and felted together, then stiffened and shaped; the "napping" or covering of the best hats consists of a mixture of *cheek* beaver, with white and brown stage beaver, or seasoned beaver, commonly called *wooms.* The inferior kinds are napped with mixtures of stage-beaver, nutria, hare-fur, wool, and musquash. Silk hats are made from silk plush or shag, and, owing to the improvements introduced into their manufacture in late years, have grown into favor. The cane and willow framework formerly used in them imparted to them a hard appearance and feel, which was often attended with great discomfort to the wearer. This has been obviated by the use of beaver, silk, and muslin foundations, and the consequence has been, that a greater impulse has been given to this branch of the trade. One of the most important improvements, however, which has been introduced into hat manufacture is that of "water-proofing" the bodies previous to their being napped. The elastic properties of the gums used in this process, when dissolved in pure alcohol or naptha, imparts a body to the materials which enables the maker to reduce a considerable proportion of their weight.

As an illustration of the value of this improvement, we may mention that, about twenty years since, ninety-six ounces of stuff were worked up into one dozen ordinary-sized hats for gentlemen, while at present from thirty-three to thirty-four ounces only are required to complete the same quantity. Felt hats and *cordies* are the coarsest species of the manufacture, being made wholly of inferior wools. Cordies are, however, distinguished by a fine covering of camel or goat-hair. It is a singular fact, that the *petasus* of the ancients was identical, both in material and form, with the common felt hat worn by agricultural laborers at the present day. We must not, however, wander into the classical literature of the hat, seeing that it has been exhausted in some of the professional *brochures* of our New York dealers.

As regards the machinery used in the process of manufacture, we may as well take this opportunity of stating that no trade has benefited less by the labors of the inventor. There are two causes for this. In the first place, many of the operations are of so delicate a nature that manipulation can hardly be dispensed with; and in the second, such improvements as have been effected have met with determined opposition on the part of the workmen. This is the case not only here but in England; and in fact the balance of liberality lies with us. Some few years since, an American named Williams, invented a machine for forming hat-bodies. It economizes half the labor previously expended in this operation, and at least three-fourths of the hat-bodies made in this country are formed by it. The attempt to introduce it into general use in England proved a failure, owing to the opposition of the body-makers, who refused to assist in the necessary process, termed *basining*. It is now only used by the English in the preparations of the shells required for silk hats. A machine has also been invented by a Frenchman for shaping the brims; but it is very little used here, although it is very effective, and can do the work of five men.

It is a curious fact that the oval form now given to hats is of comparatively recent introduction; dating, we believe, not more than twenty years back. Previous to that time, round blocks were employed, and the head of the wearer, to its great discomfort, was left to perform the task of accommodating the hat to its proper shape.

There is no manufacture, perhaps, which confers more general benefits on the communities situated in the immediate neighborhood of its operations, from the opportunities which it affords for the employment of both the males and females, and sometimes of the children, of a family. In other countries, the children may be advantageously employed in plucking the beaver skins, cropping off the fur, sorting various qualities of wool, plucking and cutting rabbits' fur, shearing the nap of the blocked hat, picking out unseemly filaments of fur, and even trimming—that is to say, binding and lining the hat. As most, if not all, the materials imported into the United States arrive here ready prepared, but few opportunities are afforded here for the employment of children. We do not, of course, include in this classification apprentices, whose ages range from 14 to 20. In England and on the continent of Europe, the depression of the finer branches of the manufacture has affected considerably the earnings of the workmen engaged in them, as a less amount of skill and labor is required in the production of silk hats than beavers; and the increased quantity produced in the lower description, has not furnished an amount of employment equivalent to the decrease in the higher branch. With us, this tendency towards the use of an inferior and more economical article, has not been so much felt, owing to a variety of causes, the principal of which is no doubt the greater comfort and prosperity of our working classes.

As no certain data exist, on which a correct estimate can be formed of the value of the different branches of the manufacture, or of their aggregate amount, we have taken the trouble to collect the following particulars, which, though not from official sources, may be relied upon as tolerably accurate:

HATTERS' MATERIALS—ANNUAL IMPORTS.

560,000 yards of Silk Plush (French), at an average cost of $2 per yard,..$1,120,000

The above amount of plush will make 1,120,000 hats, worth at retail $4,480,000.

90,000 yards of Silk Plush (German), at an average of $1 38 per yard,.. 121,000

This amount will make 180,000 hats, worth at retail $540,000.

800,000 yards of Angola Cotton Plush (French and German), at $1 per yard,.. 800,000

2,400,000 hats can be manufactured out of the above quantity, worth at retail, at $1 25 each, $3,000,000.

Coney and Hare's Furs, imported from France and Germany,....1,000,000

These materials are used for the bodies of hats and the making of California and soft hats. About 4,000,000 of these latter descriptions of hats are made annually in this country. At an average of $1, they will make $4,000,000.

Amount of other goods used by hatters, such as linings, bindings, bands, &c., the greater part of which are imported,.......... 2,100,000

TOTAL.

	HATS.	VALUE.
Men's Silk Hats, 1st quality,..................	1,120,000	$4,480,000
Men's Silk Hats, 2d quality,..................	180,000	540,000
Men's Silk Hats, 3d quality,..................	2,400,000	3,000,000
Men's California or Soft Hats,..................	4,000,000	4,000,000
Men's and Boys' Caps,..................	4,000,000	3,000,000
Total..................	11,700,000	$15,020,000

In the manufacture of the above there are 24,000 persons employed, one half of them are men and the remainder women.

The consumption of Straw Hats amounts to about 1,500,000, about half of which are imported. The average value is $1 50 each hat.

The capital invested in the Hatting Trade in this country is little short of $8,000,000.

One of the most singular features of the competition induced by exhibitions like the present, is the struggle to elicit new ideas from common-place materials, or by a high-sounding nomenclature to impart importance to objects that would otherwise fail to arrest the attention. In the manufacture of hats, this latter peculiarity assumes an amusing character, from the extremes to which it is carried, while it also serves to atone for the lack of interest resulting from that uniformity of material and style to which it has been reduced by the absurd canons of modern taste. If, therefore, we occasionally fall into a train of reflections suggested by the grotesque images presented to our minds, the exhibitor must take it in good part if our impressions do not always coincide with the effect which he seeks to produce.

Selecting rather with a view to the gratification of the whim of the moment than with reference to the superior quality of the articles exhibited, let us commence our task by an inspection of that small case belonging to Amidon, of Broadway. Within the narrow compass of that glass inclosure, are contained objects whose features are familiar to our recollection and names that occupy a large space in the revolutionary annals of our day. We might incline to the belief that in the choice of his models are worthy French *concitoyens* intended at once to glorify the country of his birth and flatter the political tastes of the country of his adoption, were it not for the infelicitous association with them of one of the great historic titles of France—a name, too, deservedly dear to the English aristocracy. If hats only possessed a share of the susceptibilities of their owners, we cannot help thinking how strangely uncomfortable these cylindrical eccentricities would feel in such close propinquity to each other. But let us proceed with our examination. In that "baseless fabric" of rabbit's fur and plush, which occupies the peg in the corner, were conceived vast designs and ambitious hopes, which ended in the overthrow of a dynasty, and the ruin of the republic that succeeded it. Many a time have we seen that remarkable beaver, uplifted in the energy of passionate declamation to stir the hearts of the masses that thronged the Hotel de Ville, or to stimulate into frenzy the volcanic elements that were seething and foaming in the bosom of the National Assembly. Every thump of that hat brought down with it either the thundering acclamations of the *Montagnards* or the tumultuous murmurs of the partisans of legitimist or imperial pretensions. And yet, in its conical inclination, modest brim, and trim compliance with the prevailing fashion of the day, we recognize rather the harmless foppishness of the *flâneur* than the restless energy and fierce impetuosity of the tribune. In the unusual width of the crown, however, the phrenological observer will detect that large cerebral development, which would negative the conclusions to which these appearances might otherwise lead. As you contemplate that hat, you would do well to reflect upon the instability of human greatness, and the vanity and emptiness of all things mundane. Its owner is now an exile and a wanderer, like the family of the monarch whom he helped to expel. He that directed the foreign affairs of France, and stretched the vigorous arm of her power to the uttermost confines of the earth, either to protect her children or to vindicate her rights, cannot now lay claim even to the anomalous title of a French citizen, or look forward to a last resting-place beneath that maternal sod which consigns to oblivion our virtues and our faults. Uncover! You look upon the hat of Ledru Rollin!

In appropriate juxtaposition with this interesting relic, and towering above it in the majesty of its proportions, hangs that unmistakable and formidable beaver, whose daily appearance in the streets of revolutionary Paris inspired such hopes and fears among the timid, and served as a rallying-point to the bold. In the unparalleled audacity of its style, we can read at a glance the character of that celebrated *commis-voyageur*, who contrived to create an *imperium in imperio* of the Prefecture of Police, and to frighten the wits out of the Executive Government. Combining the high *bombé* crown of the Empire with the broad, oval, deeply gimped brim of the D'Orsay epoch, exaggerated to alarming proportions, its first aspect overwhelms one with astonishment, succeeded by feelings of respect and admiration for the hardy spirit which had the genius to conceive, and the courage to wear such an unique superstructure of felt. We can readily conceive the enthusiasm with which this glorious creation was said to have been regarded by his *Montagnard followers*, from the effect which it had upon ourselves. It was a feeling somewhat analogous to that which Belzoni must have experienced on beholding the head of his first sphinx, or Layard that of his winged bull. We no longer wondered that the physical development indicated by such colossal proportions should have struck such terror into the multitude, or that it should have sated its ambition only in the chair of the Prefect of Police. If the statue of Caussidière be worthy of a niche in the Temple of Fame, surely that of the hatter, who helped to build him into greatness, is deserving of some slight inscription on its pedestal.

Passing from great things to small, but still consistently adhering to revolutionary models, we will next examine that smart-looking little *tuyau de poêle*, inscribed with the name of Felix Pyat, orator and writer, known to us only by some trifling efforts. The hat and the reputation seem to have a sort of natural relation to each other. It is not a hat like that of Caussidière, which is destined to leave its impress upon the age, and, therefore, we will not waste our time before it.

We now come to that well-known beaver, the admiration of aristocratic belles, and the envy of aristocratic beaux, which so long formed the capital of that Corinthian pillar of European dandyism, Count D'Orsay. With what inimitable grace have we seen that hat manœuvred by its handsome wearer, as he caracoled his beautiful Arabian through the complexities of the ring in Hyde-Park, thronged as it was with carriages filled with the smiling and approving beauties of Belgravia. With what feelings of pride and exultation have we seen a certain literary Peeress watch the evolutions of her accomplished cavalier, as he pranced by the side of her splendid equipage, exchanging graceful salutations with the fair daughters of the nobility, or bestowing a friendly nod of recognition on some humble pedestrian on the foot-path, whose only claim to his notice was the possession of some literary or artistic talent. And, with Count D'Orsay, no title was paramount to this. With generous sympathies, and an enlarged and cultivated mind, he knew how to reconcile the conventional trammels which his high position imposed upon him with the warm interest which he felt in the unrewarded struggles of genius. In him, the artist and the man of letters found not only a sincere friend, but a munificent patron, ever ready to make sacrifices of his time and his purse to the calls which his well-deserved reputation entailed upon him. With the multitude, to whom he was known only by his exquisite taste for dress, he passed only for a fit successor to that selfish and cynical beau who had enslaved the tastes and perverted the hearts of the previous generation. In the circles in which he moved, however, and more especially amid that large class of scientific and artistic minds, which may be said to comprehend the real intelligence and society of the English metropolis, he was valued as much for his mental acquirements as for his noble and generous impulses. A writer, painter, and sculptor, himself, he was recognized and received in that brotherhood of the arts as one of the most successful of their votaries. When we consider the time that he frittered away in the frivolous pursuits of fashionable life, we cannot help admiring the industry which he must have practiced to keep pace with the inspirations of his genius. With more moral worth than the celebrated Villiers, Duke of Buckingham, he resembled him in the versatility of his arguments, and in the facility with which he could pass from the most serious occupations to the *persiflage* of the dinner-table or ball-room. A close student, and an indefatigable artist, he would always bring into society a mind unclouded by severe application, and sparkling with the suggestions of a refined wit and lively imagination. No man could be more brilliant or *enjoué* in female society; none could be more serious and interested in that of the learned circles in which he frequently mixed. Like la Rochefoucauld, he appeared to owe his extraordinary quickness of perception and knowledge of character rather to a gift of nature than to the results of observation and study. Had he been divested of those advantages of fortune and position, which in the early part of his career served to relax his energies, and to take from him all motives for exertion, he must have risen to an eminence that would have thrown these adventitious circumstances into the shade, and secured him an enduring reputation. As it was, the latter years of his life manifested a consciousness that his time had been misspent, and that he was capable of achieving a higher destiny than he had hitherto attained. He began to withdraw himself gradually from the seductive influences of the society which had possessed such a charm for his youth, and to devote himself assiduously to those more serious and ennobling pursuits to which the philosophical constitution of his mind naturally inclined him. His end, painful and melancholy as it was, was still consistent with those lofty qualities which redeemed the few serious blemishes of his character. While we can afford to pass over in charitable silence the one, it gratifies our feelings to render justice to the other; and, as we look upon this memento of his follies, disinterred from oblivion by the enterprise of an aspiring hatter, we cannot help exclaiming with the sorrowing Dane, "Alas! poor Yorick!"

A short time since, there was some talk of a patent having been solicited for a curious application of the Daguerreotype, the idea of which seems to have been borrowed from the Egyptian custom of delineating the features of the dead on the cere-cloth which encased the mummy. It was proposed by the inventor to affix Daguerreotype likenesses of deceased persons to the lids of the coffins, but the undertakers seem to have anticipated the notion by a simple contrivance—namely, that of inserting a glass window over the face of the corpse, and thus exposing the features themselves to view. The ingenious hatters of our city could not fail to profit by the suggestion thus thrown out; and accordingly Messrs. Rafferty & Leask, of Chatham-street, have hastened to present the Exhibition with a case of hats, whose chief attraction seems to be the insertion of a Daguerreotype likeness of the wearer in the lining of the crown. It is scarcely necessary for us to point out the manifold advantages and uses of this interesting novelty. Beside the gratification which it must afford our self-esteem to contemplate at will features so dear to us, we shall no longer be exposed to the risk of being the victims of those confused notions of *meum* and *tuum* which seem to prevail among diners-out and ball-goers on the subject of hats and umbrellas. The least favored by Nature will be the most likely to be benefited by this arrangement; inasmuch as, however convenient a difficulty of identification in the property of the hat may be at present to certain smart young fellows, it would never do to have any doubt existing as to the identity of the portrait. True, the security thus obtained, as regards one sex, will be in some degree counterbalanced by an obvious danger arising from the other. We are afraid that the innovation will create a new species of petty larceny which our laws will be unable to reach, as no owner of the article abstracted will be inclined to prefer an indictment against the offender. Even this evil, however, will be attended with its advantages; as ladies will now be unable to possess themselves of these "counterfeits" of the objects of their desires without compromising themselves in their eyes by asking for them. To persons who dislike being disturbed by troublesome visitors, the benefit arising from the new system will be incalculable. By an inspection of the hats in our hall, we can at once determine whether it would be either agreeable or convenient for us to make our appearance in the parlor. If our space permitted it, we might cite a hundred other instances to prove that this invention entitles Messrs. Rafferty & Leask to rank among the benefactors of humanity.

What elaborate inscription is that which we see crowding the base of that tall show-case, which bears on its summit the triumphal flourish, Leary & Co., *Leaders* "and introducers of Fashions for Gentlemen's Hats?" A bold preface that! But, after all, there is nothing like being one's own trumpeter. None but fools will, in this age of smartness and progress, be content to await the verdict of a dull and undiscerning public. Man must now clear at a bound the path to Fame—that difficult and thorny steep, which used to cost so much toil and patience to ascend, or he will be left behind like a miserable laggard, to plod on and sweat and die in his harness. There is no danger that your modesty will keep you back in the race, Messrs. Leary! You comprehend the spirit of the age; and you seem determined not only to be on a level with it, but to rise above it. Let us now look at the inscription: "These hats are entered for exhibition and "competition, and are samples of our manufactures in silk and "fur. We have affixed to each the price for which duplicates "are daily sold at our counters, in their appropriate season. De- "precating the use of material whose only claim to notice is its "excessive cost, we have confined ourselves strictly to that hourly "used in our make-shops, combining a standard of excellence in "their production, workmanship, utility, cheapness, and adapta- "tion to home markets, together with beauty of design and other "elements of merit, commending them to public notice and pa- "tronage." The pen of criticism falls powerless from our grasp before this Io Pean of self-glorification. It puts an extinguisher upon genius and knocks Phalon into a cocked hat (excuse the vulgarism—the simile is in place). These munificent patrons of the penny-a-liner and bill-sticker have had the good taste to leave their broad sheets and paste-pots at the door of the Exhibition, contenting themselves with the laconic but significant *circumspice* of Sir Christopher Wren. In the greatness of their works they hope to live. Not so the Messrs. Leary. "Leaders and introducers of fashion," they have thriven so long on the mutability of human taste that they evidently fear it will turn round upon them and play them some slippery trick at last. Summoned into a new arena of competition, they enter the ring with doubts and misgivings, which they endeavor to drown in a flourish of trumpets and a proclamation of their past achievements. It won't do, gentlemen! This is to be a fair, stand-up fight, with a clear field and no favor. We care nothing about your antecedents. The best man here is he that can prove his skill!

We believe that we have now touched upon all the salient points of this feature of the Exhibition. We have not attempted to enter into a comparison of the qualities of the productions of the different houses, for the simple reason that we should only get laughed at for our pains. With an article that can only be judged of by the touch, and that accurately, only by a person in the trade, it would not only be absurd, but unjust, toward the manufacturers, were we to pretend to criticise them through the plates of the jealously locked glass-cases in which they are exposed.

There are twenty-two exhibitors of hats and caps from different parts of the Union. The New-York contributors are Messrs. Beebe, Genin, Leary, Warnock, Knox & James, Amidon, Espenscheid, Kellogg, Alles, Freeman, Small & Co., Rafferty & Leask, Beaudin, Mealio, Todd, Cowly, Baker, Vesnock, and Grosset & Degan.

The display of military hats and regulation caps is very creditable to the makers who have devoted themselves to this department of the business. Beaudin has a regulation hat mounted on a spring, which reduces it when pressed down to about half its height—a great convenience in a theatre or concert-room, but scarcely advisable, we should think, when blows are more plentiful than compliments.

The fashions for hats are not, as is generally supposed, imported, but are got up by the leading houses, such as Beebe's, Leary's, Genin's and Knox's, with of course some slight reference to the styles prevailing in Paris. There is no article, perhaps, in which so much deception can be practised as in the hat, owing to the difficulty which the uninitiated find in applying any test to its qualities but that of wear. As a proof of this, we may mention that the Jews are in the habit of selling hats that only cost them twelve shillings for $3 and $5 each.

In addition to the statistics of the trade already given, we may state that the number of body-makers in New-York is almost three hundred; of finishers one hundred; of curlers and shapers two hundred; and of trimmers four hundred. There is no branch of industry in which the rates of wages are so fluctuating; no trade reflecting so faithfully the depressed or prosperous condition of the country. The journeymen generally work by the piece. Body-makers, although they only earn six dollars some weeks, can in others make as much as thirty. Finishers make from ten to twenty, and shapers and curlers from fifteen to thirty dollars a week. There are between fifty and sixty finishing-shops in New-York. There is no general understanding between the shops as to a fixed scale of wages, each establishment regulating its own scale of payment. It is a peculiarity of this trade that a person seeking employment never addresses himself to the principal; he goes direct to the foreman, and if there is room for him, if he belongs to the Association, he is immediately engaged. The rules of the body are very stringent; but some of the manufacturers, such, for instance, as Genin, have broken through them, and continue to carry on their trade successfully in despite of the efforts made to deprive them of their hands.

XIX.

FLAX AND ITS MANUFACTURES.

Above three thousand years ago, when all Europe was enveloped in Cimmerian darkness, the manufactures of the fine linen of Egypt were imported into that Continent. By a curious reverse, a country the least advanced toward the comforts of civilization, now sends its fine linens to all corners of the globe. If there be any one manufacture in which Ireland is able to come into the market of the world without fear of competition, it is in the growth and manufacture of Flax. Its introduction into that island forms an apt illustration of the manner in which it has been governed. It was once said of the people of Halifax, England, who lived then, as now, by the manufacture of Woolens, that they had an inordinate estimate of themselves and their produce, and that if they were asked what was the greatest crime which a man could commit, and whether was it treason or parricide? their ready answer would be, neither of those, but the *importation* of Wool. The whole people of England must have been of this opinion in the reign of William III., when Ireland had, from the peculiar advantages which her climate gives her, increased the number of her sheep, and the quality of their wool to such an extent, that she could undersell the English in their own markets. A deputation of growers and manufacturers of wool waited on the monarch, and laid at his feet their complaint, that they could not grow wool against Ireland. The answer was short and to the point: "Gentlemen, I will speedily remedy all that;" and, when Parliament met, a heavy duty was laid on all wool and woolens from Ireland. This was a severe blow to the prosperity of the sister isle, and ultimately changed her industry from the growth of Wool, for which she is peculiarly favored by nature, to that of Flax, whose growth is the result of excessive labor.

9

Deprived of the woolen trade by the edict of 1695, Irish industry had no other vent than in the cultivation of Flax, a plant which had been introduced, half a century before, by Lord Strafford, then Lord Deputy, who ruled the country with that tyranny which ultimately brought his head to the block, and who boasted of his rule, "that he made the King as absolute in Ireland as any prince in the whole world could be." The flax-plant has now been cultivated in Ireland two hundred and twenty years, and is still on the increase. Having heretofore been confined to the northern province of the island, it has, since 1849, been extended south and west. It will grow on any soil, but requires high manuring, and in good soil the yield is more abundant. As to most plants, the presence of lime in the ground stimulates their growth. Such is the case with madder and all the cereal grains; but the flax-plant, on the contrary, is injured by that mineral, and should the ground be fresh-limed, the growth of flax will have to be omitted for a rotation.

The Scotchman sings that "Corn rigs are bonny," but a pleasanter sight the eye scarcely lights upon than an extensive field of flax fully grown and in flower. The graceful green stem, lanceolate leaves and convolvulus-like blue flower, present a graceful contrast. It is gathered when in seed, and thus a double crop is raised off the one plant, viz., the flax-seed or lin-seed and the fibre from the stem. This, however, is bad practice; one or the other ought to be sacrificed; and it is so by those who raise a fine article; for the younger the plant, the more delicate are the spiral vessels which constitute the flax fibre. Hence the practice of sowing thick, by which the plant shoots up and forms but little wood, and the advantage of high manuring, which starts the plant forward very rapidly. Cultivated thus for the fibre, and not for the seed, it is a profitable crop. There are in Ireland one hundred and twenty-five thousand acres under flax, and the produce is about thirty-seven thousand five hundred tons, of an average value of two hundred and fifty dollars per ton; this gives about sixty-two dollars for the usual produce of the statute acre. The value of the crop depends entirely on the care taken of the fibre.

Flax employs a number of hands in its manufacture. Thus three acres, properly managed, will produce one hundred and twenty stone, (fourteen pounds each,) which will realize to the farmer four hundred and fifty dollars. Suppose it is to be converted into cambric pocket-handkerchiefs, it may be spun to thirty hanks to the pound, and is usually spun by hand. This will employ one hundred and fifty-eight women for twelve months to spin it. Eighteen weavers are occupied in weaving it, and forty women in hem-stitching, or veining it, when made into kerchiefs; thus annually employing two hundred and ten persons, producing two hundred and ten webs of cambric, each containing five dozen handkerchiefs, each dozen worth twelve dollars; and the entire, when finished, thirteen thousand dollars. Were it not for this extreme profit, flax would not be grown, for it is one of the most exhausting of crops.

To separate the fibre from the flax, the plant has to undergo several processes. Pulled before the seeds are ripe, the latter are separated by *rippling*, or pulling the head of the plant through an iron comb. The stem is then *steeped*, to soften and separate the fibres easily, and to dissolve a gummy resin, which pastes the fibre to the bark. The introduction of Mr. Schenck's process (of this city) into Ireland was a great aid in facilitating the separation of the fibre. The plant is then bruised or *broken* by beating it with machinery. It is then passed through a mill with fluted cylinders, three in number, one of which is moved by power, and the others moved by it. This is termed *scutching*. By the two last processes, the fibre is wholly freed from the woody portion of the plant. In this state it is transferred to the mills, to be spun into thread for the seamstress and lace-maker, or into yarn for the weaver. Here, after being sorted, it is *heckled*, or combed by hand or machinery, until the fibres are all parallel and continuous, and the whole cleared from adhering matters. It is then again sorted, and afterward *drawn* into one sliver or band. This consists in twisting the fibres, which are about ten inches long, at the end, by which a continuous band or rope is obtained. The refuse of the heckling is *tow*. With this description in view, the samples of raw material in progress of manufacture, shown in Fenton, Son & Co.'s collection, will be one of the interesting features of the Exhibition.

When the yarn is spun, the flax manufacture terminates and that of linen commences. Although it is but recently that machinery has been applied to the weaving of flax, yet the largest factories in the world are occupied with this art. Marshall's, of Leeds, stands foremost, whose one-story factory covers two acres of ground, and had the largest room in the world until Crystal Palaces were raised. Richardson's at Guilford, Fenton's at Belfast, and the Mulholland's at the latter place, are also noteworthy. The goods of this last manufacture, and those of Marshall, Young & Lindsay, are missed from the British collection. Indeed, the Irish collection is very imperfect, and in no degree represents the industry of that country. This is chiefly due to the manufacturers not being able to learn clearly whether this Exhibition was a private or national affair; and, if the former, how far it would subserve their interests to exhibit—and perhaps due in a small extent to the Dublin Exhibition, which has occupied their attention.

The collection of Fenton, Son & Co., is chiefly in heavy linens, or those in which the yarn fibre is strong and thick. This is a class of goods, we believe, not extensively known in this country. A prize medal was obtained by this firm from the London Exhibition. There is also a fair collection of damasks and fine light linen, and an assortment of cambrics. In the same compartment is the collection of Richardson, who has two factories in the north of Ireland. The linens exhibited by this house are of the fine or light class, for which a prize medal was obtained. These light goods are exceedingly fine, and are well worth the inspection of importers and buyers. These linens are all grass-bleached, and the flax was rotted by the usual cold water process, and, whatever objection there may be in point of time, certainly no chemical treatment of the fibre could produce a more beautiful yarn than is in Richardson's goods.

Among damask goods, Richardson's table-cloths are gems in their way. One of these, measuring six yards by three and a half, is the most beautiful cloth our eyes, accustomed as they have been to linen goods, have ever seen. The damasking represents a tesselated centre, with vases resting on agricultural implements and surmounted by flowers; urns are at the corners, surrounded by wreaths, and the whole is bordered to the depth of two and a quarter feet, with intertwined shamrock, rose, and thistle, and inclosing the antique Irish emblems, the harp and wolf dog. This cloth was exhibited in the London Palace in an unbleached state, and has been bleached for exhibition here. A second table-cloth is also exhibited, which is seven and a half yards by two and a half. The linen in these cloths is very fine. The cases exhibited by Richardson contain light sheetings, housewife linen, fronting linen, and damask cloth. The-play of light in the lower part of the building interferes very much with the favorable exhibition of worked and fancy goods; instead of coming in one direction upon the articles, it breaks in on all sides, and produces lights and shadows independent of the work upon the goods. That part of the building which is darkened by the Reservoir would have been most appropriate for this class of articles.

The third collection of linens, is that of Dunbar, McMaster & Co., and Dunbar, Dickson & Co., under one head. This is a joint firm, with two manufactories, in one of which the flax as pulled is rotted and put through all the processes to convert it into thread and yarn, and then the latter is handed over to the second factory, where it is woven into linens, cambric, diaper, and damasks. The establishment thus takes the raw material from the farmer, and when it leaves the factories, it is the article ready for sale. This is unusual; generally, a manufacturer of flax goods is only so to a limited extent. Some take the raw flax and convert it into yarn, and then stop. Some take the yarn and weave it, and, when woven, bleach it; and some only take the unbleached woven cloth, bleach and calender it; but in Dunbar & Co.'s establishment all the departments are combined. It is necessarily a very large one, both in occupation of space and employment of individuals. There are three thousand people employed in both factories, and five thousand extra hands are out-doors; that is, employment of the latter number is given to cottiers round about in the weaving and finishing of the cloth; thus eight thousand people are dependent on this firm for support. The factory law of Ireland prevents children under the age of thirteen being employed with advantage, and schools are provided on the ground for the education of children up to that age, when they are taken into the factory to work; and adult schools are also in operation in winter evenings for the benefit of those more advanced. The wages paid by the firm amount to $300,000 per annum.

The collection of linen thread is very good, of assorted degrees of fineness and of all colors. Some of the samples are of remarkable fineness, eighty thousand yards being spun out of one pound. This is equal to forty-eight miles of linen thread spun out of one pound weight! Among Dickson's threads is one variety adapted for our sewing-machines, which are almost of an unlimited length, varying according to the number of the thread. Ordinary thread is unsuitable to sewing-machines, owing to the necessity of frequent junctions. The lengths of these are their recommendation, averaging eight thousand yards in one pound, or two thousand yards in a skein of continuous length, which weighs a quarter of a pound.

The sheetings exhibited by Dickson are of great dimensions, being thirteen quarters wide and without seam, of the class termed extra strong. Indeed, the collection of heavy linens by this firm is very fine—to which recommendation may be added the samples of bleached and unbleached family and fronting linens.

Among the products of Irish manufacture is the article poplin or tabbinet, of which there is a case exhibited by Messrs. Pim & Co., of Dublin. Poplin is a material whose weft is worsted and the warp silk. It is a fabric of great beauty, whose manufacture is confined almost exclusively to Dublin. In this department we miss the articles of Messrs. Fry & Atkinson, who manufacture more extensively than Pim. This exhibition, however, is a very fine one, embracing plain and watered double poplins, figured samples for dress and vestings, and poplin tartans, after the pattern of the different clans. There is a specimen of rich brocaded tissue poplin, which we recommend to the inspection of those ladies who delight in fine dress. The brilliant hue of the roses upon this cloth produces a beautiful effect.

The exposition of Irish lace by Higgins & Co. is beautiful in the extreme: lace, as the term implies, is a network of threads; it may be woven by hand or machine. When the thread is silk, it is silk net; when cotton, it is bobbin-net, and when of flax, it is the real *lace* of the last three centuries. The manufacture of lace by hand is one of the most tedious and least remunerating that woman ever engaged in, and the bobbin-net machine, one of the most complicated that man ever devised. Specimens of both are exhibited by Higgins. In the same case is also the skirt of a dress, worked with the needle. It is what is called Limerick lace, and is worth $400. The lace worked in Limerick is esteemed the best in the British Empire, ranking above that of Nottingham.

This notice comprises the Irish exposition of textile fabrics, unique and superior in their kind. We have not seen any Belgian linens on exhibition. Samples of the flax plant, in the various changes which it passes through until it is yarn, may be seen in Fenton's collection, alluded to above, and in a department near the south nave.

We miss from this Exhibition the flax cotton, flax velvet, flax flannel, and the other novelties of this manufacture, which have been brought into notice by Chevalier Claussen, of Brazil, and which adorned the London Exhibition.

The question of flax culture and manufacture in this country, is one which might now occupy the minds of business men. The price of Irish linens has gone up ten per cent., owing to the increased value of labor in that island. This increase will be permanent, at least for some years; and although farmers may not find it profitable to grow flax for the sake of the seed as now, yet when both bolls and fibre are in demand, the crop pays well.

XX.

WOOL AND WOOLLEN MANUFACTURES.

Ever since those good old times of patriarchal simplicity, when it is said

When Adam delved and Eve span—

when Man cultivated the soil and guarded his flocks, and Woman, with all her solicitude for the comfort of her consort, formed the first rude fabrics from the fleecy material so abundantly supplied by her petted companions, and when the wealth of a family was calculated according to the extent of its herds and its flocks, until the present time, the growth of wool and the production and improvement of cloth of various textures, have constituted one of the most important branches of ingenious pursuit and manufacturing enterprise. To compare the first results of spinning, weaving and knitting with what is now produced by the combination of skill and experience which so many ages have afforded, and to trace the progress of the manufacturing art from its earliest to its latest periods, would be both interesting and instructive; but in this country, where "onward" is the exhilarating word which inspires the actors in all departments of productive invention, we need only look so far backward as to find that which will add encouragement and force to our wish, that the progress of our country should be aided by past experience and based upon the rational deductions of scientific investigation.

The United States, in the space of a single century, furnish as great a diversity in the articles of dress, beginning with domestic spinning and weaving, and contrasting the result with the present productions of machinery, as can be found in exploring a thousand years of old-country practice and experience. Many of the early settlers of America necessarily commenced the world anew, and some of the most ancient customs, which had long been superseded in Europe, were here resorted to as the first alternatives, while the various stages of progress, which other countries had taken many ages to pass through, have been compressed into a few years; and we now find American manufactures in a condition to compete in many respects, with European fabrics, and all that is required in most instances is to remove the prejudices which exist in the minds of purchasers against home productions, and then we should have the demand for American goods so increased as to improve the condition of our own manufacturers, and enable them eventually to completely supply our own market. What we say is, give American manufacturers a fair chance; do not allow the old feeling that certain foreign countries are the only places where the best cloths can be made, to prevent our encouraging to the greatest possible extent the growing manufactories of our own country. Let it be remembered that most of the American manufacturers have had difficulties to encounter in the prosecution of their undertakings, such as would have disheartened men of merely ordinary courage. They have commenced in a small way with little or no capital; have struggled for years, endeavoring to equal the most favorite articles, and when they have accomplished their purpose, or nearly so, they are met at the merchants' store with the most approving remarks, followed by the very unprofitable appendage that the customers will have English, or French, or German goods—anything in fact rather than American productions. Here is a reward for years of ingenious toil! And what is the result? Why, prejudice is met by what is regarded as harmless deception. Goods made in America are packed up with English, French or German labels, and the fop who prides himself on his suit of French superfine cassimere or West-of-England broadcloth, and who has probably paid as much again for his cloth as would have satisfied the American manufacturer and merchant in the ordinary course of business, may, in many instances, congratulate himself that his country has so far progressed in the manufacture of these articles as to have deceived him, and perhaps his tailor too; and he is, after all, wearing what has never crossed the Atlantic or paid a shilling of customs duty.

What we want is, to raise a more generous appreciation of American manufactured articles, such as will render deception unprofitable. If a man has any patriotism in his heart or intelligence in his head, we think he ought rather to take the highest pleasure, not in wearing the productions of foreign countries, but in showing the excellence of those of his own. Increased demand always has the ultimate effect of lowering prices; and if the consumption of American goods were largely increased, there is no doubt that American manufacturers would be enabled so to increase their facilities as very materially to diminish the cost of production, while they would be able to devote more attention to those points of improvement, and to new branches of the trade, to which we are about to call their especial attention. It is therefore the interest of the consumer, as well as of the manufacturer, that these prejudices should give way before facts which the present Exhibition has brought more prominently before the public.

The English and French departments of the Exhibition are very scantily supplied with this description of goods; and had we no other opportunities afforded us of examining the productions of these countries, we might, from what is exhibited, be led to draw, in some respects, an unjust comparison. Whether it arises from a consciousness of superiority, such as defies competition, or an indifference as to the American trade, we know not; but certainly there appears to have been little or no effort on the part of foreign manufacturers to show their capabilities. The German States have sent a larger assortment than any other countries or states, but their display is more to be noted for variety and quantity than for any particular superiority in any of their productions. Russia has been assigned a place in the department of the German States, and is well represented by the productions of one manufacturer. Belgium, however, in a very unostentatious manner, has placed before us some of the finest broadcloths, combining, as it appears to us, all the points of excellence which are desirable to this important article of daily wear; and if the relative merits of the six nations, America, Great Britain, France, Germany, Russia, and Belgium, are to be judged of by the present exhibition at the Crystal Palace, we have every reason to believe that, in the department of superfine cloth, the palm of excellence would justly be awarded to Belgium. It must be remembered, however, that the specimens of extra-superfine West-of-England and French Cloth, which gained the prizes at the World's Fair in England, in 1851, are not included in the present Exhibition.

What we have seriously to speak of, is the neglect of nearly all the exhibitors to provide competent persons to attend the stalls, and afford information as to the relative *prices* of the different articles. We can judge of the quality, and form our opinion of its relative merits with regard to other articles of a similar character; but, unless we can ascertain the price at which such and such articles can be obtained, it is impossible to say how far America has succeeded in competing with foreign countries in this respect. If the Crystal Palace Company, instead of stationing all over the building so many men, who may be tolerably competent as policemen, but who have no knowledge of the articles exhibited, would select from the various trades, men versed in the technicalities of each department, whose business it should be to become posted up in their particular line, so as to be able to give *disinterested* information, and perhaps occasional lectures on the various specimens, detailing their relative value, and pointing out their merits and defects, they would render the Exhibition a school of art and manufacture, as well as a place of amusement and recreation. Instead of being a mere dumb show, it would become enlivened by the remarks of wit or wisdom, such as the various objects exhibited are so well calculated to bring forth, while the interest and usefulness of the exhibition would be very greatly enhanced.

In examining some of the most important specimens of woollen manufactures, we have kept in mind the following points of excellence, which, though familiar with the trade, are required to be understood by the uninitiated:

I. The good quality of the wool itself. However much care may have been taken in the cleansing of the wool and manufacture of the article, unless, in the first instance, the wool has been selected with care, and with due regard to the quality of the goods required to be produced, no after process can remedy this first error. The proper assortment of the wool is indeed a principal secret of success in the manufacture of woollen goods; and we recommend this fact to the attention of every American woollen manufacturer.

II. The softness and flexibility of the fabric, and freedom from any unpleasant stiffness and smell, arising from the defective cleansing of the wool in the first instance. The cleansing of the wool from its original animal oil, is an operation in which England at present far excels America ; and there is no defect which it is more important that American manufacturers should remedy than this want of thorough cleansing of the wool in the first instance. It constitutes a principal difference between the productions of America and England, and renders the succeeding process of dyeing far more difficult and uncertain in its results.

III. Fastness and durability of color. In this hot climate, especially, a fast color is indispensable, as the excessive perspiration is otherwise exceedingly liable to remove the coloring matter, and the heat and intense light of the sunshine are very trying to the fixedness of a dye. Attention to our advice, relative to cleansing the wool, would probably effect all that is now desirable in American goods in this respect.

IV. Excellence in shearing. The length of the nap is an important consideration in all superfine cloths ; and, if our American manufacturers would make cloth with a shorter nap, they would be able to produce better results.

V. Permanent finish. It is most desirable to have a cloth which will look nearly the same, after six months' wear, as it did when first made up. In this respect, English goods certainly have at present retained the highest character. For, although France and Belgium may have produced goods which look better in the piece, and the high finish and gloss of which cannot be excelled by the best West-of-England manufactures ; still, for wear, and the retention of all the excellences of which it is at first possessed, nothing certainly has yet been *proved* superior or even equal to the English goods. One important reason for this durability of finish, is to be found in the shortness of the nap ; because it must be obvious that a cloth with a long nap will become sooner disarranged by the rain and dust, and wear at the joints of the body, or where the cloth is subject to friction, than one with a short nap. But the most important reason for the durability of English cloths is their firmness of texture, combined with elasticity and pliability.

VI. Solidity or body in the fabric. This element cannot be too highly prized, if it be found combined with the other good qualities we have enumerated.

VII. Water-proof. There are some cloths in which this quality is desirable. It is a property secured, in some instances, by the peculiar nature of the wool itself. The natural oil of such wool, if allowed to remain in sufficient quantity, renders it impervious to all ordinary showers, from its own repelling character. And, although the fabric is as porous as any other, it resists the rain without, while it permits that free ventilation and exit for the vapors of the body, so essential to health, and the want of which is the principal objection to the India-rubber material. The same desirable result is likewise effected by a composition where the inherent quality of the wool does not answer this purpose.

VIII. Elasticity is likewise an important property in woollen goods. If cloth, when stretched, continue in the same position, and does not again contract into its former proportions, it is liable to the objection of losing its proper shape in wearing. For instance, the elbows of coats and the knees of pantaloons will retain their protrusion when the limbs are straight. The elastic nature of wool itself, which is strengthened when spun, is a principal preservative against this defect; but there are some goods better than others in this respect.

IX. Superiority of finish and glossy texture. These, by a large class of purchasers, will always be regarded as the principal elements of good cloth; and certainly when these properties are combined with durability, and all the other qualities we have enumerated, the climax of perfection in cloth manufacture is attained. To have a glossy dress suit, if it retains its splendor but for one party, where the object is to make an extra appearance, or to win the hand of some fair charmer, may be desirable in some cases; and the French, in their ready adaptation to every emergency of this kind, have provided cloths of surpassing lustre, the durability of which, however, is neither expected by the purchaser, nor desired by the trade.

X. Lightness. This is a most desirable property in all summer goods intended for the American market, and it is in this respect more than in any other, that the English goods are objectionable. France takes the lead in lightness of fabric, and some American manufacturers are successfully following the example. The best of wool is essential to a light cloth, if it is to combine the elements of strength and durability with its lightness. For this reason, a thin cloth will often be found stronger than a thick one.

There are some fabrics to which many of these remarks on quality do not apply; but the better class of goods generally require to be examined, with a view to these characteristics; and those which present the greatest number, combined, will of course come the nearest to our idea of perfection in cloth manufacture.

The exhibition of Woollen Goods in the Palace, although not equal to our expectations, presents many features of interest; and the first in order of production is wool in the raw state, and in the various processes of manufacture. There is one case of this character in the English department, exhibited by Messrs. Burgess & Co., worsted spinners, Leicester. It contains, in the first division, specimens of all the various kinds of wool used in the production of the varieties of yarn exhibited in the other divisions of the case. There is a sample from each of the wool-growing counties of England, viz: Shropshire, Northamptonshire, Worcestershire, Leicestershire, Devonshire, Herefordshire, and Buckinghamshire, as well as samples from Amsterdam, Germany, and Ireland. These are all in their unwashed condition. The next division of the case contains lambs'-wool in the staple, and in the various stages of manufacture, until finished into single or two-fold worsted yarns. Another apartment of the case exhibits English sheep's-wool in the same processes, and finished into single and three-fold worsted yarns. Another exhibits the same processes, and made into five-fold yarns. Another division shows the same processes with German wool; and the last shows ingrain, or wool dyed in the staple, and combed and passing through all the processes until made into yarn. There is also a case exhibited by Messrs. F. Derby & Co., which shows more clearly the process of manufacture, and contains samples of wool in the following conditions:—1. Scoured white; 2. Indigoed, presenting a bluish cast of color; 3. Dyed quite black; 4. Carded in plaits, just as it is drawn from the rollers of the carding-engine; 5. Spun into yarn, and prepared for weaving; 6. Harnessed for the treddle, which separates the yarn for the reception of the shuttle; 7. In a woven condition, but still showing the thread; 8. Felted or fulled; 9. Dressed or teasseled, with the nap raised; 10. Finished black cloth.

In these specimens there is nothing exhibited of the mungo, shoddy, or "devil's dust," as it has been called in English political debates. And as these articles have been extensively used in the large woollen manufactories of Yorkshire, perhaps a few explanatory remarks—the result of personal inspection when in England—may not be unacceptable here. We do not introduce it because we wish to encourage the use of these articles in America, as we are aware that they are getting into use without such encouragement. We believe, however, that if carefully selected and used in moderation, that shorter nap, of which we have spoken as desirable in American goods, will most probably be secured. We are aware, too, in speaking of these articles, we may be considered as exposing the secrets of the trade; but as we write for public enlightenment, and the advancement of our domestic manufactures, we are sure that we are justified in saying what we know of English manufactures in this respect.

In the somewhat hilly district of Yorkshire, between Huddersfield and Leeds, stand on two prominences the pretty little towns of Dewsbury and Batley Car. The stranger, on alighting from the railway-car, is struck with the unusually large warehouses, built of stone, by the Railway Company. For such small stations, these are mysterious erections. But if he enter the principal warehouses, he will probably find piled up hundreds of bales, containing the cast-off garments of Great Britain and the Continent of Europe. Here, in fact, from all parts of the world, are brought the tattered remains of the clothes, some of which have been worn by royalty in the various Courts of Europe, as well as by peers and peasants. The rich broadcloth of the English nobles here commingles with the livery of their servants and the worsted blouses of French republicans; while American under-shirts, pantaloons, and all other worsted or woollen goods may there be found, all reduced to one common level, and known by the one common appellation of "rags."

The walls of the town are placarded with papers announcing public auctions of "Scotch Shoddies," "Mungoes," "Rags," and such like articles of merchandise; and every few days the goods department of the railway is besieged by sturdy-looking Yorkshiremen, who are examining, with great attention, the various bales; some of which are assorted into "whites," "blue stockings," "black stockings," "carpets," "shawls," "stuffs," "skirtings," "linseys," "black cloth," &c. A jovial-looking man, of doubtful temperance principles, at last steps forward, and puts the goods up at auction. The prices which these worn-out articles fetch is surprising to the uninitiated. Old stockings will realize from £7 to £10 a ton; while white flannels will sometimes sell for as much as £20 a ton, and even more. The "hards," or black cloth, when clipped free from all seams and threads, are worth from £20 to £30 a ton. There are common mixed sorts of coarse fabric, which can be bought as low as from £3 to £5 a ton; whilst the "rubbish," consisting of seams, linseys, and indescribables, are purchased by the Chemists for the manufacture of Potash Crystals, for from £2 to £3 a ton.

It will be seen that *assorting* these old woollens is equally important with the assorting of the different qualities of new wool; and there is the additional consideration of colors to render assorting still more necessary. It is surprising, however, with what rapidity all this is accomplished. There are some houses where old woollen rags are divided into upwards of twenty different sorts, ready for the manufacturer. The principal varieties are flannels, of which there are "English Whites," "Welsh Whites," "Irish Whites," and "Drabs." Each of these commands a different price in the market: the English and Welsh, being much whiter than the Irish, and of finer texture, are worth nearly double the price of the Irish. The stockings are the next in value to the flannels, on account of the strength and elasticity of the wool. The peculiar stitch or bend of the worsted in stocking manufacture, and the hot water and washing to which they are submitted during their stocking existence, have the effect of producing a permanent elasticity which no after process destroys, and no new wool can be found to possess. Hence, old stockings are always in great demand, and realize for good clean-colored sorts as much as £16 a ton, in busy seasons. The white worsted stockings are the most valuable of the "softs," and when supplied in sufficient quantity, will sell for as much as £28 a ton. Carpets and other colored sorts are generally, owing to their rapid accumulation, to be had at very low prices. The rag collectors and merchants of America would be sure to find a good market for flannels and stockings in England, but the common articles would scarcely pay for the transit.

The "hards," consisting of old superfine cloth, will generally realize good prices in England, and should be stripped of their seams and sifted free from dirt, before exporting. We have seen from twenty to thirty Irish women in a room, all cutting the seams from old cloth. This is in fact an important branch of the business, and in Liverpool, Manchester, and nearly all large towns, it finds employment for many hundreds of hands. They are generally paid by the weight of rags they cut.

"Shoddy," so well understood in Yorkshire, is the general term for the wool produced by the grinding, or more technically, the "pulling" up of all the soft woollens; and all woollens are soft except the superfine cloths. The usual method of converting woollens into shoddy, is to first carefully assort them, so as to see that not a particle of cotton remains on them, and then to pass them through a rag-machine. This consists of a cylinder three feet in diameter and twenty inches wide, with steel teeth half an inch apart from each other, and standing out from the cylinder, when new, one inch. This cylinder revolves five hundred times in a minute, and the rags are drawn gradually close to its surface by two fluted iron rollers, the upper one of which is packed with thin stuff or skirting, so as to press the rags the closer to the action of the teeth. The cylinder runs upwards past three rollers, and any pieces of rag which are not completely torn into wool, are, by their natural gravity, thrown back again upon the rags which are slowly creeping into the machine. The rollers are fed by means of a creeper or slowly moving endless cloth on which a man, and in some instances a woman, lays the rags in proper quantities. One of these machines is commonly driven by a seven-inch strap, and requires at least five-horse power. Half a ton of rags can be pulled in ten hours by one of these machines. The dust produced, subjects the work-people, who first commence this occupation, to what is there called the "rag fever." But after a time the immediate effects are warded off, and although it no doubt shortens life, the remuneration being considerable, (two English shillings for every two hundred and forty pounds of rags pulled,) there is never any difficulty in obtaining work-people.

The "Mungo" is the wool produced by subjecting the hards or superfine cloths to a similar operation as that above described. The machine, however, for the mungo trade is made with a greater number of teeth, several thousands more in the same-sized cylinder, and the cylinder runs about seven hundred revolutions in a minute. The rags, previous to being pulled in this machine, are passed through a machine called a "shaker." This is made of a coarsely-toothed cylinder, about two feet and a half in diameter, which revolves about three hundred times in a minute, in a coarse wire cylinder. This takes away a large portion of the dust, which is driven out at a chimney by means of a fan. The mungo-pulling is, therefore, a cleaner business than the shoddy-making, and, as a general rule, is more profitable. The power required for a mungo machine is that of about seven horses.

Both the better kinds of shoddy and the mungo have for some years been saturated with oil; but when we were last in Yorkshire, we found that milk had been applied to this purpose, and found to answer exceedingly well. The consequence was, that milk had risen one hundred per cent. in price; and even in that district, where cows are kept in large numbers, it was feared there would be a great scarcity of milk for the supply of the towns.

When well saturated with oil or milk, the shoddy or the mungo is sold to the woollen manufacturer. There are scores of men who attend the Huddersfield market every Tuesday to dispose of their mungo. It is as much an article of marketable value there, as cloth is here. It is not unusual for good mungo to realize as much as eight English pence per pound, while the shoddy varies in price from one penny to sixpence per pound according to quantity.

The common kinds of shoddy require, of course, to be subjected to the scouring process, for which large wooden beaters, or "stocks," are employed. The excrescence of hogs is largely employed in this purifying process, as well as human urine, which is extensively used in the blanket manufacture of Yorkshire.

The white shoddy is capable of being used either for light-colored goods or for the common kinds of blankets, while the dark-colored shoddy is worked into all kinds of coarse cloths, carpets, &c., which are dyed any dark color, so as to hide the various colors of the old fabrics. It is mixed in with new wool in such proportion as its quality will permit, without deteriorating the sale of the material.

The mungo is used in nearly all the Yorkshire superfine cloths, and in some very extensively. It produces a cloth somewhat inferior, of course, to the West-of-England goods in durability, but, for finish and appearance, when first made up, the inferiority would only be perceived by a good judge of cloth.

The great English slop-sellers, Moses & Hyam, are among the largest purchasers of Yorkshire broadcloths.

The effect of shoddy in the cloth of an overcoat in the wear, is to rub out of the cloth and accumulate between it and the lining. We have seen a gentleman take a handful of this short wool from the corners of his coat.

The grounds on which this shoddy and mungo business can be justified, are the cheapening of cloth, and the turning to a useful purpose what would be otherwise almost useless. The business in Yorkshire is dignified by the title of the "Dewsbury trade." And to it Dewsbury certainly owes its wealth, and we might almost say its existence. In twenty years it has grown from a village to a town of some thirty thousand inhabitants, and some immense fortunes have been made by this extraordinary transformation of old garments into new.

Considerable quantities of white shoddy have been sent from England and Scotland to this country; and a machinist informed us that he had sent several of his rag machines, so that the trade is not entirely unknown here, and it is probable that there will one day arise a Dewsbury in the New England States, which will render it unnecessary to send old woollens to England, to be pulled into wool, and then returned here again at the cost of some three hundred per cent. above the price given for the woollen rags.

The Dewsbury trade is somewhat fluctuating, being affected very much by the state of the wool market. About this time last year, the wool market was high in England in consequence of the report that the shepherds of Australia were all deserting their avocations to go to the diggings, and this had the effect of promoting the Dewsbury trade. So great is the competition in the English markets, that as soon as a rise takes place in the price of new wool, the small manufacturers, instead of raising their prices, commonly regulate their expenditure by using a larger proportion of the old material, and they are thus enabled to compete, in prices at least, with the larger manufacturers, who can lay in a large stock of new wool when the prices are low.

Sixty years ago, the imports of wool into Great Britain scarcely exceeded twenty thousand bales a year. Spain was then the best producer for the English market. At the commencement of the present century, the total annual imports amounted to about forty-two thousand bales. As Britain has gone on increasing her own population, and sending out emigrants to people her colonies, she has proportionately increased her importations of wool, until, in 1852, we find that no less than 325,695 bales of wool were imported.

German wool has for some time been popular in England, and since the war, the importations have been greatly increased, although fluctuating. They may be stated as follows:

1814	9,807 bales.	1826	30,219 bales.
1820	14,607 bales.	1833	72,776 bales.
1825	82,284 bales.	1852	36,114 bales.

Spanish wool has been superseded by the German in the English market, and the German wool is now being superseded by the Australian, and this accounts for the decrease since 1833 of German importations. The amount of wool received from Australia last year by the English was 145,767 bales, nearly one-half of the whole importation. The amount of wool sent by the United States to England, from June 30, 1851, to June 30, 1852, was 5200 lbs., worth $1600, and to Scotland in the same period only 268 lbs., worth $39; while Canada sent during the same period, 49,977 lbs., worth $12,627.

A moderately cold climate is best adapted for sheep. Mountainous districts, affording all the variety of temperature from extreme heat to extreme cold, in their intermediate localities on the sides of verdant hills, are the most suitable for sheep-walks. In such districts, the shepherd can suit his flock to the season, the weather and their power of endurance. In the cold of winter he shelters from the strong blast in the valleys, and as the warm weather approaches he can guide his gentle charge to more elevated plains, reaching near the summits as the hot weather approaches, there to enjoy the cool, bracing, mountain air.

The New-England States are the best adapted for sheep pasturage, although there are many sheep grown in Illinois, Ohio, and some other Western States. We have seen, however, good wool said to have been grown as far south as Virginia; but this was doubtless in the mountainous districts where cool pasturage can be selected. Wool-growing in America is an important branch of agriculture. The scope for its successful operation is immense, and the choice of locality affords excellent opportunities for useful experiments with the different breeds of sheep.

The demand for wool in England is generally greater than the supply, and it is this circumstance, combined with the profitable nature of the business, which has given rise to the Dewsbury trade. While we have endeavored to describe this trade for the benefit of our home manufacturers who may have had no opportunity of seeing the Yorkshire processes, we should much rather recommend the more extensive growth of new wool, and attention to its improvement, with all its healthful rural pursuits, than the extensive introduction of the Dewsbury trade in this country.

The Flannels and Blankets of the American Department of the Crystal Palace deserve especial notice. There is a case exhibiting three grades of quality in Blankets manufactured at the Rochdale Mills, Rochester, N. H., by the Norway Plains Company, and placed in the Exhibition by Nesmith & Co. The wool of these Blankets is evidently well selected and cleansed. The coloring at the ends is variegated, and the Blankets are silk-bound. We saw nothing in the English Department, even, which equals these excellent articles, either for whiteness or softness; and although there is a pair of Whitney Blankets, which are said to be like those presented to the Queen and Prince Albert in April, 1851, and manufactured by Mr. E. Early, of Whitney, which are probably the best that can be made in England, being selected from a variety of fleeces, we must say they do not come up to these Rochester Blankets, either in whiteness or finish, whatever may be said of their strength and durability.

For beauty and exquisite finish, however, we must mention a case of embroidered blankets, exhibited by Messrs. Snelling, Parker, Wilder & Co., of Boston. The ends of the blankets, which appear to be the size for children's couches, are embroidered with a bold pattern of a vine and flowers: one in scarlet, and the others in crimson, green, blue, and orange colors. The case being locked, and no person to exhibit the goods, we were unable to feel the quality of the wool; but, judging from the appearance, we should say it is the best that could be selected. The surface is more closely sheared than that of ordinary blankets, probably in order to show the embroidery to greater perfection. We have never seen better taste displayed in this department of manufacture, it being unusual to ornament blankets so artistically.

The Canadian Department contains some prize blankets, said to have taken the prize at the Crystal Palace in London, in comparison with the Royal Whitney Blankets just referred to. They possess the qualities of strength and durability in a pre-eminent degree—qualities to which our home manufacturers would do well to pay some attention—but we cannot pronounce them superior to the Whitney blankets for any other quality. There is also in this department an assortment of home-made fabrics, gray woollens, knitted shawls, &c., serving to contrast the work of former ages, and of the backwoodswomen of the present times, with the results of machinery and modern improvements displayed in the other departments, and serving to illustrate the progress of the woollen manufacture in this country, as well as showing how the far-west Canadians still stand in relation to this branch of manufacture.

In the English Department, there are some good specimens of Whitney blankets, Welch flannels, &c., but, their qualities being well-known, we need not enlarge upon them, further than to say they excel our home manufacture principally in the qualities of strength, evenness or regularity of thickness, and weight; qualities which must continue to command the market until our home manufacturers have learned to combine them with their own superiority, both in whiteness and finish.

In the French Department, we observe several blankets, manufactured by T. Bouillier & Co. of France, supplied for exhibition by Messrs. A. T. Stewart & Co. of this City. These blankets appear to us to combine all the strong spinning and durability of the Whitney blanket, with the softness and finish of the Rochester goods above referred to. We can recommend these blankets as models for our home manufacturers to imitate. They certainly present the qualities most desirable in a good blanket, being made of good, soft wool, even, free from thin places, strong, well spun, closely woven, well carded or napped, prettily colored at the ends, and free from all unpleasant smell. Better and more serviceable blankets we have never examined.

There is also in the American Department a case of flannels, exhibited by John Slade & Co., and manufactured by the Ballard Vale Company. They are four-quarter wide flannels, and are unequalled for fineness of texture, and for whiteness, by the best Welsh flannels.

The most approved flannels, however, are, in our opinion, those in a case sent by Messrs. Dale & Co., of this city, from the manufactory of George H. Gilbert, Ware, Mass. We have never seen flannels made of finer wool than these appear to be. The case being locked, was inaccessible; but, judging from the appearance, we have good reason to compliment the manufacturer on the unrivalled excellence of his goods.

The amount expended in the importation of blankets and flannels during the year ending June 30, 1852, was as follows:

	For Blankets.	For Flannels.
England	$963,455	$79,159
Scotland	1,336	——
British American Colonies	32	——
Canada	6	27
France on the Atlantic	31,929	317
France on the Mediterranean	47,972	——
Holland	1,431	——
Hanse Towns	136	7,489
Mexico	14	——
Total	$1,046,361	$87,492

In our criticisms on these important productions we have been guided entirely by the principles with regard to quality, with the statement of which we commenced this article. We believe we cannot better serve the manufacturers of the United States and the best interests of the country, than by the candid statement of unbiased opinion, whether favorable or not to the present state of our manufacturing science; and we trust it will be seen that our object is to encourage the home trade, not by any flattering laudations of inferior articles because they are American, but by giving credit where it is justly due, and holding up for public approval what, in our judgment, is most worthy of praise, irrespective of the Country or State which may have produced it; knowing that the only sure foundation for successful manufacturing enterprise consists in a steady determination to excel—a constant and undeviating effort to attain perfection. It is this alone which will remove all prejudice in favor of foreign goods; and, if we may judge from the progress already made, and the degree of excellence attained, we have every reason to congratulate the

American manufacturers and our readers generally on the prospect before us as a nation in this respect. If we go on as we have done, the perfection of our woollen manufactures, so as to supplant our foreign supplies, must be near ; and we would urge forward the work as well worthy the skill, industry and perseverance of a great and independent republic.

XXI.

WOOL AND WOOLLEN MANUFACTURES.

[SECOND ARTICLE.]

In the wise economy of Nature, nothing is more remarkable than the application to new and useful purposes of those substances which, in the activities of life, have been reduced to apparently worthless material. No sooner has decomposition in dead animal or vegetable tissue commenced, or its first form ended, than life in a new shape makes its appearance. Man avails himself of this circumstance, and, when any material has become unfit for any other purpose, it becomes the most valuable agent in the hands of the agriculturist for the production of the various fruits of the earth essential to human existence. This same principle has been applied to mechanical as well as to natural science—to manufactures as well as to agriculture. The paper on which we write is an illustration of this in relation to worn-out cotton fabrics being made, as is well known, from old rags which once formed the under-garments of the active population of the world. Our former article showed that the same principle has been extensively applied to the reproduction of woollen fabrics; and we have introduced this subject again because the necessary limits of our previous essay prevented the mention of one department of this peculiar trade, which is less known in America than that which we explained, but which has been a growing trade in the old countries of Europe, and in England in particular—we refer to the application of wool to the purposes of stuffing. Mattresses, beds, cushions, and some other useful articles require to be filled with some elastic material; and there is no more justifiable application of old woollens than to the manufacture of what, in the early part of the trade were called "woollen flocks," but which in the progress of the manufacturing art have been entitled successively "water-flocks," "mill-puff," and latterly "curled wool."

In Yorkshire, England, the shortest portion of the shoddy, (explained in the former article) which cannot be made into yarn, is sold by the manufacturers to flock-dealers, who travel to the various towns of England and sell the flocks to the upholsterers, and bed and mattress-makers, at prices varying from one penny to fourpence per pound according to quality. The lowest goods of this class are made from linseys, containing a large admixture of cotton, (worth about £3 a tun,) and these are sometimes sold even for less than one penny per pound. The waste wool, which is carded off the face of the blankets, is also sold to the flock-dealers, and generally brings from fivepence to eightpence per lb. The goods known as "Yorkshire flocks" have within about seven years been superseded by Mr. Mathew Grist, of Stroud, Gloucestershire, who made a great improvement in this manufacture, and produced an article of a more elastic nature, called "mill-puff." This remedied the principal objection to Yorkshire flocks, their tendency to become hard by use. Mr. Grist invented a machine by which the wool or shoddy was separated into small globules, and each of these having a tendency, by their nature, to spring from each other, the liability to become hard or solid was, to some extent, obviated, and one of the best materials for stuffing purposes was the result. By this improvement, the flocks were increased fifty per cent. in marketable value, and Mr. Grist and his sons, keeping the invention a secret, realized a large fortune in a very short time, as the demand soon became very considerable. There is scarcely a town in England or Scotland where mill-puff has not become an article of daily use among the bed and mattress manufacturers. Many have been the attempts, especially in Yorkshire, to imitate these goods, but without success, till the spring of 1852, when Mr. Henry S. Clubb, of Manchester, invented a machine and a new process of mixing certain sorts of wool and of manufacture by which a still more elastic material was produced. This he called "curled wool." It has been pronounced by the trade as superior in elasticity and in the quality of "filling" to any other description of wool ever employed for stuffing. The newest and longest wool is inferior for stuffing purposes to this short, curled material. This manufacture is now carried on in Manchester by the brother of the inventor, of the firm of Clubb, Howorth & Co.

The most that can be said of wool for stuffing is, that it supplies an article of medium quality and price, being neither so good* or so expensive as hair or feathers, and much superior and a little more expensive than sea-weed, straw, and the cotton-waste which is used so extensively in England for the commonest kinds of beds and mattresses. The improvements above described, and the cheapness of these articles, compared with hair and feathers, have tended to bring wool for stuffing into greater favor, and the result is that the demand for the various kinds of woollen flocks in England and Scotland amounts to several thousand tuns a year.

In the department of the Crystal Palace devoted to Holland, is displayed the largest and most complete assortment of Blankets. Holland wool is very long and fleecy, it being commonly known to grow to ten inches in length. These blankets are peculiar, as having an extraordinary length of nap, resembling the coat of a white polar bear. The wool of which they are made is undoubtedly of excellent quality, being white and strong. The spinning and weaving are good; and so full and strong is the nap that, when looked at edgewise, some of them appear to be three-quarters of an inch in thickness. They possess the quality of softness in a pre-eminent degree, and we have no doubt will be found proof against the severest weather.

The counties of Somersetshire, Wiltshire, Devonshire, Gloucestershire and Dorsetshire have long been famous for the production of the best broadcloths; and, although the West Riding of Yorkshire has become a successful rival in the market, it is not on account of any intrinsic superiority of its goods, but the cheapness of its prices and the excellence of its finish.

The remarks of our contemporary, the *Courier des Etats Unis*, speaking of British manufactures, that they "possess in the "highest degree the art of giving a good appearance to the most

* The Editor of this volume protests against any admission that *feathers* are "good" *at all* for the beds of any bipeds but fowls, especially geese. For human beings, feather beds are unwholesome, uncleanly and uncomfortable.

"inferior articles," must be regarded as referring to the Yorkshire manufacturers rather than to those of the West-of-England. All respectable tailors in England profess to use West-of-England goods; and yet Yorkshire is stated by McCulloch to have employed or supported 85,096 families in 1831, in the cloth manufacture, whilst the West-of-England employed only 20,851 in the same period. There is no doubt but a large quantity of Yorkshire goods are sold for West-of-England productions, in order to meet the prejudice which exists, and with reason, so strongly in favor of these goods. It is due to the West-of-England manufacturers to say that they have well sustained the character of English goods; whilst they have had the cheap prices of the mungo traders of Yorkshire to compete with. Some account, therefore, of the processes by which this high character has been secured, will be useful to the manufacturer, as well as interesting to the general reader.

The great distinction between the woollen manufactures of the West-of-England and of the North, consists in the entire use of new wool; principally German and Australian, many of the manufacturers of the West being too anxious to preserve their character for strength and durability, to allow the mixture of old material or mungo with any of their goods.

The woollen mannfacture is divided into two important branches, produced by two leading qualities of wool. The "woollen manufacture," in its precise or restricted meaning, applies only to cloths made of the short wool, and such as possess the quality of felting or adhering together, and of elasticity; the other branch is called the "worsted manufacture," in which long wool and such as possesses no particular tenacity of fabric is used. The first process, therefore, is to separate the wool into long and short. The latter is passed on to assorters, or, as they are commonly called, "sorters." In this process, the senses of touch and sight become peculiarly active. Each bale of wool contains many different degrees of *fineness*, *softness*, *strength*, *color*, *cleanness*, and *weight*; and each of these is particularly regarded by the sorter, who separates the wool into the following kinds: "prime," "choice," "super," "head," "downrights," "seconds," "fine abb," "coarse abb," "livery," &c. A great deal depends upon this process; and it is partly owing to the pains taken by the West-of-England manufacturers to secure the requisite proportion of each quality in the goods they manufacture that they have been so signally successful. Each kind, being thus separated, is subjected to the action of a strong ley, made of stale urine and soap, at a temperature of about 120 degrees. After soaking a considerable time, according to the requirement of the wool, it is rinsed in cold water. It is then pressed by passing through rollers, and the result is to remove, not only the dirt, water and discoloring matter from the wool, but, what is of equal importance, the natural grease as well. If this operation be not well done, all subsequent operations will be impeded. The quantity of soap used in England for the cleansing of wool amounts to over fourteen million lbs. a year.

The next operation is *dyeing*, when it is intended to make cloth dyed in the wool. The usual proportions for a good black dye for every one hundred pounds of wool, previously indigoed, are five pounds of copperas, five pounds of nutgalls, bruised, and thirty pounds of logwood. The wool is first dipped in the solution of gall, and is then passed through the decoction of logwood, in which the copperas is dissolved. Pyrolignite of iron is used to fix the black dye.

Willying or willowing is performed next. It disentangles the locks of wool and cleanses it from sand and all loose dirt. The machine used for this purpose is a kind of hollow truncated cone, having an axis running through its centre. On this axis are fixed three wheels of different diameters, bearing on their circumference four longitudinal bars studded with sharp spikes. The cone revolves with the rapidity of three or four hundred revolutions a minute, within an outer cylindrical casing, the inner surface of which is armed with similar spikes. The machine is fed by means of an endless cloth or creeper, with wool, which enters at the small end of the cone, and travels to the largest end by virtue of the centrifugal force produced by the rotation. As it passes onward between and among the spikes, it becomes opened and disentangled, the fibres of each lock separated, and the impurities detached. But this is not all. When the wool has reached the lower end of the cone, it passes into a receptacle where a fan is revolving with great rapidity, by which a current of air is generated, sufficient to blow away all the dust mixed with the wool; while at the same time a kind of revolving cage distributes the wool in a flat, equable layer. The inferior kind of wool requires to undergo this process several times, but once is sufficient for the finer qualities. These layers are carefully examined by wool-pickers, who remove whatever objectionable particles may have been left by the willy.

The wool is next spread over a floor and sprinkled with olive oil. It is in this process that milk is now used in Yorkshire so extensively. The wool in this state is well beaten with staves. It is then passed on the scribbling machine, which consists of several cylinders covered with bent teeth or cards. The teeth of one cylinder are bent in the contrary direction to those of the cylinder against which it works; so that when all the cylinders are revolving and wool is applied to the first by a creeper, it is caught from tooth to tooth, carried rapidly from cylinder to cylinder, separated completely from all entanglement, and finally given forth in a delicate sheet or fleece. It becomes wound on a revolving roller after having passed through the scribbling machine. It then goes through the carding-engine, consisting of a great number of cylinders and finer teeth or cards, and it finally comes out in the form of a slender rope of about an inch wide, the wool adhering together by its own tenacity, which is considerably increased by the oil it now contains. Delicate almost as a spider's web is this first form of manufactured wool. This slender rope or pipe of wool is passed on to the "slubbing billy," by which it is spun into a very soft yarn. It is then subjected to the spinning jenny or mule-spinning machine, by which it is considerably elongated, and spun into very fine yarn. We shall treat of this ingenious mechanism when we come to describe the manufacture of cotton goods. The wool has now become yarn wound on large bobbins or reels.

The yarn is next sized, so as to produce the requisite stiffness and distinctness for wearing. Hand-loom-weaving has long been adhered to by the woollen manufacturers, but power-loom is rapidly superseding this slow process in almost every department of the woollen manufacture. The loom is set for cloth considerably wider than the finished goods, in order to allow for the shrinking produced by the fulling process. The list on each side of the piece of cloth is made of coarse yarn.

The cloth is next subjected to the scouring process. It is placed in a wooden trough, soap and water are let in, and wooden mallets are employed to beat it until clean. It is then rinsed in clean water, and if not dyed in the wool, is then dyed.

Fulling or felting is the next important process. It is in this operation that that peculiar body and consistency are produced, for which the West-of-England cloth is esteemed. In this process the necessity for well assorted wool becomes peculiarly apparent. Unless the wool possesses naturally a *felting* quality, no beating will ever cause it to become so united as to form one solid body. Microscopic discoveries have been made within the last few years, which have led to a revelation of much of the mystery of felting. Examined through a powerful microscope, the short fibre exhibits the appearance of a continuous vegetable growth, from which there are sprouting, (and all tending in one direction from the root to the other extremities,) numerous leaves like calices or cups, each terminating in a short point. It is easy to perceive how easily one of these fibres will move in the direction from root to point, while its retraction must be difficult being obstructed by the tendency of the little branches. In a fibre of merino wool, the number of these serrations or projections amounted to 2,400 in the space of one inch. In a fibre of Saxon wool of acknowledged superior felting quality, there were 2,720 serrations. South Down's wool, being inferior to these two for felting power, only contained 2,080 serrations in one inch of fibre, while Leicester wool contained no more than 1,860 in one inch, and Leicester wool is known to be but little adapted for felting purposes. In order that these peculiar fibres may be compelled to embrace each other, so as to become consolidated into one mass, the cloth is subjected to the following operation: a large mass of cloth is folded into many piles and put into the fulling-mill, where it is subjected to the action of two heavy wooden-mallets or stocks. The superfine cloth has four fullings of three hours each, with a thick solution of Castile soap, spread between each layer of cloth each time. During these violent concussions, the fibres are driven into the closest possible contact with each other, and those little serrations become inextricably united, and each thread, both of warp and weft, is so compacted with those that are contiguous to it, that the whole seems formed into one substance, not liable, like other woven goods, to unravel when cut with the scissors. In this process cloth is thickened considerably, but diminished in length and breadth. It feels like chamois leather.

Teazling, or raising, is the next process. Teazles are the seed-pods of the *dipsacus fullonum*, having small hooked points on the surfaces. Various attempts have been made to substitute metallic points for these vegetable brushes; but nothing has yet been found to answer the purpose so well as the natural teazle. Efforts have been made to monopolize the growth of teazles in the west of England, their value for this particular operation being well known. They will grow, however, on any soil, but are best suited to a loam after grass. Every piece of cloth wears up from fifteen hundred to two thousand teazles. The reason why they answer better than steel wire is, what at first sight would appear to be their greatest disadvantage, their weakness. When the steel wire hook substitute for the teazle catches on the cloth, it tears it and perhaps makes a hole in the piece, while, when the teazle catches the cloth, it gives way and saves the piece. The teazles are fixed round a cylinder so as to form even cords, or brushes, and these revolve against the surface of the cloth which is stretched against the teazle cylinder by means of rollers, round which it is drawn. There is a small cylinder of similar construction so adjusted against the surface of the large cylinder as to clean the wool from the teazles. This machine is called the gig-mill.

The shearing is performed by a revolving cylinder on which are placed knives of a worm-like and sloping form so as to come in contact with other knives fixed in such a position as to resemble the action of shears. The cloth passes lightly through this machine, after which it is put upon rollers and subjected to the action of steam, which increases its firmness, and imparts a brilliant lustre to the surface. It is again teazled and sheared, which process is repeated several times until its surface is worked down to a close, thick, and short nap. It is then subjected to the process of steaming and brushing at the same time. It is then stretched upon tenter-hooks and racks in the open air, brushed, and allowed to dry. It is afterward subjected to hydraulic pressure. The press plates being heated by steam, the whole piece of cloth, which is placed between glazed press-boards, is made thoroughly hot while subject to the pressure. It is then packed for market.

Attempts have long been made to make felting supersede spinning and weaving. It has succeeded in reference to the manufacture of hats, in which rabbit's down is also a material of large consumption. It has also succeeded with regard to beavers and other heavy goods; but its application to superfine cloth remains, at present, an object of interesting experiment, the successs of which is doubtful. The greatest objection to the specimens we have seen, is the want of that elasticity which is so important an element in all cloths used for close-fitting garments. But there are many purposes to which fine felt may be applied, such as shawls, cloaks, loose overcoats, and all garments on which there is no particular stretch. The greatest perfection yet attained in the felting art, is due to the exertions of the Union Manufacturing Company, Norwalk, Conn. The process of manufacturing felts adopted by this Company, is different to that of any other manufacturers we have heard of. A number of the fine webs of wool from the carding engine are drawn over a smooth metallic bed, covering a surface proportionate to the width of the piece. The first layer is succeeded by a cross layer of a similar character; this is succeeded by another lengthwise, and then another across, repeating the operation till the requisite thickness is attained. As many as thirty layers are sometimes employed in the manufacture of one thickness of felt. These layers are next subject to the action of a large metallic beater, weighing two tuns. This beating is continued until the wool is all consolidated into one compact mass or felt. In some of the goods the wool is dyed first, and the webs being alternately dark and light, stripes and plaids are formed, each bar of color being about an inch and a quarter wide. The beavers and petershams manufactured by this Company exceed any thing of the kind we have seen, either at the Exhibition or elsewhere. They are heavy, strong, and very solid. There are also some specimens of lighter goods made on the same principle; but either the wool selected is not of an elastic quality, or the process is not so far completed as to secure so much elasticity as is found in woven goods. The spinning doubtless increases the elasticity of wool, and we are not yet convinced that this contracting power can be secured where spinning and weaving are dispensed with. We tested the strength of the thinnest felt, and found that a needle pierced close to the edge did not break out. A specimen of painted felt is exhibited, which, if of an indelible coloring, shows the applicability of the process to the manufacture of shawls and other light and fancy articles. Being free from all grain or thread-marks, it receives the impression of the pattern to perfection. The felted lamb's wool for linings to gloves is admirably adapted to prevent frost from causing numbness in the fingers. The Union Manufacturing Company deserve every encouragement for the progress they have made in the felting art, and we are glad to find their goods coming into greater demand, especially their heavy beavers and petershams, which obtained a prize medal at the first Exhibition of the Metropolitan Mechanics' Institute, held at Washington last spring.

There are also some felt beavers and petershams manufactured by Lounsbury, Bissell & Co., Norwalk, Conn. The petershams are not equal to those manufactured by the Union Company, but there is a piece of blue felt-beaver which is a most excellent article, and does credit to the firm. The same remark will apply to some drab felt beavers by the same manufacturers.

The best Wool Beavers in the Exhibition are undoubtedly those known as Carr's Patent Beavers, exhibited by Messrs. F. Derby & Co. They are manufactured at Tiverton, near Bath, England, and are placed in the English department. They possess the quality of resisting water, without being impervious to the exhalations of the body. Their water-proof quality is shown by a piece of the cloth being placed in a glass case with several quarts of water suspended in it, in which are floating mock gold fish. The exhibition of these beavers, ornamented as they are at the ends with gold and tinsel letters, form the most attractive feature of the English Woollen Department. There is good reason for making these articles showy and attractive, because they well repay a careful inspection; and although the first appearance raises expectation, the succeeding scrutiny tends to increase our admiration rather than to produce disappointment. These goods are of the very highest character; their finish is quite consistent with their quality and design; they combine all the requisite qualifications of good overcoating, and may be regarded as perfect of their kind.

We would draw the attention of the American manufacturers to these excellent cloths, as suggesting a branch of the business which is worthy of their increased exertions. There is a large demand in this country for winter cloths, and these English goods are commanding a very large share of the trade. There is no reason why America should not equal the Old Country in this particular. We have wool as good, and looms as strong, and men as willing and intelligent, and they do not present any of those nice difficulties of finish which appertain to the superfine cloths—difficulties which experience, and a long course of steady perseverance, can alone overcome. That these or similar goods can be produced in this country, we have ample proof: there is in the American department an exhibition of beavers manufactured at the Bay-State Mills, which come as near as possible to the English beavers, containing all the points necessary in good beaver-cloth, not excepting, we believe, the waterproof quality. If the Bay-State Mills Company will supply the trade with the same quality of goods as they exhibit, they will be sure to take the lead in this important branch of the woollen trade in this country. We do not think that they have arrived at the perfection of Carr's patent beavers in every particular; but they produce what convinces us that they are well qualified to take the position we have assigned them, if they will continue their attention to this class of goods, in which they have shown themselves eminently successful.

There are also some good specimens of Petersham felt exhibited by F. Skinner & Co. of this city, from the manufactory of Bissell & Co. The piece of drab felt is unexceptionable, and the colored felt beavers are very creditable productions. There is also a piece of thick gray cloth, which is a perfect production of its kind. It is remarkably well sheared, and so strong, that one coat made of it would certainly last a long lifetime, if it did not become an hereditary possession for successive generations. We are sorry we cannot record the name of the manufacturer, the piece being placed, when we examined it, without a ticket to denote its origin. We should not be afraid to trust ourselves to its protection through the longest shower that ever cooled an American atmosphere.

Messrs. A. T. Stewart & Co. exhibit in the English department an assortment of excellent overcoating, in patent beavers and reversible cloth, one side being mohair and the other cloth-finish. There is also a specimen of coating resembling a Whitney blanket on one side, and on the other fine cloth. This is the best display of reversibles. They are goods which are becoming popular in England for paletots.

In the Belgian department there is a piece of beaver manufactured by Juan Simonis, which comprises all the characteristics of good cloth. It is marked 20,317, and is well worth the careful attention of the trade.

On the stall in the German department, which has been hospitably afforded to Russia, M. A. G. Thilo, of Riga, has placed some pilot-cloths and beavers, which equal any we have seen of this description, with regard to the quality of the wool and the excellence of spinning and weaving. The mohair coatings are peculiarly Russian, and are more like furs than cloths. Some appear to be at least half an inch in thickness. The dye has all the appearance of permanence, and for extra-thick overcoats nothing exceeds these Russian productions.

At this season of the year, the heavy class of goods which we have been examining are in great demand at the wholesale houses where the country merchants are busily selecting their winter stock. We trust that their attention will be directed to a careful examination of American productions. Let not the established ideas on this subject prevent them from appreciating cloths of good quality which are made at home. We know there is always a greater value set upon far-off objects—as if the notion that

> "Distance lends enchantment to the view,"

applied to articles of commerce as well as to the objects of a landscape; but it is time that a discriminating discernment and sound judgment should take the place of a prejudice which originated at a time when the American manufacture was in its infancy, and when a large class of our citizens had all the feelings of national pride pertaining to old countries to contend with; but now that America has added to her natural resources, as an agricultural country, nearly all the appliances of a great manufacturing community; now that, with a few trifling exceptions only, her practical arts have reached the height of European civilization, and in some instances gone far beyond; it surely is but reasonable to expect that her own merchants and citizens should be willing to encourage, in the most substantial manner, every industrial achievement of their own country, placing in the hands of our own manufacturers the just reward of their industry and enterprise, and enabling them to pursue, with increased facilities and renewed vigor, that course of steady, intellectual perseverance, which, more than all political agitation, promotes greatness, wealth, and prosperity.

XXII.

WOOL AND WOOLLEN MANUFACTURES.

[THIRD ARTICLE.]

THE highest point at which the Woollen Manufacture has arrived is undoubtedly that of producing the best superfine cloth. The wearing of a superfine suit was once a principal mark of distinction in the countries of Europe between a laboring man and "a gentleman." Of late years, however, since the manufacture has advanced, prices lowered, and the condition of the people improved, this distinction has become less conspicuous. Every sober mechanic has his one or two suits of broadcloth, and, so far as mere clothes go, can make as good a display, when he chooses, as what are called the upper classes. It is in this way, that trade, commerce, and individual comfort, as well as social improvement, are advanced by the progress of mechanical invention. A good article produced at a low price commands an extensive sale, and benefits the whole community. Millions of men, such as in times past would never have dreamed that they could afford to indulge in good clothes, are now possessed of this desirable addition to their personal property; and, as one result, the demand for such goods is increased a hundred-fold; a trade has been created by the increased facilities for production which modern inventions have introduced, and manufacturers and merchants are all reaping advantages, while the community at large is better and more respectably clothed.

In the American Department we were highly gratified to see several pieces of black cloth, manufactured by Messrs. Slater & Son, of Webster, Mass., for which prize-medals were awarded in the London Exhibition, when shown in contrast with English and French production. These choice specimens of cloth were manufactured from American fleece-wool. Their quality is, beyond doubt, of the best character. The wool is well selected and well cleaned; the spinning is strong; but the fulling in some places is not quite so compact as is desirable. The cloth, however, is flexible and elastic. The only point in which we could discover any material difference between this and French or English cloth is in the length of the nap. It is a little too long. The French are the most perfect in this particular. They spin such a fine yarn, that they can raise the finest nap, and then shear so close to the fabric as to give permanence to the finish. The English cloths come next to the French in this respect, and the German next. Now, while in most other particulars the cloths of Messrs. Slater & Sons resemble the English and French goods, in the matter of finish and length of nap they resemble the general character of German goods. The finishing process has probably been a little too rapid; an additional teazling, so as to lay the nap all one way more completely, if we may judge from the strength and excellence of the spinning and weaving, would have rendered some of these cloths equal to the best goods of this character.

There are some cloths exhibited by Messrs. Barnes, Bowers & Beekman, manufactured at the Kelloggs' Mills, Skaneateles, Onondaga County, N. Y., which deserve special notice. The cassimeres are equal, in quality of wool, and excellence of finish, to any foreign goods. The nap is well raised and sheared. A little more pliability and elasticity, however, would be an improvement. There is a feel about them resembling that of leather, and they smell somewhat of the sheep. The oil of the sheep is evidently not entirely removed in the scouring processes. This remark applies also to the silk-warp tweeds and silk and wool cassimeres from the same manufactory. They are in every other respect highly creditable productions, and such as do honor to the American manufacture.

There is a piece of doeskin, manufactured by the Middlesex Company, Lowell, numbered 811,537, which is fairly comparable with any foreign doeskin. It is most creditable to the Company.

The Cassimeres of the Bay State Mills are, like their beavers, peculiarly English in their character. The piece of chocolate color is excellent. There would be no difficulty in disposing of these goods as British productions. The Company deserve great credit for the perfection to which they have brought the manufacture of American cassimeres.

The Fancy Cassimeres, manufactured by the Broad Brook Company, stand high in our estimation. They are in square blocks and check patterns. They resemble in appearance and smell English goods, and, had they been labelled as such, we should never have discovered them to be otherwise. There is a piece of Jacquard goods which appears quite equal to any English cassimere we have seen. If these goods were brought into the market as American goods, and recommended by respectable tailors as such, and sold at a less price than imported goods of similar quality, they would do very much to destroy the prejudice against American woollens.

Mr. Edward S. Hall, of Millville, Mass., exhibits some very creditable fancy cassimeres of English patterns, and, we may add, of English quality. There are also some in French patterns of the latest fashion, single and double milled. They are manufactured by the Millville Company.

Messrs. J. Wetherell Brothers, of Wetherellville, Mass., display some black cassimeres and doeskins which are remarkably well finished. The nap is short, and the spinning and weaving fine and close, so that the cloth loses nothing in appearance by the shortness of the nap, while the finish will be the more permanent.

The fancy check cassimeres of Messrs. Jacob T. Seagrave & Co., are very superior in every respect, showing good taste in patterns and excellent workmanship. The mouse-colored doeskin is well finished, pliable and elastic. It is an unexceptionable piece of goods for all the purposes intended. We are glad, however, to be able to speak most favorably of Messrs. Platner & Smith's other productions. We refer to their cloudy satinets, made of cotton warp and wool fillings. They are evidently more in their line; and in contrast with articles of this class made in America twenty years ago, they exhibit a true picture of the rapid growth of manufacturing art in this country. The productions of former years were rough, stiff and coarse, whilst these are perfectly smooth and pliable. The former harshness of face is entirely removed and they now nearly resemble the French cassimeres. Their cassimeres in plaids and boot patterns, and also those in plain colors, including the twilled pearl drab in two shades, are very closely woven and sheared. There is no doubt they would wear well.

Juan Simonis displays in the Belgian Department the finest broadcloths we have seen in the Crystal Palace. We may say they excel in every feature. Although the exhibition of Belgian goods is limited, it presents a rich variety. The colored broadcloths, especially a piece of blue marked 19,536, are exquisitely finished, and deserve all the commendation that can be bestowed upon any manufactured production.

Chenest & Buisson, of Bischeviller, exhibit in the French Department several pieces of colored Thibet doeskins, six-quarters wide. They are well adapted for summer wear in this country. The colors are good and the manufacture excellent. There are also from the same manufacture, black and blue " Amazon cloth," which is a good sample of French manufacture.

M. Paret, of Sedan, Ardennes, exhibits a good assortment of cassimeres and doeskins, of first-rate French quality; also, some brilliant red cloth for military purposes, and cloth for billiard-tables. The coloring cannot be surpassed.

Mr. F. A. Reichard also exhibits some kerseymere cloths and zephyr cloths of various colors. Those who wish to understand the superior finish peculiar to French cloths, should examine these goods. There is a piece of brown cloth on this stand which is soft and yet solid, strong and yet light, glossy but not long-napped. It is a first-rate production of its kind.

Legrix & Bruyant, of Elbeuf, exhibit some good fancy cassimeres. Also some well worked cloth vestings. Some patterns represent sporting scenes, of various degrees of cruelty. The display of vestings is large, and exhibits considerable taste—such, indeed, as might be expected from France. But, as a whole, the French Department is very limited in the display of woollen goods, and must not be taken as a true or complete exposition of French industry in this branch of manufacture.

Compared with the extent of our trade with England, the exhibition of English goods is exceedingly deficient. The Yorkshire trade in particular is barely represented. It may be that the traders in Yorkshire goods are too well aware of their quality, to submit them to the scrutiny of critics at the World's Fair, fearing that their real qualities should be made known.

Messrs. Derby & Co. in addition to their unrivalled display of beavers, exhibit some good English cassimeres, such as are in common use, and are well known to the trade in this country. They have also favored us with a sight of some West-of-England prize goods, those which won the highest prize at the Exhibition in London—the quality of which cannot be surpassed. They are manufactured of the finest wool, collected from the backs of a great many sheep, each animal furnishing but a very small quantity of such exquisite fineness. Such cloth as this could not be brought into common use, because the supply of such wool is too limited, and the cost would be enormous.

Messrs. Babcock, Milnor & Co., exhibit some splendid piece-goods manufactured by Henry Pease & Co., Darlington, Durham. The silk-warp coatings are well colored, and in point of texture are equal to the best French merinoes.

Messrs. Ball & Wilson, of London, make a good display of fancy cassimeres and figured vestings embroidered with silk on cloth in various colors.

There are some other good specimens of cloth of similar character to those we have mentioned, but nothing particularly new or worthy of comment.

In the German Department we noticed some excellent specimens of cloths for ladies' mantles, manufactured by Augustus Hausman, of Brandenburg, on the Havel, Prussia. There are some entirely new patterns in imitation of furs. They deserve special attention.

There is a peculiarity about some German Broadcloths which is more easily understood by their feel than described by the pen; they seem to the eye to possess a long, soft nap, and yet when examined, it is found to be quite short. The finish of German broadcloth is not equal to that of French goods of similar quality, but it is more lasting, especially with regard to colored cloths.

O. C. & H. Tschille, Frankfort-on-the-Oder, Prussia, exhibit some excellent Saxony fine Cloths. One piece marked 85, and another marked 87, appear to be the strongest fine broadcloth we have seen. The finish must be of the most abiding nature, and the color is excellent. These pieces do great credit to the Prussian manufacture.

Messrs. Schoedler & Son, of Leipsic, Saxony, display a magnificent piece of light drab cloth. It resembles velvet for softness, and the finish is unexceptionable.

Messrs. Foistman & Huffman, Werden-on-Ruhr, Prussia, are large manufacturers for the American market. So well known are their goods, that they are commonly called F. & H. goods, and are considered to be among the best of the foreign goods brought to America. They combine fineness of finish with that enduring quality which secures a permanent character in the trade. They are exceedingly pliable, well cleaned, well sheared, and finished with excellent effect.

Messrs. Ridner, Thiel & Co., exhibit a piece of cloth, (No. 28,088,) which will compare favorably with any goods in the Exhibition. It is manufactured by F. A. Barmann, of Goldberg, Silesia, who evidently understands cloth manufacture to perfection.

There is some good black cloth exhibited by J. B. Meyer; the piece marked 27,680 is of a superior quality and remarkably firm and strong. Similar remarks might be made of more than fifty exhibitors in the German department. For quantity, the German States stand unrivalled in the Exhibition; but, except the goods we have enumerated, there is nothing particularly worthy of note, the general good qualities of German goods being well known in the United States.

The following is the value of foreign imports in cloths and cassimeres for the year ending June 30, 1852:

England	$3,391,568	Holland	$7,928
France on the Atlantic	1,735,530	Canada	997
Hanse Towns	1,318,134	Chili	254
Belgium	444,987	China	20
Scotland	10,324		
		Total	$6,909,742

The lighter class of woollen goods, adapted for ladies' dresses, deserves a passing notice. There is more scope for artistic skill in this department of woollen manufacture, and the progress made in this country in this complex class of goods is truly encouraging.

There are some printed Mousseline de Laines by J. Dannell & Co., Providence, which are good of the kind, but do not contrast favorably with those in the opposite case, "printed with copper shells," by the Hamilton Woollen Company, Southbridge, Mass. The Cashmeres of this Company are excellent both in pattern and color; and we were particularly pleased with some Plaids of a novel style, with brilliant and variegated colors. The Mousseline de Laines of this Company show the extent to which America has arrived in this department of copper-printing. It is gratifying to us to be able to record the complete success of this branch of artistic manufacture, and we congratulate the Company on taking the lead in this respect. There are some patterns of birds brought out to the life. Landscape-printing, even, is not neglected, and we have a view of a castle, and trees, and various colored flowers, done with great taste and good artistic effect.

The Cashmerets of the Chelmsford Company, West Chelmsford, Mass., are well made articles, and could not be distinguished from English goods. Their patterns of cloth exhibit an extensive assortment of colors, and show the resources of the Company to be considerable.

Messrs. McGregor, Simpson & Co., exhibit some very fine Cashmerets. The colors are good, and the fabric well manufactured.

The Philadelphia Print Works have a large display of printed patterns, which show excellent taste in design. They closely resemble woven patterns.

In the same case in which Messrs. Snelling, Parker, Wilder & Co., show their fancy blankets, were some Wool Shawls embroidered with silk. One is crimson wool, with a silk embroidered vine of the same color, and green and gold-colored flowers. Another is of a green ground, with zephyr worsted embroidery, beautifully shaded in leaves and flowers, of various colors. Another is scarlet, with silk of the same color for the vine and flowers. The last is the blue, with blue silk vine and orange-colored blossoms. They appeared to be entirely new designs. They have been recently removed from the case in order to show the embroidered blankets to greater advantage, and are now exhibited in a case above, where they make a good display. Their novelty and the taste they exhibit, render them worthy of particular remembrance.

Messrs. James Roy & Co., of Watervliet Mills, N. Y., display a splendid case of woollen shawls, somewhat novel in their character. They are plaids or "Rob Roys." They are of great brilliancy of color, and could not be excelled even at Paisley for their beauty and quality.

Hotchkissville Shawls form an ornamental and novel feature of the American Department. They are manufactured in imitation of French cashmere, and their novelty consists in the rounded character of their corner patterns, the effect of which is highly commendable.

There is a beautiful display of Shawls in the English Department, manufactured by W. Bliss, of Chipping Norton, Oxon. They are of a quiet English pattern and excellent make.

In the German Department south-west Gallery, is a beautiful display of Zephyr Berlin Wool Yarns, exhibiting all the varieties of color, with their graduating shades, amounting to nearly one thousand five hundred tints. It is so arranged as to show the colors to the greatest advantage, in all their unrivalled depth and softness. These samples are from the manufactory of Messrs. Bergmann & Co., Berlin, Prussia, and their harmonious arrangement is due to their agents, Messrs. Meyer & Stucken, of this City. The use of Berlin wool or yarn has long been a favorite occupation of English ladies, and a very large business is done in supplying their wants in this respect.

In the French Department there are several good studies for the American manufacturer. There are some superior figured fabrics for ladies' dresses, plain corded worsteds and figured merino goods. In this Department America is at present very far behind the European manufacturers. There is nothing of American productions at all to be compared with the specimens of merinoes exhibited by A. Rogues, and if we are to judge from this exhibition, it does not appear that there have been any successful attempts to compete in this line with our foreign supplies. The colors and texture of these goods deserve and will bear the closest attention.

M. Edward Hartwick, Rue du Mail, Paris, exhibits three patterns for Cashmere Shawls, beautifully printed, though of very ugly design: one represents a lion, lioness and cubs, and on one side a lioness hunted and caught by the bloodhounds, with a spear running through her body, and on the other side is a wild boar attacked by the hounds.

The following is the value of foreign imports in Merino and other Woollen Shawls, in the year ending June 30, 1852, from

England	$426,896	Brazil	$55
France on the Atlantic	165,113	Canada	8
Hanse Towns	72,254		
Scotland	51,488	Total	$715,814

Great credit is due to the American manufacturers for the progress they have made within a few years in the various divisions of this useful and ornamental branch of manufacturing industry, and, while we have endeavored to accord to each his share of honor, we have not hesitated to point out defects where we found them to exist. We have done this on the principle that the best friend is not the flatterer, but he who helps us to discover our imperfections, with a view to their removal.

XXIII.

BOOTS AND SHOES.

The manufacture of Boots and Shoes, like that of the material from which they are made, has as yet derived but little aid from the inventive faculties of man. The tanner still adheres to the ancient process practised in the time of Simon of Joppa ; and the *ne sutor ultra crepidam* seems to have formed an eternal barrier to improvement on the mind of the shoe-maker. The Crispin of the present day we take to be pretty much the same sort of ruminating animal as he that heel-tapped the sandals of Herod, for he chews the cud of his reflections without apparently growing wiser. How he can sit hammering and pegging away from year's end to year's end without either originating an idea, or borrowing a suggestion for the curtailment of his labor, is a puzzle to those who have no faith in the metempsychosis. For our own part we have always looked upon him as the envelope of some condemned spirit that once fretted the world with its activity. No greater purgatory could have been devised for the soul of an ambitious warrior or meddling statesman.

One would suppose from this dead-lock on the progress of the art of shoe-making since the time of Moses, that it had reached perfection at that respectable era. That there are plenty of gouty brokers, and irritable dowagers, who are ready to testify that there is still room for improvement. If all the tortures they have suffered from pedal constriction could be carried over to the credit side of the Great Ledger which contains their last account, we expect that the balance against them would be very small. Shoemakers are in fact the greatest scourges of humanity. The *peine forte et dure* to which they subject us, exceeds in atrocity all the refined inventions in cruelty resorted to in the middle ages. The sweetness of an angel, or the firmness of a stoic, must alike yield to the agonies which they inflict.

The art of shoemaking may be said to be still in its infancy. Until its professors discard their admiration for the *beau ideal*, and apply themselves to the study of nature, we do not expect to see any great improvement in their works. If they will persist in showing a club-footed Alderman like an Adonis, or a dropsical lady like a Venus de Medici, the result must be failure and unmitigated suffering. We cannot see why the protuberances of the foot should be treated less tenderly or scientifically than those of the head. If phrenologists would only take the trouble to seek in the former, the disturbing causes which they profess to find in the brain, they would more frequently arrive at the idiosyncrasy of their subject. Compressed bunions and festering corns have more to do with men's humors than these theorists dream of in their philosophy. Were the bumps of benevolence ever so large, they are sure to be counteracted by the bosses on the feet. Let them unite some little knowledge of pedology with the study of the brain, and people will believe in them. Their favorite pursuit will then have some chance of being classed among the exact sciences.

From what we have stated, it is evident that shoemaking is not a progressive art. Some attempts have been made of late years to effect improvements in it; but their authors having little or no knowledge of the practical difficulties and requirements of their subject, their efforts were directed rather to expediting by machinery the process of manufacture than to the application of scientific principles to the perfection of the article produced. About five and twenty years ago, the English engineer, Brunel, took out a patent for the manufacture of boots and shoes by machinery; but it was abandoned almost as soon as it was put in operation, the results proving that little or no economy could be effected on the starvation prices at which the Northampton and Nottingham goods could be brought into the market. In 1849, the writer of the present article attempted, in conjunction with others, to work a French patent, which consisted for the most part of modifications of Brunel's invention, with the addition of some new machinery which it was hoped would meet the difficulties that had caused the failure of the latter. A large manufactory was established in the suburbs of Paris, for the purpose of submitting it to a fair commercial test; but, like its predecessor, it failed in the conditions necessary to ensure successful competition with the low-priced productions of the under-paid artisan. By this process, we have seen a pair of boots or shoes completed in less than forty minutes, the different operations of soling, heeling, and pegging being performed by a series of simple machines, which in these details certainly effected a great economy of labor. But there was wanting in this invention some mechanical contrivance for curtailing the time and expense bestowed on the preparation and stitching of the upper leathers, which had to be effected by hand, and which in reality constituted the most important feature of the economical question that was sought to be solved. The sewing machine which had so long formed a desideratum in the mechanical arts, and which had occupied the attention of so many ingenious and practical minds, had not as yet been perfected; and without its aid it was clear that no important commercial results could be secured from the patent. Could it have embraced this feature, there was no limit to the extension which it must have attained; the contracts of the army and navy could have been easily secured; the whole of the coarser descriptions of goods consumed in the departments, would have been supplied by it; and, even in the finer class of articles, its productions would have depreciated if not utterly ruined the trade of the artisan. To work these machines, little or no previous knowledge of shoemaking was required; the merest novice being able in a few days to acquire all the experience necessary to produce a perfect article. To an invading army, involved in the intricacies of a hostile country—to an infant colony, as yet imperfectly supplied with mechanics—or to remote villages dependent upon distant towns for supplies—the advantages of so simple and expeditious a process are obvious. The compactness and portability of the machines, and the ease with which they could be worked, would render them invaluable in all such cases, while, for general consumption, the economy and durability of the articles which they would produce, would soon enable them to entirely supersede the products of hand-labor.

At the present moment there are two houses in Paris who sell what they call machine-made boots and shoes, but in reality only a portion of the process of manufacture is effected by that means. Lefebvre, on the Faubourg Montmartre, has a patent for machine-made screws, by which the upper-leather is attached to the soles; and Housiaux & Co. use a peculiar sort of brass peg for the same purpose. They both avail themselves of Brunel's original process for cutting out the soles and riveting the pegs, so that there is but slight difference in their modes of manufacture. Being obliged to have the upper-leathers stitched by hand, the economy effected by the partial employment of machinery is so trifling that it does not counterbalance a serious objection made to their productions—namely, that they are stiffer, and less pliable to the foot, than hand-made boots. Of this defect we ourselves have had experience, having worn for years manufactures of both houses. They possess, however, a recommendation which, with most people, will outweigh the temporary discomfort to which we allude, namely, that of superior durability. The screws, being made of brass, are no tliable to shrink or expand from the influence of moisture, as in the case of the wooden pegs used in this country, and which also in time affects the ordinary stitching: they maintain their hold with extraordinary tenacity, and rarely or never allow the soles to separate from the upper-leather. We therefore give this mode of attaching them a decided preference, as much on account of its superior wear, as of the saving in time which it effects in the manufacture.

When the Sewing-Machine is conjoined with the improvements above noticed, we may look forward to an immediate and complete revolution in the trade. Boots and shoes can then be manufactured at nearly one-half their present cost, and an important saving will be thereby effected in every family. When we reflect on the heavy item which these articles form in our annual expenses, we cannot but regard with lively interest the progress of inventions which tend to double our incomes without imposing on us the necessity of curtailing our comforts or enjoyments. There is no doubt that the changes which they will bring about, will, as in all cases where manual labor is supplanted by machinery, inflict great suffering upon large classes of deserving artisans. This evil will, however, be only partial and temporary in its effects, while the benefits resulting will be universal and enduring. To the poorer classes the boon conferred by the improvements which we have described will be of inestimable value, the articles to be produced by them being precisely those of which they wear most, and in the purchase of which they are most constrained to practise economy.

Having taken a retrospective view of this useful branch of industry, and indulged in speculations as to its future prospects, it is now time to turn our attention to the more immediate objects of this article. Before we proceed, however, to notice the specimens exhibited in the Crystal Palace, a few words respecting the present condition of the trade may be deemed necessary.

Although the French have long enjoyed the reputation of being the best boot-makers in the world, we are now able to compete with them successfully, both as to quality and finish. In stating this, we are in candor bound to add, that it is in a great measure owing to the employment of foreign workmen and the use of French leather. Almost all the leathers used in the finer description of boots, even to the very linings, are imported from France. Le Morne's French calf-skin, and the varnished leather known in the trade as "the silver medal patent," are those which are principally employed. The patent leather made in Newark is only used in the cheapest description of goods. The sole leather comes principally from Baltimore.

There is no trade, perhaps, in which the average rate of wages earned by journeymen runs so low. They are paid by the piece, and it is difficult for a good workman, no matter how hard he labors, to earn more than $8 or $9 per week. What is called the first-rate of wages, gives the following prices:—Bottoming patent-leather, $2 50; bottoming calf-skin, $2 25; closing patent-leather tops, $2; closing calf-skin, 7s. Second rate of wages: Bottoming patent leather, 18s.; bottoming calf-skin, $2; closing patent leather, $2; closing calf-skin, 6s. At the third rate of wages, a boot can be both closed and bottomed for $2. At least one of the leading New-York houses does not, however, confine itself within the limits of these rates. The prices paid by it are as follows: Bottoming patent-leather,

$4; bottoming calf-skin, $3; closing patent-leather, $2 50; closing calf-skin, $1. This manufacturer can, however, afford to give these prices, as he can get for his patent-leather boots from $10 to $12, and for his calf-skin boots from $7 to $8. We must not, however, run away with the notion that this apparent disparity creates any real difference in the remuneration of journeymen. A good bottomer on the second rate of wages, can earn as much as on the extra rates paid in Pacalin's shop. This employer is so particular with regard to the finish of the work which he turns out, that more time must be spent over it, and consequently the journeymen cannot get through as many pieces in the week as he could do elsewhere.

It is quite a mistake to suppose that the extravagant prices above quoted ensure any real superiority in the quality and durability of the boots; as good boots may be purchased in the shops of employers who pay their journeymen according to the second rate of wages. All the difference is in the ornamental stitching, which adds little or nothing to the intrinsic value of the boot. It may gratify the vanity of the fop, but it adds nothing at all to the comfort, solidity, or nice adjustment of the article. It is extraordinary how the influence of fashion, or the *prestige* of a name will cause people to shut their eyes to this fact. More money is paid for what is called style, or, in other words, the arbitrary distinction set up by tradesmen to gull the multitude, than would purchase twice over the equally serviceable but less pretentious article, which bears not the *cachet* of some fashionable purveyor.

> "So may the outward shows be least themselves;
> The world is still deceived with ornament."

Of the manufactures of which we are treating, there are twenty-four contributors to the Exhibition from the City and State of New-York, five from Massachusetts, two from Pennsylvania, one from Missouri, and one from Texas. From Great Britain there are two; from France, eight; from Germany, six; and Austria, one.

There is, perhaps, no branch of industry in which we make a more creditable display than in this. Almost all the specimens shown are of first-rate merit, and will vie with the best French productions, both in taste and execution. The samples of ladies' shoes and slippers are especially worthy of notice. Every species of ornament that fancy or extravagance could desire, seems to have been lavished upon them, from the most delicate lace-work to the heaviest gold embroidery. Although we take pride in the skill of our artisans, and would be the last to deny to the *beau sexe* those reasonable adornments which they deem necessary to set off their charms to the best advantage, we still cannot help expressing our regret to see this taste for prodigality and luxury carried to such a ruinous extreme. With the wasteful and extravagant habits of the European *noblesse*, we will soon begin to copy their vices, and lose sight of that becoming simplicity of attire and severity of morals which are in character with our institutions. Already have our women become distinguished in the eyes of foreigners by the costliness and fanciful extravagance of their dress; and we are sorry to say that this mania is not confined to the wealthy, but is rapidly extending itself to those classes which have but small and precarious incomes to depend upon. This is a bad system, and must be checked in time. Nothing tends more to corrupt and demoralize the whole tone of society.

Among the novelties exhibited in the gentlemen's branch, is a pair of boots made of alligator's skin, by W. Benedict, of Galveston, Texas. Although the surface of the upper-leather presents that scaly appearance which was to be expected, the effort is rather pleasing to the eye than otherwise. The boot is beautifully finished, and, from its peculiar appearance, will, no doubt, tickle the fancy of our young bloods. Whether the supply will keep pace with the demand, is another question, as it is not quite so easy to catch an alligator as a calf. Lang, of Warren-street, exhibits specimens of what he calls his adjusting spring boots. The spring is either contracted or expanded by means of a key inserted into a box in the heel, like the box of a spur. The contrivance is ingenious, and if it effects the object proposed—that of keeping the boot always in shape—it must come into general use. The American Union Boot, Shoe, and Leather Company show samples of their pegged brogans and heavy boots and shoes, which seem to combine strength and durability with more neatness of execution than is usually to be found in this class of goods. The same remark applies to the Australian and Californian mining boots exhibited by Underwood & Godfrey, of Milford, Massachusetts. Better made or more substantial articles it would be impossible to produce. Of the finer descriptions of home-made gentlemen's boots, the best specimens we have noticed are those of Mayer Eisemann, Sylvester Cahill, John Ready, Philip Steiger, and Patrick Magee, of New-York; Leonard Benkart, of Philadelphia; and J. E. Henn, of St. Louis. The men's boots exhibited in the French department, are, as usual, very carefully finished, but the assortment is small, and presents little variety. The specimens shown by Clercx, of the Boulevard des Italiens, appear to us superior to any of the others, both as regards quality and execution. Kault Este, of the Rue de la Paix, exhibits a case of ladies' shoes and slippers which are very beautifully finished and ornamented; but, as we have before stated, the American specimens display quite as much taste and richness. Nothing can be more beautiful than the samples of workmanship in this particular class of goods, exhibited by Messrs. Miller, Brooks, and Shaw, of this city. We can only say, that if the ease and comfort of the foot were as carefully studied by shoemakers as external embellishment, the profession of the Corn Doctor would be at an end.

[For some account of a new Shoe Pegging Machine, see the article on Machinery.]

XXIV.

PAPER AND ITS MANUFACTURE.

There are some articles in the Exhibition much neglected by visitors, although their importance is really considerable. Among them not the least important is the show of Paper, which thousands pass by without paying the least attention, except perhaps, to De la Rue's or Marion's fancy stationery, where there are so many varieties of beautifully gilded, painted, embroidered or lace-cut letter-paper. Nevertheless, if those thousands would think only for a moment of the many useful employments to which the dirty and otherwise useless rags, picked very often along the gutters, are turned, they would be amazed indeed, and thankful for the marvellous and continually increasing improvements introduced in this manufacture, which not only enable us to produce the beautiful sheets upon which we write our letters, but also the many other equally useful kinds of paper. The time is not yet remote when paper, in consequence of its cost, was the privilege of the rich classes; and we were very forcibly struck with the change since then, when we saw, some four months ago, a number of *The Boston Gazette*, printed in 1779, upon a sheet only some eighteen inches long by ten inches wide, with which we would not to-day even wrap our candles. But then paper was sold, some at forty cents a pound, and of course our grandsires could not afford to purchase a better and larger sheet, even in order to print the great and immortal facts of the Revolution. What was the price of subscription to such a sheet, we do not know, but we are sure that it was at least three or four times higher than that of *The Tribune*. Forty years ago, three men, working very hard all day long, could scarcely manufacture from the pulp of rags four thousand small sheets; while, with the new means of the present day, the same men can produce in the same time over sixty thousand, and make them in an endless sheet of any length—and it has been calculated that, if the paper produced yearly by six machines could be put together, the sheet would be long enough to encircle the globe.

Our improved methods of making paper have, however, been closely pressed upon by the immense and increasing consumption of the article. And no where is so much of it used as in the United States. In France, for example, with its thirty-five millions of inhabitants, only seventy thousand tons of paper are produced yearly (of which one-seventh part is for exportation,) giving only four pounds per head; and in England, for its twenty-eight millions, the production is sixty-six thousand tons, giving four and three-quarter pounds per head; while in this country the production may be calculated, although there are no precise documents, at very nearly the same amount as in England and France together, no part of it being exported, yielding for the twenty millions of free Americans very nearly thirteen and a half pounds per head as the yearly consumption. This can be accounted for only by our liberal institutions, the circulation of journals, and the vast use of books in our common schools.

Of the hundreds of manufacturers in each country, there are only a few who have condescended to exhibit their products. We find in the Palace specimens from only three in America, three in England, seven in Germany, four in France, one in Belgium, and three in Holland, while his Negro Majesty, the Emperor of Hayti, does not disdain to enter the field, and send some bundles of very good paper, made from the Banana tree. Why would not the more advanced manufacturers (who, perhaps, made this paper for him,) send their own also? If we had the honor of belonging to the Grand Jury of the Exhibition, we would award the prize medal to Faustin I., if only to make our own makers ashamed. We are told that there are above seventeen hundred paper-mills in the United States, from which we infer that there are at least five hundred proprietors or companies, though only three have contributed to the Exhibition.

It is true that these three are masters of their trade. We are pleased to see that the firm of Platner & Co., of Lee, Mass., did not think it beneath their dignity to exhibit their beautiful writing paper; but we would advise them not to keep it, as they do, in its gilded envelopes. The same could be said to almost all the paper-makers of all nations. These decorated wrappers are of little interest; it is the paper itself we wish to see, and, as there is nobody to show it, it would be better to leave some few quires to be soiled by the hands of visitors than to give them no opportunity of judging as to the article.

Nothing can surpass the beauty and goodness of those letter and blank-book papers which we were able to examine. For the firmness of the close and uniformly-woven sheet, the purity of the pulp, the color and hardness of the sizing, they can compete with any of the best papers made in Europe, and they really do honor to New England.

The Carew Manufacturing Company of South Hadley, Mass., exhibit a quantity of very respectable-looking packages of letter-paper, of which we wish we could say something, but can only report that we have been able neither to see nor touch it. If, however, this paper is as good as that we are used to see from the same manufactory, it is worthy of being shown to our foreign visitors in some more practical way than under its gilded covers.

The same may be said of the Victoria Mills' paper—is it English or American?—which Cyrus Field & Co. have locked up, by way of precaution, under a glass case.

Where are the specimens of Manilla paper in reams and rolls from the mills of Manning, Peckham & Howland, of Troy? We have not been able to discover them; and yet this description of wrapping-paper is a sort of national manufacture which is much envied by the English paper-makers on account of the extraordinary strength of its thin sheets, which are as tough as parchment.

In the English Department, as we have said, there are only three competitors. But, at least, one can see the specimens exhibited, and find somebody who will show them.

A. Cowan & Sons, of Edinburgh, who have the largest establishment in Great Britain, have very good specimens of all kinds of Writing Paper. Their blue-laid and cream-laid post is of a good texture; the pulp is pure, but the blue lacks something in color, not being exactly the same shade on both sides of the sheet. All these papers are very strongly sized; but in respect to their surface, which is rough, they are rather inferior.

The specimens of Note-paper (paper made by hand) exhibited by M. J. Hollingworth, of the celebrated Turkey Mills, are worthy of the name of their former proprietor, the world-renowned Whatman, whose brand is universally considered as the guaranty of a good article. The drawing-papers are of the highest quality, and their bank-post is of the best we have seen. We do not so well like their machine-made drawing paper: it seemed to us a little deficient in sizing, so that it would hardly do for water-painting.

Thomas H. Saunders, of Dartford, without any doubt, exhibits the best paper in the Crystal Palace, both for quality and purity of pulp, exactness of weaving, firmness of sheet, hardness of sizing, and good finish. The prize can only be disputed between him, Platner & Smith, and Blanchet Frères, or Kleber, from France, of whom we will speak presently.

But we cannot leave Mr. Saunders without paying him the highest compliment for his water-marked paper. If we were to consider it as merely ornamental, it would possess very little interest. But if we think of its fitness for fine bank-notes and checks for the prevention of forgery, and if we consider how, for this purpose, it is important to have the most perfect design, so as to render imitation impossible, we are struck with the delicacy of the lines, embedded in the pulp itself, and the beautifully fading shades of the designs, which make this production quite an artistic work. With regard to the process of impressing these designs in the paper, suffice it to say, that it is done in manufacturing the sheet itself, and cannot be done afterward without leaving many signs of the forgery. This, with the difficulty for a forger of preparing his own pulp and molding the sheet, which requires special practical ability, we consider the peculiar perfection of the water-mark; it is quite clear that where it is used, forgery becomes almost impossible. Any one can convince himself of this by the mere inspection of these beautiful water-marks, representing the Virgin, the Fornarina, Queen Victoria, Prince Albert, Mendelsohn, Abelard, Heloise, the Capitol in Washington. All Banks should avail themselves of the security which is offered, by the use of this paper, which the Bank of England has lately adopted.

In going toward the French Department, we find the collection of the Messrs. Vanhemmelrynk, of Stal, near Brussels, who exhibit a large quantity of specimens of every description of paper. They are the only exhibitors who have properly understood that, in a World's Fair, not the finest articles alone, but rather those for the use of the million, ought to be exhibited. Here are some very good colored wrapping-papers, and some good writing-paper, rather tender, perhaps, especially when compared with our own, or with the English article, though of a good quality. But what most struck us was some good printing paper, at eighty francs per one hundred kilogrammes, which corresponds to something like seven and a half cents a pound.

We have remarked above, that Blanchet Fréres, or Kleber, from France, might compete with the best American and English manufacturers. We regret that they have inclosed their specimens in a glass case instead of arranging them so that they could be shown to every one to the best advantage. Their thin Bank-post, and Bristol and colored Paste-boards for drawing, are especially worthy of notice, as well as their Incombustible Paper for gun and cannon cartridges; this is made entirely from skins.

But the great feature of this Exhibition, especially for us, is a plain-looking collection of writing-paper, *made entirely from straw*, by Coupier and Mellier, of France, who have also patented their process in this country. For a long time we have believed in the possibility of making paper from crude vegetable substances, as the fibres contained in them may evidently be made available for the purpose. But we had not been aware, until hearing the explanations of Mr. Mellier, the inventor of this paper, of the difficulty of getting these fibres into a convenient state to turn them into pulp for manufacture.

It appears that some one hundred and fifty different processes of doing this have been patented as well in England as in France, but that all of them have utterly failed, either in respect of the quality and color of the paper, or the cost of production. The first attempt was made in Germany in 1756, where the scarcity of rags was felt even then, although the production of paper has since increased about twenty-five per cent. A treatise upon the subject was printed in Frankfort-on-the-Main, giving a plan for reducing all vegetables into pulp, and bleaching the same. Some twenty years afterward, a new way was found in France, and we have seen a small volume printed in 1776, upon white-looking paper made from the bark of the Linden tree, at the end of which were some twenty specimens of paper, made from as many different kinds of vegetables. But the poor quality of these papers, and the cost of producing them, seem to have discouraged the inventors. All the subsequent attempts made from 1804 to 1843, equally resulted in complete failure, leaving only as a token the manufacture of the yellow, coarse-looking, brittle paper, generally used for wrapping. But the possibility of getting pulp from these substances was nevertheless established, and although there has been a constant prejudice against their employment, in consequence of these failures, there has, however, remained among all practical men in the paper trade, a strong feeling, that, by some means or other, a convenient process would be found to make them really useful.

The great difficulty Coupier and Mellier had to overcome, was to submit the straw to the chemical agents which they employ in such a manner as to produce on it the necessary effect, and, at the same time, not to wear it out; that is to say, to retain the strength of the fibres, and, finally, to obtain the pulp for manufacturing at a cost not exceeding, and, if possible, less than, the cost of the pulp made from rags. Before discovering the very ingenious combination of means which answers completely, they had to go through all the previous processes, uniting chemical science with their practical experience as paper manufacturers, and at a great expense of time and money.

How far they have succeeded as to the quality of the paper, we can judge by the specimens which they exhibit, which are strong, consistent, and of good color; as to the cost, by the fact, of which we have trustworthy information, that their process has been successfully applied, during the last two years, in France, Great Britain, and Switzerland, and is about to be applied in Belgium. We learn, also, that one of the inventors is now in America, and is building his apparatus for a paper-mill in Pennsylvania, which, in the course of two months, will furnish the market with straw-paper.

We do not know that we can anticipate an immediate reduction in the price of paper from the introduction of this process; but at all events we can depend upon its checking the constant increase of price, which must otherwise follow the constantly-increasing consumption of paper, while the sources which supply rags remain the same. But, if the inventor is correct in his opinion, we may expect that before long, at the same time that he will receive an adequate reward for his ingenuity, the profits made by the manufacturer will be increased, while the price of paper will be diminished. Then, while the public at large will be benefited in every way, we shall be able to add another improvement to *The Tribune* by printing it on paper about as fine and heavy as that used by the London journals, without increasing its price.

XXV.

BOOKBINDING.

ALTHOUGH we have evidence that the art of Bookbinding was pursued by some of those nations whose very names are now almost lost in the lapse of ages—witness the hieroglyphics in the Egyptian "palace-tombs" to prove its great antiquity—and has been practised more or less successfully, by the nations of modern Europe during several centuries, yet it is only till within a very few years that it has been known in the United States; for, though the trade of Bookbinding was probably introduced into this country contemporaneously with the first printing press, yet its earliest footing here as an art, dates back only a very few years, antecedent to which all books were bound, as "Hodge's Razors," (of Peter Pindaric fame,) were made—to sell; and in each case with a result equally afflicting to the purchaser.

It would not, perhaps, be hazarding too much to assert, that in no industrial pursuit has such a general improvement recently taken place as in that under notice, whether considered with regard to the greater stability of the workmanship, the better materials used, or, above all, to the more correct taste displayed at the present day, both as regards the style of embellishment and appropriateness of covering; for, prominent as were all other defects, yet in this latter essential was the greatest necessity for reformation evident. Therefore, it was that American Bookbinding gained such scant commendation at the Great Exhibition of 1851—in fact, the criticisms made at the time in London were by no means encouraging to future competition. The justice of the condemnation, however, lay far more in the want of taste displayed than in the quality of the workmanship; though it has since been generally admitted that this latter was far from deserving to be considered as a favorable specimen of what could have been shown by American binders, many of whom deemed it folly to compete with the old and famous houses in Europe, where their vocation has so long attained the dignity of an art, and where samples of all styles of binding, suitable to any kind of work, are so easily accessible; while in this country, the majority of even our most celebrated binders, lacking such facilities, are absolutely ignorant of the names and origin of the various styles practised in Europe. This deficiency in a knowledge of the first principles of their art has prevented many gentlemen of wealth and taste, who have collected costly libraries, probably containing many rare works of early date, from giving that legitimate encouragement to the bookbinder, which in other countries is so liberally bestowed, the owners of such valuable works preferring to endure the reproach of meanness rather than see their highly prized volumes disfigured by inapt and ridiculous *outward* coverings—a mortification to which several of our most distinguished collectors have been subjected. The truth of these strictures will, we venture to say, not be disputed by those who are most deeply interested in this matter, the bookbinders themselves; and although, as before stated, a great improvement in taste is perceptible here even within two years, especially noticeable in one or two instances, yet till the binders, as a body, have more thoroughly educated themselves into a knowledge of their trade in all its bearings, especially in the adaptation of the style of covering to the contents of the volume to be bound, they will do well to imitate more closely foreign styles, when they find themselves at a loss. If in addition they would encourage competition among themselves, and bestow, periodically and permanently, honorary rewards upon such as execute their work in the best taste, we believe the trade would speedily be benefited to an extent little anticipated.

Estimated by the display in the Crystal Palace, our views are, certainly, by no means borne out; but this arises from the fact that the nations of Europe, with the exception of one or two specimens from England, have not entered the field as rivals. We should have been pleased to have had an opportunity of comparing the merits of our best binders with men of such reputation as Beauyonnet, Duru, Capé, and other eminent French artists of the present day; and we likewise regret that the less splendid but more substantial works of the best English houses, such as Hayday, Clarke, Bedford, and others, have not a single representative at our World's Fair, to enable us to judge of their merits. We do not find a solitary specimen from France, and the few from England are, on the whole, inferior to those in the American Department; and, as the British samples, worthy of any notice, are so few in number, we will proceed to dispose of them first:

A collection of books, exhibited by Mr. H. G. Bohn, the eminent London publisher, affords decidedly the best samples of bookbinding to be found in the English department. We do not know by what house they were done, as the binder's name is not given, nor do we suppose they were sent as model specimens of English workmanship, but merely consist of a random selection from the large stock of the exhibitor, and are placed there, we think, rather to show the different styles adopted in England for various kinds of work, than for any other purpose. Foremost among the display, stands Selby's British Ornithology, in two volumes folio, bound in green morocco, of beautiful quality and grain. They are ornamented with a rich border, composed of heavy rolls and scrolls of a style very appropriate for large and richly-illustrated works. There are several other folios in this case, all suitably and richly bound, and serving to show a good and appropriate style for costly folios, intended for valuable libraries; many binders, exhibitors and otherwise, might also profit considerably by examining the smaller books, containing sundry volumes of Bohn's classical and standard libraries in calf extra, calf antique, and other bindings suitable for library editions. As mere specimens, they are by no means remarkable, still they generally look well, and are all in correct taste.

Mr. Seten, of Edinburgh, has a large folio volume, entitled, "Scotland Delineated," which at least succeeds in attracting the attention of most persons in that department of the building. It is bound in red morocco, and inlaid with what appears to have been originally white morocco. The arms of Scotland are stamped in the centre, and a border in which the national thistle predominates, forms the design for the side, while several ecclesiastical edifices are attempted to be delineated on the edges. The sides are sunk in panel, and this remarkable book is completed by the addition of large metal gilt corners. All this work is, in our opinion, utterly superfluous, and by indulging in it the binder departs from his legitimate sphere. Compare this book with the folios in Bohn's case; in the one every thing is attempted and nothing effected; the others are models of simple elegance. No binder ever yet succeeded, none probably ever will, in producing gothic churches or landscapes on the edges or outside of his books. Such workmen should bear in mind that the proper place for illustrations is the interior of the volume.

We are much indebted to Mr. Rudd, of London, for his specimens of binding, as he has shown us how ridiculous and ugly a thorough master of his trade, as this exhibitor no doubt is, can contrive to render a book. They consist of various works in paper, sheep, calf, and wood—we should probably give a more correct idea by describing the latter specimens as in timber—and are apparently placed there solely with the generous motive of allowing the surrounding cases to be displayed to better advantage. Mr. Rudd has either formed a poor opinion of the abilities of our binders, or an unreasonably exalted one of his own; or he is only "poking fun" at us.

Closely adjacent, among the stationery of De la Rue, are some cases for the reception of blotting and writing paper, which though not strictly bookbinding, yet sufficiently approach it to be entitled to a notice in this article. They are specimens of exquisite tooling, and the designs are of the most chaste and elegant nature. The inlaid metal covers, too, cannot be surpassed. We fancy we can recognize the pencil of Owen Jones in these beautiful lines.

The above are the only foreign contributions at all deserving of notice; in the departments devoted to Holland and parts of Germany, numerous volumes can be seen; but they are all, without exception, destitute of any merit whatever.

American Bookbinding, on the contrary, is abundantly, and, taken as a whole, very creditably represented, though during an evening inspection it is seen at great disadvantage, the part of the building in which it is placed being very imperfectly illuminated; this is much to be regretted, as visitors are then unable to appreciate the merits of one of the finest samples of bookbinding, probably, ever produced, namely: "The Alhambra," to which, however, we shall have occasion to refer more in detail ere we conclude, and now incidentally mention it with a view to call the attention of the Crystal Palace Executive to an oversight that can and ought to be remedied, as a fine and diversified collection of bindings is now almost lost in the deep gloom in which it is placed. We see some old familiar covers that have already done veteran service in various exhibitions, fairs, and institutes; but, as this does not detract from their merit, we need not particularize them.

E. Walker and Sons, have a case of books in showy and miscellaneous bindings, the principal attraction in the group being three quarto Bibles. The edges of one of these are very tastefully ornamented and painted, but we can pass no opinion on the outside of the book, as it can be so imperfectly seen, even during daylight; but we do not deem the inside scroll-work graceful, or compatible with the character of the book which it covers. "I still live," words now become historical, at once attract the observation; they are richly painted on the edges of Webster's works, in six volumes, and add, unlike stamped figures and landscapes, very much to the beauty of appearance in this otherwise well-bound set. The neatest and most tasteful books in these gentlemen's case are an Altar service and a Common Prayer, bound in white vellum, having a very neat design worked in gold and colors, forming a pretty contrast with the white vellum. The production of these two volumes must have been a task, involving great time and labor.

Lippincott, Grambo & Co., of Philadelphia, have a very good case of scriptural books, fully equal to any of those on exhibition, especially a Bible bound in brown-morocco, illuminated; a design on the side very tastefully and symmetrically drawn. On another, the painted edges are particularly good, perhaps the best we have ever seen, though plain gilt would, we think, have been more in unison with the work itself. In this case are exhibited manuals.

Dunigan & Co., have a case of Roman Catholic and other

books, very elegantly bound in fancy covers, such as velvet, tortoise-shell, ivory, and other materials. Many of them, too, are ornamented with beautiful medallions of the Savior in the centre, others being embellished with perforated ivory ornaments, or beautiful reliefs in brass or other metal. This is a very attractive and handsome contribution.

G. P. Putnam & Co., have a display of well-bound books, principally noticeable as containing the whole of the works issued by this enterprising firm since its original establishment.

There is also a rich display of blank books, undoubtedly the best collection ever brought together. Among so many it is difficult to select the best; we would, however, assign a prominent place to Root, Anthony & Co., whose contributions are at least inferior to none. The ledgers for the Bank of New York and the Chemical Bank, in full Russia, and most excellently finished, are particularly good specimens of workmanship.

Nearly all the leading Account-book manufacturers have sent in their contributions; and, for durability, ruling, and all those qualities which are required to make up a good book, they appear to be much on an equality, and all of the very best class. We cannot help thinking, however, that there is a great deal of superfluous ornament on the majority, considering the purpose for which they are intended.

If there is a diversity of opinion relative to the merits of the blank books, our doubts are not extended into the other branches of the bookbinder's art, for we have no hesitation in assigning to the case exhibited by Mr. Matthews the honor of being the best in the Crystal Palace, and this, too, independent of the Alhambra. We would particularly mention the "Knights of the Round Table," a compact quarto, bound in vellum, characteristically illuminated with a monogram in the centre—a perfect bijou. Also a volume of Victor Cousin "On the Beautiful," in green morocco, with a richly ornamented border; also two copies of Pickering's edition of Milton, one being in morocco, the other in calf, and both splendid specimens of library binding. A highly useful simple feature is also introduced in the shape of a so-called Flexible Binding, especially adapted for dictionaries and other works of reference, as by its use a book may be turned completely back, an instance of which is shown in the case, where a reversed volume is exhibited, suspended over a string.

But the gem, not of this case only, but of the entire Exhibition, and beyond question the finest display of workmanship ever made in this country, and the beauty and perfection of which cause us to regret still more the absence of specimens of the best European work, with which we believe it would enter into a triumphant competition, is Owen Jones's "Illustrations of the Alhambra," exhibited, like the above, by Mr. Matthews, of this city, as a specimen of the skill of his establishment. From a printed card attached to this beautiful production, we learn that the object of the exhibition was to show what could be accomplished by the art of bookbinding, "pure and simple," unaided by the painter, jeweller, or engraver; and his success fully sustains our own opinion, as recently expressed. The book is a large folio, filled with plates, illustrative of the building whose name it bears, and the subject thus gave the binder scope for a fanciful design, an opportunity of which he has admirably availed himself of. The exterior bears a light and elegant design, purely in the style of the Alhambra decorations. The panel-work is formed of intersected lines, and the compartments filled with scroll-work, the whole being simply in outline. No solid or engraved tool has been used in its entire construction; even the lettering is a novelty in this particular, being formed with a dot or period. In order to make so light a design bold enough for so large a volume on light Russia, with which the book is covered, it is inlaid with blue and red morrocco, the blue forming the groundwork, as it were, of the design, while the scroll-work remains of the yellow Russia color, thus standing boldly out from a dark ground. The red consists of a narrow strip in the intersected frame-work, which serves to enliven the whole. The exterior thus presents to the eye the three colors, principally used in Moorish decorations—red, blue, and yellow. The interior-design of the cases is rendered more showy by a very brilliant border of the same colors, and the centre is of white vellum inlaid with a straw-colored diamond lozenge, the fly-leaves being of watered silk of similar hue. From the size of the volume, the profusion of work in the designs, and the minuteness which characterizes the entire execution, we can readily imagine that the exhibitor has not exaggerated in his statement of the time occupied in its production. The general effect is splendid, and the skill of the artisan wonderfully displayed, especially when we consider that leather and gold leaf are the only materials used throughout, and that there is no meretricious effect gained by painted edges, raised panels, or jewelled ornaments, a remark which applies to all the volumes in the case. It is stated in the card that six months' labor was expended on this one book, at an outlay of $500.

Though we receive so large a proportion of our book-binders' materials from Great Britain, we discover but one sample of muslins from that kingdom, and that only of an average quality. The manufacture of that article was, till recently, entirely monopolized by England, though of late years the domestic production has been steadily increasing—the only house in that trade, Abbot and Wilcomb, effecting sales equal to about one-half of the entire present importation. There appears to be but little difference in quality between the two articles, while the American is the cheaper; yet an old prejudice still exists against it among many of the binders. Judging from present appearances, however, it is very probable that in a few years the foreign goods will be entirely expelled from our market, as native competition has already reduced the price nearly one-half in a period of ten years.

Two inventions which gained a medal at the World's Fair in 1851, are also exhibited at our Crystal Palace; namely, the Patent Backing and the Patent Finishing-Machines, both by Mr. Starr. The former is designed as a substitute for the hammer in backing books. The pressure is gained by weights and levers; and, by pressure against a pair of gauges, a uniformity in the backs is secured. The principal advantages which this machine possesses over the hammer, consist in the superiority of the workmanship, and in the economy of time required to perform it—a man, with one-tenth part of the experience he may have had with the hammer, saving from twenty to seventy per cent.

The Patent Finishing-Machine is designed mainly for embossing the backs of books after they are covered, but is also advantageously used in lettering and gilding, and the pressure is produced as in the backing-machine. A brass tool, two inches in diameter, is engraved upon the surface, to suit the size of the back. The book being placed in the box, and held fast, is turned with the tools pressed upon it, and thus the impression is effected. By the use of this machine, two thousand duodecimo volumes are sometimes embossed in a day at the Bible-House, where they are in constant use, though the dispatch varies with the size and thickness of the volume. The lettering, too, can be done in less time than by hand, and with greater accuracy.

Several other most important inventions and improvements, as connected with the bookbinding trade, have recently come under our notice, and it would be of mutual advantage to the public and the patentees, if they received the fullest publicity. We are sorry to say, that many of the latter have not had sufficient enterprise to send in specimens of their ingenuity, and we are consequently unable to call that attention to them which otherwise we should like to do. We have already devoted a large portion of our space to different objects of interest in various departments of the World's Fair; but, with every disposition to give meritorious inventions all the advantages attainable by the circulation of our journal, we do not care to go out of our usual course to help those who will not help themselves.

XXVI.

CANNON.

In an age in which the progress of science and the humanizing influence of the peaceful arts have already gone far to neutralize that thirst for military glory, which seems to be one of the ruling instincts in the breast of man, the subject of the present article has lost much of the importance that once attached to it. We have reached a period when the supremacy which has been so long maintained by physical force, begins to crumble and melt away before the influence of those great elements of progress. The steam-engine and the power-loom are now the arms by which the ascendency of nations must be decided: the war of races has been transferred from the bristling fortress and tented field to the great factories and industrial arenas of the world; its victories are counted, not by the number of victims it has slain, but by the number of starving wretches that it has made prosperous and happy. It has broken down the barriers of ancient prejudices, and swept away the landmarks of feudal monopoly; but it has left no track of desolation in its train, nor has it deluged the soil with the tears and blood of its children. In this triumph of mind over matter—this substitution of moral for physical power—war and its destructive implements will eventually be classed amongst the traditions and types of barbarous epochs; and will be looked upon by our children with that feeling of mingled pity and contempt, with which they will be taught to regard all such deplorable evidences of human folly. Until, however, this golden era arrives, we fear that we must continue to look upon the manufacture of fire-arms as one of the necessary evils of our present imperfect state of social development.

The period at which cannon first came into use has never been accurately determined. Some writers attribute the invention to the Chinese; and affirm that there are cannon still in existence in that country, which were made in the eightieth year of the Christian era. From the Chinese the Saracens probably learned to manufacture them; and Callinicus, a deserter from Heliopolis in Phœnicia, made them known in the year 676 to the Greek Emperor, Pagonatus. It is said that Solomon, King of Hungary, used them at the siege of Belgrade, in 1073; but, notwithstanding these statements, the Germans persist in ascribing the invention to a monk, named Albertus Magnus, about the middle of the thirteenth century. Bombards were first brought into use in France in the year 1338. Of this fact there can be no question from the proofs quoted by Father Daniel, in his life of Philip of Valois, and the more recent discovery, within the last few years, by M. Lacabane, of an old parchment, in which it is stated that the Seigneur de Cardaillac himself made the ten cannons necessary to the defence of Cambrai, and that the powder was prepared by Etienne Morel, his squire. It is pretended, by some writers, that it was with great reluctance that the French knights could be brought to use cannon; and that even Duguesclin refused those that were offered to him at the siege of the Abbey of Perigord in 1369. Louis Napoleon, in his able treatise on artillery, completely refutes these assertions, and shows by a careful reading of the *Chronique rimée* of Cuvellier, that the Breton hero did not refuse cannon but engines for casting stones; some confusion existing in the minds of the chroniclers of the fourteenth century, as to the correct designation of the former, which were originally applied to the same purpose.

The first cannon of which we have any distinct account, were made of wood, wrapped in numerous folds of linen, and well secured by iron hoops. They were of a conical form, being wide at the muzzle and narrow at the breach. They soon, however, assumed a cylindrical shape, and the wood was supplanted by iron bars, firmly bound together, like casks with iron hoops. The first notice that we have of cast cannon is in the year 1370, the people of Augsbourg having succeeded in founding several in that year. They were first cast in an alloy of copper and tin, but other metals were subsequently added.

It was a considerable time, however, before iron was resorted to, owing to an idea that prevailed, and which, curious to say, prevails to this day, that that metal is liable to burst. The truth is, however, that if iron guns are made from good ore, they resist bursting as well as brass cannon, and possess some important advantages over them. The first cast cannon that are mentioned as having been used in battle were of such small calibre, that they might properly be considered as portable fire-arms, were it not that the clumsiness of their construction rendered them difficult to manage. They were accordingly mounted on frames with wheels, or on portable stands made of wood. They consisted of several small tubes of iron, united together, or placed in rows, and discharged leaden balls, or iron missiles of a pyramidal form, with a square base. Louis Napoleon, in the work above referred to, gives an engraving of one of those original gun-carriages, described by Froissart and other chroniclers, under the title of a *ribandequin*. It consists of a frame mounted on a couple of wheels, and protected transversely in the centre by a wooden screen, through which the tubes pass, the latter being loaded at the breach behind the screen, and fired off in the same manner. The back of the carriage is protected by lances and broad blades of steel, set parallel in the wood-work with the protruding tubes. The plan of loading at the breach, which seems, in this case, to be suggested by the impossibility of passing between the lances to load in front, seems, however, to have been the general system adopted from the beginning. There is a document in existence in the archives of the town of St. Omer, dating from the year 1342, which shows that the cannon used there were loaded in this way; and it is probable that the cannon employed by the English at Cressy, were of the same construction; for, according to the *Annuaire administralif* of Gaud, these *ribandequins* were already in general use in Flanders in 1347.

It is worthy of note that most of the modern improvements effected in fire-arms, have been suggested by clumsy attempts to carry out the same idea in the very infancy of the invention. We have shown that the new system of loading at the breach, is, in truth, but a revival of the ancient practice, and any one who will take the trouble to inspect the stand of arms contributed to the Exhibition from the Tower of London, will be rather surprised to see there the original of Colt's celebrated invention—a pistol with nine revolving barrels, dating from the reign of one of the Edwards!

The lead cannon which were invented and employed by the Swedes, between the years 1620 and 1632, in the Thirty Years' War, were lined with tubes of wood or copper, and secured on the outside with iron rings. The art of firing red-hot balls from cannon was invented by Major-General Weiller, of the Electorate of Brandenburg. In the commencement of the sixteenth century, Maurice of Switzerland discovered a method of casting cannon whole, and boring them so as to draw out the interior in a single piece. Arms for expeditious firing, loaded from the breech and closed in with a wedge, were introduced toward the close of this century, by Daniel Spekle, who died in 1589; and some improvements on his system were subsequently added by Uffanus. A person, named Millon, invented a kind of air cannon, two feet long, three inches in diameter in the thickest part, and twelve lines in calibre, charged with inflammable air, and fired with a Leyden jar or a piece of catskin, by which twelve discharges could be made in a minute. In 1740, cannons were made of ice at St. Petersburg, and balls of many pounds' weight were projected from them without injury to the pieces. The cannon clock, invented by a Frenchman named Rousseau, and exhibited, for some time, in the gardens of the Palais Royal, and the Luxembourg, although conducive to no useful purpose, is yet deserving of notice for its ingenuity. A burning glass was fixed over the vent of a cannon, so that the rays of the sun, at the moment of its passing the meridian, were concentrated on the priming of the piece, and fired the charge. The glass was regulated for this purpose every month. The expansive power of steam has also been employed as a projectile force, in connection with artillery. The idea was not a new one when our countryman, Perkins, invented his famous steam-gun, but to him belongs the merit of having carried it out successfully. He constructed a small cannon, which, when connected with the generator or boiler, could discharge musket-balls at the rate of two hundred and forty in the minute; and with such tremendous force that, after passing through an inch board, the ball in striking against an iron target, became flattened on one side and squeezed out. The original size of the bullets was 0.65 of an inch, but after striking the target they were plano-convex, and their diameter 1.70 inches and 0.29 of an inch thick. At the London Exhibition, a model of a war-engine was shown by a person named McGettrick, which it was stated would discharge ten thousand nine hundred charges of ball cartridge in ten minutes.

It was formerly the custom to distinguish pieces of artillery by high-sounding names, suggested either by the whim of the founders, or by the accidental circumstances that gave them celebrity. Twelve guns, cast by Louis XII., were called after the twelve peers of France. Charles V. had also twelve pieces of artillery, which he more humorously than reverently designated, the twelve Apostles. A large gun at Bois le Duc was called the Devil; a sixty pounder at Dover is styled "Queen Elizabeth's Pocket Pistol;" an eighty pounder at Berlin is called the Thunderer; another at Malaga, the Terrible, and two sixty pounders at Bremen, bear the appropriate title of "The Messengers of bad news."

In the beginning of the fifteenth century, these names were abolished, and the following substituted for them; Cannon Royal, or carthouns carrying forty-eight pounds; Bastard cannon, or three-quarter carthoun, thirty-six pounds; half carthoun, twenty-four pounds; whole Culverins, eighteen pounds, demi-culverins, nine pounds; falcons, six pounds; Sakers, lowest sort, five pounds; ordinaries, six pounds; largest sort, eight pounds; Basilisks, forty-eight pounds; Serpentines, four pounds; Aspicks, two pounds; Dragons, six pounds; Sirens, sixty pounds; Falconets, three, two and one pound; Moyens, ten or twelve ounces; Robinets, sixteen ounces.

The nomenclature of artillery has subsequently undergone another change, and the pieces are now distinguished by the weight of the balls which they carry, such as twelve pounder, six pounder, &c. To the uninitiated in such matters, the technical description of a gun may prove useful. The interior of a cannon is called the *bore;* the solid piece behind is called the *breech,* and terminates on the button. The cylindrical parts by which the gun is fixed upon its carriage, are called *trunnions,* and the handles on brass pieces are called *dolphins,* from the fish whose form they represent. The diameter of the bore is called the calibre of the piece, and the difference between the diameters of the shot and the bore is called the *windage* of the gun.

Until the commencement of the present century, the process of casting cannon was attended with innumerable difficulties, and so little were the fundamental principles of the art understood, that we believe not one out of three of the shells cast for mortar service could be admitted into the stores. Owing to the improvements effected, not only in the mode of casting but in the quality of the metal itself, the results are now reduced to something like certainty. Guns are usually cast from metal, brought into the fluid state in a reverberating furnace, and the moulds are formed of loam or dry sand. Guns cast in loam do not come from the mould with a surface so correctly resembling that of the model as those cast in dry sand; and, in order to render the surface correct, and to remedy defects, it was always found necessary to subject them to the process of turning. In guns carefully cast in dry sand, the latter process might be dispensed with; the gun would then be strengthened by the outer skin of metal, which, being cooled more rapidly than the other parts, is the hardest. This outer skin is also less liable to rust than the surface laid bare by turning. The mould of a gun in dry sand, at the same time that it is more accurate, is also sooner made, and dried, than a loam mould. From experiments made at Douay, under the direction of Messrs. Gay, Lussac and D'Arcet, it has been ascertained that the addition of a small proportion of iron into the alloy doubles the force of the resistance.

Brass guns are subject to melt at the interior extremity of the touch-hole from the heat of rapid discharges, and the melted parts are driven out by the explosion, so as to render the touch-hole too wide. To obviate this, a bush of copper is sometimes inserted, and on this bush the touch-hole is drilled. The copper being less fusible than the brass, is not liable to be melted by the heat of the discharges.

The display of artillery at the London Exhibition was very poor, and consisted, for the most part, of models. The specimens of British ordnance, contributed by Captain Tylden, of Woolwich, formed the most interesting features in it, as this gentleman has acquired considerable reputation, both as an inventor and cannon-founder. The only other specimens exhibited were the model of a ship's gun loaded at the breech, by Mr. Gardner, of Lambeth, the model of an improved gun or mortar, by the Hon. W. E. Fitzmanine, and Haughton's traversing-gun on platform.

Although the New-York Exhibition can only boast of one contributor—the Ames Manufacturing Company of Chicopee, Massachusetts—the specimens of brass ordnance exhibited, and ranging from six to eighteen pounders, two of which only are mounted, will stand a comparison with those of any other country. The mathematical precision with which these guns are cast, and the care which has been bestowed on the subsequent operations which conduce to their embellishment, prove at once to the eye of the military visitor that this establishment possesses all the requirements necessary to enable them to compete successfully with any of the European foundries. In the mounting of the guns and caissons, they have availed themselves of the tardy discovery, made by coach-makers, that force and solidity may be obtained without heaviness. The wheels and frameworks of their gun-carriages are as light and elegant as if they were destined for gentler usage than the contingencies of war. They are, in reality, however, stronger and more durable than the clumsy vehicles that have been hitherto employed. The specimens exhibited, as made according to regulations of the United States service, are: 1, a six pounder, mounted on a field carriage, with implements and equipments complete; 2, a field caisson with implements and equipments, also ready for service; 3, a field-forge, with stores and tools complete; 4, a twelve pounder mountain howitzer-carriage with harness and equipments complete. All these carriages combine the latest improvements, and comprise everything necessary for effective service on the field.

XXVII.

CONFECTIONERY.

Although the juvenile portion of the community is undeniably deeply interested in all that relates to Confectionery or "Candies," as they delight to term the majority of those articles to which we shall have occasion to allude, yet there are so many "children of a larger growth" who have expended large amounts of capital with a view to cater for the clamorous demands of young America for sweetmeats, that it is not suprising to find them largely represented, by means of specimens of their goods, among other more or less important branches of industrial art.

So far as relates to confections made principally of sugar, the United States department may be said to contain the only specimens worth noticing, as, with the exception of some excellent rock candy in the Belgian department, and a very inferior specimen of confectionery in the shape of lozenges, "made by steam-power," from a Dublin manufactory, we have seen none worth any notice except in that portion of the building devoted to American skill.

First among the specimens of the *chefs d'œuvres* of the art of working in sugar are cases exhibited by Struelens & Co. of this city, which decidedly stand unapproachable by any other goods in the same material in the Crystal Palace. Though this kind of work, like so many other branches of industry, requiring artistic taste of a high order, has generally been produced in the greatest perfection in France, yet we have never seen, even in that country, anything of the kind superior to that contained in the case under notice. The subject, too, of a portion of their contribution, independently of the novel materials employed in its construction, appears, judging from the crowds by which it is always surrounded, highly attractive to the mere sight-seers, consisting of a view in Greenwich-street, embracing the arrival of a number of German immigrants, and containing probably not far short of a hundred representations of human figures, exclusive of horses, vehicles, &c., all wonderfully life-like. One part of the scene, however, is very unreal, proving the artists to possess strong imaginative powers, or merciless satirical propensities, indulged in with a reckless disregard to the feelings of our city dignitaries—a strong body of street-sweepers, to the number of twelve or fourteen, and all hard at work, being introduced. The same exhibitors have likewise a frame of butterflies, and stands of birds, also in sugar, and which, in their fidelity to nature as to form and coloring, and in every other respect, are really most artistic works, deserving of the highest praise. There are besides, fruits, flowers and leaves, equally truthful in their details; also, figures in French chocolate, of "rats and mice and such small deer," worthy in every respect of their companion cases.

Maillard & Co. have also some ornamental work, one repre senting the Arch of the Place du Carrousel, at Paris, except that the reliefs consist of the battles of our War of Independence and the Mexican Campaigns, in place of the original subjects. There is also an imaginative sketch, with a lake on which float gondolas, while winged creatures, otherwise in human form, disport themselves therein. Though attractive, these sketches are by no means comparable with the first-named contribution; true anatomical proportions of the men and women being totally disregarded, while the color of some of the inferior animals would utterly amaze any mere earthly jockey.

The chocolate preparations of Mendes & Martin, as well as some other articles of confectionery, in the same case, also merit attention.

The French department contains a variety of preparations in chocolates, also an extensive show of flavoring essences and coloring matter. Some of the ornamental boxes for the reception of confectionery are very beautiful, exhibiting all the delicacy and chasteness which have rendered the workmen of France so famous. Among the most beautiful is a collection of fancy bon-bon cases, exhibited by Salleron of Paris.

The confectionery trade, as such of our readers not "without incumbrances," (as the advertisements have it,) may possibly be aware, from the repeated occasions in which they have their attention called to the various "candy stores" they encounter in their walks when accompanied by their sweet-palated young olive-branches, is carried on to a large extent in this city, as nearly three hundred houses are engaged in the trade either as manufacturers or retail dealers; some of the latter, however, carrying on business on a very limited scale. About twelve establishments are occupied exclusively in manufacturing for the trade; though there are, beside, many store-keepers who make a considerable proportion of the goods required for their own customers. Of these twelve, there are three confined almost solely to the making of what is termed French confectionery, while the remaining nine deal in general goods connected with the trade. They also vary much in the extent of their establishments—one house in the busy season giving employment to more than a hundred hands, male and female, though the same firm at another period of the year will not be able to find occupation for more than thirty or forty. The men are divided into various callings—modelers, cooks, engine-drivers, where they use steam-power, and common laborers; the latter, a very under-paid and over-worked body of men, being subject to an intense heat which they endeavor to mitigate, as in the sugar refineries proper, by divesting themselves of all superfluous clothing. The services of such as these, under certain firms, are considered highly remunerated with five dollars a week, many not getting more than, some not so much as, sixteen dollars a month! The remainder are paid from six to nine dollars a week, a medium between the two being an average price throughout the trade. Girls are employed in arranging the confectionery in the boxes, and similar light work, for which they are allowed about fifty cents a day. During the busy season, there are engaged in this city, in the manufacturing houses, about five hundred persons of both sexes, though a very much larger number, probably some thousands, are indirectly supported by it, the paper-box makers being generally busily employed, and many children gaining a livelihood by hawking "candies" through the streets.

The city of New York is the head-quarters of the confectionery trade, supplying as much as all the rest of the Union together, and distributing the results of its industry to all parts of the States, as well as to Canada, most of the West India Islands, Mexico, Chili, and many other places. To provide the means of meeting such a demand, the agency of steam is necessary, and a large outlay of money is therefore expended in machinery alone, though it is extremely difficult to ascertain the real amount invested in this kind of property in the city. It is worthy of notice that the chocolate-mills used here by those distinguished in the trade as French Confectioners, from their imitating to perfection the foreign articles, are all imported, not on account of any superiority in the machinery itself, but from the impossibility of procuring separately a peculiar stone known as the Pyrenean Granite, which alone will answer the purpose required; and hence it is necessary to introduce, at a great expense, an article of foreign manufacture, that but for the stone, could be made quite as well, and much more cheaply at home.

It is estimated that fully $1,000,000 worth of confectionery is made annually in this city, and by that term, we mean preparations of sugar, chocolate, jujube paste, &c., but exclude many articles, which properly come under the denomination, such as ice-creams, jellies, blanc-manges, pastry, and other delicacies, which would run up the amount to perhaps double. Two of the principal houses manufacture daily between them four thousand pounds of "candies," at prices varying from fourteen to fifty cents per pound, the average being about twenty cents; and this is exclusive of lozenges, three hundred boxes of which are sold weekly by a certain firm, each containing ninety-six paper packages, such as are sold in stores, and each package twenty lozenges, making a total of nearly six hundred thousand! What can become of them all?

In view of this enormous consumption, principally by children, parents will be inclined to ask, what candy is, and what effect it has in a medicinal point of view? It is unnecessary to mention the endless forms which this confection assumes, whether as drops, plums, comfits, sticks, or other enticing shapes, but in any of these it is supposed to consist only of sugar highly refined, (though by different processes from that used in the sugar-house,) undergoing in each case some slight variety of preparation, and flavored variously to meet the tastes of different customers, the coloring, effected by some harmless vegetable matter, also being diverse, to make a greater attraction for the purchaser. When thus compounded, these sweetmeats are evidently quite harmless, if taken in moderation, though it is otherwise when allowed, as is the case in many instances, to become almost the staple article of food for a child, as common sense alone ought to indicate.

But most of the confectionery imported from foreign countries, and a proportion, though a very inconsiderable one, of the home-made article, is not manufactured of such innocent materials; on the contrary, substances of a nature highly dangerous to life, if admitted in large quantities into the system, are known to be used. Indeed, to such an extent has this been carried abroad that in France it has been found necessary to pass stringent laws to protect the candy-consuming portion of the public from the effects of the unscrupulous traders in articles of sweetmeats; while in the city of York, in England, within two years, after a public dinner at which certain conserves were supplied, several of the guests were seized with sickness brought on from partaking of sweetmeats colored or flavored with poisonous ingredients. It is, however, principally in the coloring matter, so far as relates to foreign confections, that these noxious ingredients are to be found, as mineral agents are adopted in preference to vegetable with the object, thus attainable, of procuring a brighter and more enduring color, for which purpose verdigris, among other poisons, is used—an article, as our readers are well aware, possessed of the most deleterious qualities. The flavoring essences, too, are not always less hurtful. Dr. Letheby, an eminent English toxicologist, and who from his position may probably be reasonably accepted as an authority, states as the result of an inquiry into the cause of a fatal case he had attended in the person of a patient who had been suddenly attacked immediately after partaking of some sweetmeats, that the presence of the essential oil of bitter almonds, a deadly poison, in the comestible he had examined, was clearly apparent.

In this country, however, where the use of confections is in a great degree encouraged among all classes, a little additional beauty, vividness, and durability of coloring, are very properly sacrificed, by all respectable manufacturers, to the more important consideration of procuring a wholesome article—hence all mineral coloring matters are rejected, and some simple vegetable agent, such as saffron, for instance, if a yellow is required, substituted; while the flavoring ingredients are equally harmless; and we have no reason to suppose otherwise than that this precaution extends to nearly all the candies actually made here, and only wish our remarks to be understood as referring to such conserves as are in reality imported, and not to the imitations of foreign articles made in this city.

By the way, we may here mention, as bearing on the subject, one of the many strange shifts that some people are compelled to make in this Babylon of ours to obtain the means of existence. There are men who go round periodically to the sugar refineries and collect all the drainings of molasses to be gathered in the largest establishments, deriving these "perquisites" almost solely from the floors and walls, which are often completely daubed with the sweet sprinklings. As these individuals are not, as a class, troubled with weak stomachs, or squeamishness in any shape, they very impartially take any other kind of dirt, of whatever nature, that may have found its way to the places to be scraped; the gatherings are then taken home, and cleansed as much as possible of the impurities, when they are converted into "'lasses candy," or peanut cakes, for the especial use and behoof of juveniles possessed of slender purses and a constitutional tendency to sweetmeats in any shape. It was possibly one of these young Goths whom we heard exclaim, at the Crystal Palace, while gazing at the beautiful specimens we have indicated, and which are protected by glass cases, "Don't I wish I could get through to them, just!"

To compare merits, it may be stated that foreign confectionery displays much more beauty in design and attention to appearances than the American, which latter, while as a general rule unpretending in outward display, has the immense advantage of rarely containing unwholesome ingredients. But in some articles, the French especially have no competitors, such, for instance, as their delicious preparations of chocolate, which are quite free from any objectionable qualities, and form a very wholesome beverage.

But there is one branch of business connected with this trade in which the Americans are lamentably behind all the European manufacturers, and in which the French bear away the palm of superiority from all the world. We refer to the boxes in which the confectionery is exhibited. It is true the specimens of domestic manufacture are so very limited in number, as to allow us to say that this trade is there quite unrepresented ; but the beauty of those in the French department led us to investigate farther into the comparative merits of the products of this branch of the skill of the two countries, and with this object we waited on one of the leading importers of fancy paper boxes and visited some American manufactories. In the former, many most beautiful specimens were exhibited to us, one being elegantly enamelled, another adorned with a pretty colored engraving, and a third ornamented with a handsomely worked flower on a silk or satin ground; while in the less pretending, a tasty appearance was always observed. In value, there was of course a considerable range of prices, extending from a merely nominal sum to as high as ten and twelve dollars per box. In the American establishments very few attempts, and those not by any means creditable, at originality or diversity, were made, and, equally in the best as in the worst, most of the articles of which the boxes were composed, even down to the little colored engravings, were of foreign manufacture—the pasteboard alone being home-made. All the cosaques, fancy baskets and envelopes, and even the paper in which the "kisses" and other confections are wrapped, are imported goods. As a growing trade is springing up in these articles, and as, in the last-named especially, there seems but little difficulty to encounter, it is a matter of surprise that its domestic manufacture is not attempted.

With respect to the nationality of the workmen employed in New York, in the three establishments engaged principally in the manufacutre of imitations of French confectionery, in its most *recherché* style, the majority of the men are from France and Belgium, with a considerable number of Germans; while in the other houses, making up general articles of confectionery, but little regard appears to be had to country, the best workmen, very properly, being engaged, irrespective of any other consideration.

XXVIII.

SOAPS AND PERFUMERY.

It was, we believe, the celebrated chemist Liebig who observed, that "we might estimate the conditions of comfort and civilization of a people by the quantity of soap which they consume." Although there is a great deal of truth in the remark, we cannot admit the uniform justice of its application. We once knew a man of a highly intellectual and cultivated mind whose personal habits were so disgusting as to justify the observation of a witty Irishman, that "he was the dirtiest fellow living, although he had more soap in his shop and more water running by his door than any man in the Union." We might go farther, and, but for the fear of exciting certain lively susceptibilities, point out some national exceptions to the axiom, in which we do not find luxurious tastes and great refinement accompanied by a corresponding attention to cleanliness. The only way in which this anomaly can be accounted for is by the fact that the cement familiarly but inelegantly termed *soft soap* enters rather too largely into the composition of their vernacular, and that consequently they cannot afford to make any very liberal use of the article on their persons.

We presume that it is for a reason precisely the inverse of the above that the manufacture and use of soap have grown into such importance among us. Of all nations we may be said to be the least addicted to the use of saponaceous compounds in our speech, while commercially speaking, we are large consumers of them. We are emphatically a cleanly people—perhaps of all nations the most so—passionately fond of the bath; delicately nice respecting the quality and odor of our soaps, and shaving-creams, and particular to a shade about the color and rigidity of our linen. With us have originated all the recent improvements in that important auxiliary of social economy—the smoothing-iron; and, if we mistake not, that never to be highly enough appreciated process for enamelling shirt-collars! If a stranger wishes for any other evidence of the neatness of our personal habits, let him stroll into the Exhibition. He will there find the places of honor assigned to the barber, the tailor, and the perfumer; he may even stumble upon a learned professor, demonstrating to an admiring female audience a new and scientific mode of cutting out their dresses. If he be a lover of statuary, he will stop to admire the busts of Franklin, Washington, Clay, and Calhoun—of architecture, a huge pillar (order unknown)—of window-staining, a rich specimen of medieval art, all in—soap. Be he curious on the autographs of the great, he will have an opportunity of examining testimonials from ex-Presidents, ex-Secretaries of State, and learned judges, as to the soothing and softening properties of the *savon rose*, or the miraculously hair-restoring effects of the *chemical Kathairon*. In short, our admiration of soap is carried almost to the extreme of a passion. If there be any truth in the maxim of Sir Edward Coke, that "external neatness denotes internal purity," we ought to be one of the most immaculate and spotless of nations.

Before we proceed to notice the various improvements in the articles of soap and perfumery upon which the exhibitors found their claims to public patronage, a few observations respecting the nature and progress of these manufactures may not be unacceptable to our readers. Soap is obtained by the action of alkalis upon oily substances, and, as these ingredients are numerous, the character of the article produced from them is susceptible of a great variety of modifications. The soaps in general use, however, may be classed under three heads. 1. Fine white and scented soaps. 2. Coarse household soaps. 3. Soft soaps. The materials employed in the manufacture of white soaps are generally olive oil and carbonate of soda. Perfumes and various coloring matters are occasionally added when the soap is in a semi-fluid state, and in this way a great variety of fancy soaps are obtained. In order to produce marbled, or, as it is more generally known, Spanish Soap, a solution of sulphate of iron is mixed with the soap, the action of which decomposes the iron and separates the black oxyde in streaks and patches through the mass. The action of the air converts the exterior into red oxyde, but the interior retains its black color, so that a section of a roll or cake of this soap presents a black mottled centre, surrounded by a red external layer. The common household soaps are principally made of soda and tallow. If potash be used, a large addition of common salt will be found necessary to harden the soap, which it probably effects by the transference of the soda. Yellow soap has a portion of resin added to it. Soft soaps are made with potash instead of soda and fish and vegetable oils; it has a tenacious consistence, and appears granulated. Soap is soluble in pure water and alcohol; the latter solution jellies when concentrated, and is medically known under the name of *opodeldoc*. When carefully evaporated, the soap remains in a gelatinous state, which forms, when dry, the article sold under the name of transparent soap. All new soaps contain a considerable portion of adhering water, a great part of which they lose when kept in a dry place; hence the economy and excellence of old soap, and hence the dealers in soap generally keep it in a damp cellar, that it may not lose weight by evaporation, or, as it is said, sometimes, immerse it in a brine, which does not dissolve it, but keeps it in its utmost state of humidity.

The exports of American soap and tallow candles were, for the years 1847 and 1849 respectively, of the value in 1847, of $606,798, and in 1849, of $670,223.

The manufacture of perfumery requires great nicety and care in the distillation of the essences and the preparation of the oils and pomades. The essential oils obtained in the south of France, are those of roses, neroli, petit-grain, lavender, wild thyme, thyme and rosemary. These essences are distilled in the usual manner. From forty pounds of rose-leaves and thirty pints of water about fifteen pints of rose water are first obtained by distillation. The operation is then continued until the quantity amounts to two hundred pints of water, termed No. 1. In this first distillation, an almost imperceptible quantity of the essence of roses is obtained, but in the second it becomes more apparent, and finally in the fifth it becomes notable. In the distillation of orange flowers is also obtained the essence of *neroli*, now become an article of great importance. To make it, the ordinary process is followed; the waters of the first distillation being repassed upon the new. When, however, it is intended to prepare orange-flower water of a good quality, only a fifth part of the water placed in the cucurbit is drawn off. There are two modes of making pomades, namely: *by*, and *without* infusion. By the former process, rose, orange-flower, and cassia are prepared; by the latter, jasmine, tuberose, jonquil, narcissus, and violet. Each process is exceedingly troublesome, and requires minute attention, some of the pomades taking as long as two or three months to prepare. No less than twenty scented pomades are distinguished by the perfumers of Paris. The essences usually employed in their manufacture are those of bergamot, lemons, codrate, limette (sweet lemon) Portugal, rosemary, thyme, lemon thyme, lavender, marjoram, and cinnamon. The scented oils are also prepared either by infusion, as in the case of rose, orange-flower, and cassia, or, by saturating with the oil for a period of seven or eight days the fresh flowers. All delicate flowers, such as the jasmine, tuberose, jonquil, and violet, are subjected to this latter process. In making odoriferous extracts and waters, the spirits of the flowers, prepared by macerating the latter in alcohol, should be preferred to their distillation, as forming the foundation of good perfumery. In the preparation of *eau de Cologne*, two processes are resorted to, namely, distillation and infusion. The only essences which should be employed, and which have given such celebrity to this water, are bergamot, lemon, rosemary, Portugal, and neroli. They should all be of the best quality, but their proportions may be varied to suit the taste of the purchaser. Of almond pastes there are three varieties, namely: gray, sweet white and bitter white. The first is made either with the kernel of apricots or with bitter almonds. They are winnowed, ground, and formed into loaves of five or six pounds' weight, which are put into the press in order to extract their oil; three hundred pounds of almonds yielding about one hundred and thirty pounds of oil. The pressure is increased upon them every two hours during three days, at the end of which time the loaves or cakes are taken out of the press to be ground, dried and sifted.

As may be gathered from our opening observations, there are no manufactures so well represented at our Exhibition as those of soap and perfumery. There are no articles capable of such an infinite variety of modifications—the discovery of a new perfume, or the novel combination of several known ones, constituting, in the eyes of the soap-maker or perfumer, a claim to a speciality. Of soaps, we have accordingly a vast assortment, the peculiarities of which are calculated to meet all the caprices of fashion and the whims of the most fastidious. They are, however, like the nicer shades of color in a picture, difficult to appreciate and arbitrary in their distinctions. The name and label of a favorite maker are sufficient to stamp immediate popularity on a new article, without any reference to its merits, just as the eccentric productions of some well-known painter pass current with the multitude, without any distinct comprehension of the qualities that constitute their excellence. To keep pace with this insatiable thirst for novelty, all the resources of chemical science seem to be taxed to the uttermost. There is scarcely a discovery effected in the laboratory which is not immediately applied to the production of new tints or perfumes in the manufactures of which we are treating. Whether this indiscriminate employment of metallic oxydes and subtle essences is beneficial or injurious to the action of the pores of the skin, seems to matter little in the commercial calculations of the manufacturer. As in the coloring of confectionery, we believe that in many instances the use of these powerful chemical agents must be highly detrimental to the health.

Of soaps and shaving-creams, the samples shown exhibit an amusing variety in their nomenclature. We have the genuine Yankee soap; the Congress shaving tablet; the gentlemen's favorite; the ladies' favorite; the Windsor brown; the lily white; the transparent; the military; the rough and-ready; the jockey club; the rainbow; the tricolor; the mosaic; the tesselated; the oleophane; the amber; the honey; the orange;

the lemon; the almond; the rose; the violet; the verbena; the myrtle; the heliotrope; the patchouli; the musk; the lavender; the sweet clover; the sweet pea; the national shaving-cream (for the million!) the cytherean; the ambrosial and the Panariston shaving-creams.

Of perfumes, we have an equally boundless choice. There is the treble extract of the upper ten, a rare essence! The poppinack; the mille fleurs; the amaryllis; the vetivert; the boquet Californienne; the otto de rose; the prairie flower; the mignionette; the winter-blossom; the hawthorn; the meadow-flower; the bergamot, and extracts too numerous to mention, of almost every flower that grows.

Of pomades and oils, we have the philocome; the ursine; the pure ox marrow (of simple but sterling pretensions;) and the *pomade divine!*

Of hair-dyes and invigorators, we have of course Phalon's, Ballard's, Brown's, and Christiani's, with, to us poor sexagenarians, cheering and conclusive specimens of their restorative effects. Some of the tints, it is true, appear rather purple in the sunshine; but as, like the owls, we only make our appearance at night, our youthful proclivities, as a contemporary would say, may escape detection.

In soaps and perfumery, as in most other manufactures that minister to the luxurious tastes of the wealthier classes, the French continue to maintain the pre-eminence which they have so long enjoyed. Although the American manufacturers have made rapid progress in the imitation of their best articles, they have been unable as yet to drive their competitors out of the market. The old prejudice which exists in favor of French perfumery has, no doubt, much to do with this; but at the same time it must be confessed that it is, in a great degree, owing to the superior quality of the articles themselves. The quantity of French perfumery consumed in the States must be immense; there is in fact scarcely a drug-store throughout the Union in which the sale of it does not constitute an important item of its trade. As usual, however, the tide of popularity seems to run in favor of one maker. The articles produced by him are no doubt excellent, but we cannot help thinking that the pastoral name in which he rejoices, has contributed in no small degree to his success. "What a delicious perfume! whose is it?" "Lubin's." "Ah! I thought so; what a charming name for a distiller of honey-suckle!" And thus are reputations made. It will perhaps surprise those who are so *entiché* with this manufacturer's productions, to learn, that in the European capitals they are comparatively unknown. If they ever were current there, they seem to have gone out with the pastoral age.

The perfumes most in vogue in the fashionable circles of London and Paris are those of Guerlain, Piver, and Houbigant Chardin. The productions of these makers are scarcely known here, but a small quantity of them finding their way into the market. Mougenet and Coudray and Mailly, names of inferior mark, seem to be, next to Lubin, the favorite manufacturers.

Although in the preparation of extracts the American perfumers have not as yet attained the same degree of skill as the French, some of the fancy soaps which they produce are fully equal to them in quality. Bazin of Philadelphia, the successor of the well-known Roussell, makes as fine soaps as any in the world. Very little inferior to them, if at all, are the soaps of Jules Hauel of the same city. There is no doubt that these productions must eventually succeed in driving the French soaps out of the market.

In the inferior and cheaper class of soaps, the articles made by Colgate, Hall, and the Mêssrs. Taylors, of Philadelphia, seem to be most generally in use. The transparent soaps, manufactured by the latter gentlemen, are as fine as any that can be produced. We have already alluded to a gothic window contributed by them, the panes of which are composed of transparent, or rather translucent soap, in a great variety of tints. The effect is almost as perfect as that of stained glass.

The importation of English soaps and perfumery is still considerable, although we have succeeded in producing here as good brown Windsor as any that issues from the manufactories of Cleaver or Low. The articles most in favor with us used to be those of Low, Ede and Patey. The first was celebrated for his soaps, the second for his essences, and the third for his pomades and cold creams. Cleaver's articles, however, seem to be now fast superseding those of every other maker. His honey soap made the reputation and fortune of his house. When first introduced, the run upon it was so great that, although the price was raised considerably, it was found impossible to keep pace with the demand. The sterling quality and low prices of this manufacturer's goods render him a formidable competitor to the other foreign houses.

The importation of eau-de-Cologne used to be considerable at one period, but it has fallen off greatly since our chemists have commenced manufacturing it. The original preparation of Farina seems to be fast losing the reputation it once enjoyed. That of Zenoli, another Cologne house, seems to be preferred by those who consider themselves judges of the article, and we have even heard it asserted that the preparations of some of our own manufacturers are equal if not superior to it. As regards ourselves, we have an old and it may be an unfounded prejudice in favor of the original receipt. We fancy that in all these new preparations we get what is called the spent odor of the perfume after it has been a few minutes in use.

Although Meakim's extracts for flavoring confectionery can hardly be said to come within the limits of this article, they are deserving of some notice at our hands. They are valuable auxiliaries in household economy, and may be used without apprehension, great care having been exercised in their preparation to avoid all noxious ingredients.

In the articles of soap and perfumery, there are from the City and State of New York seventeen contributions, viz.: Messrs. Colgate, I. T. Johnson, M. R. Mason, I. Thompson, Louis Michael, D. S. Barnes, W. Johnson, G. W. Brown, Rice and Smith, J Lendmark, S. W. Jones, E. Phalon, Knight and Queru, Payson and Thurston, Justin Shelhaas, J. Wilson, and Ira F. Payson.

From Philadelphia, eight, viz.: Messrs. Bazin, Hauel, Du Costa, Harley, Taylor, Zerman, Worsley & Co., and Christiani.

From Boston only two, Messrs. Cummings, and Beck & Co.

From New Bedford, Mass., one, Mr. Howland; Charleston, South Carolina, one, Mr. Cleveland; Chicago, Illinois, one,

William Sill & Co.; Baltimore, one, Mr. J. A. Jones; Natchez, Mississippi, one, Mr. T. B. Nesbert.

We believe that no other branches of our manufactures can boast of so large a number of representatives at our Exhibition. There are certainly none among whom the spirit of competition seems to be more actively displayed.

XXIX.

SKINS AND PELTRIES.

Having heretofore spoken of the tanned hides and skins in the Exhibition, we have now only to speak of those whose value inheres mainly if not wholly in their Fur. The only countries beside our own which are directly represented in this Department are England and her dependencies. From England, the specimens are exclusively of the manufactured class. They consist mainly of sheep-skin rugs, shorn by Bevington & Morris, and I. S. Deed, of London, and Cyrus & James Clark, of Somerset. These are of every possible hue and pattern. The Messrs. Clarks also exhibit specimens of goat-skin rugs, not found elsewhere, and some ladies' fur muffs, and children's muffs. They are extensive manufacturers of shoes from the hair-dressed skins of the seal and other animals, with inner linings of wool and cotton.

The most noticeable collection of Furs is in the Canadian Department. They are chiefly from the Hudson's Bay Company, and embrace the following varieties: Black bear, beaver, otter, fisher, marten, mink, silver fox, red fox, cross fox, lynx, raccoon, muskrat, fur seal, and black squirrel. Some of these are very fine, as well as peculiar—a silver fox-skin for instance; but we are at a loss to conceive how it should be worth the price at which it is valued—thirty pounds! It should be remarked that the black bear skins have been subjected to a sort of tanning different from that which converts ordinary skins into leather. We did not learn the process to which this particular specimen had been subjected, but it may be stated, as somewhat curious, that hogs' brains are sometimes used to tan bear skins, and that they have a high reputation among backwoodsmen in the preparation of robes. Quite a curious use of the cuttings of a furrier's shop has been made by G. Lomer, of

Montreal, in a circular sleigh-robe, which he has named the Masterpiece. It is composed of nine thousand three hundred and seventeen patches of skins of almost every sufficiently strong variety, so arranged as to resemble the pelt of a leopard.

In these varieties of Skins and Furs, we notice very slight differences from those which are collected by the Indians and white pioneers in the far West and other sections where the larger game has not been wholly driven off by the inroads of civilization. In the older States, the shrill whistle and smoky puff of the locomotive, as they reverberate through the valleys and mountain gorges, strike such terror into the deer and the bear, that these animals have suddenly become rare where they were, until within a few years past, quite numerous, but a very few miles from centres of civilized activity; and in this way hundreds of men, who would have continued to depend on their dogs and their deadly rifles for subsistence, have been compelled to make a virtue of necessity, and seek it in the tillage of the soil over which they have hunted in former years. It has been a severe trial to some of the lazier of these to give up their favorite pursuits. The more enterprising have availed themselves of the employments which the roads have opened to them, and thus illustrated the civilizing influence of the new order of things which modern internal improvements have introduced. In the mean time the effect upon the peltry trade has been important, rendering it necessary to look to foreign countries for many furs and skins which were formerly supplied at home. And yet, American trappers and hunters still furnish even British subjects with a considerable supply of peltries. For example: we find among the exports to Canada for 1852 some nine thousand dollars' worth of furs and skins.

In the class of manufactured furs, we are able to report some creditable specimens. Among these are ladies' dress furs from the following contributors, all of this city: F. W. Lasak & Son, Frank Bennett & Co., J. N. Genin, and George Bulpin. The variety is not great in any of these deposits except that of the Messrs. Lasaks. In their case we find many sorts of mantillas, talmas, victorines, capes, muffs, cuffs, &c. Some of these articles are magnificent—for example, one of the mantillas, which is valued at one thousand five hundred dollars. It is made from small, choice sections of the Russian sable marten, carefully sewed together. There is a fine opportunity in this collection to compare the sables gathered by the Hudson Bay Company and those procured in Siberia and other Russian provinces. The latter are much superior to the former, though it takes good judges to detect the difference in outward appearance. The immense cost of some of these ladies' furs will cease to be so surprising, when, in connection with the fact that they are made from the choicest parts alone, the cost of the skins is taken into account. This is often as much as fifty, and sometimes seventy dollars for a single skin, although it is not larger than that of the domestic cat. Besides the marten skins, including the stone marten, there are in the same collection articles manufactured from the lynx, the silver fox, (a very rare pelt, in much request) the chinchilla and the royal ermine. These are truly creditable specimens of American manufacture. And here we remark, that, although most of this class of articles are manufactured in the United States, from Russian and British North American materials, England has some advantage as to both sources of supplies. A large portion of the Russian skins are imported through London, while the monopoly of the Hudson Bay Company is so managed that all its peltries are taken to the London market. There they are disposed of in large lots, at trade sales, by the authorized agents of the Company.

The fabrics from the soft and beautiful Chinchilla are necessarily quite costly, not only on account of the expense of sewing together skins so small as those of this little animal, but of their original cost. Many of these are subjected to an English profit, before reaching our markets, though they are, to some extent, imported direct from the ports of South America, of which continent this beautiful little animal is a native.

We cannot dismiss this branch of our subject, without calling attention to some curious facts of commercial interchange. While our furriers are seeking the elegant furs of Russia in the London market, or importing them direct from St. Petersburg, the furriers of the Autocrat's dominions are busy in New-York, and even in St. Louis, in person, or through their agents, purchasing the furred skins of America, with avidity, including those of "that same old coon." These coarser and cheaper furs are used as linings for the garments of such as cannot afford to wear native furs. Immense sums of money were formerly made by exportations of coon-skins to Russia; but we are credibly informed that two houses in this City sank the aggregate of forty or fifty thousand dollars last year alone, principally on this species of pelt.

We come, now, to the contributions from Newfoundland, which occupy Court 15 in the northern nave of the Palace. These are curious and justly attractive to visitors. Among them are two large stuffed skins from white polar bears, and a number of seal-skins prepared in the same mode, some of which are of an unusually large size, while many are quite small. Indeed, the collection embraces every variety of this animal. There are, besides, stuffed fox and rabbit skins. The latter indicate much greater size in the animal than it attains in our climate. They are snow-white, excepting the tips of their ears, which are black. The foxes are of the unmixed red race, the same as the native fox of our warmer middle States. To these must be added a number of seal-skins, unstuffed, as found in the shippers' hands, and skins of otters and other amphibious animals. These articles are exhibited by D. Hill & Co., of St. John's, who also exhibit some otter-skin caps; by Bully & Mitchell, of the same place, William Clements, of London, and the Newfoundland Agricultural Society, and Newfoundland Committee. Newfoundland has furnished other articles of interest, which do not strictly fall within the scope of this article, but we may properly mention a model of a sealing-vessel, reposing in the ice-bound waters, while its crew are represented hunting seals amid the ice-fields, firelock and club in hand, with every prospect of success.

The operations of the seal-fisheries of Newfoundland, and of the commerce and manufactures which are legitimately connected with them, are of immense extent and importance. A heavy trade in this line is carried on in our own city, where the skins are received as packed in bundles at the fisheries, and then assorted for distribution to the manufacturers of caps and other articles, for which they are specially adapted. A few years ago, the quantity of seal-skin caps manufactured and sold in all the Atlantic cities was much greater than now—that species of head-gear having gone out of vogue in those portions of the country most subjected to rapid changes of fashion. But they are still largely used in portions of the South and West. A considerable quantity of these skins find their way to the tanneries.

The commerce connected with the Newfoundland seal-fisheries dates back as far as 1795, though it did not assume an important aspect until 1815. The first year's operation did not amount to more than 4,900 skins, but in 1830 they were swelled to 559,342, giving employment to 1,985 men. The most reliable statistics at hand indicate considerable vacillation in the trade, the highest figures being those of 1844, which gave 685,530 skins, taken by 3,775 fishermen. In 1850, which is the latest date of the exhibits before us, the number taken was 400,000. There is no estimate of the force employed that year, but it was probably quite as large as that of the previous year, which numbered 9,388 men, the product of whose labor was only 306,072 skins. The number of vessels employed, and their tunnage, also vary greatly. For example, the vessels stood in 1830 at 92, and their tunnage at 6,198. Two years after, there were 153 vessels in the business, measuring 11,462 tuns. The very next year, the vessels dropped down to 106, and their aggregate tunnage to 7,262. The statistics show pretty steady operations till 1839 and 1840, when the number of vessels suddenly diminished to about 75. In 1849, they stood at 278. During most of these variations in the number of vessels employed, the number of men changed but slightly, and the results in seal-skins did not vary much, though a good deal of unsteadiness is exhibited by the reports, as we have already seen. The amount of tunnage employed in sealing does not run up as in other sea-going enterprises. The reason of this is, that heavy vessels are too unwieldy for the ice-bound seas of the north. Nor is the number of the vessels employed very important, judging from the above results. Much more depends on the tact and industry of the operators, joined with their knowledge of the haunts and habits of their prey, than on the vessels they employ.

A description of the processes of taking the seal will here be interesting and appropriate. We have already stated the origin of this business at the comparatively recent period of 1795. But not even then, nor for nearly twenty years later, was it prosecuted to any considerable extent. The general reign of peace after 1814 dates its active commencement. The seals are migratory animals, and are found on the coasts of Newfoundland only in the spring. The females seek the ice-fields of the great Polar Seas to bring forth their young, and are accompanied thither by their mates. Then, being swept by the currents to milder regions, myriads of them are killed while still upon the ice. During their sojourn in the more northern latitudes, they apparently live a foodless life—but, nevertheless, they become quite fat. The vessels employed in the seal fisheries are generally of from fifty to two hundred tons' burden, and carry from forty to fifty men each. They leave the coast of Newfoundland early in the spring, and proceed seaward until they encounter the ice. On falling in with it, they get into the midst of it as far as possible, by the aid of implements arranged for the express purpose. The vessel soon becomes securely fixed in limitless fields of ice, without the aid of anchorage, and the men dispose of themselves in all directions in search of their game. The seals are taken with spears, clubs and guns. The younger ones generally die quickly, and are, therefore, easily managed. The larger ones often give battle to their assailants, especially when the parental instinct arouses their resentment. Amid these death-struggles the most piteous moans are sent out by the young.

The flesh being unfit for human food, they are sought for their hides and fat alone. In stripping off the hides, the fat usually comes off with them. The denuded bodies are left upon the ice, when the weather will permit the stripping to be done there. At other times, they are carried bodily to the vessel, and skinned there under shelter.

The seal-fishing season is very brief, lasting only from the first of March till about the last of April. Hence, the scene of operations is a busy one. The most fortunate vessels make two voyages each fishing season. After the arrival of the vessels in port, the process of separating the fat from the skins and preparing oil from it, gives employment to a great number of persons. The fat is cut into pieces, and placed in vats, where the warmth of the sun does the work of separating the oil from the fibre of the blubber. The oleaginous property having once oozed out, the skins are salted in layers, in a similar mode to that employed in packing green cattle hides. When deemed sufficiently cured, they are packed in the bundles in which they arrive at the ports of foreign countries.

Within the entire circle of human enterprises, there are none more perilous than the operations of the seal fisheries. The hunters are sometimes caught in storms of hail and sleet, which come on at night and expose them to trials which make the stoutest heart quake and quail. While the vessels are absent from St. John's, the intensest anxiety prevails among the families and friends of the adventurous crews. Nor is this fearful anxiety of friends, which feeds upon the slightest rumor of disaster, merely imaginary. The north-east gales frequently drive the vessels to the shore, and dash them to pieces, making terrific havoc of property and life! In 1843, the wrecks of sealing vessels were very numerous. In 1849, a number more were lost, together with valuable cargoes and portions of their hardy crews. Last year's history was particularly marked by such calamities. The memorable gale of April 20th, 1852, was wofully disastrous. A single arrival from St. John's, at Halifax, put upon the telegraphic wires the tale of the wreck of at least fifty vessels, hundreds of whose men found a watery grave, while others were left stranded upon one of the islands in Bonavista Bay, and exposed to intense cold and hunger, from which some of them died. And yet these mishaps and losses seemed to put no check whatever upon the business. It has gone on as though nothing had happened—thus affording a striking illustration of the daring energy and devotion employed in the service of modern commerce.

XXX.

MACHINERY AND INVENTIONS.

A PERFECT account of all important inventions would be a virtual history of the origin and progress of civilization. The making of Iron marks the point of emergence from barbarism. The use of Steam, as an element of power, draws a broad line of demarcation between the last century and all which preceded it. The Mariner's Compass—Gunpowder—Mule-Spinners and Power-Looms—the Steam-Engine—Canals—the Cotton-Gin—the Steamboat—the Railroad—the Electric Telegraph—the Daguerreotype—the Ocean Steamer; such are among the rounds of the ladder up which man has climbed from the savagism of Australia to the intellectual and social condition of New-England or Paris.

A complete history of Inventions would solve many curious problems—among them, that of the comparative pecuniary rewards of inventors who have done the world good service, and those who have served only themselves. Probably, a careful inquiry would show that more solid cash has in the aggregate been pocketed for worthless than for worthy inventions; and that very few, who have really and signally extended Man's dominion over Nature, were personally benefited by their triumph. Some of the best inventions were never even patented—that of the Screw-Auger, the brain-work of a Connecticut Yankee, for one. Others have effected the pecuniary ruin of the inventor, and sent him, broken-hearted, to an early grave—yet have afterward proved immensely valuable. We scarcely know of any American inventor who derives a liberal income from his inventions, though many are sources of generous incomes to assignees or other owners. Morse is understood to have realized a handsome fortune from his Telegraph; but several of his associates, in working the patent, are believed to have done quite as well by it as he has. Arkwright left his children a vast property, the product of his cotton-spinning machinery; but neither Fulton, Whitney, nor any other eminent American inventor now deceased, is known to us as having amassed and retained wealth; while the great majority of the class have dodged duns and sheriffs from the luckless day wherein they first became absorbed by the idea of inventing, down to that in which they were shielded from farther persecution in the harsh but secure embrace of the coffin.

A volume would scarcely suffice for a full description of all the inventions and labor-saving machinery in the Crystal Palace; while to reconcile their conflicting claims to originality and efficiency, would over-tax the powers of any writer. We can only speak of the most notable, as a necessarily hurried examination of each has enabled us to do, giving our impressions, without claiming for them any other merits than sincerity and impartiality. Once for all, be it understood, that we do not aspire to guide the judgment of buyers or operators; they will of course examine for themselves, expecting of us only indications that this or that article seems worthy (or otherwise) of their consideration.

Flax-Dressing.—We have patiently awaited the appearance of Clemmons' and some other of the new machines designed to cheapen and accelerate the separation of the fibre from the woody matter of the flax-stalk—but none of them are visible; so we proceed to speak definitively of the inventions of Mr. L. S. Chichester, being the only Flax-Dressers in the Exhibition. They are the productions of a New-Yorker, educated (we believe) as a civil-engineer, and hitherto devoted to that calling. They consist, first, of a Flax-Puller, commended as quite ingenious and efficient, but it does not appear in the Exhibition; the second in order—the first which *does* appear—is a Brake, a little lower and larger than a common Fanning-Mill, but not very unlike it in appearance, consisting of two horizontal cylinders, two feet each in diameter, presenting surfaces of alternating elastic and firm-set iron ribs or breaking-plates—the elastic resting on spiral springs, and being opposed to the firm-set ribs or plates in the opposite cylinder; so that the flax, being fed endwise upon a shallow hopper or platform at one side of the machine, is drawn between the two cylinders by their revolving motion, and thoroughly beaten or broken by the pressure of each elastic on the opposite fixed rib, being subjected to a gentle *pulling* or drawing motion, and then to a reverse or doubling motion, which together loosen the wood from the fibre or line, causing a good portion of it to fall through this machine upon the floor beneath. Thence the fibre passes out on the other side of the machine, thoroughly broken, and is gathered thence by the handful, and presented to the Dresser—a machine very similar to the Brake in outward semblance, but consisting within of two conical cylinders, each formed of four large conical, spiral blades of wood, framed on parallel shafts, revolving toward each other; the blades of one cone being opposite the spaces between the blades of another. These blades draw in the fibrous mass, striking it first on one side, then on the other, beating out the wood and impurities, which pass off through an opening behind, like chaff from a fanning-mill. The work is done very thoroughly, and nearly all the fibre is delivered unbroken, and perfectly free from wood or *shives*. We saw flax dressed by these machines, which, having been rotted chemically, so as to leave the fibre white as well as long and fine, would readily command twenty-five cents per pound, or five hundred dollars per ton.

The two machines—Brake and Dresser—cost $600, and require four men and two-horse power to run them steadily. So run, they will dress one ton per day of the rotted or steeped stalk or straw, yielding three hundred and seventy-five to five hundred pounds (according to the quality of the material) of soft and very serviceable line or fibre. This, supposing the tun of rotted or steeped straw to be worth twelve dollars, the labor four dollars, the power one dollar, the use and wear of machinery, &c., three dollars more, and add five dollars per day for contingencies, would give twenty-five dollars as the net cost of say four hundred pounds of line or dressed flax, worth certainly not less than fifty dollars, giving a profit of twenty-five dollars per day to the runner or owner.

These machines cost too much to be bought by the ordinary

farmer; only one who farms on the largest scale could afford to buy them, except with a view to the dressing of more flax than his own. But one in each township, where every farmer raises his acre or more of flax, ought to do very well, and give a vigorous impulse to the production of flax. It seems to us that these machines might be profitably increased in capacity by doubling the length of the cylinders and putting on more power. The speed required to break a tun of straw per day as above is but three revolutions per minute, which might also be increased.

We have the opinion of many practical flax-men that this machinery will do.

Washing. — We had nearly lost our faith in Washing-Machines, except on the largest scale; but there is a rough-looking customer lately brought into the Exhibition, which revives it. It consists mainly of a cylindrical base or boiler, holding some ten to twenty gallons, into which the clothes are put *without* soaping; the soap is put in with them, and hot water and steam are introduced from a box or boiler below, so that whatever space in the cylinder is not filled with clothes is about half full of boiling suds and half of steam. Then the cylinder is made slowly to revolve, so that the clothes are alternately immersed in steam and in boiling suds, until the alkali of the soap has dissolved or neutralized all the grease, and the clothes are "without spot or blemish." The time required for this is from five to ten minutes, according to the tenacity of the grease, though we were informed by some of the workmen in the Palace that their oily overalls had been thoroughly purified by it in five minutes. The machine costs fifty dollars without, or seventy-five dollars with a boiler above for rinsing, and requires very little room. We think it might make the fortune of the patentee or owner, provided he knows enough to advertise it sufficiently.

Printing Uneven Surfaces. — "Burnap's Veneering Press, especially adapted to Veneering Uneven Surfaces and laying large Veneers at a single operation," strikes us as ingenious and valuable in its way; but our main interest in it centres in the light it sheds on the problem of printing irregular forms or uneven surfaces. We heard, some months since, of an invention in Austria whereby such surfaces were successfully printed, but have seen nothing that exhibited the *rationale* of the operation before this, which works by hydraulic pressure and adapts a flexible, elastic surface or *tympan* to the rigid, irregular surface opposed to it, and of which an impression is required. The principle seems susceptible of wide application.

Bonnet Pressing.—A new machine for Bonnet Pressing, by Mrs. C. C. Dowe, of this city, receives very general commendation, and seems to be very well adapted to its purpose, though we have not happened to see it in operation.

Pumps.—All kinds seem to be represented except the diaphragm pump and the common chain pump. Good judges regard the ordinary chain pump as in most cases the best article for wells that has yet been devised. It brings water from *any* depth, however great; ventilates its own shaft, ærates the water continually, so that it is rare that choke-damp collects in such a well. When set up with an iron case on a substantial stone or timber base, this pump is reliable at all seasons, and very durable. There is no patent upon the principles involved, and no particular maker. The chains and iron cases are on exhibition among hardware, imported and domestic, in several courts of the Exhibition, but the pump itself is not in motion in the arcade. They are on sale at almost any hardware store in the north and east, and cannot too soon come into general use. We have seen them in use in tanneries and paper mills, where their durability is severely tested by night and day work, in connection with engine power. Their simplicity commends them to the frontier settler, who is far away from machine shops and pump-makers. A farmer and a blacksmith can keep one in repair a century.

Rotary Pumps—Gwynne's* Centrifugal Pump; Cary's Rotary Pump, seem to be very effective indeed. The visitor must remember, however, in looking at them in operation, that steam is driving them. The proof of a pump is not in the size of the

* Another pump is noticed by another hand in the next article. Mr. Gwynne's claim to have invented any important portion of this pump appears to be disputed—we cannot say how justly.

stream alone, but also in the strength of arm or engine which drives it. Of this latter, the eye cannot judge. Gwynne's pump depends for its action upon the centrifugal tendency of rotating bodies, and at high speeds is a fluent, forcible pump. If it is true that centrifugal force is "no tax upon rotation" but is "a gratuity of nature," then beyond all question Gwynne's centrifugal pump is the best ever invented. We await the determinations of the dynamometer to settle this question. We are not disposed either to purchase or recommend Gwynne's pump, except as the most elegant form of the familiar centrifugal pump yet devised. There is no packing to wear out; but the high speed required seems to us to forbid its use as a domestic machine.

Cary's Rotary is very elegant indeed. The packing is simple, easily renewed by any man who owns a jack-knife. It adjusts itself according to its labor, the water being admitted behind each packed surface, so that it tempers its tightness to the pressure. In our judgment, no rotary pump will ever surpass this. The smallest size (No. 0) will be a very elegant article in a kitchen or wash-room, and as a force-pump will distribute water through the house. The next size (No. 1) will supply a factory or steam-engine of one to fifteen horse power very efficiently. The visitor must remember, in trying the hand-pump on exhibition, that he is raising the water only four or five feet, and not try, supposing that water will come up twenty or thirty feet out of a well just as easily. For steamships and local fire-engines, this pump will be found very satisfactory indeed. There are four sizes, Nos. 0, 1, 2, 3.

Of the Cylinder and Plunger Pumps, we are especially pleased with the simplicity and apparent durability of a horizontal-action force-pump, the invention of Mr. Dodge (L. P. or F. W.) of Newburgh, N. Y. "Dodge's Patent Premium Suction and Force Pump" is the infelicitous name of a very happy invention. Its excellence is in its simplicity, its metallic bearings, its arrangement of valves—very simple and durable—and its very light friction. It lacks elegance in its appearance, but combines, in a marked degree, the elements of simplicity and economy both of purchase money and of labor. The patent bears date June 7, 1853.

Farmers will do well to give attention to the Hydraulic Rams on exhibition. They are not as well known as they deserve to be, although a very old invention—of the French, we think. In all cases where a man has on his farm a lively brook, within four or five hundred yards of his house, he will do well to buy a "ram," rather than dig a well or build a cistern. Suburban gentlemen who miss Croton conveniences, may easily supply a small tank in their garrets, safely and surely, and thus "pipe off" their country-houses for purer water even than Croton. For the stock-yard, the steady flow is very valuable.

There are two on exhibition; neither one exhibits any very marked excellence. They both work well. The Yankee article, very neatly finished, may be obtained at any hardware store of repute. The ram is not as well known as it deserves.

There are twenty other kinds of pumps, all of which will suck or lift or force water. There is a choice among them. We have indicated ours, and given our reasons. Let the reader go and see for himself, and differ from us if he chooses, for reasons he may esteem better.

A Shoe-Pegging Machine is exhibited by A. T. Gallahue, of Pittsburgh, Pa.—patented on the 18th of September. The inventor states that no other machine for pegging boots and shoes is in operation, and we do not remember having seen any, though long ago satisfied, by observing the operation of other machinery, that pegging by machines is practicable. This one is made almost entirely of iron, costs $150 to $200, and will probably weigh some two or three hundred pounds. It works very quietly and rapidly, and will peg a shoe or boot, two rows on each side, (leaving a small space at the heel and toe) in three minutes, cutting its own pegs. One man only is required to operate it, without auxiliary power. A good workman will peg a shoe by hand in fifteen minutes, but close application to pegging is considered unhealthy. We asked an Eastern shoe-manufacturer who examined this machine when we did, whether it did its work better or worse than it is done by hand, and he said it drove the pegs more evenly and on the whole better. We understand that it is now in practical operation in Pittsburgh, but we believe no other than the one in the Exhibition has yet appeared this side of the Alleghanies.

Stave-Dressing, Planing, &c.—Four machines for Stave-dressing are on exhibition. Gwynne & Sheffield's is a well-finished machine, capable of dressing for the truss-hoop ninety staves a minute. The machine drives three knives, one to each edge and one to cut the face of the stave. The wood, after being thoroughly steamed, is offered in a block, the upper edge-knife strikes it, trims a half-inch, then descends the main blow separating the stave, then the lower knife trims the lower edge. For flour and fruit barrels, these (maple) staves will make good work, after seasoning. They are "shaky," however, in consequence of being peeled off like a shaving from the block. Had the block been dry they would have split; the steaming alone saves them.

The Barrel-making machinery of C. B. Hutchinson & Co., Syracuse, begins with a cutter, which cuts (from bolts or blocks) the staves to the proper curvature, so hollowed and rounded that no further dressing is needed—of course, with a great saving of material as compared with the old, manual process. Different machines cut from one thousand to two thousand staves per hour, according to size and thickness. To these succeed a Jointer, a Crozier, a Heading-cutter, and a Head-turner—each doing its work rapidly and accurately—the last turning out eight hundred barrel-heads per day, and requiring but one horse-power to propel it.

The third set of machinery is that of Wm. Trapp & Co., Elmira, N. Y., consisting of similar contrivances to those just mentioned, and said to produce three hundred barrels per day, from a single set of machinery. The barrel or keg made by this process seems decidedly superior in tightness and finish to one made with like care by hand; while the operator does nothing but hand on the blocks and pass the staves, &c., from one machine to another, until the barrel is ready for setting up and hooping. We cannot doubt that, where casks are wanted that will hold fast the most insinuating liquids, it will be found expedient to have them made entirely by one or other of these sets of machinery.

Near the beam-engine, at the extreme north of the Arcade, is a third Stave-dresser, for tight work, which appears well. It is simply a planing machine so arranged as to plane out a barrel-stave complete, just as floor-boards have been dressed for the last ten or twelve years. Hawkins is the inventor's name. This planing-machine, on the principle of revolving cutters, is a dangerous one to use. India rubber and planing-machines breed law-suits as fast as they do money.

Woodworth's planing machine is here in all its glory, and also a molding-mill to dress out a very common pattern. This is the best known of all the machines of the kind in the country. Its interests are familiar, *ad nauseam*, to all the United States Courts; its claims have been heard in Congress. It does excellent work and pays well.

Beardslee's Patent Planing Machine is a device which has nothing at all in common with Woodworth's. It consists of eight broad knives or plane-bitts, set up vertically in solid cast-iron stocks, and so adjusted that the board is driven along their face, and each takes a shaving as broad as the board; each knife is set to a finer cut than the preceding one, till the last shaving is as thin and soft as silk. The machine has an attachment by which both sides of a board are planed at once. The inventor applies the same plan to tongueing and grooving. This is the most efficient machine as yet invented. It planes boards as fast as one man can handle them, say one hundred and thirty to one hundred and forty linear feet of length per minute. Its faults are most manifest upon knotty stuff. The knives require a careful and a skilful workman to set them. The working model of this machine on exhibition is a pattern for all inventors who wish their inventions judged of by a model. This model, and one of a power-loom, are the only two properly finished models in the Exhibition.

Barlow's Patent Planing Machine differs from Beardslee's, in giving a reciprocating or drawing motion to some of the vertical knives or bitts. Minor differences we will not note.

These labor-saving machines have worked a revolution in the carpenter's trade. It is very rare now that a carpenter sets out to dress out boards by the hundred feet. The planes are well-nigh disused. What with planing, molding, mortising and tenoning machines, little is left to the carpenter but to put together the work. A regular old-fashioned carpenter is getting to be a curiosity. A man who can slap together a dozen or two four-panel doors a day is a very different man from the old steady workman, who prided himself on splitting the gauge-line with his joint-plane the whole length of a sixteen-foot board.

Charles W. Bemis exhibits a very beautiful arrangement of the String and Circular Saw. The String Saw is carried by a working-beam, which ends in an arc of a circle, over which an elastic steel strap is conformed at every stroke. The saw is stretched between two such beams, and thus dispenses with the "gate" and "guides," and moves very lightly upon centres, instead of slides. The shortness and perplexity of the curves cut by this simple tool, are a steady wonder to visitors. The Circular Saw is peculiar only in its gearing. A boy of twelve can turn the crank so as to rip a three-quarter inch pine-board with great ease. These are cheap machines. Every carpenter should look at them; they will save him time and labor.

Sherwood's Prismatic Lathe, is an engine for dressing out ballusters, bed-posts, newels, &c., into prismatic shapes. The superior richness of a prismatic post over a circular one of the same pattern, is really surprising. The machine is very simple. The post is held fast on centres, while a series of cutters ranged along a shaft, revolve with great rapidity, and dress off one side. The post is then turned one-sixth or one-eighth of a revolution, and a second side is cut. Each pattern must have a set of knives or cutters, and these are so costly, that, except in cities, the machine will not pay, through lack of work to keep it running.

Thomas S. Minniss exhibits a model of anti-friction bearings for heavy shafts. His device is to float the revolving body upon water, oil, or mercury, according to the necessities of the case. Of course his shafts will move smooth as oil and free as water. Very possibly it is a good device, though we apprehend that its novelty will deter men from its use. It is a good invention—look at it.

With regard to Steam Engines, we may say that no visitor is competent to criticise a novel steam-engine simply by looking at it. The rotaries are numerous and ingenious. We hope there is a good and economical one among them all, but we doubt it. Nevertheless, a direct-action rotary steam-engine is a desideratum—and, for that matter, so is perpetual motion. The three engines at work may be spoken of very briefly as follows: The Southern Belle, running without any labor, is true to the name *belle*—very showy, and (at present) very useless. No shop would ever dream of making or buying such an engine for use. It would keep one man busy the whole time to keep it bright and clean.

The Lawrence Engine—two cylinder—is neat, unostentatious, and workmanlike. There is nothing novel, however, in its structure.

The Beam Engine, from Providence, by Corliss & Nightingale, exhibits a new application of the governor. Instead of applying it to the usual regulator-valve, in this engine the governor is very ingeniously made to adjust the "cut-off," so as to regulate each cylinder-full of steam, stroke by stroke. The workmanship and the ingenuity displayed in this machine, are above all praise. As to its practical utility, only experience can decide.

Dick's Iron Shears, made at Hadley's Falls, (Holyoke) Mass., is a massive engine, decidedly in advance of all the boiler-makers' shears we have seen, in the length of cut, the ease of handling the iron sheet, and the accuracy with which the scribed line can be followed. Plate-iron a half-inch thick can be trimmed as closely as a lady cuts a cap or collar-pattern. There is a rival machine from Erie, Pa., which may be equally good in principle, but does not appear to possess equal power.

Mechanics will do well to examine a Screwing Machine, as the maker has chosen to call it—an engine for threading iron bolts and nuts of all sizes, from a half to two inches in diameter. It is difficult to cut a thread upon a bolt without crushing or damaging, to some extent, its true cylindric shape. The "spurs" and "dies," with the device for applying them, are worthy of study. The same exhibitor offers a Shaping Machine, for turning curves, beads, &c., by a fixed head and slide-rest motion, which is a very thorough and workman-like tool. A box of standard-measure gauges for bolts and drills, consisting of twenty-seven hardened steel rings, and as many steel cylinders, varying in diameter from three inches down to one-eighth of an inch, is a valuable addition to any large machine-shop. The accuracy of these tests is such that they detect a difference of magnitude less than the thinnest tissue-paper. Joseph Whitworth, Manchester, England, is the maker.

A new Portable Grist-Mill—new to us—(John T. Noye, Buffalo, N. Y.) seems very neat as well as most efficient. Its advantages are compactness, portability, freedom from heating and efficiency. It is abundantly certified to grind, with stones (French burr) three feet in diameter, eighteen bushels of wheat, or twelve barrels of water-lime, per hour. Its cost is too high to render it purchasable by farmers on a moderate scale, but the great grain-growers of the West may have it as well as millers. There are cheaper mills exhibited, which any farmer may buy; and we think the day cannot be remote when each considerable feeder of grain will grind it on his own premises.

"Holden's Patent Sheer-Cut Draft" (Moore Holden, Lawrenceburg, Ia.) is an undoubted improvement on the old method of dressing mill-stones, though there may be new devices which rival it. Millers should know.

"Storer's Corn-Kiln," to dry grain so as to secure it against the danger of heating and spoiling, is a New-Jersey invention. The cost of drying by it is said to be less than half a cent a bushel. It dries starch, paint, meal, &c., as well as grain.

How many Corn-Shellers there may be in the Palace, we cannot say: the last we noticed is that of William Reading, Flemington, N. J., certified by Hon. J. M. Clayton to shell one thousand bushels per day with a force of three men and four horses, and claimed by its patentee to be capable of shelling one hundred and fifty to two hundred bushels per hour. The ears are shovelled into its hopper with a scoop, or poured in from a basket, and the cobs are delivered apart from the grain. It was patented in July of last year, and one house sold two hundred and seventeen between November and April last.

Several Cotton-Gins are now on exhibition, but that of E. Carver & Co., Bridgewater, Mass., attracts most attention, being actually employed at times in ginning the great Southern staple, whereof the ginned fibre escaping from the machinery, is arrested and confined within a mammoth glass case or sentry-box of windows. The basis is of course Whitney's immortal invention, but Mr. Carver avoids the choking or clogging of the spaces between the grates and the tearing of the fibre thence resulting as well as the tendency to overheating and destruction by spontaneous combustion. There can be no doubt of the practical utility of Mr. C.'s grate and cylinder-brush,—the latter producing a strong centrifugal current ejecting the ginned cotton to any required distance and preventing that dropping upon and winding around the shaft, or collecting between the ends and ceiling of the gin, which was formerly a serious defect and a source of perpetual danger from fire.

There is one novel invention of which we may have already spoken, but which is so placed as to attract no attention commensurate with its merits. We allude to that for Veneering Uneven Surfaces by means of hydraulic pressure—which will reward the careful study of inventors. We see in it the germ and suggestion of other uses, perhaps more important than that to which it is primarily applied. In printing, modelling, literal copying from nature, art or antiquity, it may be made extensively useful.

In the small court assigned to specimens of Typography, Books, Binding, &c., may be seen some primitive results of a new invention in Graphics—an extension of Printing into the domain hitherto held by Engraving, Lithography, &c., which is destined to work a revolution in Color and Fancy Printing, if no other. Mr. Donlevy (the inventor) produces, by the use of Plastic and Stereotyping, typographic effects superior in accuracy and force to those hitherto attained through either Lithography or Wood Engraving, and at far less cost.

A machine for making *cots*, or little leathern rolls used in spinning (and of which twenty thousand per day, hitherto made by hands, are worn out in Massachusetts alone,) is one of the most ingenious contributions of Connecticut to the Fair. Those who are familiar with Whittemore's machine for cutting, bending, and setting card teeth, or the machine for making chain of brass or other wire, invented at Derby, Conn., will readily anticipate its best points. The leather is drawn into the machine in the shape of a strap or belt, is cut off at the proper length diagonally, so as to form the best edges for gumming, is then rolled or doubled over so that the two edges, being gummed in the operation, exactly meet; when they are pressed firmly together and the now perfected cot dropped through the machine and another length drawn in, to undergo the same process. The inventor's name has escaped us, but it will not be soon forgotten.

A Weighing and Packing Machine, for packers of Tea, Coffee, Pepper, Spices, &c., &c., is exhibited by Slater & Steele, Jersey City, which seems excellent in its sphere, though that sphere is a narrow one. The material is fed from a hopper over head, is weighed in its descent from the hopper and discharged in pounds, half-pounds, or otherwise as may be required, into a funnel resting in a square box, into which a paper has already been conveyed by the machine. The box forms one link in an endless chain of boxes revolving around a platform, and moving on a few inches, receives through the tunnel a square stamp just fitted to it, and thence passes to another and another, until the fourth delivers it pressed into a solid mass and enveloped. Mr. G. D. Jones is said to be the patentee.

A Tobacco Pressing Machine is exhibited, costing eight hundred dollars or so, and said to press Tobacco from loose rolls into plugs as fast as twenty men have hitherto been able to do it. We should judge that one of these machines could press as much Tobacco in a day as all mankind ought to chew from this hour to the final conflagration of the world.

Finally—let no one spend even an evening in the Palace without traversing the department of Machinery. Elsewhere are results; but here are seen the processes whereby they were attained,—trophies of the genius which rendered them attainable. Doubtless, all that has yet been achieved in physics is but a prologue to what remains to be effected; and perhaps some unnoted, thinly clad youth now sidling noiselessly and shily through the crowd collected in front of some whirring Cotton-Gin or rasping Stave-Cutter shall be inspired by his hurried visit and its cherished memories with a fruitful idea, whose practical issue shall overshadow in importance the achievements of Watt and Fulton, and send his name down to remote generations enshrined with those of Galileo, Columbus, Bacon, Newton, and all those illustrious benefactors of humanity who have signally enlarged the domain of terrestrial knowledge, extended the sway of civilization, or increased the general comfort and happiness of mankind.

XXXI.

MISCELLANEOUS FARMERS' TOOLS.

There is a Clover-Seed Harvester in the Agricutural Gallery worthy the attention of those engaged in the business of raising clover-seed for market. It is a box about a foot deep, four feet in length and width, mounted upon a pair of low wheels with a roller in front so arranged that as the clover-heads are drawn in between teeth as the machine is pulled forward by a horse, they are scraped off and saved in a box. When that is filled, it is unloaded into a wagon or upon sheets laid down in the field. It has been considerably used in various parts of the United States, and much approved. J. A. Wagner is the patentee, who says that one man or boy and one horse can harvest twelve acres of clover or timothy-seed in a day. As the heads only are saved, but little room is required for storage of enough to make a hundred bushels. We cannot give the cost of the machine, but it cannot be very expensive.

There are two models in the gallery of Indian Corn-Cutters. The first appears to be a very simple, and we should think very effective machine. It certainly is a cheap one. A horse harnessed in a pair of thills, attached to a pair of wheels, walks between two rows, while the wheels run outside of the same. Upon the axle there is a knife for each row, that cuts by drawing the machine forward, the stalks falling back and are held till enough accumulates for a bundle, when, by touching a spring, they are dropped in a pile ready for the wagon or setting up to cure in shocks. The corn is brought up to the knives by a reel. In the model exhibited, the knives are not set upon a sufficient angle.

The other model represents a machine perhaps more effective, but a good deal more complicated, costly and cumbrous. It is probably better for the great Southern corn, which requires a blow almost equal to that of an axe to sever it from the ground. This machine gives that kind of a blow. The cutting apparatus runs upon the left hand of a four-wheeled platform, which is to be drawn by two horses. As the vehicle progresses, a sort of reel or rake gathers the stalks, no matter how they lie about, and brings them up in between two teeth to each row, when a strong heavy knife fixed upon a shaft that revolves half round and back, is constantly striking down obliquely, cutting off the stalks, which fall back upon a carrier, which drops them at intervals upon the ground. These arms and knives are adjustable to wide or narrow rows, and if team enough is applied, there is no doubt about the cutting apparatus. It appears to us that the machine is too heavy and expensive for any except very large, smooth farms, where corn is grown by the thousand acres. The inventor claims that by some little change he can cut hemp to perfection. We hope those interested in either crop will give the model a fair examination. They will find it at the head of the South branch of the north-east stairway from the dome.

There is a model of a California Reaping-Machine in the same vicinity which exhibits a great amount of ingenuity. The cutting machinery is in two parts, working from curious cranks and cam motions in the centre, one knife acting as a balance for the other. The frame is hinged in the middle, upon the same principle as the hinged harrow, to work over uneven ground. The horses work upon a shaft behind, pushing the machine forward of them, the driver steering by a stern-wheel. The grain as it is cut is to be carried by rakers out upon bands on each side, and thence to the back part of the machine, where each bunch is held long enough for a man riding upon the platform to tie it into a bundle. We hope grain-growers will give this machine a fair examination, particularly those who grow it upon the same large scale that it is grown in California, and give the inventor the same praise we do for his ingenuity. We hope, too, they will have a better opinion of its practical utility than we have.

Upon the same table with the above model, there is a model of a Potato-Digger. A cylinder armed with iron fingers, mounted upon wheels to which it is geered, is to scoop the potatoes out of the ground and carry them over and discharge them upon a shaking-screen behind, when the dirt is got rid of. It looks as though it would work in mellow ground.

In the collection of Ruggles, Nourse, Mason & Co., may be seen the identical Plow used in 1742 by Roger Sherman of Connecticut. The contrast between this plow and the highly-finished, beautiful models in the present collection, is very striking. We look with wonder now at this century-old plow, and express surprise that people could have been so stupid as to use such an implement; yet that in its day was called "an improved plow," and its owner used to go about among his neighbors with his wonderful plow to assist them in their work. Now look at those of the present day and then at that. The beam is four feet and a half long, the handles are two nearly upright posts, three feet high, with pins in behind; the standard is fourteen inches high, the mold-board, standard and land-side are wood, partially plated with iron, very roughly; the length of land-side is two feet four inches; from point to wing of mold-board three feet; the whole about as uncouth a looking article as one could imagine, and yet a perfect specimen of the plow in universal use in our own time in that land of invention that gave birth to this; and a superior one to many that are in use in the United States at this very day. But in contrast with those in the Exhibition this is a great curiosity.

In the same collection there is a pump which we denominate the Farm-house Pump. It is so simple, so effective, so cheap, so little liable to get out of order, so easily repaired if it does, that it must recommend itself to people in the country where pump repairing is one of the things most often needed and most difficult to obtain. Getting at the boxes of a pump is often the worst part of the bad job of repairing. The one now under review will never give any of that difficulty as the working-box, or the substitute for it, is on the outside. Any body who can turn a screw, and use a jack-knife can repair all that is ever likely to get out of order. It is composed entirely of iron, except the India-rubber valve, or as it is sometimes called, the diaphragm. This pump and its operation is entirely different from any other. It is all comprised in about the space of a couple of large soup-plates, one turned bottom up upon the other. Now suppose a lead pipe coming up through a hole in the bottom plate, over which is a valve. Then the upper plate, all but the rim, is composed of vulcanized India-rubber, the edges of which are screwed between the plates. To the centre of this rubber the piston-rod is attached, and as the handle is lifted up it rises and forms a vacuum, which is immediately filled with water. The lower valve closes when the motion is reversed and the water thrown out through an air-chamber and pipe. Fifty strokes of this little machine, which can be made by a child eight years old, will throw fifty quarts of water. In setting it at a well not over twenty-two feet deep, it is simply screwed to a plank three feet high, with a pipe running down to the water. If the well is deeper, the pump must be set down, the piston-rod lengthened, and the handle fixed to a proper height over the well. This is particularly worthy the attention of farmers, as a hose-pipe can be attached, and water conducted through it by operating it as a force-pump with great ease, as all friction of the boxes is absolutely dispensed with. It is a good pump for a small windmill. If the India-rubber part gives way, it is replaced with the least possible trouble imaginable. The action may be compared to a bladder having a pipe in the water; if the upper side of the bladder is lifted up, water would rush in; if compressed by a weight or lever, it must be discharged with force.

There is another article in the Exhibition which we should like to call the most particular attention of farmers to, as it is a machine very much neglected in these latter days of steam locomotion. This is nothing more than a HAND-LOOM. This is one of the most simple and useful inventions for the new country farmer in the Exhibition. This loom verifies the adage that necessity is the mother of invention. It originated in Iowa, where the country is too new for power-loom manufactories in every village, and where the hand-loom is still a necessity of frontier-life. It was invented by John G. Garretson, Salem, Iowa. The whole motion of treadles, harness and shuttle is caused by the operation of moving the lathe back and forth by the hand, weaving twilled cloth with the same ease and facility as plain webs. The frame is four feet square, so that it can stand in a space five by six feet, and give ample room to work. Except the gallows-frame suspending the harness, it is only about two and a half feet high. The woodwork is very simple, easily made by any carpenter, and the iron-work almost none at all. It is so simple that almost any farmer, with a jack-plane, saw, and auger, could make it, and a child use it and make twenty yards of cloth in a day.

It can be seen in the south end of the machine department, and should be seen by every body who needs a farmer's hand-loom. It is just the thing for southern plantations. By the side of this loom may be seen a piece of machinery, not exactly an agricultural one, yet we have known several cases among farmers where it would have been of signal advantage. This machine is a locomotive chair, so constructed that, with a slight effort of one hand, the poor invalid can propel himself in doors or out, turning the shortest corners with ease, going back or forward, upon smooth surfaces, absolutely without labor. Then in one minute he can change it from a self-propeller to a little wagon, to be drawn by an assistant. For simplicity and perfect adaptation to its purposes, it is a model machine. It is the invention of T. S. Minnis, Meadville, Pa.—a poor but most deserving, and, as we happen to know, an honest man.

Among the many Garden Tools in the Exhibition, illustrating the great improvement which has been made in this class of farm instruments within a few years, we are particularly pleased with some manufactured by Lyman, of Williamsburg, Mass. Rakes are made with wooden heads and malleable iron teeth, with or without wooden bows. These rakes possess two advantages over those made all of iron or steel—they are lighter and cheaper. They are also made with a rake one side and hoe the other. Some are designed expressly for boys.

Of Churns there is a small ship-load, of every conceivable form and fashion that Yankee ingenuity could contrive. If the reader has a distinct recollection of Jeremiah's figs, he may apply that description to the family of churns now in the Crystal Palace. We shall describe a few of them, so that our readers will understand them a good deal better than they would some of them if they had no other way of making butter except by their operation. The ancient and honorable dasher-churn is usually made of cedar staves, partially cone-shaped—that is, bigger at the bottom than at the top, and of all sizes, from two to twenty gallons. One of medium size, say three pails' full, would be about eight inches across the top and ten at the bottom. The lid is made movable, with a hole in the centre for the staff of the dasher, which is a perforated board, or couple of pieces fastened across and to the bottom of the staff. This operated up and down, sometimes for hours, and hard labor at that, produces the butter. To do this work in an easier manner, since many housewives adhere to the old-fashioned churn, a very ingenious, contriving fellow, has made an attachment of a churn to a straw-cutter, which appears to work with surprising ease. This machine will be fully described under our article upon straw-cutters, in a notice of one called the "Farmer's Friend." To this machine, which has a heavy fly-wheel, the inventor has ungeared the cutters, and attached an arm to the dasher, so that by turning the crank, it is made to work very easy. Any straw-cutter that is operated with a crank and fly-wheel, may be adapted to the purpose; and we don't know why the principle may not be applied to a grindstone, so as to propel the churn by turning the crank.

There is another churn, called a "Self-adjusting Churn, intended for churning, gathering, working, and salting butter." Whether it will milk the cows, strain and skim the milk, we are not informed. It is a very strong, neatly-made article, and looks as though it might do a part of the work claimed for it. We advise butter-makers to give it a look. By the side of this, they will find another, the proprietor of which challenges the world to make as much butter in as short a time, from the same quantity of cream, as he can. This churn is like a small deep tub in shape, with an upright shaft, driven by a crank and gearing. Upon the shaft are eight beaters, simply round pins; and upon the sides of the tub, three ribs, of a triangular shape, spirally set, assist to break the cream in its circular motion, and, by reversing the crank, help to gather the butter.

There is another churn geared upon the same principle as the last, only the wheels are between the legs under the drum, driving a shaft with a hollow tin tube that projects up through the lid, which is calculated to carry a column of air down to the bottom of the cream, and discharge it through openings in a wheel, by which a chemical separation takes place between the butter and watery part of the milk. It will, without doubt, make butter, but we have some fears whether it will make it well and economically. All of the "atmospheric churns" which we have seen operate, do not make as good butter, or as much of it, as those which give a certain amount of agitation to the cream. What they do make, is generally done very quickly, at a great saving of time and labor. The churn previously described, which effects its work altogether by stirring and breaking the cream, has frequently produced butter in eight minutes. The average time of churning, however, is not much short of an hour, in the old-fashioned churns.

There is upon the same table another contrivance for butter-making, represented with glass sides. It is a square box in two compartments, with a dasher for each, both attached to one lever, like a pump handle, so that when one goes up the other goes down, forcing the cream back and forth through holes in the partition, by which the inventor apparently thinks to gain his object with less labor; forgetting that the friction of the cream through the holes in the partition will be as great as through the holes in the dasher. This, however, he thinks he has obviated by air tubes in the partition, through which a column of air is drawn by the movement of the cream, so that it is mixed with and buoys it up, and if no other effect is produced by the air, it serves to make the dasher work easier.

Another fancy churn is in the form of a small keg, the ends of an oyal shape. Through the centre, flatwise, is a crank shaft which carries a curiously shaped float or half wheel, which seems to be intended to scoop up cream on one side and air on the other, and stir them together. This may do pretty well, but we see no advantage in the peculiar shape of the tub.

Crowell's Thermometer Churn is to be seen upon the same table, and also in several other places in the collection of Agricultural Implements. It has the appearance of a small wooden chest, standing upon legs formed of the end boards. Various sizes are made from No. 1, which is sixteen inches long and sixteen inches high, and fourteen inches wide, to the largest size, thirty-two inches long, thirty-four inches high, and twenty-one inches wide, holding a barrel. No. 5, which is a good medium size, is twenty-one inches long, twenty-six inches high, and eighteen inches wide, and costs five dollars and fifty cents. These churns are constructed of an outside case of wood, with an inside lining of zinc. The top is covered with a lid, the cream is poured into the zinc case, and water, cold or hot, between that and the wooden one, until the cream is brought to the temperature of sixty-five degrees indicated by a thermometer set at one end of the churn. The operation of churning is done by a wheel in the cream, which is operated by a crank upon a shaft that passes out through a tight stuffing box at one end. This crank and the floats of the wheel are easily taken apart, and taken out to remove the butter. This kind of churn is more generally used than any other which has "patent" attached to its name in this country, unless one called Kendall's is an exception. Both are very popular—both compact and neat, and operated by a crank in the same way. The latter has no thermometer, or zinc lining. It is made of staves, straight like a drum, with blocks or supports for feet to stand on a table, is from twelve to twenty-four inches diameter, the staves from ten to eighteen inches long, hooped with iron. The cream is put in at a lid on the top, and the beaters are shaped like a small ladder; for small-sized churns used single, for large-sizes double, on the form of an X. They are made generally of pine or cedar, are cheap, and much liked.

After looking at the churn, take a view of the butter-worker. It is simply a table with the back legs a little the shortest, so that the buttermilk will drain off into a tub, it being guided to that by ledges around the edges of the table. A fluted roller, eighteen inches long, six and a half inches diameter at the big end, four and a half inches at the other, with a hook in the small end by which it can be caught upon a staple in the table, and a handle at the other end, is the butter-worker. The butter, placed upon the table, is rolled over and over by this roller until the milk ceases to run, when it is sprinkled with salt, which should be of the best quality, ground very fine, and not used too lavishly. Now if you would like to spread your butter upon your bread faster than you can cut it with a knife, there is a bread-cutting machine to be seen close by. It is simply a piece of board with a movable set knife, like that of a spoke-shave, set diagonally across, so that a loaf of bread, cucumber, apple, cabbage, or other substance to be cut in slices, being shoved quickly across the board, is sliced in whatever thickness the knife is set.

Another very convenient article in the household line is the Sausage or Mince-meat Cutter. These are of different forms, but all upon the same principle—knives set in rows on the inside of a cylinder, in which runs a shaft armed with iron spikes set in spiral rows, which carry the meat previously cut in inch cubes around between the knives and out at the end, completely masticated by the iron teeth and knives. One of these cutters, large enough for family use, is fourteen inches long, eight inches wide, and eight inches high; on the outside of the box, with twenty knives three quarters of an inch long, set half an inch apart, with square iron pins in a wooden shaft, three inches diameter, with a wooden crank, costing about five dollars. One made all of iron, same size cutting apparatus, costs double that sum. There is another, a six inch circle, about two inches thick, made to screw on the edge of a table and fed by the hand at the side, which is a very convenient little machine for cutting up mince-meat for a family breakfast. The cost is not over four or five dollars.

Next in order comes the Sausage-Stuffer. This is a tin barrel, four and a half inches diameter, twelve inches long, with a nozzle of the same length. This is hung on a pivot upon a wooden frame, so as to turn up for convenience of filling; it is then laid back in its place, and the case slipped on the nozzle and held fast. A follower on the end of a rack is forced in, by turning a crank that works a pinion, and in five seconds the whole contents of the cylinder are discharged into the case, if it is long enough and large enough to hold all. This sized stuffer costs five dollars. There is a smaller size for three dollars, on the same principle, only the rack is moved by an upright handle and a quarter-circle pinion. The latter is a very nice article, more compact and convenient than those with a crank, and big enough for any family. What a saving of labor, compared with the mode of sausage-stuffing in our youthful days, when the case was taken in the lap, and one end drawn over a little basket split hoop, to form an opening, and the meat put in by hand, after having been cut with the hand-chopping knife.

There are any number of Apple-Paring Machines, some of which are very ingenious labor-saving tools, taking off the rind, cutting out the core, and quartering the apple, almost as fast as the operator can pick them up and place them on the fork under the knife. A few rapid turns of the crank does the work, throwing the skins one way and cores another, and dropping the quarters into a tub.

There is a convenient Fruit-Picker in the Canadian department. A long pole is armed with a wire fixed upon the upper end, which takes hold of the stem of the apple upon a twig twenty feet above the ground, and, by a little turn of the hand, is wrenched off and dropped into a cotton cloth hose, and conducted down to the operator, or deposited in a basket on the ground.

But of all things in the fruit line, the most interesting in the exhibition or out of it, is a case of Models of Fruit; apples, pears, plums, strawberries, &c., done in a substance, principally plaster, as hard and indestructible as stone. This work is done by only one artist in this country, an amateur by the name of Townsend Glover, of Fishkill, N. Y. This case seems superior to any of the work ever before exhibited by this gentleman, who has probably received more medals, cups, premiums, diplomas, and high encomiums for his work, than any other amateur artist in America. The composition is principally plaster, and the apples, pears, &c., are modelled from the article to be represented, and the coloring is so perfect as to deceive the very best judges. It is well worth the great attention which it attracts. It may be found in the south-west part of the agricultural gallery.

Of patent Bee-Hives, there are a sufficient number in the

Exhibition to satisfy the seekers after certain preventives of that great pest of the apiarian, the bee-moth. All the contrivances which we have ever seen for keeping moths out of hives, are utter failures; and now the minds of those who contrive new hives, seem to be turned to the best method of getting them in, instead of keeping them out of the hive. The plan which we like best, is one where the hives are set upon a box covered over with wove wire, the meshes of which are too fine to admit a miller to pass through. This box is about twice as wide as the hive, and may be of any length, to hold fifty stands, if you like. Under each hive there is a drawer, into which dust and trash from the hive falls. This drawer is open to the moth, and here they deposit their eggs and hatch the worms that in due time are to be transformed into moths. Of course, the bee-keeper must destroy them before they arrive at that age. In the back part of the box, there is a feeding-drawer, so arranged, that in winter, the bees, being shut in the hive, can go down under the wire-screen and exercise, and eat the food provided for them, which they will convert into honey. The patentee of this hive claims a great many advantages in the peculiar arrangements of his hives and honey-boxes, which we do not care a fig about; but we do think the wire-screen arrangement a good one, and see no reason why any common box-hive may not be used upon it to good advantage.

XXXV.

RAW AND MANUFACTURED SILKS.

THERE is no manufacture which has ministered more to what are called the elegancies of life, than that of which we are now about to treat. Possessing the united characteristics of splendor, durability and comfort, we find in it all the conditions supplied by cotton and wool, while it surpasses those useful materials in the richness and glossiness of its surface, and the round and swelling gracefulness of its folds. If it gratifies the ostentation of the rich, it occasionally soothes the wounded pride of the poor. The silk gown is in fact the only true leveller of social distinctions among women. The grocer's wife in her Sunday finery feels herself emboldened to return with interest the contemptuous stare of the lawyer's lady; while, in spite of her affected superciliousness, the latter is frequently envious of the superior good taste, and even elegance, of her humbler neighbor's attire. In a philosophical point of view, the history of the silk manufacture offers some curious subjects for reflection. Owing its origin to one of the most insignificant creatures to be found within the whole range of the animal kingdom, and its first discovery and application to a people upon whom, notwithstanding their natural shrewdness and ingenuity, modern civilization has failed to shed its light, it presents to us, on the one hand, the interesting spectacle of an humble insect covering the earth with its works, while, on the other, we see the nation to whom we owe the first appreciation of its usefulness, imitating the sluggish progress of the snail, and even jealously shutting out from themselves the benefits to be derived from an extended intercourse with their fellow-men.

If we are to believe Chinese writers, the manufacture of silk has been practiced for thousands of years in that country. The date of its first introduction into Europe is said to have been in the reign of the Emperor Justinian, and for six centuries the breeding of silk worms was confined to the Greeks of the Lower Empire. When, about the middle of the twelfth century, Roger, king of Sicily, sacked the cities of Corinth, Athens and Thebes, he carried off a number of the inhabitants to Palermo, who introduced into that kingdom the culture of the insect and the manufacture of silk. Hence the manufacture soon found its way into Spain, France and England; in the two latter of which countries it has made rapid progress.

Silk may be generally described as a fine thread or filament spun by various species of caterpillars of the *phalæna* genus. It is, strictly speaking, the secretion of a long pair of glandular tubes called *sericteria*, which terminate in a prominent pore or spinnaret on the upper lip. Previous to their completion, another secretion from a smaller gland glues together the two fine filaments from the two *sericteria*, the thread, which appears single, being in reality double, and its quality being affected by the equality or otherwise of the secreting power of the *sericteria*. The silk-worm begins spinning when it is full grown, in some convenient spot affording points of attachment for the first-formed thread, which is drawn from one point to the other until the body of the *larva* becomes loosely inclosed by the thread. The work is then continued from one thread to another, the silk-worm moving its head and spinning in a zigzag way in all directions within reach, and shifting the body only to cover the part which was beneath it. The silken case so formed is called the cocoon, which usually takes five days for its completion. The silk-worm decreases in size and length considerably, then casts its skin, becomes torpid, and assumes the form of the chrysalis. The *phalæna* is not the only insect that produces silk. There are several species of the *aranea* or spider which inclose their eggs in fine threads of the same material.

Of the *Bombyx mori*, that species of the *phalæna* which is commonly employed in Europe, and which, as its name implies, is fed exclusively on the leaves of the mulberry tree, there are several varieties—the result of long domestication and careful breeding. The worms most esteemed in France, where the art of *sericiculture* is carried to a high state of excellence, are those known under the names of the "*Sina*," the "*Syrie*," and the

"*Novi.*" The *Sina* is valued for the whiteness of its silk, but its thread, although fine, is weak, and not very lustrous. The *Syrie* is fertile in production; its thread, however, is large and coarse, with a tendency toward a greenish tint. The cocoons of the *Novi* are firm and well made, the color of the silk inclining toward yellow.

Heat seems to be the agent employed in most of the processes for killing the pupa, and extracting it from the cocoon preparatory to unwinding the thread from the latter—an operation requiring the exercise of the greatest skill and experience. The method employed by the Chinese is described by the old French Missionaries to have been as follows:

"The extremities of the cocoon are first cut off with a pair of scissors; they are then put in a canvas bag and immersed for an hour or more in a kettle of boiling ley, which dissolves the gum. When this is effected, they are taken from the kettle, pressed to expel the ley, and left till the next morning to dry. While they are still moist, the chrysalis is extracted from each cocoon, which is then turned inside out, to make a sort of cowl. They are then easily wound into thread."

The specimens of raw silk contributed to the London Exhibition comprised not only almost all the varieties of the article produced in different countries, but afforded an opportunity of comparing the results and testing the value of the improvements introduced in the rearing of the insect. The French, who, as we have already stated, have of late years devoted great attention to the science of sericiculture, bore away the honors to which their efforts justly entitled them. The Jury, in order to testify their admiration of the specimens exhibited by the Central Society of France, and their appreciation of the important influence which it had exercised in the improvement of this beautiful and valuable product of the animal kingdom, unanimously concurred in recommending the award of the Council Medal to that body, and at the same time gave the honor of their first notice to the samples of unbleached silks and cocoons exhibited by Count Bronno Bronski, of St. Selves, near Bordeaux. The cocoons shown by this gentleman were unusually large and regular in their form, while the silk obtained from them was distinguished by its length, pure white color, and its fineness and lustre. The circumstances under which this superior quality of silk was obtained are certified in a report by a committee of the Agricultural Society of the Gironde, dated 28th April, 1847, to be as follows: "In 1836 Major Bronski reared separately the eggs of the three varieties 'Sina,' 'Syrie' and 'Novi.' In 1837 he set apart the cocoons of the varieties 'Syrie' and 'Novi,' and on the exclusion of the 'imago,' a perfect insect, he associated the males of the 'Novi' with the females of the 'Syrie,' and the hybrid ova were hatched at the ordinary period in 1838, the operations being repeated in 1839 and 1840. With regard to the race 'Sina,' M. Bronski in 1837 separated the white from the black worms as soon as they were hatched. He then selected the largest and best shaped cocoons, and made a special collection of the eggs from the moths excluded from those cocoons. This procedure was repeated in 1838 and 1839, but in 1840 he associated the males excluded from the large cocoons of the black worms with the females excluded from those of the white worms. In 1841 he associated the male of the 'Sina' race with the hybrid females obtained from the above-described crossings of the 'Novi' and 'Syrie' breeds. By these and similar experiments, M. Bronski at length appears to have succeeded in obtaining a race of silk-worms not subject to disease, producing large and equal-sized cocoons of a pure white color, the silk of which is equal in all its length, strong and lustrous, and presenting an average length of thread of one thousand and fifty-seven metres."

Among the specimens transmitted from Italy, the preference was given to those of Tuscany, the qualities of which were highly commended, although not deemed equal to those we have just described. The Turkish silks were also greatly admired for their fineness, strength, and elasticity, and a prize medal was awarded to the school of Sericiculture at Broussa, as well as to several private exhibitors from Turkey.

In the Chinese and Indian departments some very fine samples were also shown—those from the latter country exhibiting a marked improvement on the qualities that usually find their way into the market. The Bengal silk was originally but little esteemed, from the careless manner in which it was wound and its inferiority of quality generally. In 1757, the East India Company sent out a gentleman named Wilder, who had devoted a great deal of attention to the subject, to assist the natives by his experience; and twelve years later he was joined by a number of other Europeans in the various capacities of drawers, winders, reelers, and mechanics. The filatures were all in Bengal and to the southward of twenty-six degrees of north latitude—the north-west provinces being too hot and too dry for the silk-worm. For many years attempts were made, under the direction of an Italian named Mutti, to introduce the culture of the silk-worm on the western side of India, but the enterprise proved a failure. The silk produced in Mysore is of a superior quality as compared with the products of other parts of India, and it is probable that the culture of the silk-worm could be advantageously prosecuted in the valleys of the Himalaya, if the owners of the soil would turn their attention to it. Beside the silk from the ordinary silk-worm, (*Bombyx mori*) called in India *pat*, stronger and coarser kinds of silk are produced from the *tussur* moth, (*Saturnalia mylitta*) which feeds on the leaves of the *terminalia catappa*, and from the *Bombyx Saturnia*, which feeds upon the same trees as the *tussur*. The *Eri* silk is produced from the *phalæna cynthia*, which feeds upon the *ricinus communis*. From these latter varieties are manufactured the silks known as the *tussur*, *moonga* and *eri* cloths.

Although the samples of raw silk contributed to the New-York Exhibition do not form a collection as complete as that of London, there is here a sufficient variety to indicate the progress that has been made in the rearing of the worm, and to determine the merits of the different breeds. In the French Department, there are no less than eight exhibitors of raw silk; most of the samples shown by them are of excellent quality, being in general remarkable for the purity of their color and the fineness and lustre of their thread. From Austria, we only find specimens from two producers, although large quantities of silk are raised in her Italian provinces. Sardinia shows some very good samples; they are not equal, however, to those we saw at the London Exhibition, and which bore away the prize medal. England sends us one sample of home-produced silk, but her attempts in this way are, at best, but sickly efforts—her ungenial climate opposing insurmountable obstacles to the successful culture of the worm. It may be within the recollection of some of our readers that at the London Exhibition the Jury of the Silk Department made honorable mention of some specimens shown by Mrs. Catherine Dodge, which were produced from silk worms reared on the leaves of the white mulberry at Godalming in Surrey; but this tribute of approval was awarded rather to the perseverance that could struggle against such difficulties than to the quality of the samples themselves.

It is to be regretted that we have no samples of the raw produce of our silk-raising States among the specimens shown at the Exhibition. The unprofitable results of the efforts that have been made to render the culture of the worm indigenous to our soil seem to have disheartened and discouraged those engaged in them, to an extent that, on careful inquiry, appears neither well-founded nor reasonable. If, as we have reason to believe, they are still convinced that the disappointment and partial failure in which they have ended, are to be attributed rather to the mistakes that were made in the earlier stages of the enterprise than, as is alleged by some, to insuperable difficulties arising from the peculiarities of our climate, it is not consistent with the characteristic energy and perseverance of our countrymen that they should thus relax their efforts and abandon to others the monopoly of an industry from which such vast returns might be obtained. It is anything but a pleasing retrospect to trace the history of the culture of Silk in this country, presenting as it does such a lamentable series of individual failures (due, for the most part, to ignorance or inexperience.) As, however, it may have the effect of again calling attention to the subject, and perhaps of dispelling the erroneous notions that still prevail among many, as to the impossibility of our growing the proper description of food for the silk-worm in this climate, we will endeavor to put our readers in possession of the facts upon which this conclusion is founded.

We owe the introduction of the silk-worm, in this country, to James I., who, excited by the success which had attended its culture in France, made strenuous efforts not only to promote it in England, but to extend it to his American colonies. With this view, he addressed a letter to the Virginia Company in 1622, enjoining them "to apply themselves diligently and promptly to the breeding of silk-worms, and the establishment of silk-works," and advising them rather to bestow their labors in producing this silk commodity than in growing "that pernicious and offensive weed," tobacco, an article to which this monarch had a violent aversion. In compliance with his Majesty's wishes, the Company immediately forwarded his letter to the Governor and Council of Virginia, together with minute instructions for carrying out its objects, and several copies of a work on the management of the insect, written by Mr. Bonœil, a member of their body. This gentleman was so fully convinced of the practicability of the undertaking, that he engaged personally in it, being, as he publicly stated, "satisfied that, with an adequate number of hands, such a quantity of silk might be produced in Virginia, as in a very short time would be sufficient to supply all Christendom." The troubles into which the colony was soon after plunged, and which brought about the dissolution of the company, served to check, for some time, the execution of the project. A considerable number of mulberry trees were planted, and throve exceedingly well; the amount of silk produced, however, was but small.

About thirty years afterward, a fresh impulse was given to the speculation by a person named Diggs, who confidently asserted that he had overcome all the difficulties that had attended the first experiment. It does not seem, however, that his promises were attended with the results anticipated, for but little increase was made in the amount of production: The planters, no doubt, found it more profitable to devote themselves to the culture of tobacco, of which they were now exporting large quantities.

The attention of the settlers in Georgia was early directed to this branch of industry. Some land belonging to the Government was allotted in 1732, as a nursery plantation for white mulberries; and the results, at first, appeared to be of a most promising character. The English Government, desirous of rendering itself independent of foreign states for the supply of a material so important to its growing manufactures, introduced a bill into Parliament in 1749, having for its object the encouragement of the growth of colonial silk, and which relieved from duty all silk entered at the port of London, which was certified to be the production of Georgia and Carolina. Not satisfied with the passing of this measure, bounties were further offered for the production of silk; and an Italian gentleman, named Ottolenghe, who had had great experience in the management of similar establishments, was engaged, at a high salary, to proceed to the town of Savannah, to take charge of a large filature which had been established there. An immediate impetus was given to the culture of silk by this establishment; the mulberry was extensively cultivated, and considerable quantities of raw silk exported to England. Owing, however, to the inferior quality of the silk, and the disastrous results of one or two unfavorable seasons, its culture soon began to decline, and the lessening of the bounty soon put an end to it altogether. Another circumstance contributed, perhaps, as much to the abandonment of the enterprise as the causes we have mentioned, namely, the introduction of the indigo plant. The planters found, in this new branch of industry, advantages so immediate and certain, that they no longer cared to employ their time and capital in a speculation which was attended with so much trouble and risk.

In South Carolina, the rearing of the silk-worm was commenced about the year 1732, but was at first principally confined to the small farmers, who produced on an average from forty to fifty pounds' weight of silk each in the course of the season. A few capitalists subsequently took an interest in the speculation, and among others, M. De St. Pierre, who sacrificed his whole fortune in his efforts to improve the imperfect system of management upon which it had been carried on. Some specimens of the silk produced by him were forwarded to England in 1771, and the Society of Arts thought so highly of them that they presented him with their gold medal and a premium of fifty pounds. Notwithstanding the encouragement thus held out, the enterprise shared the same fate with that of the attempts already noticed in the other States. Owing to causes which we shall presently have occasion to examine, the cost of production proved too great for successful competition with foreign silk.

In 1769, Franklin, who was then in England, carefully observing everything that might be turned to the advantage of this country, suggested to the American Philosophical Society, (then lately instituted, and of which, though residing abroad, he had been elected the first president,) the patriotic idea of introducing the culture of silk into Philadelphia, and recommended a commencement by the establishment of a filature. The Society warmly embraced his views; application was made to the Legislature for assistance, but, it appears, without success, and the necessary sum was finally raised by subscription. The filature was established in Seventh-street, between Market and Arch-streets; a skillful Frenchman was placed at the head of it, and the Society procured the necessary machine (the Piedmont reel) to wind the cocoons. It is asserted, that the silk reeled in this filature was equal in quality to the best silk imported from France or Italy. There may be some exaggeration in this, but as regards the quantity of silk reeled, there can be no doubt. In a period of less than two months, from the 25th of June to the 15th of August, 1771, more than 2,300 pounds of cocoons were brought to the filature to be reeled, or were bought by the managers. The whole of this silk was produced in Pennsylvania, New-Jersey, and Delaware. The Revolution put an end to this useful establishment.

About the year 1789, a project was formed to extend the culture of the mulberry-tree all over the States of the Union; and steps were taken to carry it into execution, by the formation of extensive nurseries at New-York, Long Island, Princeton, N. J., and Philadelphia. The immediate motive of this new scheme was the hope entertained that, in the then disturbed state of Europe, the emigration from the silk-producing countries would bring crowds of skilled cultivators to our shores, and that a fresh impulse would thereby be given to this branch of industry. These expectations, however, were not destined to be realized.

In the year 1829, public attention was attracted by some

essays published in *The National Gazette*, by Mr. D'Homergue, of Philadelphia, a gentleman formerly engaged in the cultivation of silk in France, in which he pointed out the causes of these repeated failures, and contended that the *filature* system was the only means by which the culture of silk could be made a source of profit to this country. The popularity of these letters induced the writer to publish them in the form of a pamphlet, which attracted the notice of Congress, who referred it to their Committee on Agriculture, with power to enter fully upon the subject, and report on the best course to be pursued. The Committee immediately appreciated the importance of the suggestions thrown out by Mr. D'Homergue in his pamphlet, and unanimously determined to establish a *normal* filature for the instruction of the people.

Before we proceed to notice the further steps taken in this matter, it will be necessary for us to explain, briefly, the views of Mr. D'H. Everywhere in Europe the conversion of raw silk into sewing silk is the business of the *throwster.* The farmer confines himself to his cocoons and his reel, and leaves the rest to those mechanics who have acquired a sufficient degree of skill in their respective arts, and employ competent machinery. In this country, on the contrary, everything—spinning, twisting, and even dyeing—had been, up to this time, done by the same hands, and with rude instruments not at all fitted to the purpose. The silk was reeled from the cocoons by the common spinning-wheel, and was twisted into an inferior sewing-silk, which could not stand competition with that imported from Europe. That to the imperfect mode of reeling, more than to any other cause, the inferiority of our home-produced silk, and the consequent failure of our attempts to give importance to this branch of industry, were owing, was clearly demonstrated by Mr. D'Homergue. He showed, from the returns of two counties—Windham and Tolland, Ct.—which he visited for the purpose of inquiry, that it was impossible, under the then system of management, that the production of either raw or manufactured silk could be attended with other than loss to the producers. This statement is so curious, and illustrates so perfectly the general ignorance and carelessness that prevailed throughout the Union, in the treatment of the cocoons and the general economy of the manufacturer, that we cannot do better than give it in his own words:

"We were informed by persons, the best acquainted with the business of the place, and worthy of full credit, that the sales of sewing-silk in these two counties amounted annually to $15,000 or $18,000. That amount was produced by 8,000 lbs. of raw silk, each made out of 20 lbs. of cocoons, which makes, in the whole, 160,000 lbs. of those balls. Now, we beg to be allowed a few observations on these important facts. In the first place, what a small sum is $18,000, the highest in the computation, and that nominal too, for the proceeds of 160,000 lbs. of cocoons, to which is to be added all the labor and expense put upon that material to convert it into sewing-silk! Were the farmers to sell these cocoons at only 20 cents a lb., (the lowest price for good cocoons that we can think of,) they would produce $32,000, nearly double the amount above mentioned, and that in ready cash, (for they are a cash article,) without the labor and expense attending the reeling, twisting and boiling, and the dyeing in various colors.

"It may be said that, since we were in Connecticut, that State has allowed to the reelers a bounty of fifty cents on every pound of raw silk reeled on an improved reel, which they should produce. We shall say nothing of the *improved reel*, but we say that even with that bounty which, on 8,000 lbs. of raw silk, which we have shown above to be their yearly production, would amount to only $4,000, they would make less than by the sale of their cocoons; for $4,000 added to $18,000, the admitted produce of their cocoons wrought into sewing-silk, make only $22,000, and their cocoons at 20 cents per pound would produce $32,000; difference $10,000.

"If, on the contrary, the cocoons were sold for ready cash, that money would circulate among the people, stimulate their exertions, increase the quantity of silk, and enrich the whole country; filatures would be established in their neighborhood, and the State of Connecticut, now so thrifty, would experience the highest degree of prosperity. We hope it is not too late, and that these fair prospects will yet come to be realized.

"It might perhaps be enough to have shown that this domestic manufacture of sewing-silk, after all the labor and expense bestowed upon it, produces in its results from 30 to 40 per cent. less than the first raw material (the coccons) would produce in an open market; but we think it will not be amiss to show here what are the causes of this enormous difference. We can easily demonstrate that it is entirely to be ascribed to the imperfection of the implements used and the methods pursued, all of which arise from a lamentable ignorance of the art of reeling and the mechanism of throwing, by which alone the raw material can be converted into good and merchantable sewing silk. A few reflections on the facts above stated will be sufficient to convince the reader of the truth of this assertion.

"1. Twenty pounds of cocoons, employed in making one pound of raw silk, are double the quantity employed in Europe for the same purpose. Here then is a loss of *one hundred per cent.*

"2. The sum of $18,000, which, on the highest calculation, is the amount of the annual proceeds of all sewing-silk made in the two counties above mentioned, at the current price of $4 a pound, represents only 4,500 pounds of sewing-silk; and that is made as above stated out of 8,000 pounds of raw silk; here is again a loss of nearly *fifty per cent.*

"This loss is almost entirely produced by the imperfect reeling of the raw silk; in technical language, it is called *waste.* We know that thrown silk loses something of its weight by the dissolution of the gum in boiling; but that never exceeds twenty per cent.; and we know that this loss is more or less compensated by the dyeing, particularly in black. In Europe, when sewing-silk is dyed in black, the dyer is obliged to return the same weight of silk that he has received, so that the greatest part, and sometimes the whole, of this loss of weight in Connecticut, must be attributed to waste occasioned by bad reeling.

"The loss suffered in Europe on the best raw silk in the operation of *throwing* or twisting seldom exceeds four per cent. when thrown in Italy and five when thrown in England. That which was sent to England from the experimental filature at Philadelphia, to be manufactured, suffered only a loss of three five-eighths per cent., which shows the great strength of American silk. It must be acknowledged that it was thrown with great care by Mr. Edward Molyneux, an eminent silk throwster at Manchester, from whose report we have stated the above fact. Let this be compared with the immense loss suffered by the fair manufacturers of sewing-silk in Connecticut. Waste of the cocoons in reeling, waste of the raw silk in twisting. Can the nation ever expect to derive profits from this mode of proceeding?"

This was written in 1829. It presents a faithful picture of the general improvidence and recklessness of economical results which seem to have marred all the fair hopes that were at one time entertained for this fruitful branch of industry, and which seem to have annihilated all motive for further effort. But we must not digress.

From what has been just stated, our readers will arrive with us at the conclusion that the only chance of removing the evils therein pointed out, was to be found in the measure suggested by Mr. D'Homergue and decided upon by the Committee of Agriculture: namely, the establishment of a *normal* school of filature for the instruction of those engaged in the culture of silk. We will again see, however, the same fatality which seems to have impended over the heads of all connected with this branch of industry from the beginning, contributing to defeat this new project. The Committee, having decided on the formation of the school, made a communication to Mr. D'Homergue through their Chairman, Mr. Spencer, expressing their desire to place him at its head, and requesting to know on what terms he would accept its direction. They proposed a plan which Mr. Duponceau thought could not be carried into execution without too much expense, and which was, beside, attended with many difficulties. He suggested another on a more moderate scale, to which Mr. D'Homergue agreed, and this plan was adopted by the Committee, and a bill known as *the Silk Bill*, embracing all its details, reported to Congress. It remained pending there three sessions, and, on the 22d of May, 1832, was finally rejected. It should be stated that, while the bill was before the House, a new Committee of Agriculture had been appointed, of which the Hon. Erastus Root, of New-York, was Chairman, and this Committee declared themselves opposed to the bill. Mr. Duponceau and Mr. D'Homergue went to Washington and appeared before the Committee. They were examined and cross-examined by its members, and the result was that the Chairman, Gen. Root, and several of its members who had been before decidedly hostile to the bill, entirely changed their opinion, and the Chairman supported it eloquently in the debates that ensued in Congress. Although the bill numbered among its supporters such men as John Quincy Adams, Governor Everett, of Massachusetts, Governor White, of Louisiana, and Andrew Stevenson, it was rejected by a small majority, the day after it was reported to the House. The truth was that the period chosen for pressing it upon the attention of Congress was unfavorable to its patient consideration, as several questions of the most absorbing interest were then under discussion. That the importance of the measure was not exaggerated by its supporters, is evident from the fact that the French Ambassador, M. Serrurier, publicly reproached Mr. D'Homergue with his want of patriotism in endeavoring thus to forward the interests of the American silk manufacture at the expense of those of his native country—an observation which ought to have helped the passage of the bill.

After an interval of six years, a third Committee on Agriculture, at the head of which was the Hon. J. F. Randolph, of New Jersey, in a report dated the 20th of April, 1838, expressed their approbation of the principles of the bill, as suited to the time when it was proposed, but thought it at present useless, for the reasons given below. They express themselves in the following terms:

"Thus perished the first *important* measure proposed by the nation to promote the production of silk in this country; a measure which the Committee believe, with the lights then in existence, was *wise*, *prudent* and *important*, but which the subsequent ingenuity and experience of our countrymen now render unnecessary; believing as they do, that the recent improvements in reeling will do more in a few weeks than the establishment of many Normal Schools upon the old plan would do in many years."—(*Report*, *p.* 6.)

In another part of the same report it is said, that—"The dull, tedious method of reeling by hand—which required a regular apprenticeship to learn, and years to acquire facility in the use of—has given way to the new patent reel, by which a person (even a child) may learn in a few hours to reel with great ease and expertness, a much more even thread than by the old process."

Subsequent experience has demonstrated the fallacy of these anticipations. Public opinion has undergone a great change respecting the employment of this improved reel, and it is now admitted that no machinery can produce the effects that were pretended. Our readers will perceive, from the following explanation, that there are physical impossibilities that are opposed to its adoption:

The fibres of the cocoon are as fine as the finest human hair, and of course easily broken. They are not of the same degree of fineness through the whole ball; it is well known to naturalists that there are three layers of silk in the cocoon; the first or uppermost is formed of the best and strongest silk, the insect being then in full vigor and strength; after two or three days he becomes fatigued; his silk is thinner and less perfect; this forms the second layer. At last, as he draws near his change into a chrysalis, he spins a still thinner silk, which generally falls with the chrysalis to the bottom of the boiler, and sometimes, in the best cocoons, is entirely reeled off. Good reelers learn to distinguish these different layers by the sight, and by the touch, while the cocoons are immersed in a basin of hot water; and in some filatures where the best raw silk is to be obtained, these different layers of silk are separately reeled, being destined for different kinds of manufactures. This is only said by way of example. There are a number of other details which no less require the skill and dexterity of the reeler, and are beyond the power of machinery. As the perfection of raw silk principally depends on the equality of the threads, which must be of an equal fineness and strength through their whole length, that the weak parts may not be broken by the equal pressure of the throwing machine, which cannot be lessened or increased at pleasure, it is necessary that those threads should consist as nearly as possible of an equal quantity of the delicate fibres of the cocoon. But the cocoons are not of an equal size, and, as we have said before, the fineness of their silk varies: it follows that, to preserve the equality of the thread, they must be frequently changed, and their numbers increased or lessened: of this the reeler must judge, and her fingers as well as her eyes direct her in this most delicate operation. Beside this, many accidents happen in reeling which she must learn how to remedy with dexterity and skill; we shall only instance those entanglements of the silk threads which are called *marriages*, and which frequently result from the nature of the operation. It would be too long to detail here all that has to be done by a skillful reeler, but enough has been said to show that no machinery whatever can supply the place of her experienced hand, and that she is not in the least aided by the machinery of the reel, which helps only to wind the threads which she draws from the cocoons, nor can it be improved to any other purpose.

How deeply therefore is to be regretted the rejection of a project, which, by establishing a normal school of instruction, would have diffused throughout the Union a knowlege of the only true principles on which this branch of industry can be profitably carried on, and which, by the promotion of filatures, generally, would have reduced to practical demonstration the soundness of those principles. The Piedmontese silk owes the reputation it has so long enjoyed to the uniformity of system which would have been thereby secured, and which is enforced by regulations imposed by the government. The proprietor of a silk filature in Piedmont, before he commences the business of reeling, is obliged to announce to a local Board of Commissioners the number of boilers he intends to use and the thickness and weight of the silk which he means to produce in the season. A smaller quantity than five hundred pounds' weight of silk is not allowed to be reeled in a single filature. The various establishments are visited during the season of reeling by the members of the commission, and, should any person be found operating upon a greater or lesser number of cocoons than he has previously reported, or otherwise, in any way infringing the regulations, a fine is imposed. Nothing of this kind exists in France, and, in consequence, there is found an infinite variety in the size of the reel and the thickness of the silk.

The history of American Legislation with reference to Silk would of itself afford material for an interesting article. Let it here suffice that this legislation has been of the most capricious and mischievous character—to-day stimulating the Silk culture by generous State bounties and shielding it by ample duties; and to-morrow abolishing the former and reducing the latter to the lowest revenue standard. Had no attempt ever been made to encourage by legislation the silk culture, it would very probably have stood stronger and worn a more hopeful aspect than it now does; had the production of silk enjoyed a protection as steady and adequate as that of cotton fabrics, it would probably have outgrown ere this all need of protection, all peril of failure. But it must be borne in mind that the production of silk is everywhere a nice and critical operation, and that Italy and France—now the chief seats in Christendom of this important industry were, for many centuries since the Christian era, dependent on China and India for their silks.

We have now traced what we believe to have been the real causes of our failures, and which must still continue to operate against our progress in this valuable branch of industry until something like system and uniformity are adopted. Years must elapse before vitality and prosperity can be infused into this languishing branch of production. Some idea of its present exhausted condition may be formed, from the fact that, in 1840, the whole produce of the Union amounted to only 61,552 lbs. of cocoons, equal to about 4500 lbs. of Silk.

A large proportion of the raw silk imported into the United States (we believe as much as two-thirds) comes from China. It is generally preferred by manufacturers for the pure whiteness of its color and the strength and glossiness of its fibre. The remainder is brought from different parts of Europe (chiefly

Italy) and Bengal. France supplies us with very little raw silk, as she requires all she produces for her own consumption. Most of the Indian and Italian silks are imported through English houses, as were formerly those of China. The silks brought from Canton consist of two leading varieties, known in commerce by the names of Canton and Nankin. The first, which is raised in the province from which it derives its name, is divided into five sorts. The Nankin silk is produced in the province of Kiangnan, and consists of two kinds, known in our market under the names of Tsatlee and Taysaam. The duty on raw silk, under our present tariff, is fifteen per cent., but if we take into consideration the fact, that it arrives here impregnated with gum, which must be removed before the silk is manufactured, it is, in reality, from three to four per cent. higher. The Canton and Taysaam silks average at present, in our market, about five dollars and twenty-five cents. the pound, being dearer by a dollar, than they were twelve months since. Tsatlee silk usually averages twenty-five cents more, the quantity produced being small. The Bengal silk is very inferior in quality to the Chinese, and is chiefly used in the manufacture of fringes. It is of a bright yellow tinge, and its thread is coarse and uneven. The same objections may be urged, although in a less degree, against some of the Italian silks. Some good white silk is, however, obtained from Milan and Turin. The Italian silks are imported in the form of tram and organzine, and range in price from nine dollars to eleven dollars the pound.

We now come to the article of manufactured silk, or in other words, raw silk converted into what is known in commerce under the terms of singles, tram and organzine.

Singles (a collective noun) is formed of *one* of the reeled threads slightly twisted in order to give it strength and firmness.

Tram consists of two or more threads thrown just sufficiently together to hold, by a twist of from one to one-and-a-half turns to the inch.

Organzine, or thrown silk, is formed of two or more singles, according to the thickness required, twisted together in a contrary direction to that of the singles, of which it is composed.

The art of throwing silk was originally confined to Italy, where it was kept a secret for a long time. It was introduced into England in the reign of Elizabeth, but remained in a very imperfect state until the year 1719, when a patent was granted to Sir Thomas Lambe and his brother, for various improvements effected by them in silk-throwing, at their celebrated silk mill in Derby. Since that period, the progress of science has enabled the manufacturer to dispense with the clumsy machinery employed under Lambe's patent, and the means of production have been multiplied to an extent that would have been deemed fabulous in those days. Our American throwsters have introduced some valuable modifications on the English machinery, which have had the effect of still further simplifying the process of manufacture and diminishing its cost. The first factory started in this country for spinning the tram and organzine was we believe, established in Northampton, Mass., but its operations were for some time carried on at a loss; and it was only when it commenced the manufacture of sewing-silks that an adequate return was obtained for the capital invested. Since then, two other factories of a similar character have been established in Paterson, N. J., (Mr. Ryle's and Mr. Crossley's,) which employ a great number of hands and are rapidly extending their trade. Mr. Ryle confines himself exclusively to the manufacture of the raw silk; but Mr. Crossley has conjoined with it the manufacture of sewing-silks, gimps, fringes, and tassels for drapery. Both these gentlemen exhibit specimens of their productions, which appear to us fully equal in quality to any of the goods imported into our market.

XXXIII.

SILK MANUFACTURES.

SEWING, FRINGE, AND EMBROIDERING SILKS, FRINGES, GIMPS, TASSELS, AND BUTTON-SILKS.

THE manufactures comprised under the above heads constitute thriving branches of our home industry, and are entitled to a separate notice at our hands. Nearly all the sewing-silk used in this country, including the black silk so much sought after under the name of "Italian silk," is now made by American manufacturers; and we question if the quantity imported amounts to five per cent. of the home production. There are a great many manufacturers scattered throughout the Union, who confine themselves exclusively to the fabrication of this article. The Connecticut establishments make in general what is called hundred, or small-skein silk, of different colors. It is so termed because it is made up from one to one-and-a-half ounce of silk to the hundred, measuring about ten yards in length to the skein. This article is generally sold to pedlars and jobbers. There is another description of skein made up for retailers, which measures from twelve to twenty yards in length. It is principally used by clothing-houses, who find an economy in employing the larger skeins. Black Italian sewing-silk fetches about $6 for the pound of twelve ounces; colored small skeins, $6 50 for twelve ounces; large skeins of ditto, from $7 to $7 50. There are specimens of sewing-silks from three American manufacturers at the Exhibition—namely, Mr. Ryle and Mr. Charles Crossley, of Paterson, N. J., and Mr. Chaffe, of Mansfield, Conn. The samples shown by these gentlemen are remarkable for the strength and evenness of the twist and the purity and brilliancy of their colors. The crimsons and scarlets exhibited by Mr. Crossley are especially deserving of commendation, being as fine specimens of those dyes as have ever fallen under our observation. Mr. Crossley confines himself to one quality of sewing-silk, but Mr. Ryle manufactures three varieties, which are called for by the general nature of his trade. The latter gentleman also exhibits a beautiful American flag made of the tram and organzine prepared in his establishment. There is another description of sewing-silk known under the name of *fringe silk*, which is made of two strands, of from two to eight threads of raw silk to each strand ; each skein consisting of one unbroken thread, and weighing from one-half to three-quarters of an ounce. The motive for making the skein in one thread, is to prevent the delay that would arise from stopping to tie the short lengths in weaving. Fringe silk is sold in different states. In the gum, the average price is about $6 50 per pound. In what is called the boiled-off state—that is to say, divested of the gum—it fetches about $8 62. Out of sixteen ounces in the gum, not more than twelve ounces of silk are obtained in the boiled state. For this reason fringe sewing-silk consists of only twelve ounces to the pound. Dyed fringe-silk fetches on the average about $8 50 per pound, and black about $8. *Embroidery silks* are made of two strands, of from six to twenty threads each, the same as plain sewing-silk, but not so much twisted. The raw material employed in this branch of the manufacture is the best that can be procured. Embroidery silk is sold to jobbers at an average price of from $7 to $8 for the pound consisting of twelve ounces, or of $9 for the pound of sixteen ounces.

We now come to the articles employed in trimming clothing and drapery, and which are known under the general name of Fringe. Those which are used for the first of these purposes, are distinguished as sewing-silk fringes, while the articles employed by upholsterers are designated as bullion or twisted fringes. The latter are only partially made of silk, the foundation being generally either cotton or worsted. They are all woven in the loom, the hand-loom being employed when the pattern is unusually difficult or wide, and the power-loom for the general run of fringes. All goods with figures, such as galloons, or fringes with figured heads, are woven on looms with the Jacquard addition. Without this, the weaver would have to use a great many treadles for making the figure. Gimps, which are generally made by hand, sometimes require as many as twenty treadles, using from ten to twelve shuttles. When the Jacquard addition is employed, the number of cards required to form a single pattern frequently amounts to several thousand. The prices of plain and figured silk fringes range from six shillings to forty dollars the dozen yards.

Tassels are all made by hand. There are different descriptions of this article, distinguished as cloak and dress tassels, picture and drapery tassels, coach tassels, &c. The cloak and dress tassels are generally made of what are called sewing-silk skirts. Drapery tassels are either made entirely from silk, or from a mixture of silk and worsted. Picture and coach tassels are also made from the latter combination of material. The covering of the tassel-molds is generally done by the needle; the bullion or cord-work is executed by machinery. The molds are made in a great variety of forms, in order to give the workman room to exercise his fancy in the construction of the patterns. Each piece is covered separately, and there are sometimes as many as 150 of them in a single tassel. Some furniture tassels cost as high as $25 the pair.

It is only within the last dozen years that the manufacture of fringes and tassels has been commenced in this country, all the trimmings previously used being imported from France and England. For some time the efforts of our manufacturers were confined to the making of plain fringes and tassels; but this branch of industry has attained such rapid development within the last few years that they can now execute any description of pattern, no matter how complicated. Even the designs are got up here, and it is only when something very striking and original is imported that they think of copying. The importation of fringes and tassels is still large, owing to the high price of labor in this country. There is a class of goods which it will not pay to make here, the prices at which they are imported, even with addition of the duty, being lower than we can produce them at.

The American manufactures of which we are now speaking,

are distinguishable from the European goods by the superior quality of the stock and make. The French aim at making a showy article with as small a quantity of silk as possible. Their goods only look rich and fresh when they are new, whereas the American articles retain their qualities for a long period.

This branch of industry seems to be one of the most lucrative and thriving of our infant manufactures, if we may judge from the number of houses that are already engaged in it, and the rapidity of their increase. A large proportion of the trade of the Union is done by the New York makers, who possess greater facilities for finding skilled hands, as also perhaps a greater command of capital. Of fringes and tassels, either made entirely of silk, or of silk and worsted, we have ten exhibitors, namely: Messrs. Tilt & Dexter, Crossley, Gurney & Co., Foote, Henning & Staderman, McFarlan, Meiker & Maidhoff, of New York; Mills & Carlock, of Bridgeport, Conn.; Klahre, Union Hill, Bergen County, N. J.; and Plimptons, Stephenson & Co., Boston, Mass.

The specimens exhibited by these gentlemen are, generally speaking, of superior finish, and possess considerable merit as regards design. Some of the dress and cloak trimmings, for instance, contrast most favorably with the English goods of the same class, and deserve to rank with the best productions of the Paris makers.

There are about one thousand hands employed in this branch of the silk manufacture in New York, two-thirds of them being females. The average wages of the spinners and weavers is from six to seven dollars a week, and that of the girls engaged as gimb-makers from three to four dollars.

The manufacture of figured cloth for the coverings of buttons, constitutes a separate branch of industry in itself, and is confined to a few establishments. The Italian silk is generally used for this purpose, and the twist is prepared on a machine, called the patent spinner, somewhat similar in principle to the rope-machine. The loom employed in the weaving of the cloth is a modification of the Jacquard principle, and was patented a few years since by Mr. Lightbody, of Jersey City. The whole of the frame-work is of cast-iron, and its construction is so simple that a weaver accustomed to the ordinary hand-loom can work it without difficulty. It possesses the further advantages of rarely getting out of gear and occupying but little space.

The only houses that we know of which are engaged in this branch of the manufacture are those of Mr. Schwietering, of John-street, and Naugatuck, Connecticut, and of Mr. Graves, of Williamsburg, Massachusetts. The former has about twenty looms at work, and the latter about ten. The hands employed by Mr. Schwietering are nearly all Germans.

These establishments do not put the buttons together. Button-making forms a distinct branch in itself, and gives employment to a great number of hands. There are about ten makers in the Union, the greater proportion of whom are located in Connecticut and Massachusetts. Almost all the work of these establishments is done by females, the proportion of men employed being only about five to thirty. The larger buttons are made by hand, and the smaller descriptions by a rotary machine, worked by steam. In a factory employing five men and thirty females, from six to seven hundred gross of buttons can be turned out daily. The iron composing what is called the *collett* of the button, and the canvas which forms the *tough* or padded stem, are imported from England.

Insignificant as this article may appear to be, it is worthy of remark that it has, from time to time, occupied a good deal of the attention of the English legislature, which not only passed statutes to regulate the way in which it was to be made, but to impose restrictions on the fancy of the wearer as to the form and material of button which he might select! The 4 Geo. 1, c. 7, directs that "No person shall make, sell, or set upon any clothes or wearing garments whatsoever, any buttons made of cloth, serge, drugget, camblet, or any other stuff of which clothes or wearing garments are made, or any buttons made of wood only, and turned in imitation of other buttons, on pain of forfeiting forty shillings per dozen for all such buttons." A subsequent act passed in the same reign (7 Geo. 1, c. 22) directs that "No tailor shall set on any buttons or button-holes of serge, drugget, &c., under penalty of forty shillings for every dozen of buttons or button-holes so made or set on." And again, that "No person shall use or wear on any clothes, garments, or apparel whatsoever, except velvet, any button or button-holes made of or bound with cloth, surge, drugget, frieze, camblet, or other stuffs whereof clothes or woollen garments are usually made, on penalty of forfeiting forty shillings per dozen under a similar penalty." We believe these absurd enactments still remain unrepealed on the English statute-books, but it is needless to say that they have long since fallen into disuse.

XXXIV.

COTTON.

THE application of simple natural productions to the manufacture of articles of utility and ornament suggests an inquiry at once attractive and important to every student of natural and experimental philosophy; it is of itself replete with interest; but when we see that a certain plant provides for its future propagation in a small globe or capsule, which in due time bursts forth to distribute its seeds, and at the same time exposes to view a fleece of vegetable wool as white as snow, as fine almost as silk, and as soft as down; that this same vegetable wool, with which was made the garments of the ancient Arabs, and which clothed the immediate disciples of Mahomet, has in process of ages become a source of occupation to millions of our race; that it has originated a system of cultivation, manufacture, trade and commerce, the most extensive and complex; that in one country it is made a plea for oppression the most degrading and anomalous, and in another the great vehicle of commercial gambling and industrial exploitation; that it is closely connected with the domestic pursuits of the mothers and daughters of civilization; that from it are made the first dress of helpless infancy, the most essential covering by night and day throughout life, and in many instances the mantle of death; that it has placed the essential elements of cleanliness and comfort within the reach of the masses; that from it, in many instances, are formed the sails which, by their whiteness, distinguish American from all other vessels on the seas and oceans of the world, and in every port; that, while it thus forms articles of strength and usefulness, it is also wrought into the most exquisite and delicate laces; that when it has served its manifold purposes in clothing the outward man, it forms the basis of a new material on which are impressed words clothing the living thoughts of our poets, philosophers, and orators; that it has thus brought education, light and truth within the grasp of countless millions, furnishing not only vestments for the body but food for the mind; that it has, in a variety of ways, occupied this conspicuous part in human history, must continue to exert an increasing influence over the destinies of nations, and is peculiarly connected with the growth in wealth and fame, in influence, power and greatness of our own country;—when these and the many great interests involved are considered, there surely is no American who enjoys his daily paper, rendered accessible by cotton, but will heartily follow us while we trace out some of the facts connected with this valuable plant, and some of the principal processes by which it is made to contribute such important services to mankind.

The cotton plant belongs to the genus *Gossypium* of the order *Malvaceæ*. It grows, in some of its varieties, in India and China, and appears to have been, in early times, an object of very extensive cultivation in those countries. It was in universal use in all the Eastern nations, long before the Christian era. The area whereon cotton has been found exceeds, to some extent, the torrid zone in breadth; but by cultivation it has been extended on the one hand to the south of Europe, and to Lower Virginia and even Maryland in our own country; whilst on the other it is grown as far south as the Cape of Good Hope and the southern parts of Brazil.

To grow cotton to perfection, a long summer of hot weather is absolutely necessary; a cold winter is no obstacle, provided it does not last so long as to abbreviate the duration of summer. The species known as *Gossypium barbadense*, *hirsutum*, and *religiosum*, will flourish where the mean annual temperature is from 68° to 82°; but the *Gossypium herbaceum* is most successfully cultivated where, the summer heat being 75° or 73°, that of winter is not less than 46° or 48°. The thermometer, in Upper Virginia, is sometimes as low as zero of Fahrenheit in winter, and yet cotton is grown there during the long summers.

Botanical knowledge of this plant is not very extensive, many of its varieties being at present undefined. The "Nankeen Cotton," *Gossypium religiosum*, was introduced at an early period from China; it is abundant in produce, but the wool is of a dirty yellow color and of low price. The *green-seed cotton* is quite white, and it grows in the middle and upland districts, and is called *upland cotton*, and sometimes a short-staple cotton, or *bowed Georgia cotton*. Then there is the *Sea Island* or *long-staple* cotton, which has a remarkably black seed, surrounded by a fine, white, strong and silky long staple. This is grown in the lower parts of Georgia and South Carolina, near the sea, and on several small islands near the coast. It is the best quality of cotton, and commands at all times a high price. The *Gossipium herbaceum* and its varieties, which grow from four to six feet in height, are chiefly grown in India, and it produces a short-staple, white wool. The species chiefly cultivated in Jamaica is called *Gossipium hirsutum*, is shrubby and grows about six feet in height. It is the same plant, we believe, which is known in this country as the green-staple or upland cotton. *Gossipium barbadense* is shrubby, grows from six to fifteen feet in height, and is extensively cultivated in the West Indies and also in Egypt. It is believed that the number of varieties extend to nearly one hundred, but those we have enumerated are the principal.

It is a peculiarity of cotton-seeds grown in this country, to become covered with a kind of fur, which renders them difficult to clean, but they are not deteriorated in any other respect by removal from China, India, or the West India Islands. The Sea Island Cotton has been known to survive for five years in Georgia and Carolina. It sometimes grows so large as to assume all the appearance of a tree; but, when this is the case, its blossoms produce pods so late as to be cut off by the frost before they have time to ripen.

The naturalization of the most valuable species of the Cotton plant, that known as the Sea Island Cotton, was an important era in the history of this country. Fortunately for the experiment, the winters of 1785 and 1786 were mild in Georgia, so that the frosts did not penetrate the ground sufficiently to destroy the roots, and the shoots which succeeded the first year's somewhat discouraging attempt, came up earlier, and arrived sooner at maturity; did not rise so high; displayed their blossoms fully, and more speedily formed their pods. In the succeeding year, the fruit ripened in good time, being by this time more acclimated. The hopes that America would become an important cotton-growing country, now received a new confirmation. The credit of commencing the growth of cotton in this country is due to Georgia and North Carolina, which persevered in the enterprise unaided by their own government. Labors destined eventually to accomplish so much, were for a long time placed in jeopardy the most vexatious and harassing. But indomitable energy requires no patronage, and is frequently provoked by difficulties.

It was upon two of the islands on the coast of South Carolina, on a soil composed of a mixture of sand, decayed vegetables, and sea-shells, forming a loam of peculiar lightness and fertility, that Sea Island Cotton was first produced, and, being separated from the continent by only a few miles of salt marsh, the success of this first experiment with this quality of cotton was considered as conclusive evidence that it could be grown on the main-land. In addition to the name of Josiah Tatnall may be mentioned that of Nicholas Turnbull, both of Skideway Island, near Savannah. Their cotemporaries in the work were James Spalding and Alexander Bissett, of St. Simond's Islands, and Richard Leake upon Jekyl Island, adjoining St. Simon's. For many years, however, the growth of this description of cotton was confined to the warm high lands in these islands, under the influence of a saline, humid atmosphere. In process of time, it was extended to the lower grounds, and to the shores of the continent; and, as the habits of the plant became adapted to the circumstances in which it was now grown, its successful cultivation spread even to the coarse clay soil deposited by the great rivers at their confluence with the tides, and eventually it has been made to grow in any part of Georgia and South Carolina where there is a saline atmosphere—a condition essential to its growth. It is still, however, in the district between St. Mary's Georgia, and Georgetown, South Carolina, extending about fifteen miles inland, that the finest and longest staple is produced.

The hand-method of sowing is usually performed by three female slaves; the first goes before, and makes the drill with a hoe; the most intelligent distributes the seed; and the third walks behind, and covers it up with her foot, pressing the soil close to the seed, so as to keep it moist. The quantity of seed used by sensible cultivators is about one bushel to the acre. The crop is very precarious during its early stages of growth, and it not unfrequently happens that a cold wind, or a visitation of cockchafers or cutworms in April, renders a second sowing necessary. In six successive hoeings the weaker plants are destroyed, leaving from six to twenty-four inches between the plants, according to the size of the variety, the rows being five feet asunder. Their nourishment is principally derived from the atmosphere, which is absorbed by its broad leaves.

By the 20th of July, all operations in the cultivation of the plant are at an end. The Sea Island district is generally blessed with temperate weather up to this time. Toward the end of July and the beginning of August, clouds usually gather on the western hills, and the weather becomes changeable. Rain, attended by lightning, deluges the fields, and beats down the leaves of the Cotton Plant, and sometimes causes it to shed its unripe fruit. At the full moon of August, the caterpillar makes its appearance. In nine or ten days it has grown so large as to become a voracious and dangerous enemy. In some instances, hundreds of acres of flourishing cotton are stripped of foliage and fruit in a few hours, by this visitation. Once in about seven years the ravages of this destructive insect exercise a considerable influence on the cotton market.

Beautiful is the scene of a cotton-field which has escaped the ravages of storms and insects: viney foliage, with blossoms of three brilliant hues, and pods of darker shades in various states of ripeness, all blended together, waving in graceful forms to the gentle breezes, which are occasionally wafted across them from the ocean. On the first day of its opening, the blossom has a fine yellow tint, which the mysterious influences of a single night changes to a crimson hue, which, on the succeeding morn, is changed into a chocolate brown. The blossom then alls to the ground, and leaves a pod half an inch in diameter. From three to six weeks, according to the season and variety, are then required to mature this pod or fruit. The earliest pods are usually ripe at the beginning of August, and they denote their maturity by bursting open. Picking the cotton is an operation which continues from this time till December. This is a tedious though not laborious operation. The slaves are expected to gather about twenty-five pounds a day each, when the weather will permit. In very favorable times, as many as fifty pounds are looked for; but in the latter part of the season, ten pounds a day becomes a single slave's work.

The average produce of an acre of cotton is about one hundred and forty pounds of white, separated from seeds, and twenty-eight pounds of stained or discolored. The average value of the produce of an acre of land to the planter, is about twenty-four dollars; a very small amount, certainly, for so precarious a crop.

Although it is difficult to estimate precisely the amount of capital employed in the Cotton agriculture of this country, the following, compiled from the census of 1840, by the Hon. Levi Woodbury, is believed to be an approximation to what it was at that time:

1,200,000 slaves, at $500	$600,000,000
4,500,000 acres of land, at $10	45,000,000
14,000,000 acres of land in timber, pasture, &c., at $3	42,000,000
6,300,000 acres of land in grain, at $10	63,000,000
400,000 mules and horses, at $100	40,000,000
4,500,000 hogs and sheep, at $1	4,500,000
300,000 cattle, at $5	1,500,000
500,000 plows, at $2	1,000,000
Wagons, and other plantation implements	1,000,000
Total	$798,000,000

The following statistics will show the gradual increase of the Cotton exportations of this country from the year 1790 to the year 1851:

Years ending Sept. 30,	*Value of Cotton Exports.*	*Years ending Sept. 30,*	*Value of Cotton Exports.*
1790	$42,285	1825	$36,846,649
1795	2,250,000	1830	29,674,883
1800	5,000,000	1835	64,661,577
1805	9,445,500	1840	63,870,307
1810	15.108,000	1845	51.739,643
1815	17,529,000	1850	71,984,616
1820	22,308,667	1851	112,315,317

In the whole of this period of sixty years, the total exportations of Cotton amounted to *one thousand seven hundred and eleven million, six hundred and ninety-one thousand, six hundred and seventy-six dollars.* This is exclusive of the large quantity consumed by our home manufacturers, which in 1850 was valued at $34,835,056.

The display of raw or merely ginned Cotton in the Crystal Palace is not equal to what might be expected in a country where cotton forms so important a feature of its agriculture and commerce. We cannot find more than ten samples, and only six of these are mentioned in the Catalogue. Not one has the botanical name of the plant on which it grew attached to it, and only two or three are furnished with the provincial name by which it is known. This is probably the result of indifference on the part of Southern planters who appear to pay very little attention to the sciences connected with their pursuits, and to care still less for the encouragement of the Crystal Palace. There is no reason why these agricultural productions of our country should not have been so arranged as to afford persons who have little opportunity of gaining practical knowledge, such information as would lead to a systematic view of cotton growing. If the Crystal Palace should become a permanent institution it would be well so to order the articles exhibited as to make them instructive to the masses. If for instance samples of the principal varieties of Cotton, with the scientific names of the plants, were nicely arranged in a glass case, as much information could be obtained by a few minutes examination, as by many hours study and research with books. This would be a much more convenient method than placing huge bales of cotton in some dark, out of the way place, under a stall used for an entirely different purpose, as is the case in the present instance. It is impossible to view the cotton in such a position, so as to judge of its true quality, and it is contrary to the rules of the Palace to remove an article from where it is placed. However, notwithstanding these difficulties, we proceed to give our opinion of the samples we procured by the permission of the Superintendent of the Department.

The sample of Sea Island Cotton produced by Mr. William Seabrook of Charleston, South Carolina is unquestionably the best Cotton in the Palace. It possesses all the qualities peculiar to the Sea Island Cotton: it is a very long staple, soft, silky and of fine fibre. This description of Cotton is generally of a brownish color, but this sample of Mr. Seabrook is unusually white. It is adapted for spinning high numbers and would produce the best quality of any fine fabric.

There is another sample of Sea Island Cotton which was grown by Mr. Henry Lawrence of New Orleans. It is good, but appears to have been pulled to pieces so that we cannot judge of its length of staple.

Mr. J. Batchelor, of Rodney, Mississippi, has sent a bale of short staple, upland cotton, which is white, but not particularly silky. No information is afforded as to the plant on which it grew, or the nature of the soil which produced it. It does not appear to be above the ordinary quality of upland cotton.

Under a stall devoted to the exhibition of "Hammel's "essence of coffee," we discovered a bale of cotton very firmly packed, sent by the Eagle Cotton Gin Manufacturing Co., Bridgewater, Mass. It is labelled with a certificate from a New Orleans cotton broker, to the effect that in point of color, ginning, handling and staple, it was the best specimen of short staple cotton brought to the New Orleans market that season. This sample is remarkably well cleaned, and does credit to the machine by which it was ginned.

There is a sample of "Golden Cotton," produced by Dr. Samuel Bond, Green Bottom, Tennessee, which is an exceedingly fine short-staple cotton. The color, also, is unexceptionable, and is creditable to Dr. Bond's experiments.

There is also a sample boll of Golden Cotton and cotton in the seed, (not ginned) from Memphis, Tennessee, which was produced by Mr. John Pope. It feels remarkably well, and has a very fine fibre. With the samples just noticed, it speaks well for the growth of cotton in the State of Tennessee.

Alabama is also represented by a sample of upland, short-staple Cotton grown by Mr. John West, Eufaula, Alabama. It is a very fair specimen, and is well adapted for good medium shirtings.

There is a bale of Cotton sent from Warren County, Mississippi, by Mr. Jefferson Nailes, which weighs four hundred and two pounds. It is a very fine staple.

Two small pink boxes contain samples of very fine short staple Cotton. It is neither labelled nor inserted in the Catalogue. It must have been produced on very poor soil. It is soft and silky, but the staple is as short as that of thistle down.

There is exhibited in the same stall, under a glass, a boll of cotton described as "the world's wonder." It contains fifteen locks, "the like of which was never before seen in the cotton world." Mr. G. D. Mitchel concludes his description by saying, "I challenge the world to produce its equal." It is a curiosity in its way, and worth examination. We could not feel the quality of the staple.

Some specimens of cotton noticed by us sometime since deserve to be referred to in this place. The seed from which this cotton was grown was brought from among the Pino Indians of New Mexico by an officer of the Mexican Boundary Commission. The staple is fine and silky, long, strong, and is not equalled by the article usually grown. The plant is being introduced into Texas, where it bids fair to become a valuable addition to the descriptions of cotton already cultivated. It is believed that the plant will not degenerate, but this must depend upon the nature of the soil where it is grown. The specimen here exhibited is destitute of all harsh feeling and is beautifully white and clear. It was forwarded for exhibition in the Crystal Palace by a mercantile house of San Antonio, Texas.

We are glad to see that the cotton seed is being applied to a useful, and, we trust, profitable purpose. Messrs. William Wilber & Co., of New Orleans, exhibit samples of cotton seed oil which is remarkably clear, and appear to be of a color similar to the oil of linseed though rather paler. No information is given as to whether this oil is found adapted for mechanical purposes. There is a great deal of oil used on the cotton spindles in the spinning of cotton; and if the seeds of the plant usually wasted, can be made to produce an oil suitable for this purpose, it will be a point of economy worth attending to. The same manufacturers exhibit several pieces of brown soap made from cotton seed oil, which may be very good, but having become dry and shriveled, it does not look well, especially now that it has become fashionable to mold soap into so many fanciful forms as are displayed by the toilet exhibitions of the Crystal Palace.

The Exhibition at the Crystal Palace, although somewhat extensive, does not display anything like a complete assortment of cotton goods. There are many stores in the city where a much greater variety is kept. We will here give the result of our observations in the American Department on the Cottons and Cotton fabrics.

The Brown and Bleached Shirtings of the Goddard Brothers, of Providence, R. I., are remarkably fine, being 120 slaie and 120 pick. There are twelve samples very handsomely packed. Some of them are as fine as 140 slaie and 140 pick. We examined them carefully under a glass, and the thread will compare favorably with any linen twist, and when powerfully magnified still appear perfectly even and regular and have all the lustre of fine linen. The brown goods are particularly worthy of remark. They are 120 slaie and 120 pick, and are made of well selected cotton. Every packet in this case is worthy of special examination. They are packed in the style of linens, bookfold, and in this respect and some others will compare favorably with the best linen goods.

The specimens of Brown Sheetings and Osnaburgs, as well as Cotton Warp Yarn, exhibited by M. Canfield & Co., are from one of the Southern States, and are interesting, as showing that the cotton-growing States are making an effort to manufacture their staple at home. There is no reason why the Southern States should not compete with the Northern, especially in these heavy goods, except it be that the curse of Slavery keeps skillful mechanics from going to live there. The Seamless Cotton Bags of the same exhibitors look well, but are placed out of reach, so that we could not examine them.

Messrs. Fitch & Co., of this city, display samples of bleached, unbleached, and indigo Blue Dills and Sheetings, from the manufactory of Asa Fitch, Fitchville, near Bozrah, Conn. The bleached and unbleached goods are not well manufactured: the cotton is moaty, being filled with specks, while the samples have a shop-worn appearance. The dressed goods are very coarse, filled up with starch, and, for the credit of the manufacturer and agent, ought to be removed. The colored drills look better, the dye rendering the specks in the cotton invisible. The light of the Palace, however, has changed their appearance.

The specimens of Shirtings and Sheetings from the Atlantic Cotton Mills, Lawrence, Mass., are sufficiently good to sustain the reputation of the establishment, but are not equal to what they can produce, the pieces selected being unusually moaty. They are, however, heavy and strong fabrics.

Messrs. Parker, Wilder & Co. of Boston, exhibit samples of Monadnock Bleached Sheetings—the 12-4, 11-4 are very creditable articles. They count 68 picks, are made of excellent thread, good staple, and are of a very even appearance.

The Cotton Sheetings and Shirtings of the Masonville Manufacturing Company, Providence, R. I., do great credit to American industry. The motto of this Company is "Excelsior," and if they persevere as they have begun they will soon be able to take the premium in any country on the globe.

The Williamsville Manufacturing Company, Providence, R. I., exhibit some cotton goods of a heavier description, which are neatly done up, but the glass of the case being broken, we could not examine the goods without the danger of doing mischief.

Conestoga Steam Mills, Lancaster, Pa., are well represented. The two-yard-wide heavy Brown Sheeting is the heaviest we have seen anywhere. It is made of yarn No. 14, count 50 by 56. These are admirably adapted for the purpose for which they are designed. They are goods which, in consequence of the weight of cotton they contain, can be made cheaper in this country than English goods of the same quality would cost, so that they are never imported into this country, and we depend entirely upon our own manufacturers for our supply of these substantial domestics. The Shirting of the same quality, thirty-six inches wide, is admirably adapted for laboring men's shirts. The samples of fine Jean is made from No. 30 yarn, are light, pretty goods. Their Drill, made of No. 14 yarn, is extra heavy, and very strong. The samples of Bed-tick, are made of No. 14 yarn, are heavy, strong goods. The herring-bone tick is very nicely woven, and both the broad and wide stripe are solid, substantial articles. The silk-bound Cotton Blankets are beautiful productions, well woven and well carded.

Messrs. Merriam, Brewer & Co., of this city, exhibit, from the Amoskeag Manufacturing Co., Manchester, N. H., some very sightly Drills, which are deserving commendation. Their Brown Sheeting is the best we have seen of this character, being without a speck. The Cotton Flannels are a full nap. Their Denims and Ticks are such as to well sustain the reputation of the Company. They have wisely made these selections from their usual productions. This company deservedly obtained prize medals at the Exhibition in London.

Mr. Thomas Bennett exhibits in a glass case a variety of Bleached Cottons, which, from their appearance, we should judge to be fine, well-finished goods; but being locked up, we could not say whether their fineness was put on in the dressing or whether it was genuine. We should incline to believe, however, that they are the true article. They are manufactured at Wamsutta Mills, New Bedford, Mass.

Messrs. J. D. Dudley & Co., of this city, exhibit some seven-eighth and four-quarter Brown and Bleached Cottons, made of No. 28 or 30 yarn, seventy picks or threads to the inch. The four-quarter goods are quite heavy, weighing about 2,80. They have also specimens of Jean, which are well-manufactured goods, and do credit to the manufacturers, the Reading Manufacturing Company, Pennsylvania.

Mr. Joseph S. Gladding, of Moosup, Windham Co., Connecticut, exhibits various samples of Brown and Bleached Cottons, which are good of the kind, but do not possess any novel qualities. His colored Drills are of a light shade, streaky, and not at all creditable productions.

Messrs. Mills & Co. display Brown and Bleached Goods of a very firm and sightly description, manufactured by the Great Falls Manufacturing Co., Somersworth, N. H. The goods are heavier than the Hadley Falls productions. The bleaching of the Great Falls Co. is done under their own superintendence and they have succeeded well in their efforts to combine this department with the manufacturing. Their style of finishing and doing up is highly creditable.

There is a bale of Cotton Printing Cloth exhibited by G. W. Chapin, from the Saunders Mills, Grafton, Mass. It is a fine, even article, and well adapted for the purpose.

There are some good specimens of Book and Formation Muslin exhibited by the executors of the late D. M'Ewing, which are well manufactured. The same remark will apply to the narrow crown buckram and mosquito nettings. The cotton twist and filling are well spun.

Messrs. Mills & Co. also exhibit a book of patterns, of what they call "Canada Plaids," from the Whittenton Mills, Taunton, Mass. They consist of pantaloonery or cottonades, in imitation of fancy cassimeres. The patterns are neat and creditable, but are all made to contain the same stripe of blue, which, however convenient to the mechanical operations of the manufacturer, conduce in no way to the credit of the sample-book. The imitation of cassimere, however, is *excellent*, and although there is not a particle of wool in the fabric, our impression, on first looking at the patterns, was, that they belonged to the woollen department. We should like to know how these goods wear, because the application of cotton to the manufacture of men's outside garments of this description is a novel and interesting experiment.

The manufacturers for Messrs. Mason & Lawrence, Boston, deserve great credit for the enterprise and ability displayed by them in the production of Cocheco Prints. They wisely display some good old patterns, such as are always in demand, not so much, perhaps, for their beauty as for their neatness and distinctness. But, beside these saleable articles, which are executed in a style that will keep them high in the estimation of the trade, we are glad to see some successful efforts at copying from nature, the true source of originality in designs. The foliage is well executed, and is highly creditable to their artist, while the flowers are of the most beautiful description. Among the light goods we observed many styles which would compare favorably with the best productions of Hoyle, who has been long regarded as the best English cotton-printer. The pink patterns we admire exceedingly; there are few ladies of taste who would not be tempted to purchase from them when exhibited at the stores. The Sheetings, Drills, and Cotton Flannels of the same Company are of their usual character, fully sustaining their well-earned reputation.

Messrs. Charles H. Mills & Co., of Boston, Mass., display some fine printed Lawns and Brilliants, the manufacture of which is unexceptionable. The styles, though not new, are exceedingly neat and chaste, and, being madder colors, are no doubt permanent. The specimens of White Cambrics, Jaconets, and brilliants, are novelties to American manufacture; and, although there are none of a very fine quality among them, they do much credit to the enterprise of the manufacturers at Hadley Falls Mills. These samples demonstrate an important truth in the history of cotton manufacture in this country, viz: that in this department of manufacture, in which England so long excelled, America has made a *successful* effort. We should like to see the Hadley Falls Mills Company bringing out some original designs in their own excellent workmanship, and we have no doubt their efforts would be well rewarded.

The Glasgow Mills, Springfield, Mass., have produced a large and beautiful assortment of Glasgow Ginghams. For brilliancy of style and color, these plaids fully equal those produced in Scotland. It must be encouraging to the proprietors of these mills to find that consumers are learning to appreciate their goods, which are rapidly taking the place of Scotch ginghams in the American market. The samples of dyed yarns from these mills are exceedingly fine; the colors are perfectly clear, having been evidently well bleached before being dyed. We see no reason why our American spinners need fear any competition from abroad if they can produce yarn like this.

M. Canfield & Co. exhibit some Furniture Checks, which are old fashioned and do them no credit.

The Merrimac Prints, from Lowell, Mass., although not novel in style, are neat, chaste goods, such as are in constant demand.

The specimens of Calico Prints from the American Print-

Works, Fall River, Mass., exhibit much taste, in glass cases. They consist principally of spring styles, some of which are new.

Mr. Robert Rennie, of this city, exhibits in a beautiful cabinet, constructed of American wood, some very pretty Prints; many of the styles are quite novel. Their green, pink, blue, and woad colors are very neat imitations of lawn. The furniture print is a fine, bold pattern of flowers, with a landscape back-ground.

Jacob Dunnell & Co. display a great variety of specimens of roller-printing on bareges, calicoes, lawns, de laines, and silks, which merit the highest praise. The case being closed, we could only examine the patterns, and can say nothing as to the texture. Their designs deserve credit for many beautiful new patterns. The established good old patterns are also well executed.

The Goddard Brothers, of Providence, R. I., have manufactured colored Silesias, Nankeens, and Bleached and Brown Cottons, which are displayed with great taste in a glass case. The doing up is unequalled by that of any fabrics we have examined, and the quality of the goods surpasses anything of the kind in the exhibition. The light-colored Silesias are particularly free from specks and admirably finished. There are seven samples of Silesias, so fine as to count one hundred and forty picks. The two qualities of Nankeens are excellent. One, if not both, we should judge to be of the natural color of the cotton, which is well selected.

Messrs. Malcolm & Hesketh of Manchester, Paterson, N. J., have manufactured a splendid white counterpane, on which is worked the American Eagle, surrounded with baskets of flowers and a rich border, with the following motto worked along the foot: "Industry, fostered by Freedom, sends Commerce, her daughter, over all the world to gather its wealth into her treasury."

The Table Covers of Messrs. Malcolm & Hesketh, Paterson, N. J., are worthy of special attention, as exhibiting a new feature of American industry. We are glad to find so successful an attempt at introducing this branch of manufacture. The samples are hung very high, but to all appearance they are equal to imported goods, both for color and style. The pattern in green and drab is well and tastefully arranged, and forms appropriate designs for large table-cloths. The blue, scarlet and crimson are in good colors.

A. Wortendyke of Godwinville, near Paterson, N. J., exhibits some highly creditable specimens of Cotton Wick; counter-twist wick for patent machine molds, and chandlers' wick. These useful articles are particularly clear and free from cotton moats, and they are exhibited in excellent style.

Mr. Nathan Buffington, Fall River, Mass. exhibits in two glass cases excellent specimens of three-cord spool Sewing Cotton. In one case is a beautiful pyramid displaying a rich variety of colors. We should think they are worthy of the highest praise, but we could not test their strength nor feel their quality, owing to their being in inclosures.

Messrs. Brownell & Co. also exhibit samples of Seine Twine which are of a fine twist, and well spun.

The application of Cotton to the manufacture of duck, for ship sails, is well shown by some admirable specimens exhibited by the Atlantic Duck Company, East Haddam, Conn. This is the heaviest and strongest fabric made from Cotton, and these specimens are exceedingly even and well woven. The duck stamped "Goodberry" does not compare favorably with the Atlantic duck, but is placed here, we presume, to illustrate a process invented by Messrs. Taylor & Co., of this City, to prevent it from mildewing or rotting. But from the confused arrangement, or rather want of arrangement of these goods, we are unable to say which of the ducks have been subjected to this process, which, if effectual, is an important feature in the manufacture of ship sails.

Mr. George Wm. Wright, of this city, deserves credit for the excellent manner in which he has exhibited the duck of the Boston Duck Manufacturing Company. The samples are placed in a large book or portfolio, and are in a form well adapted for examination. Although the No. 1 of these samples does not compare favorably with No. 1 of the Atlantic Company, still the ten qualities exhibited in this portfolio are adapted to meet the wants of purchasers with regard to price. These goods are very saleable productions.

The pyramid in a lofty glass case, surmounted by a golden eagle, forms an attractive object on the left-hand side from the entrance of the north nave. It is a white monument to American Invention, formed, not of marble, but of tightly-twisted *Cotton Rope.* This last novelty in Cotton manufacture is the production of the American Cordage Company, whose works are in Cherry and Water-streets, New-York. The mode of rope-making adopted, and which they commenced last March, is as new as is the use of cotton for this purpose. A machine is made to answer all the purposes of a long rope-walk. The advantage of using cotton is, that it is capable of a tighter twist; that it is less liable to injure by friction than hempen cords. The old cotton rope will be worth considerably more than old hempen rope. The rope of cotton is found to run with greater freedom through the blocks, and is altogether more pliable than ordinary ropes. It has been successfully applied to rigging for vessels; to hoisting-tackle; bow, stern, and tow-lines for canal-boats; fishermen's lines, &c. The description of cotton used, is a long-staple "Macon, Georgia." The fibres of the cotton are laid together far more compactly, and with more perfect tension, by this process, than by any other made known; consequently, the rope possesses greater strength than when laid in the ordinary way. It is lighter than Manilla, so that although its price per pound is a few cents more than that of Manilla roping, it is no more expensive, when regarded according to length, while it is believed to be capable of lasting three times as long. The Company is now extending its manufactory, in order to meet the increasing demand for this useful article.

In consequence of the darkness of some portions of the American department, several particularly deserving articles escaped our attention when examining the Woollen goods. We refer to three pieces of fine cassimeres, manufactured by the Vassalboro Manufacturing Company, Maine, from Silesian wool. They are so fine as to count one hundred and fifty picks; and it was impossible to distinguish the threads after scraping off the nap, even with a powerful magnifying-glass. One piece is olive, and one a beautiful mulberry color; both dyes, we are assured, are fast. The mulberry is particularly good, and, being a difficult color to make fast, it must have required a series of experiments to produce this article in so perfect a condition. The other piece is black, soft and pliable, with a lasting finish, being very closely sheared. These are goods of the first quality. They are exhibited by Messrs. F. Skinner & Co., of this city.

There is also a fine black cassimere exhibited by Messrs. Platner & Smith, of Lea, Mass., which deserves to be mentioned as a first-class American production; and some fancy cassimeres from this firm have recently been placed in the Palace by Messrs. Richards, Cronkhite & Co., of this city, (in the place of some we disapproved of,) which do great credit to the manufacturers, being equal, and, in some respects, superior, to imported goods.

Owing to a card being misplaced, the beautiful embroidered blankets and shawls, of which we spoke so highly, were attributed to the wrong manufacturer. They were produced at the Bay-State Mills, Mass. Now that they are displayed more at length, we find the blankets are full-sized ones.

XXXV.

IMPROVEMENTS IN THE MACHINERY FOR SILK WEAVING.

We propose in the present article to attempt a brief outline of the various improvements effected in the machinery employed in the weaving of Silk, from the first rude apparatus used in the production of textile fabrics generally, down to the delicate and complicated invention of Jacquard and its subsequent combination with mechanical power. There is perhaps no branch of industry which has exercised more of the higher faculties of those engaged in it; and, in tracing the successive steps by which it has arrived at the extraordinary results, both as regards beauty of texture and increased facilities of production, which it now presents to us, we are lost in admiration at the vast amount of ingenuity and perseverance that have been brought to bear upon its development.

That the art of weaving was known at an early period to the nations of the East, we have abundant proofs in the records that have descended to us. In the hymns of the Rig-Veda, composed at least twelve hundred years before the birth of Christ, allusion is made to "weaver's threads;" and in the Institutes of the Hindoo law-giver, Menu, it is directed that "a weaver who has received ten palas of cotton thread, shall give them back, increased to eleven by the rice-water, and the like, used in weaving." In the book of Esther, chap. i. v. 6, a description is given of the draperies in the Court of the Persian palace at Shushan, on the occasion of the great feast given by Ahasuerus, which corresponds closely with the hangings of striped cotton cloth used throughout India at the present day, and known under the name of *purdahs*.

When those who are uninformed on the subject happen to take up and examine any of the lighter fabrics of the Indian loom—

those delicate tissues which have been so happily compared to "webs of woven air"—they are naturally led to the conclusion that the machinery by which such perfect results are attained must bear some relation in its completeness to the quality of its productions. It will no doubt surprise them when they are told that these webs, which the most skillful of the European manufacturers, aided by the light of modern science and the mechanical improvements to which it has given birth, have never been able to excel, are produced by looms of the simplest and rudest formation, differing but little in their construction from the primitive contrivances employed some thousands of years since. The description given of the implements used by the Hindoo weaver of the present day, and of the manner in which he carries on his operations, might just as well be supposed to apply to the infancy of the art, when the laws of mechanics were imperfectly understood and no better models were within his reach. His labors are performed in the open air, under the shade of some tree whose foliage is sufficiently thick to protect him from the scorching rays of the sun. Here, extending the threads that compose the warp of his intended cloth lengthwise, between two bamboo rollers, which are fastened to the turf by wooden pins, he digs a hole in the earth sufficiently large to contain his legs when in a sitting posture: then suspending to a branch of a tree the cords which are intended to cause the reciprocal raising and depressing of the alternate threads of his warp, he fixes underneath, and connected with the cords, two loops into which inserting the great toe of either foot, he is ready to commence his operations. The shuttle, wherewith he causes the cross-threads or woof to interlace the warp, is, in form, like a netting-needle, and, being somewhat longer than the breadth of the warp, is made to perform the office of a batten by striking the threads of the woof or shoot close to each other.

The art of weaving varies but little, whatever may be the nature of the material which is to be used. In the weaving of silk or woollen fabrics the difference in the construction of the looms lies chiefly on the greater strength and weight required in the machinery employed in the manufacture of the latter.

In order that our readers may be enabled to appreciate the

value of the improvements that have been introduced in the machinery of weaving within the last century—a period that embraces nearly all the important modifications that have been effected in it—it will be necessary for us to describe the process of plain weaving, as performed by what is called the single loom. The first operation consists in laying the requisite number of threads together to form the width of the cloth. This process is termed *warping*. Let us suppose, by way of illustration, the width of the intended cloth to consist of one thousand threads; then the yarn must be so unwound from the bobbins, and so distributed, as to form one thousand lengths, constituting, when laid parallel, the warp of the stuff, or, in other words, the vertical threads attached to the loom. Before the invention of the warping-frame, the weaver was obliged to draw out the yarn from the bobbins at full-length in an open field—and this method is still practiced in India and China. By this improvement a great deal of labor is saved, the threads being rapidly arranged by means of a frame revolving on a vertical axis. They are then taken off the frame and wound on a stick into a ball previous to the process of *beaming*, or winding them on the beam of the loom. Great care is required in laying them as evenly as possible on the loom; for this purpose a ravel or comb is used to separate them at equal distances to the intended width of the cloth. The warp-treads are then *drawn*, or attached separately to a certain mechanism of the loom. In this process all the threads are attached to stays fixed to two frames called heddles, in such a manner that all the alternate threads can be drawn up or down by one heddle, and all the rest by the other. There are three movements attending every thread of weft which the weaver throws across the warp. In the first place, he presses down one of the two *treadles* by which one of the two heddles is depressed, thereby forming a kind of opening called the *shed*. Into this shed, at the second movement, he throws the shuttle containing the weft-thread with sufficient force to drive it across the whole web. Then, at the third movement, he grasps the *batten*, which is a kind of frame, carrying at its lower edge a comb-like piece, having as many teeth as there are threads in the warp, and with this he drives up the thread of weft close to those previously thrown. One thread of weft is thus completed, and the weaver proceeds to throw another in a similar way, but in a reverse order—that is, by depressing the left treadle instead of the right, and by throwing the shuttle from left to right instead of from right to left. In the commonest mode of weaving, the shuttle is thrown by both hands alternately; but, about a century ago, a person named Kay invented what is called the *fly-shuttle*, in which a string and handle are so placed that the weaver can work the shuttle both ways with one hand. In weaving plain silks, calicoes, and other webs of moderate width, there are two leaves of heddles and two treadles for dividing the warp into small parcels.

Figure-weaving is the art of producing various patterns in the cloth, either by the introduction of threads of various colors, or by a different arrangement of the threads, or by using in the same fabric threads of different substances. It seems to have been practiced by the Egyptians at a very remote period; for we find mention made in the works of Herodotus of a curious breast-plate or cuirass covered with linen, which was sent by King Amasis to the Lacedæmonians. He states that each of its apparently slender threads was composed of three hundred filaments, which, under a careful examination, were all distinctly visible.

The improvements introduced of late years into this ornamental branch of the art, have been many and important; but, previous to giving any description of these improvements, it is necessary to explain generally the more simple, although more laborious and less perfect, means whereby the weaver was formerly enabled to produce the requsite varieties of form and color from his loom.

The silks known as shot-silks are produced by the difference in color in the threads composing the warp and the weft. A *stripe* is a pattern in which parallel lines run either along or across the warp; while a *check* is an alternation of rectangles like a chess-board, or, more strictly speaking, like the varieties known as Scotch plaid. The production of a stripe depends either upon the warper or the weaver; the production of a check, upon both. This mode of ornamenting textile fabrics is very ancient, as may be seen by the figures in Rosselini's "Egypt," many of the figures in which are attired in checkered cloths. The compartments of a checked pattern are sometimes formed by differently colored threads and sometimes by threads of different qualities. In the *twill* which forms the web of satins and bombazines, the weft-threads pass over one warp-thread and under two, over one and under three, or over one and under eight or ten, according to the kind of twill required; the effect of this is to produce a kind of diagonal-ribbed appearance either on the right or the wrong side of the cloth, and a smooth and glossy surface on the other, according as the one thread is crossed above or below by the weft. To produce these results, more than two leaves or heddles are required, and more than two treadles to work them—and the weaver's loom is thereby rendered a much more complicated machine than that employed in plain weaving.

When the design embraces figures, flowers, or patters of any other kind, different means must be resorted to. By dividing the warp between several leaves of heddles, which can be depressed at pleasure by separate treadles, threads of different colors may be either concealed or brought out on the surface of the cloth, at the pleasure of the weaver. These threads may be made to change places, one with the other, so as to reveal or conceal each in such a way, as to make out the particular pattern intended. When threads of different colors or substance are employed in forming the shoot, the shuttles containing such different threads must be substituted as often as is required by the contemplated change of pattern. To effect this substitution with but little trouble or loss of time to the weaver, a simple but effectual contrivance is used. One of the troughs connected with the shuttle-race is made in two parts, thus: The box forming part of the trough in which the shuttle is placed between the warp and the pecker or driver can be easily exchanged for another box furnished with a different shuttle, having wound on it a thread of the kind wanted. In order to facilitate this exchange of the shuttles, the movable part of the trough is suspended from a centre of motion; therefore the box on its centre, any one of its divisions may be brought opposite the driver so as exactly to coincide with it, and to form a part of the same trough in continuation of the shuttle-race. The upright bar of the shuttle-box works upon a curved arm, which is furnished with pegs or catches to confine the bar in the precise position which it should occupy. If more than three different colored threads are wanted to form the shoot, there may then be two movable boxes for the shuttles, one being placed at each end of the shuttle-race.

As in the production of twilled cloths in which the variety of patterns are extensive, it was found that a greater number of heddles was required than one man could possibly manage with his feet, it was sought to meet this difficulty by some mechanical contrivance, and thus obviate the necessity of employing a second person at the loom to raise the heddles. In 1807 an invention was patented and brought into use, which effectually answered the purpose, and which, besides the economy of labor which it effected, imparted greater precision and certainty to the operations of the loom. In this apparatus, which was called a *draw loom,* the strings were so arranged that a boy could draw down the requisite warp threads preparatory to the movement of the shuttle. As, however, even this improvement involved some practical inconveniences, such, for instance, as obliging the weaver to quit the loom from time to time in order to reset it, new combinations were suggested by which it might be rendered more automatic in its action. Of these, the invention called the *draw-boy* was the best adapted to the end proposed. It not only superseded the necessity of employing a boy to pull the handles, but removed, by the unerring certainty of its operation, all possible chance of mistake in pulling the wrong handle. The same object was effected in a different branch of manufacture, (that of carpets,) by the ingenious invention of Mr. Duncan, in which the threads were moved by pins inserted in a rotating barrel, somewhat similar in principle to that of a street-organ.

We now arrive at an era in the history of the manufacture, in which all the ingenious ameliorations we have been describing were destined to give place to a new combination of machinery so perfect and satisfactory in its operation, that, in the long interval that has elapsed since its completion by the inventor, but little has in reality been done either to simplify or to add to it.

It was in the year 1801, at the second National Exposition of Industrial Products held in the Louvre, that the name of JACQUARD was first brought prominently before the European public as an inventor. His attention had long been previously directed to the improvement of the machinery used in figure-weaving, but, owing to the part which he took in the defence of Lyons against the army of the Convention, having subjected him to proscription, his labors were interrupted for several years, and it was not until the period just mentioned that he succeeded in completing the first of the beautiful series of inventions that have effected such a revolution in the art. The story of the difficulties that beset his path in his efforts to carry out his favorite idea, as well as of the prejudice and opposition which he had to encounter in his endeavors to bring his inventions into general use, has been too often told to need repetition here. It is consoling to the admirers of his genius to reflect that he lived long enough to overcome those obstacles, and see all those prejudices vanish.

It would occupy too much of our space, and would besides be imperfectly understood, without the aid of drawings and diagrams, were we to attempt to enter into a detailed description of the admirable invention now generally known under the title of the Jacquard loom. A brief explanation of its main features must suffice. In plain weaving, the weft or cross threads pass alternately under and over the warp threads, forming a perfectly regular interlacing; but in pattern or figure-weaving, the device is made by irregularities in these alternations; sometimes two or more threads are crossed over at one time without any intermediate under-crossing. When the shuttle with the weft thread has to be thrown from edge to edge of the warp or web, some of the warp-threads have to be lifted up to allow it to pass, and the Jacquard apparatus assists in this elevation, which depends (in every throw of the shuttle) on the pattern to be woven. Numerous cards are employed (sometimes as many as five hundred for a complicated pattern) formed of pasteboard and pierced with holes. Every card has a certain relation to one throw of the weft thread, and the number and arrangement of the holes determine which warp-threads shall be drawn up to let the weft pass. The cards are linked together into an endless chain, which is passed over a hollow box at the top of the loom. The chain is made to rotate slowly, one movement for every weft-thread thrown; and each card in turn acts upon a series of levers by which the warp-threads are raised: the blank part of each card acts upon the levers, while the perforated parts allow the levers to pass into the holes without being affected.

In a modification of the Jacquard machine, invented by Mr. Samuel Dean, of Bethnal Green, London, an attempt was made to dispense with the card-slips altogether, by adopting the use of two revolving bars, placed on opposite sides of the machine. Each of these bars has eight faces, and the loom is actuated by two treadles. The variations of pattern are effected by temporarily stopping such holes in the revolving bars as will influence the raising of those threads of the warp upon which the production of the patterns depends. It was found, however, that this modification could only be applied to the production of the simplest patterns, it being capable of employing only sixteen casts of the shuttle for their completion.

In 1850, another ingenious variation of the Jacquard principle was patented in England, in which the same end was sought to be accomplished by making the designs by pins on a rotating barrel instead of by holes in a chain of cards. It does not seem, however, to have been received with favor by the manufacturers.

Up to within a very recent period, the machinery employed for the perforation of the pattern on the Jacquard cards occupied the labor of two persons; one in "reading off" the pattern, as it is termed, and the other in arranging the punches. In Mackenzie's punching machine, which was patented about four years ago, an improvement has been effected by which the person who reads off the pattern is enabled to work a set of keys like those of a piano-forte, each of which inserts a punch into its proper place, thus dispensing with the labor of a second workman.

At the London Exhibition, there were several looms shown, in which modifications of the Jacquard principle were more or less successfully carried out. One of them intended for figure-weaving had a double Jacquard apparatus attached, one on each side of the loom, which greatly increased the facilities for speed of production, and obtained a council medal, for its inventor, Mr. Alfred Barlow. Another Jacquard loom sent in by Messrs. Campbell, Harrison and Lloyd, was of so complex a nature that no less than ninety shuttles are said to have been used in it. It was capable of producing the most elaborate patterns of brocaded silks. The weaving apparatus which attracted the most attention, was, however, the fringe-loom of the Messrs. Reed, of Derby, if loom it could be called, for it had no shuttle, and was almost noiseless in performing its beautiful movements. By this machine, from twenty to thirty breadths of fringe are made at once, and as many different colors either of weft or warp can be introduced in one loom. The warp threads are arranged much as usual in breadths, and each weft thread is passed through the eye of a needle at one side of each breadth, and at the proper time is laid across the warp threads and tight around the blade of a knife, which is rather narrow and not very sharp at this part; the reed then closes up and holds the thread firm, while the knife is drawn down, and the point being much wider than the other part and quite sharp, cuts the outer edge of the fringe and then rises again ready for receiving another thread around it, when the same process is repeated.

Prize medals were awarded for several other new modifications of the Jacquard apparatus for loom and lace machines, to Messrs. Acklin, in France; Bornardel, in Prussia; and Gambia, in Lombardy.

The most remarkable improvement, however, on the Jacquard loom, which has been suggested for our consideration, is that which has been announced to us as having been just effected in Italy by the application of electricity to the operations of the weaver. This invention professes to do away with the use of complicated mechanism, of pattern-cards, and, if we understand aright, of machinery almost altogether. That electricity may be rendered an important agent in the production of the pattern, we can readily imagine; but that it will effect all that is promised in this announcement, we may reasonably doubt. As, however, the details of the invention are not as yet before us, the preliminary steps having only just been taken to secure the patents, it would be unfair to raise any discussion as to the principles involved in it, until we have an opportunity of informing ourselves fully as to their merits.

Having taken a rapid review of the successive improvements effected in the construction of the silk loom, it now only remains for us to consider it in combination with mechanical power, by which the labor of the hand has been in a great degree substituted, and the facilities of production largely increased.

The earliest invention of a loom for mechanical weaving was, we believe, that of a Frenchman named De Gennes, who, in 1678, constructed a rude sort of weaving-machine, intended to increase the power of the common loom. Toward the close of the same century, the drawing and description of a power-loom, almost identical in construction with the celebrated invention of Dr. Cartwright, were presented to the Royal Society of London, but there is every reason to believe that this gentleman was wholly unacquainted with the fact of their existence until after he published the details of his discovery to the world. His attention had been directed to the subject by circumstances purely accidental, which occurred during a visit to Matlock in 1784; and, although entirely unacquainted at the time with the commonest processes used in weaving, by the April of the following year he succeeded in producing his first power-loom, which, though an extremely rude machine, soon received many valuable improvements. Owing to the prejudices of both manufacturers and workmen, great difficulties attended its first introduction, and a mill containing about five hundred of his looms was fired by incendiaries, and burnt to the ground. Undiscouraged by this misfortune, he devoted himself zealously to the improvement of his invention, and expended his whole fortune in perfecting it; but it was not until the year 1798 that it forced its way into general use. One cause of the delay in its adoption was the inconvenience which attended it in stopping the machinery frequently, in order to dress the warp with paste or size as it unrolled from the beam, which operation required a man to be employed for each loom, so that there was little or no economy of expense. Successive inventions, however, at length overcame this difficulty, and power-weaving was brought to its present high state of efficiency.

The power-loom was at first confined to the fabrication of cotton and woollen stuffs, it being for a long time the opinion of practical men that it could not be applied to such a delicate texture as silk without impairing its beauty and lessening its value. This notion, although to some extent well founded at the period to which we refer, has since, by the aid of some valuable improvements in machinery, been shown to be almost altogether fallacious. Power-looms are now applied in Europe to the production of both plain silks and ribands; and in this country, in combination with the Jacquard apparatus, even to the manufacture of rich figured goods, as we shall have occasion to show when we come to speak of the splendid results achieved in this branch by the Eagle Manufacturing Company of Connecticut. The details of this noble enterprise —the first of the kind that has ever been successfully carried out in this country—are so interesting in their industrial bearings, and so gratifying to our feelings of national pride as Americans, that we propose to devote a special chapter to them.

XXXVI.

SILK MANUFACTURES.

FIGURE-WEAVING BY AMERICAN POWER-LOOMS—BROCATELLES AND BROCADES.

HAD the Exhibition of 1853 been anticipated by a couple of years, of how much of its interest it would have been divested! Within that brief space of time we have seen some of its most attractive features either spring into the germs of a valuable discovery, or grow into the full development of a manufacture. Among the many fortuitous circumstances that favored its opening at this particular conjuncture, we look upon the opportunity afforded it of exhibiting the first specimens of complicated figure-weaving by American power-looms, as about one of the most important and eventful. Here, for the first time in the history of this difficult branch of industry, we were able to show that we had got the start of the European manufacturers, and that their monopoly of our markets in figured silk goods was at length at an end.

If our readers have not as yet inspected the brocatelles of the Eagle Manufacturing Company, the silks to which we allude, they can hardly appreciate the full extent of the advantages likely to be derived from the improvements introduced by them. They would at once feel satisfied on beholding them, that the means which had sufficed to accomplish such admirable results, were adequate to the manufacture of the most difficult fabrics—always excepting, of course, those textures in the composition of which metallic threads are employed. As the history of every successful experiment of this sort is fraught with instruction to those who are engaged in industrial pursuits, and indeed to all who take an interest in the progress of our manufactures, we purpose in the present article to give a brief account of this establishment, as well as of one or two others which have recently commenced operations in different branches of the same industry.

The Silk-Works of the Eagle Manufacturing Company are situated at Seymour, Conn., (formerly called Humphreysville, after General Humphreys, who erected the first woollen manufactory established in New-England, and introduced, we believe, the first merino sheep imported into this country.) Seymour is the seat of a number of other valuable branches of industry; and its population, which is in a great measure dependent upon them, has been increasing rapidly within the last few years. Of these establishments, the Humphreysville Copper Company, the Humphreysville Tool and Hardware Manufacturing Company, and the American Car Company, alone represent a capital of more than half a million of dollars.

The Eagle Factory is built on the verge of what are called the Falls of the Naugatuck River, which is here exceedingly picturesque, its waters winding between precipitous banks, upon whose sides the town is built. The Naugatuck furnishes water-power to a number of other important manufactories situated at Wolcotville, Plymouth, Waterbury, Naugatuck, Ansonia, and Birmingham.

The Eagle Company was organized under the general law of the State for regulating joint companies, in July, 1851. The capital stock is $100,000, divided into shares of $25, the whole of which are now in the hands of about a dozen shareholders. The buildings and machinery were all constructed under the direction of Mr. Humeston, the present Superintendent of the works—a gentleman who had long been previously engaged in the manufacture of silk goods at New-Haven, Conn., and with whom the first idea of the enterprise originated. The operations of the firm to which he belonged, had been, up to this period, confined to the fabrication of various figured silk goods, such as ribbons, galloons, and fringes; but Mr. Humeston's attention having been directed to the ingenious modifications of the Jacquard loom, which had been patented and successfully introduced in the manufacture of carpets by Mr. E. B. Bigelow, of Boston, it struck him that the same improvements might be advantageously applied to the execution of complicated patterns on broad silks. It should be stated, that previous to the conception of Mr. Humeston's plans, numberless efforts had been made in Europe, and fortunes wasted, in abortive attempts to adapt the various improvements in power-looms to the production of these patterns; but they had only succeeded in the narrow and simple fabrics. Sanguine as to the results of his scheme, Mr. Humeston went to Boston, and explained his ideas to Mr. Bigelow, who entered warmly into them, and told him that if a company could be formed to carry them out, he would sell them the exclusive right to use his improvements for this branch of manufacture. Being a man of energy and capacity, and being, moreover, zealously seconded by the personal exertions and influence of Mr. Bigelow, Mr. Humeston was not long in assembling the elements necessary to the realization of his plans. The company was formed without difficulty, and the site above described having been selected, the works were commenced, and pushed forward with such rapidity, that they were ready to commence operations in the spring of the following year.

Although the new Jacquard power-looms constructed by Mr. Humeston are applicable to the production of every description of figured silk, it was resolved by the Company to confine themselves for the present to the manufacture of those articles in which they might hope to compete successfully with the foreigner. The heavy duty levied in this country on the importation of raw silk—a burden from which the French and English manufacturers are exempt—naturally indicated the policy of their selecting the most difficult and expensive fabrics, in which the disadvantage of the cost of the raw material would be counterbalanced by the superior rapidity of the new process of manufacture as contrasted with the tedious operations of the old hand-loom used by the Lyons weaver. They therefore determined to commence with those rich stuffs which have become so fashionable as the materials for furniture, draperies, and carriage-linings, and which are known under the names of Brocatelles and Cotolines. Brocatelle is a mixed and complicated fabric composed of silk and cotton or linen, with large damask figures on a bright twilled or brocade ground. The cotton or linen is thrown into the back of the cloth to give it substance and durability. The brocatelle of the present day is in fact nothing more than a harmonious combination of the original damask with the varieties of figured weaving discovered of late years. It is merely an improvement on the *cafard* or counterfeit damask formerly manufactured by the French, in which the warp was composed of silk and the shoot of thread, wool, cotton, or hair. Cotolines belong to the same class of goods, the only difference in them being their heavier substance and the cording of the ground on which the figures are brought out.

The buildings of the factory consist of a main edifice four stories in height and about one hundred feet long by fifty wide, substantially built in brick, with several smaller erections devoted to the different operations of bleaching and dyeing. The first story has an elevation of about fifteen feet, the Jacquard apparatus requiring fully this height, and here the process of weaving is carried on. The second and third stories are appropriated to the winding of the silk, the punching of the pattern-cards, the preparation of the warps and the dressing of the goods. The building is heated by steam pipes, no fires being allowed on this part of the premises.

Although the Company has been formed nearly three years, it is only within the last twelve months that they have been able to introduce their fabrics into the market. This delay was occasioned by several causes. Besides the difficulties attending the adaptation of the Jacquard apparatus to water-power, which formed the main feature of the plan, an unexpected obstacle was encountered in the tediousness of the process by which the larger designs were executed in the pattern-cards. This occasioned such an expenditure of time and labor that it impeded greatly the operations of the manufacture, and added so much to their cost as to threaten to defeat the calculations on which the enterprise was based. Mr. Humeston applied himself at once to the discovery of some mechanical arrangement by which the process might be expedited, and after some months labor he succeeded in perfecting a machine which performs at one operation all the manipulations that were hitherto effected in four. This machine consists of the usual stamping plates, containing as many punches as there are needles in the Jacquard apparatus, and corresponding to the same scale. It runs upon an iron track like a railway car, and its movements are regulated by the machinery connected with the keys. The improvement consists in the substitution of mechanical power for manual labor, and by its aid the patterns are punched out with as much rapidity and ease as if the person controlling it were performing a piece of music on a piano-forte. The most complicated designs are cut in less time by it than even the "reading off" could be performed in under the old method. Another improvement has been effected by the construction of what is called "the Duplicate Machine," by which a single workman can cut in a day six thousand cards for a machine of six hundred needles.

Another serious inconvenience which the Company had to encounter was the difficulty of procuring the quality of silk suited to the requirements of their manufacture. To guard against its recurrence at a moment when it might embarrass their operations, they sent Mr. Humeston to Europe to make a selection of the best qualities produced in France and Italy, and to make arrangements for a regular supply of them. Neither Chinese nor Indian silk is used in the manufacture of brocatelle. The Italian and French silks are preferred for the closeness of their fibre, a quality essential in stuffs having so dense a surface.

All the silk used in this establishment is prepared and dyed on the premises. The mechanical arrangements of the dyeing department and the various processes to which the silk is subjected previous to its being ready for the weaver, resemble so closely those which we had occasion to describe in our last article, that it is unnecessary for us to recapitulate them here. In the dye-house there is a large steam-boiler, which serves the double purpose of heating the buildings and supplying the hot water used in the vats. An abundant supply of excellent spring-water is obtained from a large well sunk fifteen feet below the bed of the river. It is raised by a force-pump to a cistern, and is thence conveyed by pipes to different parts of the premises. The qualities of the dyes have been much improved since this water has been obtained. The river water which was formerly used was full of impurities, arising from decayed vegetable matter and other refuse floated down from the iron and paper mills situated higher up on the river.

All the fabrics that issue from this establishment are made from original designs, the Company studiously avoiding copying from foreign patterns. They employ an experienced and skillful artist in this department, whose labors have contributed in no small degree to the success which has attended the enterprise. The mode in which the designs are prepared is the same as that adopted for hand-weaving. The artist first sketches his conceptions on ordinary drawing-paper, and then transfers his sketch to the design paper, where it is reduced to a scale corresponding with the arrangement of the needles in the Jacquard apparatus. The sketch is then filled in with colors indicating by their position the precise warps and shoots which are requisite for the production of the figure. The design is now complete, and is ready for the operations of the machine which cuts the pattern cards.

The improved looms used in this establishment are principally constructed of cast-iron. They are surmounted by Jacquards of twelve hundred needles each, and the combined weight of each loom and apparatus is about two tons. These looms have movable shuttle-boxes, affording facilities for introducing four different colors into the fabric, which boxes are changeable at will by the motions of the Jacquard. One of the principal obstacles to the application of power-looms to the weaving of figured goods lies in the abrupt and violent jerks imparted to the delicate tissues of the warp by the cam motion. This has been surmounted in the improved loom which we are describing by such a modification of the working parts as produces a gradual and progressive movement, adapting itself to the character of the material. It is the first power-loom which has been successfully applied to the execution of complicated designs. By its means any variety of figured weaving and any number of colors can be combined in the same web. It moves at the rate of fifty picks a minute, and will produce at the rate of one hundred and twelve picks to the inch of cloth, (forty-eight inches in width,) or about six yards in a day of eleven hours. The average production of the ordinary Jacquard hand-loom is only about a yard in the same number of hours.

Each loom is worked by a girl, who requires very little previous experience to manage it perfectly, and to every six looms is attached a man called a section hand. His business is to see the warps properly kept up, breakages in the silk promptly repaired, and the general machinery kept in good order. The designer superintends the mounting of the looms and the preparation of the warps.

In order to give our readers some idea of the manner in which the operations of this particular branch of manufacture are carried on, we will select a loom on which we observe a complicated design in progress of execution, requiring upwards of eight thousand pattern cards for its completion. The warp is a deep crimson and the weft a bright gold color. The width of the stuff is forty-eight inches, and, to cover this surface, three large figures, of sixteen inches in width each and a yard in length, are intended to be employed. The design is a *corbeille* of flowers, suspended by a chain to a cluster of vine branches. The figures are raised in satin and broken twills, and the ground is a plain surface of gold-colored brocade work. When the loom is started the first operation observed is the upward motion of the trap-board of the Jacquard, which carries with it such portions of the harness threads as correspond with the perforations of the pattern card, which is pressed against the ends of the needles by the sliding motion of the cylinder, thereby raising such of the warp threads as are necessary to the progressive development of the design, to a height sufficient to allow the shuttles in their lateral flight to introduce the weft threads, which are carried home to the woven cloth by the forward motion of the reed. During the flight of the shuttle, and the vibrating motion of the reed, the Jacquard carries over the next of the series of cards to adjust the succeeding pick in the composition of the fabric. These movements are repeated sixty times in every minute, until each of the series of cards has contributed its share to the completion of the design.

We now discover on one end of the cloth-roller, and connected with the machinery of the loom, a small dial with its face accurately divided into figures, and a hand indicating at every stage of the process the precise quantity woven. Consulting our watch, and comparing it with the movements of the pointer on the dial, we find that the loom has repeated the operations just described, four thousand and thirty-two times, and has made a yard of cloth in sixty-seven minutes. During this time, in which the shuttles have travelled upwards of six miles, the weaver has only to watch their movements, replacing from time to time the filling bobbins that get expended or broken, and the occurrence of which is indicated by the instantaneous stopping of the loom. The stoppage is effected by an ingenious contrivance at each end of the shuttle race which disconnects the propelling force whenever the filling breaks or the shuttle fails to clear the web or reach its proper place in the box. There are sometimes four shuttles passing in succession through the same race, each giving out its thread of weft, and as soon as each shuttle has passed on, the fingers of the "protector," as it is called, commence feeling for the thread. The absence of the latter causes the fingers to close, and by their connection with the skipper throws off the driving-belt and applies a brake, thereby instantly arresting the motions of the loom. There is another arrangement by which only one of the four threads of weft is allowed to come in contact with the fingers at the same moment, so that the action of the "protector" is rendered certain by the absence of any one of them.

All the brocatelles manufactured in this establishment are made in widths of forty-eight inches; the length of each piece is forty yards. The French brocatelles vary in width from twenty-one to seventy-two inches; the German from forty-three to sixty-six. The French manufacturers only send goods of the first class to this market, ranging in price from two dollars and fifty cents to twenty dollars a yard, while the Germans send an inferior description, varying from two dollars to four dollars a yard. The Eagle Company have chosen an intermediate style of manufacture, better suited to the peculiar character of our market; their prices range from three dollars to six dollars a yard. Although, as we have already stated, they have only commenced the sale of their fabrics within the last twelve months, orders have poured in upon them so fast that the ten looms first mounted in their factory have been found insufficient to keep pace with them. Ten more are in progress of construction, and will be mounted in the course of a few weeks, and they will then be enabled to supply a demand of from one hundred and fifty to two hundred yards a day. The economy effected by this improved loom is about fifteen per cent, and were the American manufacturer placed upon the same footing as the French and English, as regards the free importation of the raw material and dyes, it would be fully double that amount.

The whole of the machinery of the factory is driven by water power. The water-wheel is twenty-two feet in diameter, with an issue of ninety-six square inches under a five-feet head, with a fall of thirteen feet, giving a result of twenty horse-power. The wheel works in the flume, immediately under the machine-room, and is almost entirely surrounded by water, so that it is free from all obstructions arising from ice or from back-water in times of freshet. It is frequently run with nine feet of back-water, giving off sufficient power to perform all the operations of the mill.

There are about sixty persons employed at present in the works, two-thirds of whom are females from the age of fourteen upward. The rate of wages paid by the Company is higher than that given by the neighboring factories, the nature of the work requiring a superior degree of skill and intelligence. There is a boarding-house connected with the establishment which accommodates about forty of the persons employed, the remainder residing in the town with their families. We cannot conclude our description of these works without bearing testimony to the order and discipline which seem to reign throughout every branch of them, as well as to the creditable efforts made by the Company to insure the physical comfort and elevate the moral condition of those employed by them.

The rich brocades that formerly constituted the pride and ornament of the stately dames who loved to disfigure their persons with the ruff and farthingale, have now almost entirely disappeared from use as wearing apparel, and it is only in the gorgeous vestments of the Jewish and Roman Catholic rites that their ancient glories are perpetuated. Limited as is this application of these once-popular fabrics, it appears that it is still deemed of sufficient importance to induce attempts to introduce the manufacture of them into this country, and to expend upon them an amount of capital and energy that one would have supposed might have been more profitably bestowed on some other branch of industry.

Most of the heavy damask, and gold and silver brocades, used in this country for ecclesiastical purposes, have been hitherto imported from Lyons, where the manufacture of these stuffs has been carried to the highest state of perfection, and where the demand from the different Catholic countries of Europe is of sufficient consequence to keep a certain amount of capital embarked in it.

Speculating on securing a portion of the orders forwarded from this country and South America, an enterprising German, named Neustaedter, commenced the manufacture of these fabrics in New York about eighteen months since, and, notwithstanding the difficulties attending the enterprise, he has succeeded in turning out from his looms stuffs which, for richness and beauty of design, will stand a comparison with some of the best productions of the Lyons looms. In addition to the fabrics used for church purposes, he manufactures furniture brocades of the most beautiful and costly patterns, the figures on which are woven in gold and silver thread, or the grounds composed entirely of these materials. It should be stated that in ancient times those stuffs only were called brocades which were woven both on the warp and shoot with gold and silver threads, or with a mixture or combination of both these materials. In preparing the threads for weaving gold brocade, a flattened silver gilt wire or ribbon was spun on silk that had been dyed to resemble as closely as possible the color of the metal, and the principal excellence in the art of preparing gold threads, consisted in so regulating the convolutions of the metallic covering of the silk, as that its edges should exactly touch and form as it were one continued covering without either interval or overlapping. Subsequent improvements were effected on this process by the Venetians, by which, although they used only half the quantity of gold and silver employed in making brocade according to the usual method, they imparted to them a far more beautiful appearance. The flattened wires were not wound so close together on the silk threads, nor were there so many of these threads used in the weaving; but by passing the stuffs when manufactured between rollers, to which a great amount of pressure was given, the wire threads were partially crushed, so as to cause the ornamental pattern to assume the appearance of an unbroken and brilliant plate of gold or silver. This process having long been kept a secret by the Venetian manufacturers, the jealousy of the French Government was excited by it, and about the middle of the last century they employed the celebrated Vaucanson to contrive machinery by which the same object could be effected. His efforts proved successful, and since that period the Lyons weavers have enjoyed almost a monopoly of this branch of the silk manufacture. In the various modifications to which these various improvements in the materials gave rise, the character of the fabric itself also underwent alteration, until at length stuffs composed entirely of uncovered silk, provided they were adorned and worked with flowers or other ornamental figures, took equally the name of brocades.

When we consider the peculiar difficulties of this branch of the silk manufacture, and the lamentable failures that have hitherto been the result of all the efforts made to introduce even the fabrication of plain broad silks in this country, we cannot sufficiently admire the courage and enterprise of this spirited foreigner, in applying himself at once to the most difficult descriptions of weaving. It is gratifying to learn that, so far, he has had no reason to repent the step he has taken, his goods finding a ready sale in the market, owing to the excellence of their quality and their moderateness of price, as compared with the French brocades.

The looms used by Mr. Neustaedter are constructed on the ordinary Jacquard principle, the peculiar character of the fabrics which he manufactures preventing the application of mechanical power to them. In the figured damasks made by the power-loom of the Eagle Company, we are told that it is possible to interweave a simple pattern of gold and silver thread, but the more complicated and showy effects of brocade cannot as yet be produced by them. The operations of this manufacture are extremely curious and interesting, and will well repay a visit to Mr. Neustaedter's establishment, in Dey-street.

The specimens of silk fabrics exhibited by the Newport Silk Factory, of Kentucky, consist principally of handkerchiefs of the description known as Foulard. They have double claims to public attention, from the fact that they are not only of home manufacture, but are also made of American silk. We can desire no better answer than these fabrics afford to the assertion that our climate is unsuited to the culture of the silk-worm. The establishment by which they have been manufactured has had to struggle through great difficulties, arising from a limited capital and want of encouragement, but we are glad to hear that it is now gradually extending its operations.

J. S. REDFIELD,

110 AND 112 NASSAU STREET, NEW YORK,

HAS JUST PUBLISHED:

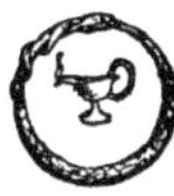

EPISODES OF INSECT LIFE.

By Acheta Domestica. In Three Series: I. Insects of Spring.—II. Insects of Summer.—III. Insects of Autumn. Beautifully illustrated. Crown 8vo., cloth, gilt, price $2.00 each. The same beautifully colored after nature, extra gilt, $4.00 each.

"A book elegant enough for the centre table, witty enough for after dinner, and wise enough for the study and the school-room. One of the beautiful lessons of this work is the kindly view it takes of nature. Nothing is made in vain not only, but nothing is made ugly or repulsive. A charm is thrown around every object, and life suffused through all, suggestive of the Creator's goodness and wisdom."—*N. Y. Evangelist.*

"Moths, glow-worms, lady-birds, May-flies, bees, and a variety of other inhabitants of the insect world, are descanted upon in a pleasing style, combining scientific information with romance, in a manner peculiarly attractive."—*Commercial Advertiser.*

"The book includes solid instruction as well as genial and captivating mirth. The scientific knowledge of the writer is thoroughly reliable."—*Examiner*

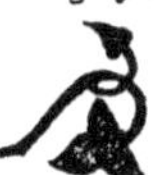

MEN AND WOMEN OF THE EIGHTEENTH CENTURY.

By Arsene Houssaye, with beautifully Engraved Portraits of Louis XV., and Madame de Pompadour. Two volume 12mo. 450 pages each, extra superfine paper, price $2.50.

Contents.—Dufresny, Fontenelle, Marivaux, Piron, The Abbé Prevost, Gentil-Bernard, Florian, Boufflers, Diderot, Grétry, Riverol, Louis XV., Greuze, Boucher, The Vanloos, Lantara, Watteau, La Motte, Dehle, Abbé Trublet, Buffon, Dorat, Cardinal de Bernis, Crébillon the Gay, Marie Antoinette, Made. de Pompadour, Vadé, Mlle. Camargo, Mlle. Clairon, Mad. de la Popelinière, Sophie Arnould, Crébillon the Tragic, Mlle. Guimard, Three Pages in the Life of Dancourt, A Promenade in the Palais-Royal, the Chevalier de la Clos.

"A more fascinating book than this rarely issues from the teeming press. Fascinating in its subject; fascinating in its style; fascinating in its power to lead the reader into castle-building of the most gorgeous and bewitching description."—*Courier & Enquirer.*

"This is a most welcome book, full of information and amusement, in the form of memoirs, comments, and anecdotes. It has the style of light literature, with the usefulness of the gravest. It should be in every library, and the hands of every reader." *Boston Commonwealth.*

"A Book of Books.—Two deliciously spicy volumes, that are a perfect *bonne bouche* for an epicure in reading."—*Home Journal.*

PHILOSOPHERS AND ACTRESSES

By ARSENE HOUSSAYE. With beautifully-engraved Portraits of Voltaire and Mad. Parabère. Two vols., 12mo, price $2.50.

"We have here the most charming book we have read these many days,—so powerful in its fascination that we have been held for hours from our imperious labors, or needful slumbers, by the entrancing influence of its pages. One of the most desirable fruits of the prolific field of literature of the present season."—*Portland Eclectic.*

"Two brilliant and fascinating—we had almost said, bewitching—volumes, combining information and amusement, the lightest gossip, with solid and serviceable wisdom."—*Yankee Blade.*

"It is a most admirable book, full of originality, wit, information and philosophy Indeed, the vividness of the book is extraordinary. The scenes and descriptions are absolutely life-like."—*Southern Literary Gazette.*

"The works of the present writer are the only ones the spirit of whose rhetoric does justice to those times, and in fascination of description and style equal the fascinations they descant upon."—*New Orleans Commercial Bulletin.*

"The author is a brilliant writer, and serves up his sketches in a sparkling manner." *Christian Freeman.*

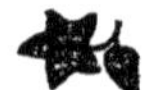

ANCIENT EGYPT UNDER THE PHARAOHS.

By JOHN KENDRICK, M. A. In 2 vols., 12mo, price $2.50.

"No work has heretofore appeared suited to the wants of the historical student, which combined the labors of artists, travellers, interpreters and critics, during the periods from the earliest records of the monarchy to its final absorption in the empire of Alexander. This work supplies this deficiency."—*Olive Branch.*

"Not only the geography and political history of Egypt under the Pharaohs are given, but we are furnished with a minute account of the domestic manners and customs of the inhabitants, their language, laws, science, religion, agriculture, navigation and commerce."—*Commercial Advertiser.*

"These volumes present a comprehensive view of the results of the combined labors of travellers, artists, and scientific explorers, which have effected so much during the present century toward the development of Egyptian archæology and history."—*Journal of Commerce.*

"The descriptions are very vivid and one wanders, delighted with the author, through the land of Egypt, gathering at every step, new phases of her wondrous history, and ends with a more intelligent knowledge than he ever before had, of the land of the Pharaohs."—*American Spectator.*

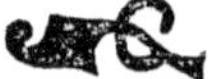

COMPARATIVE PHYSIOGNOMY;

Or Resemblances between Men and Animals. By J. W. REDFIELD, M. D. In one vol., 8vo, with several hundred illustrations. price, $2.00.

"Dr. Redfield has produced a very curious, amusing, and instructive book, curious in its originality and illustrations, amusing in the comparisons and analyses, and instructive because it contains very much useful information on a too much neglected subject. It will be eagerly read and quickly appreciated."—*National Ægis.*

"The whole work exhibits a good deal of scientific research, intelligent observation, and ingenuity."—*Daily Union.*

"Highly entertaining even to those who have little time to study the science."—*Detroit Daily Advertiser.*

"This is a remarkable volume and will be read by two classes, those who study for information, and those who read for amusement. For its originality and entertaining character, we commend it to our readers."—*Albany Express.*

"It is overflowing with wit, humor, and originality, and profusely illustrated. The whole work is distinguished by vast research and knowledge."—*Knickerbocker.*

"The plan is a novel one; the proofs striking, and must challenge the attention of the curious."—*Daily Advertiser*

MOORE'S LIFE OF SHERIDAN.

Memoirs of the Life of the Rt. Hon. Richard Brinsley Sheridan, by THOMAS MOORE, with Portrait after Sir Joshua Reynolds. Two vols., 12mo, cloth, $2.00.

"One of the most brilliant biographies in English literature. It is the life of a wit written by a wit, and few of Tom Moore's most sparkling poems are more brilliant and fascinating than this biography."—*Boston Transcript.*

"This is at once a most valuable biography of the most celebrated wit of the times, and one of the most entertaining works of its gifted author."—*Springfield Republican.*

"The Life of Sheridan, the wit, contains as much food for serious thought as the best sermon that was ever penned."—*Arthur's Home Gazette.*

"The sketch of such a character and career as Sheridan's by such a hand as Moore's, can never cease to be attractive."—*N. Y. Courier and Enquirer.*

"The work is instructive and full of interest."—*Christian Intelligencer.*

"It is a gem of biography; full of incident, elegantly written, warmly appreciative, and on the whole candid and just. Sheridan was a rare and wonderful genius, and has in this work justice done to his surpassing merits."—*N. Y. Evangelist.*

BARRINGTON'S SKETCHES.

Personal Sketches of his own Time, by SIR JONAH BARRINGTON, Judge of the High Court of Admiralty in Ireland, with Illustrations by Darley. Third Edition, 12mo, cloth, $1 25.

"A more entertaining book than this is not often thrown in our way. His sketches of character are inimitable; and many of the prominent men of his time are hit off in the most striking and graceful outline."—*Albany Argus.*

"He was a very shrewd observer and eccentric writer, and his narrative of his own life, and sketches of society in Ireland during his times, are exceedingly humorous and interesting."—*N. Y. Commercial Advertiser.*

"It is one of those works which are conceived and written in so hearty a view, and brings before the reader so many palpable and amusing characters, that the entertainment and information are equally balanced."—*Boston Transcript.*

"This is one of the most entertaining books of the season."—*N. Y. Recorder.*

"It portrays in life-like colors the characters and daily habits of nearly all the English and Irish celebrities of that period."—*N. Y. Courier and Enquirer.*

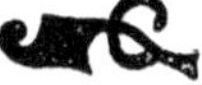

JOMINI'S CAMPAIGN OF WATERLOO.

The Political and Military History of the Campaign of Waterloo, from the French of Gen. Baron Jomini, by Lieut. S. V. BENET, U. S. Ordnance, with a Map, 12mo, cloth, 75 cents.

"Of great value, both for its historical merit and its acknowledged impartiality."—*Christian Freeman, Boston.*

"It has long been regarded in Europe as a work of more than ordinary merit, while to military men his review of the tactics and manœuvres of the French Emperor during the few days which preceded his final and most disastrous defeat, is considered as instructive, as it is interesting."—*Arthur's Home Gazette.*

"It is a standard authority and illustrates a subject of permanent interest. With military students, and historical inquirers, it will be a favorite reference, and for the general reader it possesses great value and interest."—*Boston Transcript.*

"It throws much light on often mooted points respecting Napoleon's military and political genius. The translation is one of much vigor."—*Boston Commonwealth.*

"It supplies an important chapter in the most interesting and eventful period of Napoleon's military career."—*Savannah Daily News.*

"It is ably written and skilfully translated."—*Yankee Blade.*

NOTES AND EMENDATIONS OF SHAKESPEARE.

Notes and Emendations to the Text of Shakespeare's Plays, from the Early Manuscript Corrections in a copy of the folio of 1632, in the possession of JOHN PAYNE COLLIER, Esq., F.S.A. Third edition, with a fac-simile of the Manuscript Corrections. 1 vol. 12mo, cloth, $1 50.

"It is not for a moment to be doubted, we think, that in this volume a contribution has been made to the clearness and accuracy of Shakespeare's text, by far the most important of any offered or attempted since Shakespeare lived and wrote."—*Lond. Exam.*

"The corrections which Mr. Collier has here given to the world are, we venture to think, of more value than the labors of nearly all the critics on Shakespeare's text put together."—*London Literary Gazette.*

"It is a rare gem in the history of literature, and can not fail to command the attention of all the amateurs of the writings of the immortal dramatic poet."—*Ch'ston Cour.*

"It is a book absolutely indispensable to every admirer of Shakespeare who wishes to read him understandingly."—*Louisville Courier.*

"It is clear from internal evidence, that for the most part they are genuine restorations of the original plays. They carry conviction with them."—*Home Journal.*

"This volume is an almost indispensable companion to any of the editions of Shakespeare, so numerous and often important are many of the corrections."—*Register, Philadelphia.*

THE HISTORY OF THE CRUSADES.

By JOSEPH FRANÇOIS MICHAUD. Translated by W. Robson, 3 vols. 12mo., maps, $3 75.

"It is comprehensive and accurate in the detail of facts, methodical and lucid in arrangement, with a lively and flowing narrative."—*Journal of Commerce.*

"We need not say that the work of Michaud has superseded all other histories of the Crusades. This history has long been the standard work with all who could read it in its original language. Another work on the same subject is as improbable as a new history of the 'Decline and Fall of the Roman Empire.'"—*Salem Freeman.*

"The most faithful and masterly history ever written of the wild wars for the Holy Land."—*Philadelphia American Courier.*

"The ability, diligence, and faithfulness, with which Michaud has executed his great task, are undisputed; and it is to his well-filled volumes that the historical student must now resort for copious and authentic facts, and luminous views respecting this most romantic and wonderful period in the annals of the Old World."—*Boston Daily Courier.*

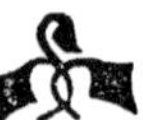

MARMADUKE WYVIL.

An Historical Romance of 1651, by HENRY W. HERBERT, author of the "Cavaliers of England," &c., &c. Fourteenth Edition. Revised and Corrected.

"This is one of the best works of the kind we have ever read—full of thrilling incidents and adventures in the stirring times of Cromwell, and in that style which has made the works of Mr. Herbert so popular."—*Christian Freeman, Boston.*

"The work is distinguished by the same historical knowledge, thrilling incident, and pictorial beauty of style, which have characterized all Mr. Herbert's fictions and imparted to them such a bewitching interest."—*Yankee Blade.*

"The author out of a simple plot and very few characters, has constructed a novel of deep interest and of considerable historical value. It will be found well worth reading."—*National Ægis, Worcester.*

Life under an Italian Despotism!

LORENZO BENONI,

OR

PASSAGES IN THE LIFE OF AN ITALIAN

One Vol., 12mo, Cloth—Price $1.00.

OPINIONS OF THE PRESS.

"THE author of 'Lorenzo Benoni' is GIOVANNI RUFFINI, a native of Genoa, who effected his escape from his native country after the attempt at revolution in 1833. His book is, in substance, an authentic account of real persons and incidents, though the writer has chosen to adopt fictitious and fantastic designations for himself and his associates. Since 1833, Ruffini has resided chiefly (if not wholly) in England and France, where his qualities, we understand, have secured him respect and regard. In 1848, he was selected by Charles Albert to fill the responsible situation of embassador to Paris, in which city he had long been domesticated as a refugee. He ere long, however, relinquished that office, and again withdrew into private life. He appears to have employed the time of his exile in this country to such advantage as to have acquired a most uncommon mastery over the English language. The present volume (we are informed on good authority) is exclusively his own—and, if so, on the score of style alone it is a remarkable curiosity. But its matter also is curious."—*London Quarterly Review for July.*

"A tale of sorrow that has lain long in a rich mind, like a ruin in a fertile country, and is not the less gravely impressive for the grace and beauty of its coverings . . . at the same time the most determined novel-reader could desire no work more fascinating over which to forget the flight of time. . . . No sketch of foreign oppression has ever, we believe, been submitted to the English public by a foreigner, equal or nearly equal to this volume in literary merit. It is not unworthy to be ranked among contemporary works whose season is the century in which their authors live."—*London Examiner.*

"The book should be as extensively read as 'Uncle Tom's Cabin,' inasmuch as it develops the existence of a state of slavery and degradation, worse even than that which Mrs. Beecher Stowe has elucidated with so much pathos and feeling."—*Bell's Weekly Messenger.*

"Few works of the season will be read with greater pleasure than this; there is a great charm in the quiet, natural way in which the story is told."—*London Atlas.*

"The author's great forte is character-painting. This portraiture is accomplished with remarkable skill, the traits both individual and national being marked with great nicety without obtrusiveness."—*London Spectator.*

"Under the modest guise of the biography of an imaginary 'Lorenzo Benoni,' we have here, in fact, the memoir of a man whose name could not be pronounced in certain parts of northern Italy without calling up tragic yet noble historical recollections. . . . Its merits, simply as a work of literary art, are of a very high order. The style is really beautiful—easy, sprightly, graceful, and full of the happiest and most ingenious turns of phrase and fancy."—*North British Review.*

"This has been not unjustly compared to '*Gil Blas,*' to which it is scarcely inferior in spirited delineations of human character, and in the variety of events which it relates. But as a description of actual occurrences illustrating the domestic and political condition of Italy, at a period fraught with interest to all classes of readers, it far transcends in importance any work of mere fiction."—*Dublin Evening Mail.*

"SHAKESPEARE AS HE WROTE IT."

THE WORKS OF SHAKESPEARE,

Reprinted from the newly-discovered copy of the Folio of 1632 in the possession of J. Payne Collier, containing nearly

Twenty Thousand Manuscript Corrections,

With a History of the Stage to the Time, an Introduction to each Play, a Life of the Poet, etc.

BY J. PAYNE COLLIER, F.S.A.

To which are added, Glossarial and other Notes, the Readings of Former Editions, a PORTRAIT *after that by Martin Droeshout, a* VIGNETTE TITLE *on Steel, and a* FACSIMILE OF THE OLD FOLIO, *with the Manuscript Corrections.* 1 vol, Imperial 8vo. Cloth $4 00.

The **WORKS OF SHAKESPEARE** the same as the above. Uniform in Size with the celebrated Chiswick Edition, 8 vols. 16mo, cloth $6 00. Half calf or moroc. extra

These are *American Copyright Editions,* the Notes being expressly prepared for the work. The English edition contains simply the text, without a single note or indication of the changes made in the text. In the present, the variations from old copies are noted by reference of all changes to former editions (abbreviated f. e.), and every indication and explanation is given essential to a clear understanding of the author. The prefatory matter, Life, &c., will be fuller than in any American edition now published.

"THIS is the only correct edition of the works of the 'Bard of Avon' ever issued, and no lover or student of Shakespeare should be without it."—*Philadelphia Argus.*

"Altogether the most correct and therefore the most valuable edition extant."—*Albany Express.*

"This edition of Shakespeare will ultimately supersede all others. It must certainly be deemed an essential acquisition by every lover of the great dramatist."—*N. Y. Commercial Advertiser.*

"This great work commends itself in the highest terms to every Shakespearian scholar and student."—*Philadelphia City Item.*

"This edition embraces all that is necessary to make a copy of Shakespeare desirable and correct."—*Niagara Democrat.*

"It must sooner or later drive all others from the market."—*N. Y. Evening Post.*

"Beyond all question, the very best edition of the great bard hitherto published."—*New England Religious Herald.*

"It must hereafter be the standard edition of Shakespeare's plays."—*National Argus.*

"It is clear from internal evidence that they are genuine restorations of the original plays."—*Detroit Daily Times.*

"This must we think supersede all other editions of Shakespeare hitherto published. Collier's corrections make it really a different work from its predecessors. Compared with it we consider them hardly worth possessing."—*Daily Georgian, Savannah.*

"One who will probably hereafter be considered as the only true authority. No one we think, will wish to purchase an edition of Shakespeare, except it shall be conformable to the amended text by Collier."—*Newark Daily Advertiser.*

"A great outcry has been made in England against this edition of the bard, by Singer and others interested in other editions; but the emendations commend themselves too strongly to the good sense of every reader to be dropped by the public—the old editions must become obsolete."—*Yankee Blade, Boston.*

www.ingramcontent.com/pod-product-compliance
Lightning Source LLC
LaVergne TN
LVHW020600110826
845149LV00002B/328
* 9 7 8 1 4 1 8 1 8 8 2 2 1 *